REPRESENTATIVE PLAYS BY
J. M. BARRIE

285716

CONTENTS

		PAGE
INTRODUCTION............ *William Lyon Phelps*		v
QUALITY STREET		1
THE ADMIRABLE CRICHTON		85
WHAT EVERY WOMAN KNOWS		187
DEAR BRUTUS.................................		291
THE TWELVE-POUND LOOK		377
THE OLD LADY SHOWS HER MEDALS...........		403

BARRIE

I

James Matthew Barrie was born on an Island situated seven leagues west of the most western of the Islands of the Hebrides. It can be reached only by the right pair of boots. In ancestry he comes straight down in the authentic line of apostolic succession, there being two of the disciples in his name; a happy combination of works and faith. Although a mortal man, he is the father of immortal children, among whom may be mentioned Tommy, born in 1896; Crichton, born in 1902; Peter Pan, born in 1904; John Shand, born 1908; Margaret Dearth, born in 1917; Mary Rose, born in 1920. So much for biography.

II

It takes more courage to live than to die; which is proved by the fact that so many more men die well than live well. No wonder, therefore, in making an address to undergraduates, Barrie took *Courage* as his theme.

> Courage is the thing. All goes if courage goes. What says our glorious Johnson of courage: "Unless a man has that virtue, he has no security for preserving any other." We should thank our Creator three times daily for courage instead of for our bread, which, if we work, is surely the one thing we have a right to claim of Him. This courage is a proof of our immortality, greater even than gardens "when the eve

is cool." Pray for it. "Who rises from prayer a
better man, his prayer is answered." Be not merely
courageous, but light-hearted and gay.

Young Barrie came up to London with no money, no
friends, and no influence, and conquered the town. Thus
his life, though he would be the last man to think so, abun-
dantly illustrates his precepts.

The element of Courage is the dynamic quality in all of
Barrie's dramas. His heroes and heroines have it; his
villains do not. Maggie saves John Shand by courage;
Crichton conquers an island and saves a family; the school-
room on Quality Street contains more courage than a
battle field; Kate Sims saves her own soul, saves it with a
typewriter; the Old Lady transfigures loneliness by courage;
the artist Dearth by this attribute has his only chance when
the curtain falls; Mrs. Morland succeeds in governing her
household and awaits the end without fear.

In Storm Jameson's fine book, *Modern Drama in Europe,*
she had the insight to see that Barrie is not a Romantic,
but a Realist—a true realist, in his revelation of human
nature.

But the drama of J. M. Barrie has other qualities
than those of grace and loving kindness, and other arts
than the wizardry that sets men's thoughts wandering
in forgotten places and their eyes searching for forgotten dreams. There is pity, infinite pity, and—lest
that become intolerable—infinite courage, defying suffering and age and death itself. Pity and courage alike
have a fine, keen edge. There is nothing sentimental in
the mind that called them out, giving them life and
form—the form, maybe, of an awkward boy, or a "queer
old diver" of a charwoman; it is a shrewd mind, quick

to see the absurdity of our unconscious posturings even
while it smiles at them.

III

We are living in the greatest creative period that English
drama has seen since the days of Elizabeth. The last decade
of the nineteenth century and the first three decades of the
twentieth have been characterized by an outburst of activity
in the theatre that has commanded universal attention.
Oscar Wilde, Pinero, Jones, Synge, Yeats, Shaw, Barrie,
Galsworthy, Dunsany, Ervine,—their plays have conquered
the native and foreign stage; despite the fact that nearly
every other country in Europe has produced during this
same period notable dramatic works, the English-written
drama now holds the leadership.

There is no explanation of genius; it is the rarest and
most mysterious thing in the world, and while its presence
and its effects are as obvious as the weather, its origin is
beyond knowledge and guesswork. Yet it is always interesting to trace some of its beginnings and make a record
of certain influences.

So far as there is any key to the mystery of Barrie, it
is to be found in a woman, Margaret Ogilvy. She was his
mother. During the years of his intimate association with
her in his childhood and early youth, she exercised a powerful influence upon him; but that is nothing to what she did
for him after her departure. The spiritual presence of those
whom we love is often more real than their physical existence; especially is this true of the influence of parents on
their offspring. They reach out from the grave invisible
hands and guide our steps; their inaudible voices mould
our opinions. We treat them with more deference than
when they were here.

In reading the plays of Barrie, I have a feeling that during their composition his mother was present; not merely telling him what to retain and what to delete, but useful as Maggie was to John Shand. I cannot read *Quality Street, What Every Woman Knows, The Legend of Leonora, Mary Rose,* without feeling that the knowledge born of reverence came from Margaret Ogilvy. She herself was Maggie, Leonora, and Mrs. Morland, in her humor, in her wit, in her secret delight in self-effacement, in her infallible knowledge of the difference between good and evil. Very woman of very woman—who never tried or wished to be a man— Margaret Ogilvy in her daily life, conversation, and influence—as subtle as it was pervading—is the mother not only of her wonderful son, but of his wonderful works.

We learn more of Barrie's methods in play-composition by reading his biography of his mother than by studying his "technique," or by hunting "sources."

It is true that Barrie has mastered the technique of the theatre; he is not a literary man who writes interesting dramatic books, he has an uncanny knowledge of plot, dialogue, and theatrical effect. Every one of his plays, stripped of its literary quality, would make an effective motion picture. He knows human nature, and can create human beings on the stage; he knows human nature, and understands how to arrest and hold his audiences. The curious fact that he regards Pinero's *Iris* as the best play of our time is a revelation of his prolonged study of dramatic technique and of his homage to the well-made play.

In a remarkable speech that he made a few years ago to an assemblage of dramatic critics, he said

> None of your adjectives gets to the mark as much as one I have found for myself—"Inoffensive Barrie." I see how much it at once strikes you all. A bitter

pill; but it looks as if on one subject I were the best critic in the room.

Your word for me would probably be fantastic. I was quite prepared to hear it from your Chairman, because I felt he could not be so shabby as to say whimsical, and that he might forget to say elusive. If you knew how dejected those terms have often made me. I am quite serious. I never believed I was any of those things until you dinned them into me. Few have tried harder to be simple and direct. I have also always thought that I was rather realistic.

Blessed is he whosoever is not offended in me, said the greatest creative artist of all time. It is because Barrie is inoffensive that he can steal into the hearts of his characters and of his audiences. He has no dogmas to defend, no theory of the theatre to uphold, no political creed to enforce, no thesis to advance; his sympathy is not limited or twisted; he has only one subject to write about, the one that Richardson called "love and nonsense, men and women."

Barrie's is the drama of ideas as distinguished from the drama of opinions. This is why he is so fond of an island, because on an island you can isolate various specimens of humanity, and study their impulses at your leisure. He gave us a broad hint when in this same speech to the critics, he spoke of islands.

You may sometimes wonder why I write so much about islands, and indeed I have noticed a certain restiveness in some of you on the subject. There are more islands in my plays than any of you are aware of. I have the cunning to call them by other names. There is one thing I am really good at, and that is slipping in an island. I dare say it is those islands that make you misunderstand me. I would feel as if I had left off clothing if I were to write without an island. Now could there be a more realistic statement than that?

One of the reasons for the author's fondness for *The Admirable Crichton* is because there are two islands in it, England and the savage one; in both—especially the latter —human traits can be magnified, and nature assert herself. In *Mary Rose* the mysterious island has the voices of eternity. In *Dear Brutus* the island is the enchanted forest, where unoriginal human nature gets its second chance; in *Quality Street* the island is the little town of eternal womanhood; in the following passage, it is as though Barrie were writing from his mother's dictation;

> Because he has taken from me the one great glory that is in a woman's life. Not a man's love—she can do without that—but her own dear sweet love for him. He is unworthy of my love; that is why I can be so cruel.

In *Leonora* the island is where human impulses are separated from human actions, and studied selectively; in *Alice-Sit-by-the-Fire* the island is the progressive isolation of advancing years; in *The Old Lady Shows Her Medals* it is a basement in a dingy street, filled with rosemary.

Barrie is indeed very good at slipping in an island; the islands of isolation, where the human heart can be studied under the microscope.

The very last word that should be applied to the plays of Barrie is the word "sentimental." I often hear him called sentimental by persons who cannot distinguish between subway and surface. Sentimentalism is found in melodramas and in slushy novels and in motion pictures; one never gets out of one's depth in sentimentalism, because one is always wading in shallow places, in the domain of the obvious.

Are the relations between Lady Mary and Crichton sentimental? Or Maggie's treatment of the vampire in *What Every Woman Knows,* or indeed John Shand's? Or Dearth's dialogue with his daughter in the moonlight?

Barrie understands human nature because his sympathy for men, women, and children knows no social and national limits. The charwoman in *A Kiss for Cinderella* takes care of a German baby in wartime. Many of those who were loudest in their denunciations of the old Calvinistic creed which spoke of "non-elect infants" were quite willing to have German babies starved; it took courage for Barrie to save one, even in imagination. The same understanding that made Lord Loam and his daughters real people made the charwoman taking tea equally alive. And finally, there is a passage in his speech to the critics that helps us to understand not only why Barrie will not reply to adverse criticism —of which he has had aplenty—but why his *dramatis personae* are so human. It is spoken playfully, but it is nevertheless revealingly sincere.

I wish I could think, gentlemen, that my forbearance toward you is owing to deeply artistic reasons; but no, it is merely because I forever see the fates hanging over you and about to stretch forth a claw. However you may ram it in—I refer to the rapier—I have a fear that something disastrous is about to happen to you in the so much more important part of your life that has nothing to do with the pen—bad news, ill health, sudden loss; and so I forgive you and tear up.

Many a man writes with relish and self-satisfaction a re-view ridiculing another man's work; his victim reads it on a sickbed, after a financial disaster, after sitting up all night with a dying child.

In the plays of J. M. Barrie we see disclosed the perfect combination—the combination of original genius with mastery of dramatic devices. He has never found it necessary to "express himself" by breaking dramatic laws; he has found the conventions of the stage, as Browning found the conventions of poetry, a sufficiently broad field whereon to exercise his original powers.

IV

Barrie's career as a dramatist covers a period of thirty-five years. A.D. 1891 is an important point in his life, for it marked the beginning of his fame and fortune, and also his first appearance as a playwright. *Becky Sharp*, which did no good to Barrie and no harm to Thackeray, *Ibsen's Ghost*, a parody which at that time seemed better to the British than Ibsen, and *Richard Savage*, written in collaboration with Mr. Marriott-Watson, which had a hail-and-farewell performance, were all produced in 1891. As I understand it, the receipts from these were not enough to buy a tin of Arcadia Mixture; hence it was fortunate that also in 1891 appeared the novel *The Little Minister*, which made Barrie's name known everywhere in Britain and America, and supplied him with sufficient funds to continue his dramatic experiments.

There is a copy of *Richard Savage* in the Chapin Library at Williams College. It has no title-page, but on the front wrapper are the words "Privately Printed. Richard Savage. *A Play* in Four Acts."

The prologue was written by W. E. Henley, and the year after the poet's death Barrie paid a compliment to his friend by having the only book which the Admirable Crichton took to the island a copy of Henley's Poems.

In the last act of that masterpiece, we have the following dialogue:

LORD BROCKLEHURST.	Presumably Crichton is no reader.
LADY BROCKLEHURST.	By the way, Crichton, were there any books on the island?
CRICHTON.	I had one, my lady—Henley's poems.
LORD BROCKLEHURST.	Never heard of him.

The three plays of 1891 were flashes in the pan. Barrie fired his first shot on 25 February 1892 with an original play, *Walker, London*. The year 1892 is significant, for it marked the beginning of modern English Drama; the dawn of a new period, now in its full and perfect day. In that year appeared *Lady Windermere's Fan*, by Oscar Wilde, and *Widowers Houses*, by George Bernard Shaw; Pinero was writing *The Second Mrs. Tanqueray*, produced in 1893. So it is interesting to observe that Barrie's true beginning as a dramatist synchronized with that of Wilde and Shaw. Today, Shaw and Barrie, living side by side in a corner of London, so close that they converse merely by opening windows, are the leaders of the contemporary stage.

Barrie showed his love for an island in *Walker, London*— it was a floating one. The entire action takes place in a houseboat on the Thames, and one of the situations in the abortive *Richard Savage* is repeated with success. *Walker, London* is of little intrinsic importance, but its interest lies in the fact that it demonstrated its author's mastery of stage technique. It is a play, not a story; indeed from a perusal of it, one would not guess that its author was a "damned literary man."

In 1894 came the play *The Professor's Love Story* that

gave Barrie some general reputation as a dramatist, tremendously increased in two years by *The Little Minister*, which had enormous vogue, and has seen many revivals. A triple alliance was formed, the principals being Barrie, the playwright, Charles Frohman, the manager, and Maude Adams, the interpreter. This was a good thing for them, for the public, and for the drama; it lasted eighteen years, broken only by the death of Mr. Frohman on the *Lusitania* in 1915.

The year 1902 was made memorable by the production of *Quality Street,* a brilliant comedy of the Napoleonic era in England, and *The Admirable Crichton,* which seems to me of all the excellent plays of our epoch, the most excellent. Both of these plays have been revived in England and America, to the delight of two generations. In 1920 a French translation of *Crichton* appeared in Paris, and for a few minutes Parisian theatre-goers forgot the triangle.

It is hard to believe there ever was a time when no Peter Pan existed, but as a matter of fact he made us first see the light in 1904. This play, in a manner that seemed before the opening night to ask too much of the conventional audience, has already become a classic, and is as essential to every London Christmas as Santa Claus, a tree, and a stocking. Peter Pan is a permanent addition to the population of the imaginative world—he will survive every human being now on earth.

Alice-Sit-by-the-Fire (1905) is a farce with the shadow of tragedy. "She isn't a woman, she's my mother." No such error was ever made by Barrie, because he apprehended Margaret Ogilvy from so many different points of view. Those who think Barrie is a sentimentalist should study this play, which is (partly) a burlesque of the sentimental drama. The stage directions are among the best he has ever written, and in this field he stands without an equal in the history of the theatre.

In 1908 came again one of his masterpieces, *What Every Woman Knows*, opening with the queen's gambit, in a manner that made every person in the house as silently attentive as the chess-players themselves. This is one of the great plays of the modern stage, and will outlive most of its contemporaries. Maude Adams reached the climax of her art in the interpretation of Maggie. *Quality Street* and *What Every Woman Knows* are good plays wherein to study Barrie's powers of characterization. Look particularly at the so-called *minor* characters. The author takes the same pains with his lesser figures that a great surgeon takes with poor and obscure patients.

Barrie is a master of the technique of the short play, where the action continues without the distressing breaks caused by the fall of the curtain. He has written many beautiful one-acters, but I think the best are *The Twelve-Pound Look* (1910), and *The Old Lady Shows Her Medals* (1917), greatest of all the war dramas.

The *Legend of Leonora* (1913) will I hope soon be added to the list of Barrie's published plays, as its technique is worth studying. The idea—dramatization of human *motive* rather than of human action—is original; and except for the last act, brilliantly executed.

A Kiss for Cinderella (1916) does not compare in interest and in value with *What Every Woman Knows*, but the scene where the social life of the king and queen are presented through the medium of the charwoman's imagination is a scene that no one but Barrie would have thought of, and no other playwright could have managed.

In *Dear Brutus* (1917) Barrie achieved another masterpiece, one that ranks among his four or five finest produc-

tions. Perhaps its greatest triumph is its last act. Few
indeed even among successful playwrights, are those who can
write a satisfactory final act; and in *Dear Brutus* after the
moonlight scene of imagination, everyone must have wondered how anything that followed could escape anticlimax.
But Barrie is like history—it is the unexpected that happens.

Not content with the portrayal of life on earth, in *Mary
Rose* (1920) Barrie took us across the border that separates
the world of matter from the world of spirit. This is a
play that awakened fervent enthusiasm and outspoken
dislike. No one who saw it remained in an attitude of
indifference. Some of his friends walked no more with him;
others felt that he had surpassed himself. To me it was
at my first view of it so deeply impressive that after a few
weeks I went again; and the second time it seemed even
more so. Now that it is in print—I regret that the stage
directions are scantier than in some other of his dramas—
one can study it at leisure. It illustrates Thoreau's famous
saying, "One world at a time." It shows that King David's
remark about his son expressed not only what will happen,
but what ought to happen. We shall go to them, but they
will not return to us. There is no place in this world for
those who have left it; should they return

Life's night begins; let them never come back to us!
There would be doubt, hesitation, and pain,
Forced praise on our part—the glimmer of twilight,
Never glad confident morning again!

This piece was written in the afterglow of the war. It was
meant to show to those who mourn that life goes on; that
on earth one cannot live in the memory of those who have
departed, but must obey the imperious call of earthly interests and earthly duties.

It was meant to show too that human beings, especially children, should be treated with tact as well as with affection.

Every reader of this drama will have his own interpretation of it, which is well. The greatest plays do not satisfy our curiosity, they arouse it.

If Barrie were not a man of genius, we might be able to classify him and "place" him; but because he has indubitable genius, he is simply himself. He has already had innumerable imitators, who by their shortcomings demonstrate his uniqueness.

W. L. P.

QUALITY STREET

A COMEDY

ACT I

THE BLUE AND WHITE ROOM

The scene is the blue and white room in the house of the
    MISSES SUSAN *and* PHOEBE THROSSEL *in Quality*
    Street, and in this little country town there is a satisfac-
    tion about living in Quality Street which even religion
    cannot give. Through the bowed window at the back we
    have a glimpse of the street. It is pleasantly broad and
    grass-grown, and is linked to the outer world by one
    demure shop, whose door rings a bell every time it
    opens and shuts. Thus by merely peeping, every one
    in Quality Street can know at once who has been buy-
    ing a Whimsy cake, and usually why. This bell is the
    most familiar sound of Quality Street. Now and again
    ladies pass in their pattens, a maid perhaps protecting
    them with an umbrella, for flakes of snow are falling
    discreetly. Gentlemen in the street are an event; but,
    see, just as we raise the curtain, there goes the RECRUIT-
    ING SERGEANT *to remind us that we are in the period of*
    the Napoleonic wars. If he were to look in at the win-
    dow of the blue and white room all the ladies there as-
    sembled would draw themselves up; they know him
    for a rude fellow who smiles at the approach of maiden
    ladies and continues to smile after they have passed.
    However, he lowers his head to-day so that they shall
    not see him, his present design being converse with the
    MISSES THROSSEL'S *maid.*
The room is one seldom profaned by the foot of man, and

3

everything in it is white or blue. MISS PHOEBE *is not
present, but here are* MISS SUSAN, MISS WILLOUGHBY
and her sister MISS FANNY, *and* MISS HENRIETTA
TURNBULL. MISS SUSAN *and* MISS WILLOUGHBY, *alas,
already wear caps; but all the four are dear ladies, so
refined that we ought not to be discussing them without
a more formal introduction. There seems no sufficient
reason why we should choose* MISS PHOEBE *as our
heroine rather than any one of the others, except, perhaps, that we like her name best. But we gave her the
name, so we must support our choice and say that she
is slightly the nicest, unless, indeed,* MISS SUSAN *is
nicer.*

MISS FANNY *is reading aloud from a library book while the
others sew or knit. They are making garments for our
brave soldiers now far away fighting the Corsican Ogre.*

MISS FANNY. ". . . And so the day passed and evening
came, black, mysterious, and ghost-like. The wind moaned
unceasingly like a shivering spirit, and the vegetation rustled
uneasily as if something weird and terrifying were about to
happen. Suddenly out of the darkness there emerged a *Man*.

> [*She says the last word tremulously but without
> looking up. The listeners knit more quickly.*]

The unhappy Camilla was standing lost in reverie when,
without pausing to advertise her of his intentions, he took
both her hands in his.

> [*By this time the knitting has stopped, and all are
> listening as if mesmerised.*]

Slowly he gathered her in his arms——

> [MISS SUSAN *gives an excited little cry.*]

MISS FANNY. And rained hot, burning——"
MISS WILLOUGHBY. Sister!

MISS FANNY. [*Greedily.*] "On eyes, mouth——"

MISS WILLOUGHBY. [*Sternly.*] Stop. Miss Susan, I am indeed surprised you should bring such an amazing, indelicate tale from the library.

MISS SUSAN. [*With a slight shudder.*] I deeply regret, Miss Willoughby—— [*Sees* MISS FANNY *reading quickly to herself.*] Oh, Fanny! If you please, my dear.

[*Takes the book gently from her.*]

MISS WILLOUGHBY. I thank you.

[*She knits severely.*]

MISS FANNY. [*A little rebel.*] Miss Susan is looking at the end.

[MISS SUSAN *closes the book guiltily.*]

MISS SUSAN. [*Apologetically.*] Forgive my partiality for romance, Mary. I fear 'tis the mark of an old maid.

MISS WILLOUGHBY. Susan, that word!

MISS SUSAN. [*Sweetly.*] 'Tis what I am. And you also, Mary, my dear.

MISS FANNY. [*Defending her sister.*] Miss Susan, I protest.

MISS WILLOUGHBY. [*Sternly truthful.*] Nay, sister, 'tis true. We are known everywhere now, Susan, you and I, as the old maids of Quality Street. [*General discomfort.*]

MISS SUSAN. I am happy Phoebe will not be an old maid.

MISS HENRIETTA. [*Wistfully.*] Do you refer, Miss Susan, to V. B.?

[MISS SUSAN *smiles happily to herself.*]

MISS SUSAN. Miss Phoebe of the ringlets as he has called her.

MISS FANNY. Other females besides Miss Phoebe have ringlets.

MISS SUSAN. But you and Miss Henrietta have to employ papers, my dear. [*Proudly.*] Phoebe, never.

Miss Willoughby. [*In defence of* Fanny.] I do not approve of Miss Phoebe at all.

Miss Susan. [*Flushing.*] Mary, had Phoebe been dying you would have called her an angel, but that is ever the way. 'Tis all jealousy to the bride and good wishes to the corpse. [*Her guests rise, hurt.*] My love, I beg your pardon.

Miss Willoughby. With your permission, Miss Susan, I shall put on my pattens.

> [Miss Susan *gives permission almost haughtily, and the ladies retire to the bedroom,* Miss Fanny *remaining behind a moment to ask a question.*]

Miss Fanny. A bride? Miss Susan, do you mean that V. B. has declared?

Miss Susan. Fanny, I expect it hourly.

> [Miss Susan, *left alone, is agitated by the terrible scene with* Miss Willoughby.]
>
> [*Enter* Phoebe *in her bonnet, and we see at once that she really is the nicest. She is so flushed with delightful news that she almost forgets to take off her pattens before crossing the blue and white room.*]

Miss Susan. You seem strangely excited, Phoebe.

Phoebe. Susan, I have met a certain individual.

Miss Susan. V. B.? [Phoebe *nods several times, and her gleaming eyes tell* Miss Susan *as much as if they were a romance from the library.*] My dear, you are trembling.

Phoebe. [*Bravely.*] No—oh no.

Miss Susan. You put your hand to your heart.

Phoebe. Did I?

Miss Susan. [*In a whisper.*] My love, has he offered?

Phoebe. [*Appalled.*] Oh, Susan.

> [*Enter* Miss Willoughby, *partly cloaked.*]

MISS WILLOUGHBY. How do you do, Miss Phoebe. [*Portentously.*] Susan, I have no wish to alarm you, but I am of opinion that there is a man in the house. I suddenly felt it while putting on my pattens.

MISS SUSAN. You mean—a follower—in the kitchen? [*She courageously rings the bell, but her voice falters.*] I am just a little afraid of Patty.

> [*Enter* PATTY, *a buxom young woman, who loves her mistresses and smiles at them, and knows how to terrorise them.*]

Patty, I hope we may not hurt your feelings, but——

PATTY. [*Sternly.*] Are you implicating, ma'am, that I have a follower?

MISS SUSAN. Oh no, Patty.

PATTY. So be it.

MISS SUSAN. [*Ashamed.*] Patty, come back. [*Humbly.*] I told a falsehood just now; I am ashamed of myself.

PATTY. [*Severely.*] As well you might be, ma'am.

PHOEBE. [*So roused that she would look heroic if she did not spoil the effect by wagging her finger at* PATTY.] How dare you. There is a man in the kitchen. To the door with him.

PATTY. A glorious soldier to be so treated!

PHOEBE. The door.

PATTY. And if he refuses?

> [*They look perplexed.*]

MISS SUSAN. Oh dear!

PHOEBE. If he refuses send him here to me.

> [*Exit* PATTY.]

MISS SUSAN. Lion-hearted Phoebe.

MISS WILLOUGHBY. A soldier? [*Nervously.*] I wish it may not be that impertinent recruiting sergeant. I passed him in the street to-day. He closed one of his eyes at me and then quickly opened it. I knew what he meant.

PHOEBE. He does not come.

MISS SUSAN. I think I hear their voices in dispute.

[*She is listening through the floor. They all stoop or go on their knees to listen, and when they are in this position the* RECRUITING SERGEANT *enters unobserved. He chuckles aloud. In a moment* PHOEBE *is alone with him.*]

SERGEANT. [*With an Irish accent.*] Your servant, ma'am.

PHOEBE. [*Advancing sternly on him.*] Sir—— [*She is perplexed, as he seems undismayed.*] Sergeant—— [*She sees mud from his boots on the carpet.*] Oh! oh! [*Brushes carpet.*] Sergeant, I am wishful to scold you, but would you be so obliging as to stand on this paper while I do it?

SERGEANT. With all the pleasure in life, ma'am.

PHOEBE. [*Forgetting to be angry.*] Sergeant, have you killed people?

SERGEANT. Dozens, ma'am, dozens.

PHOEBE. How terrible. Oh, sir, I pray every night that the Lord in His loving-kindness will root the enemy up. Is it true that the Corsican Ogre eats babies?

SERGEANT. I have spoken with them as have seen him do it, ma'am.

PHOEBE. The Man of Sin. Have you ever seen a vivandiere, sir? [*Wistfully.*] I have sometimes wished there were vivandieres in the British Army. [*For a moment she sees herself as one.*] Oh, Sergeant, a shudder goes through me when I see you in the streets enticing those poor young men.

SERGEANT. If you were one of them, ma'am, and death or glory was the call, you would take the shilling, ma'am.

PHOEBE. Oh, not for that.

SERGEANT. For King and Country, ma'am?

PHOEBE. [*Grandly.*] Yes, yes, for that.

SERGEANT. [*Candidly.*] Not that it is all fighting. The sack of captured towns—the loot.

PHOEBE. [*Proudly.*] An English soldier never sacks nor loots.

SERGEANT. No, ma'am. And then—the girls.

PHOEBE. What girls?

SERGEANT. In the towns that—that we don't sack.

PHOEBE. How they must hate the haughty conqueror.

SERGEANT. We are not so haughty as all that.

PHOEBE. [*Sadly.*] I think I understand. I am afraid, Sergeant, you do not tell those poor young men the noble things I thought you told them.

SERGEANT. Ma'am, I must e'en tell them what they are wishful to hear. There ha' been five, ma'am, all this week, listening to me and then showing me their heels, but by a grand stroke of luck I have them at last.

PHOEBE. Luck?

[MISS SUSAN *opens door slightly and listens.*]

SERGEANT. The luck, ma'am, is that a gentleman of the town has enlisted. That gave them the push forward.

[MISS SUSAN *is excited.*]

PHOEBE. A gentleman of this town enlisted? [*Eagerly.*] Sergeant, who?

SERGEANT. Nay, ma'am, I think it be a secret as yet.

PHOEBE. But a gentleman! 'Tis the most amazing, exciting thing. Sergeant, be so obliging.

SERGEANT. Nay, ma'am, I can't.

MISS SUSAN. [*At door, carried away by excitement.*] But you must, you must!

SERGEANT. [*Turning to the door.*] You see, ma'am——
[*The door is hurriedly closed.*]

PHOEBE. [*Ashamed.*] Sergeant, I have not been saying the things I meant to say to you. Will you please excuse my turning you out of the house somewhat violently.

SERGEANT.   I am used to it, ma'am.

PHOEBE.   I won't really hurt you.

SERGEANT.   Thank you kindly, ma'am.

PHOEBE.   [*Observing the bedroom door opening a little, and speaking in a loud voice.*]   I protest, sir; we shall permit no followers in this house.   Should I discover you in my kitchen again I shall pitch you out—neck and crop. Begone, sir.

> [*The* SERGEANT *retires affably. All the ladies except* MISS HENRIETTA *come out, admiring* PHOEBE. *The* WILLOUGHBYS *are attired for their journey across the street.*]

MISS WILLOUGHBY.   Miss Phoebe, we could not but admire you.

> [PHOEBE, *alas, knows that she is not admirable.*]

PHOEBE.   But the gentleman recruit?

MISS SUSAN.   Perhaps they will know who he is at the woollen-draper's.

MISS FANNY.   Let us inquire.

> [*But before they go* MISS WILLOUGHBY *has a duty to perform.*]

MISS WILLOUGHBY.   I wish to apologise.   Miss Phoebe, you are a dear, good girl.   If I have made remarks about her ringlets, Susan, it was jealousy.   [PHOEBE *and* MISS SUSAN *wish to embrace her, but she is not in the mood for it.*]   Come, sister.

MISS FANNY.   [*The dear woman that she is.*]   Phoebe, dear, I wish you very happy.

> [PHOEBE *presses her hand.*]

MISS HENRIETTA.   [*Entering, and not to be outdone.*] Miss Phoebe, I give you joy.

> [*The three ladies go, the two younger ones a little tearfully, and we see them pass the window.*]

PHOEBE. [*Pained.*] Susan, you have been talking to them about V. B.

MISS SUSAN. I could not help it. [*Eagerly.*] Now, Phoebe, what is it you have to tell me?

PHOEBE. [*In a low voice.*] Dear, I think it is too holy to speak of.

MISS SUSAN. To your sister?

PHOEBE. Susan, as you know, I was sitting with an unhappy woman whose husband has fallen in the war. When I came out of the cottage *he* was passing.

MISS SUSAN. Yes?

PHOEBE. He offered me his escort. At first he was very silent—as he has often been of late.

MISS SUSAN. *We* know why.

PHOEBE. Please not to say that I know why. Suddenly he stopped and swung his cane. You know how gallantly he swings his cane.

MISS SUSAN. Yes, indeed.

PHOEBE. He said: "I have something I am wishful to tell you, Miss Phoebe; perhaps you can guess what it is."

MISS SUSAN. Go on!

PHOEBE. To say I could guess, sister, would have been unladylike. I said: "Please not to tell me in the public thoroughfare"; to which he instantly replied: "Then I shall call and tell you this afternoon."

MISS SUSAN. Phoebe!

[*They are interrupted by the entrance of* PATTY *with tea. They see that she has brought three cups, and know that this is her impertinent way of implying that mistresses, as well as maids, may have a "follower." When she has gone they smile at the daring of the woman, and sit down to tea.*]

PHOEBE. Susan, to think that it has all happened in a single year.

MISS SUSAN. Such a genteel competency as he can offer; such a desirable establishment.

PHOEBE. I had no thought of that, dear. I was recalling our first meeting at Mrs. Fotheringay's quadrille party.

MISS SUSAN. We had quite forgotten that our respected local physican was growing elderly.

PHOEBE. Until he said: "Allow me to present my new partner, Mr. Valentine Brown."

MISS SUSAN. Phoebe, do you remember how at the tea-table he facetiously passed the cakebasket with nothing in it!

PHOEBE. He was so amusing from the first. I am thankful, Susan, that I too have a sense of humour. I am exceedingly funny at times; am I not, Susan?

MISS SUSAN. Yes, indeed. But he sees humour in the most unexpected things. I say something so ordinary about loving, for instance, to have everything either blue or white in this room, and I know not why he laughs, but it makes me feel quite witty.

PHOEBE. [*A little anxiously.*] I hope he sees nothing odd or quaint about us.

MISS SUSAN. My dear, I am sure he cannot.

PHOEBE. Susan, the picnics.

MISS SUSAN. Phoebe, the day when he first drank tea in this house.

PHOEBE. He invited himself.

MISS SUSAN. He merely laughed when I said it would cause such talk.

PHOEBE. He is absolutely fearless. Susan, he has smoked his pipe in this room.

[*They are both a little scared.*]

MISS SUSAN. Smoking is indeed a dreadful habit.

PHOEBE. But there is something so dashing about it.

MISS SUSAN. [*With melancholy.*] And now I am to be left alone.

PHOEBE. No.

MISS SUSAN. My dear, I could not leave this room. My lovely blue and white room. It is my husband.

PHOEBE. [*Who has become agitated.*] Susan, you must make my house your home. I have something distressing to tell you.

MISS SUSAN. You alarm me.

PHOEBE. You know Mr. Brown advised us how to invest half of our money.

MISS SUSAN. I know it gives us eight per cent., though why it should do so I cannot understand, but very obliging, I am sure.

PHOEBE. Susan, all that money is lost; I had the letter several days ago.

MISS SUSAN. Lost?

PHOEBE. Something burst, dear, and then they absconded.

MISS SUSAN. But Mr. Brown——

PHOEBE. I have not advertised him of it yet, for he will think it was his fault. But I shall tell him to-day.

MISS SUSAN. Phoebe, how much have we left?

PHOEBE. Only sixty pounds a year, so you see you must live with us, dearest.

MISS SUSAN. But Mr. Brown—he——

PHOEBE. [*Grandly.*] He is a man of means, and if he is not proud to have my Susan I shall say at once: "Mr. Brown—the door."

[*She presses her cheek to* MISS SUSAN'S.]

MISS SUSAN. [*Softly.*] Phoebe, I have a wedding gift for you.

PHOEBE. Not yet?

MISS SUSAN. It has been ready for a long time. I began it when you were not ten years old and I was a young woman. I meant it for myself, Phoebe. I had hoped that he—his name was William—but I think I must have been too unattractive, my love.

PHOEBE. Sweetest—dearest——

MISS SUSAN. I always associate it with a sprigged poplin I was wearing that summer, with a breadth of coloured silk in it, being a naval officer; but something happened, a Miss Cicely Pemberton, and they are quite big boys now. So long ago, Phoebe—he was very tall, with brown hair—it was most foolish of me, but I was always so fond of sewing—with long straight legs and such a pleasant expression.

PHOEBE. Susan, what was it?

MISS SUSAN. It was a wedding-gown, my dear. Even plain women, Phoebe, we can't help it; when we are young we have romantic ideas just as if we were pretty. And so the wedding-gown was never used. Long before it was finished I knew he would not offer, but I finished it, and then I put it away. I have always hidden it from you, Phoebe, but of late I have brought it out again, and altered it.

[*She goes to ottoman and unlocks it.*]

PHOEBE. Susan, I could not wear it. [MISS SUSAN *brings the wedding-gown.*] Oh! how sweet, how beautiful!

MISS SUSAN. You will wear it, my love, won't you? And the tears it was sewn with long ago will all turn into smiles on my Phoebe's wedding-day.

[*They are tearfully happy when a knock is heard on the street door.*]

PHOEBE. That knock.

MISS SUSAN. So dashing.

PHOEBE. So imperious. [*She is suddenly panic-stricken.*] Susan, I think he kissed me once.

MISS SUSAN. [*Startled.*] You *think?*

PHOEBE. I know he did. That evening—a week ago, when he was squiring me home from the concert. It was raining, and my face was wet; he said that was why he did it.

MISS SUSAN. Because your face was wet?

PHOEBE. It does not seem a sufficient excuse now.

MISS SUSAN. [*Appalled.*] O Phoebe, before he had offered.

PHOEBE. [*In distress.*] I fear me it was most un-ladylike.

> [VALENTINE BROWN *is shown in. He is a frank, genial young man of twenty-five who honestly admires the ladies, though he is amused by their quaintness. He is modestly aware that it is in the blue and white room alone that he is esteemed a wit.*]

BROWN. Miss Susan, how do you do, ma'am? Nay, Miss Phoebe, though we have met to-day already I insist on shaking hands with you again.

MISS SUSAN. Always so dashing.

> [VALENTINE *laughs and the ladies exchange delighted smiles.*]

VALENTINE. [*To* MISS SUSAN.] And my other friends, I hope I find them in health? The spinet, ma'am, seems quite herself to-day; I trust the ottoman passed a good night?

MISS SUSAN. [*Beaming.*] We are all quite well, sir.

VALENTINE. May I sit on this chair, Miss Phoebe? I know Miss Susan likes me to break her chairs.

MISS SUSAN. Indeed, sir, I do not. Phoebe, how strange that he should think so.

PHOEBE. [*Instantly.*] The remark was humorous, was it not?

VALENTINE. How you see through me, Miss Phoebe.
[*The sisters again exchange delighted smiles.*
VALENTINE *is about to take a seat.*]

MISS SUSAN. [*Thinking aloud.*] Oh dear, I feel sure
he is going to roll the coverlet into a ball and then sit on it.
[VALENTINE, *who has been on the point of do-
ing so, abstains and sits guiltily.*]

VALENTINE. So I am dashing, Miss Susan? Am I
dashing, Miss Phoebe?

PHOEBE. A—little, I think.

VALENTINE. Well, but I have something to tell you
to-day which I really think is rather dashing. [MISS
SUSAN *gathers her knitting, looks at* PHOEBE, *and is preparing to go.*] You are not going, ma'am, before you
know what it is?

MISS SUSAN. I—I—indeed—to be sure—I—I know,
Mr. Brown.

PHOEBE. Susan!

MISS SUSAN. I mean I do not know. I mean I can
guess—I mean—— Phoebe, my love, explain. [*She goes
out.*]

VALENTINE. [*Rather disappointed.*] The explanation
being, I suppose, that you both know, and I had flattered
myself 'twas such a secret. Am I then to understand that
you had foreseen it all, Miss Phoebe?

PHOEBE. Nay, sir, you must not ask that.

VALENTINE. I believe in any case 'twas you who first
put it into my head.

PHOEBE. [*Aghast.*] Oh, I hope not.

VALENTINE. Your demure eyes flashed so every time
the war was mentioned; the little Quaker suddenly looked
like a gallant boy in ringlets.
[*A dread comes over* PHOEBE, *but it is in her
heart alone; it shows neither in face nor voice.*]

PHOEBE. Mr. Brown, what is it you have to tell us?

VALENTINE. That I have enlisted, Miss Phoebe. Did you surmise it was something else?

PHOEBE. You are going to the wars? Mr. Brown, is it a jest?

VALENTINE. It would be a sorry jest, ma'am. I thought you knew. I concluded that the recruiting sergeant had talked.

PHOEBE. The recruiting sergeant? I see.

VALENTINE. These stirring times, Miss Phoebe—he is but half a man who stays at home. I have chafed for months. I want to see whether I have any courage, and as to be an army surgeon does not appeal to me, it was enlist or remain behind. To-day I found that there were five waverers. I asked them would they take the shilling if I took it, and they assented. Miss Phoebe, it is not one man I give to the King, but six.

PHOEBE. [*Brightly.*] I think you have done bravely.

VALENTINE. We leave shortly for the Petersburgh barracks, and I go to London to-morrow; so this is good-bye.

PHOEBE. I shall pray that you may be preserved in battle, Mr. Brown.

VALENTINE. And you and Miss Susan will write to me when occasion offers?

PHOEBE. If you wish it.

VALENTINE. [*Smiling.*] With all the stirring news of Quality Street.

PHOEBE. It seems stirring to us; it must have been merely laughable to you, who came here from a great city.

VALENTINE. Dear Quality Street—that thought me dashing! But I made friends in it, Miss Phoebe, of two very sweet ladies.

PHOEBE. [*Timidly.*] Mr. Brown, I wonder why you have been so kind to my sister and me?

VALENTINE. The kindness was yours. If at first Miss Susan amused me—— [*Chuckling.*] To see her on her knees decorating the little legs of the couch with frills as if it were a child! But it was her sterling qualities that impressed me presently.

PHOEBE. And did—did I amuse you also?

VALENTINE. Prodigiously, Miss Phoebe. Those other ladies, they were always scolding you, your youthfulness shocked them. I believe they thought you dashing.

PHOEBE. [*Nervously.*] I have sometimes feared that I was perhaps too dashing.

VALENTINE. [*Laughing at this.*] You delicious Miss Phoebe. You were too quiet. I felt sorry that one so sweet and young should live so grey a life. I wondered whether I could put any little pleasures into it.

PHOEBE. The picnics? It was very good of you.

VALENTINE. That was only how it began, for soon I knew that it was I who got the pleasures and you who gave them. You have been to me, Miss Phoebe, like a quiet, old-fashioned garden full of the flowers that Englishmen love best because they have known them longest: the daisy, that stands for innocence, and the hyacinth for constancy, and the modest violet and the rose. When I am far away, ma'am, I shall often think of Miss Phoebe's pretty soul, which is her garden, and shut my eyes and walk in it.

[*She is smiling gallantly through her pain when* MISS SUSAN *returns.*]

MISS SUSAN. Have you—is it—you seem so calm, Phoebe.

PHOEBE. [*Pressing her sister's hand warningly and imploringly.*] Susan, what Mr. Brown is so obliging as to inform us of is not what we expected—not that at all. My dear, he is the gentleman who has enlisted, and he came to tell us that and to say good-bye.

Miss Susan. Going away?

Phoebe. Yes, dear.

Valentine. Am I not the ideal recruit, ma'am: a man without a wife or a mother or a sweetheart?

Miss Susan. No sweetheart?

Valentine. Have you one for me, Miss Susan?

Phoebe. [*Hastily, lest her sister's face should betray the truth.*] Susan, we shall have to tell him now. You dreadful man, you will laugh and say it is just like Quality Street. But indeed since I met you to-day and you told me you had something to communicate we have been puzzling what it could be, and we concluded that you were going to be married.

Valentine. Ha! ha! ha! Was that it?

Phoebe. So like women, you know. We thought we perhaps knew her. [*Glancing at the wedding-gown.*] We were even discussing what we should wear at the wedding.

Valentine. Ha! ha! I shall often think of this. I wonder who would have me, Miss Susan? [*Rising.*] But I must be off; and God bless you both.

Miss Susan. [*Forlorn.*] You are going!

Valentine. No more mud on your carpet, Miss Susan; no more coverlets rolled into balls. A good riddance. Miss Phoebe, a last look at the garden.

[*Taking her hand and looking into her face.*]

Phoebe. We shall miss you very much, Mr. Brown.

Valentine. There is one little matter. That investment I advised you to make, I am happy it has turned out so well.

Phoebe. [*Checking* Miss Susan, *who is about to tell of the loss of the money.*] It was good of you to take all that trouble, sir. Accept our grateful thanks.

Valentine. Indeed I am glad that you are so comfortably left; I am your big brother. Good-bye again.

[*Looks round.*] This little blue and white room and its dear inmates, may they be unchanged when I come back. Good-bye.

[*He goes.* Miss Susan *looks forlornly at* Phoebe, *who smiles pitifully.*]

Phoebe. A misunderstanding; just a mistake. [*She shudders, lifts the wedding-gown and puts it back in the ottoman.* Miss Susan *sinks sobbing into a chair.*] Don't, dear, don't—we can live it down.

Miss Susan. [*Fiercely.*] He is a fiend in human form.

Phoebe. Nay, you hurt me, sister. He is a brave gentleman.

Miss Susan. The money; why did you not let me tell him?

Phoebe. [*Flushing.*] So that he might offer to me out of pity, Susan?

Miss Susan. Phoebe, how are we to live with the quartern loaf at one and tenpence?

Phoebe. Brother James——

Miss Susan. You know very well that brother James will do nothing for us.

Phoebe. I think, Susan, we could keep a little school—for genteel children only, of course. I would do most of the teaching.

Miss Susan. You a schoolmistress—Phoebe of the ringlets; every one would laugh.

Phoebe. I shall hide the ringlets away in a cap like yours, Susan, and people will soon forget them. And I shall try to look staid and to grow old quickly. It will not be so hard to me as you think, dear.

Miss Susan. There were other gentlemen who were attracted by you, Phoebe, and you turned from them.

Phoebe. I did not want them.

Miss Susan. They will come again, and others.

PHOEBE. No, dear; never speak of that to me any more. [*In woe.*] I let him kiss me.

MISS SUSAN. You could not prevent him.

PHOEBE. Yes, I could. I know I could now. I wanted him to do it. Oh, never speak to me of others after that. Perhaps he saw I wanted it and did it to please me. But I meant—indeed I did—that I gave it to him with all my love. Sister, I could bear all the rest; but I have been unladylike.

> [*The curtain falls, and we do not see the sisters again for ten years.*]

End of Act I.

ACT II

THE SCHOOL

Ten years later. It is the blue and white room still, but many of MISS SUSAN'S *beautiful things have gone, some of them never to return; others are stored upstairs. Their place is taken by grim scholastic furniture: forms, a desk, a globe, a blackboard, heartless maps. It is here that* MISS PHOEBE *keeps school.* MISS SUSAN *teaches in the room opening off it, once the spare bedroom, where there is a smaller blackboard [for easier sums] but no globe, as* MISS SUSAN *is easily alarmed. Here are the younger pupils unless they have grown defiant, when they are promoted to the blue and white room to be under* MISS PHOEBE'S *braver rule. They really frighten* MISS PHOEBE *also, but she does not let her sister know this.*

It is noon on a day in August, and through the window we

*can see that Quality Street is decorated with flags.
We also hear at times martial music from another
street. MISS PHOEBE is giving a dancing lesson to
half a dozen pupils, and is doing her very best; now
she is at the spinet while they dance, and again she
is showing them the new step. We know it is MISS
PHOEBE because some of her pretty airs and graces
still cling to her in a forlorn way, but she is much
changed. Her curls are out of sight under a cap, her
manner is prim, the light has gone from her eyes and
buoyancy from her figure; she looks not ten years
older but twenty, and not an easy twenty. When the
children are not looking at her we know that she has
the headache.*

PHOEBE. [*Who is sometimes at the spinet and sometimes dancing.*] Toes out. So. Chest out. Georgy.
Point your toes, Miss Beveridge—so. So—keep in line;
and young ladies, remember your toes. [GEORGY *in his
desire to please has protruded the wrong part of his person.
She writes a C on his chest with chalk.*] C stands for
chest, Georgy. This is S.

> [MISS SUSAN *darts out of the other room. She
> is less worn than* MISS PHOEBE.]

MISS SUSAN. [*Whispering so that the pupils may not
hear.*] Phoebe, how many are fourteen and seventeen?

PHOEBE. [*Almost instantly.*] Thirty-one.

MISS SUSAN. I thank you. [*She darts off.*]

PHOEBE. That will do, ladies and gentlemen. You
may go.

> [*They bow or curtsy, and retire to* MISS SUSAN's
> room, with the exception of ARTHUR WELLES-
> LEY TOMSON, *who is standing in disgrace in a*

corner with the cap of shame on his head, and
ISABELLA, *a forbidding-looking, learned little
girl.* ISABELLA *holds up her hand for permission to speak.*]

ISABELLA. Please, ma'am, father wishes me to acquire
algebra.

PHOEBE. [*With a sinking.*] Algebra! It—it is not a
very ladylike study, Isabella.

ISABELLA. Father says, will you or won't you?

PHOEBE. And you are thin. It will make you thinner, my dear.

ISABELLA. Father says I am thin but wiry.

PHOEBE. Yes, you are. [*With feeling.*] You are very
wiry, Isabella.

ISABELLA. Father says, either I acquire algebra or I
go to Miss Prothero's establishment.

PHOEBE. Very well, I—I will do my best. You may go.
[ISABELLA *goes and* PHOEBE *sits wearily.*]

ARTHUR. [*Fingering his cap.*] Please, ma'am, may I
take it off now?

PHOEBE. Certainly not. Unhappy boy—— [ARTHUR
grins.] Come here. Are you ashamed of yourself?

ARTHUR. [*Blithely.*] No, ma'am.

PHOEBE. [*In a terrible voice.*] Arthur Wellesley
Tomson, fetch me the implement. [ARTHUR *goes briskly
for the cane, and she hits the desk with it.*] Arthur, surely
that terrifies you?

ARTHUR. No, ma'am.

PHOEBE. Arthur, why did you fight with that street
boy?

ARTHUR. 'Cos he said that when you caned you did
not draw blood.

PHOEBE. But I don't, do I?

ARTHUR. No, ma'am.

PHOEBE. Then why fight him? [*Remembering how strange boys are.*] Was it for the honour of the school?

ARTHUR. Yes, ma'am.

PHOEBE. Say you are sorry, Arthur, and I won't punish you.

[*He bursts into tears.*]

ARTHUR. You promised to cane me, and now you are not going to do it.

PHOEBE. [*Incredulous.*] Do you *wish* to be caned?

ARTHUR. [*Holding out his hand eagerly.*] If you please, Miss Phoebe.

PHOEBE. Unnatural boy. [*She canes him in a very unprofessional manner.*] Poor dear boy.

[*She kisses the hand.*]

ARTHUR. [*Gloomily.*] Oh, ma'am, you will never be able to cane if you hold it like that. You should hold it like this, Miss Phoebe, and give it a wriggle like that.

[*She is too soft-hearted to follow his instructions.*]

PHOEBE. [*Almost in tears.*] Go away.

ARTHUR. [*Remembering that women are strange.*] Don't cry, ma'am; I love you, Miss Phoebe.

[*She seats him on her knee, and he thinks of a way to please her.*]

If any boy says you can't cane I will blood him, Miss Phoebe.

[PHOEBE *shudders, and* MISS SUSAN *again darts in. She signs to* PHOEBE *to send* ARTHUR *away.*]

MISS SUSAN. [*As soon as* ARTHUR *has gone.*] Phoebe, if a herring and half cost three ha'pence, how many for elevenpence?

PHOEBE. [*Instantly.*] Eleven.

MISS SUSAN. William Smith says it is fifteen; and he is such a big boy, do you think I ought to contradict him?

May I say there are differences of opinion about it? No one can be really sure, Phoebe.

PHOEBE. It is eleven. I once worked it out with real herrings. [*Stoutly.*] Susan, we must never let the big boys know that we are afraid of them. To awe them, stamp with the foot, speak in a ferocious voice, and look them unflinchingly in the face. [*Then she pales.*] Oh, Susan, Isabella's father insists on her acquiring algebra.

MISS SUSAN. What is algebra exactly; is it those three cornered things?

PHOEBE. It is *x* minus *y* equals *z* plus *y* and things like that. And all the time you are saying they are equal, you feel in your heart, why should they be.

> [*The music of the band swells here, and both ladies put their hands to their ears.*]

It is the band for to-night's ball. We must not grudge their rejoicings, Susan. It is not every year that there is a Waterloo to celebrate.

MISS SUSAN. I was not thinking of that. I was thinking that *he* is to be at the ball to-night; and we have not seen him for ten years.

PHOEBE. [*Calmly.*] Yes, ten years. We shall be glad to welcome our old friend back, Susan. I am going in to your room now to take the Latin class.

> [*A soldier with a girl passes—a yokel follows angrily.*]

MISS SUSAN. Oh, that weary Latin, I wish I had the whipping of the man who invented it.

> [*She returns to her room, and the sound of the music dies away. MISS PHOEBE, who is not a very accomplished classical scholar, is taking a final peep at the declensions when MISS SUSAN reappears excitedly.*]

PHOEBE. What is it?

Miss Susan. [*Tragically.*] William Smith! Phoebe, I tried to look ferocious, indeed I did, but he saw I was afraid, and before the whole school he put out his tongue at me.

Phoebe. Susan!

> [*She is lion-hearted; she remembers* Arthur's *instructions, and practises with the cane.*]

Miss Susan. [*Frightened.*] Phoebe, he is much too big. Let it pass.

Phoebe. If I let it pass I am a stumbling-block in the way of true education.

Miss Susan. Sister.

Phoebe. [*Grandly.*] Susan, stand aside.

> [*Giving the cane* Arthur's *most telling flick, she marches into the other room. Then, while* Miss Susan *is listening nervously,* Captain Valentine Brown *is ushered in by* Patty. *He is bronzed and soldierly. He wears the whiskers of the period, and is in uniform. He has lost his left hand, but this is not at first noticeable.*]

Patty. Miss Susan, 'tis Captain Brown!

Miss Susan. Captain Brown!

Valentine. [*Greeting her warmly.*] Reports himself at home again.

Miss Susan. [*Gratified.*] You call this home?

Valentine. When the other men talked of their homes, Miss Susan, I thought of this room. [*Looking about him.*] Maps—desks—heigho! But still it is the same dear room. I have often dreamt, Miss Susan, that I came back to it in muddy shoes. [*Seeing her alarm.*] I have not, you know! Miss Susan, I rejoice to find no change in you; and Miss Phoebe—Miss Phoebe of the ringlets—I hope there be as little change in her?

MISS SUSAN. [*Painfully.*] Phoebe of the ringlets! Ah, Captain Brown, you need not expect to see her.

VALENTINE. She is not here? I vow it spoils all my home-coming.

> [*At this moment the door of the other room is flung open and* PHOEBE *rushes out, followed by* WILLIAM SMITH *who is brandishing the cane.* VALENTINE *takes in the situation, and without looking at* PHOEBE *seizes* WILLIAM *by the collar and marches him out of the school.*]

MISS SUSAN. Phoebe, did you see who it is?

PHOEBE. I saw. [*In a sudden tremor.*] Susan, I have lost all my looks.

> [*The pupils are crowding in from* MISS SUSAN'S *room and she orders them back and goes with them.* VALENTINE *returns, and speaks as he enters, not recognising* PHOEBE, *whose back is to him.*]

VALENTINE. A young reprobate, madam, but I have deposited him on the causeway. I fear——

> [*He stops, puzzled because the lady has covered her face with her hands.*]

PHOEBE. Captain Brown.

VALENTINE. Miss Phoebe, it is you?

> [*He goes to her, but he cannot help showing that her appearance is a shock to him.*]

PHOEBE. [*Without bitterness.*] Yes, I have changed very much, I have not worn well, Captain Brown.

VALENTINE. [*Awkwardly.*] We—we are both older, Miss Phoebe.

> [*He holds out his hand warmly, with affected high spirits.*]

PHOEBE. [*Smiling reproachfully.*] It was both hands when you went away. [*He has to show that his left hand is gone; she is overcome.*] I did not know. [*She presses the empty sleeve in remorse.*] You never mentioned it in your letters.

VALENTINE. [*Now grown rather stern.*] Miss Phoebe, why did *you* omit from your letters that you had such young blackguards as that to terrify you?

PHOEBE. He is the only one. Most of them are dear children; and this is the last day of the term.

VALENTINE. Ah, ma'am, if only you had invested all your money as you laid out part by my advice. What a monstrous pity you did not.

PHOEBE. We never thought of it.

VALENTINE. You look so tired.

PHOEBE. I have the headache to-day.

VALENTINE. You did not use to have the headache. Curse those dear children.

PHOEBE. [*Bravely.*] Nay, do not distress yourself about me. Tell me of yourself. We are so proud of the way in which you won your commission. Will you leave the army now?

VALENTINE. Yes; and I have some intention of pursuing again the old life in Quality Street. [*He is not a man who has reflected much. He has come back thinking that all the adventures have been his, and that the old life in Quality Street has waited, as in a sleep, to be resumed on the day of his return.*] I came here in such high spirits, Miss Phoebe.

PHOEBE. [*With a wry smile.*] The change in me depresses you.

VALENTINE. I was in hopes that you and Miss Susan would be going to the ball. I had brought cards for you with me to make sure.

[*She is pleased and means to accept. He sighs,*

*and she understands that he thinks her too
old.*]

PHOEBE. But now you see that my dancing days are
done.

VALENTINE. [*Uncomfortably.*] Ah, no.

PHOEBE. [*Taking care he shall not see that he has hurt
her.*] But you will find many charming partners. Some
of them have been my pupils. There was even a pupil
of mine who fought at Waterloo.

VALENTINE. Young Blades; I have heard him on it.
[*She puts her hand wearily to her head.*] Miss Phoebe—
what a dull grey world it is!

> [*She turns away to hide her emotion, and* MISS
> SUSAN *comes in.*]

MISS SUSAN. Phoebe, I have said that you will not
take the Latin class to-day, and I am dismissing them.

VALENTINE. Latin?

PHOEBE. [*Rather defiantly.*] I am proud to teach it.
[*Breaking down.*] Susan—his arm—have you seen?

> [MISS SUSAN *also is overcome, but recovers as
> the children crowd in.*]

MISS SUSAN. Hats off, gentlemen salute, ladies curtsy—
to the brave Captain Brown.

> [CAPTAIN BROWN *salutes them awkwardly, and
> they cheer him, to his great discomfort, as
> they pass out.*]

VALENTINE. [*When they have gone.*] A terrible or-
deal, ma'am.

> [*The old friends look at each other, and there is
> a silence.* VALENTINE *feels that all the fine
> tales and merry jests he has brought back for
> the ladies have turned into dead things. He
> wants to go away and think.*]

PHOEBE. I wish you very happy at the ball.

VALENTINE. [*Sighing.*] Miss Susan, cannot we turn all these maps and horrors out till the vacation is over?

MISS SUSAN. Indeed, sir, we always do. By to-morrow this will be my dear blue and white room again, and that my sweet spare bedroom.

PHOEBE. For five weeks!

VALENTINE. [*Making vain belief.*] And then—the—the dashing Mr. Brown will drop in as of old, and, behold, Miss Susan on her knees once more putting tucks into my little friend the ottoman, and Miss Phoebe—Miss Phoebe——

PHOEBE. Phoebe of the ringlets!

    [*She goes out quietly.*]

VALENTINE. [*Miserably.*] Miss Susan, what a shame it is.

MISS SUSAN. [*Hotly.*] Yes, it is a shame.

VALENTINE. [*Suddenly become more of a man.*] The brave Captain Brown! Good God, ma'am, how much more brave are the ladies who keep a school.

    [PATTY *shows in two visitors,* MISS CHARLOTTE
        PARRATT *and* ENSIGN BLADES. CHARLOTTE *is a*
        pretty minx who we are glad to say does not
        reside in Quality Street, and BLADES *is a callow*
        youth, inviting admiration.]

CHARLOTTE. [*As they salute.*] But I did not know you had company, Miss Susan.

MISS SUSAN. 'Tis Captain Brown—Miss Charlotte Parratt.

CHARLOTTE. [*Gushing.*] The heroic Brown?

VALENTINE. Alas, no, ma'am, the other one.

CHARLOTTE. Miss Susan, do you see who accompanies me?

MISS SUSAN. I cannot quite recall——

BLADES.   A few years ago, ma'am, there sat in this room a scrubby, inky little boy—I was that boy.

MISS SUSAN.   Can it be our old pupil—Ensign Blades?

> [*She thinks him very fine, and he bows, well pleased.*]

BLADES.   Once a little boy and now your most obedient, ma'am.

MISS SUSAN.   You have come to recall old memories?

BLADES.   Not precisely; I—Charlotte, explain.

CHARLOTTE.   Ensign Blades wishes me to say that it must seem highly romantic to you to have had a pupil who has fought at Waterloo.

MISS SUSAN.   Not exactly *romantic*. I trust, sir, that when you speak of having been our pupil you are also so obliging as to mention that it was during our first year. Otherwise it makes us seem so elderly.

> [*He bows again, in what he believes to be a quizzical manner.*]

CHARLOTTE.   Ensign Blades would be pleased to hear, Miss Susan, what you think of him as a whole.

MISS SUSAN.   Indeed, sir, I think you are monstrous fine.   [*Innocently.*]   It quite awes me to remember that we used to whip him.

VALENTINE.   [*Delighted.*]   Whipped him, Miss Susan! [*In solemn burlesque of* CHARLOTTE.]   Ensign Blades wishes to indicate that it was more than Buonaparte could do. We shall meet again, bright boy.

> [*He makes his adieux and goes.*]

BLADES.   Do you think he was quizzing me?

MISS SUSAN.   [*Simply.*]   I cannot think so.

BLADES.   He said "bright boy," ma'am.

MISS SUSAN.   I am sure, sir, he did not mean it.

> [PHOEBE *returns.*]

PHOEBE. Charlotte, I am happy to see you. You look delicious, my dear—so young and fresh.

CHARLOTTE. La! Do you think so, Miss Phoebe?

BLADES. Miss Phoebe, your obedient.

PHOEBE. It is Ensign Blades! But how kind of you, sir, to revisit the old school. Please to sit down.

CHARLOTTE. Ensign Blades has a favour to ask of you, Miss Phoebe.

BLADES. I learn, ma'am, that Captain Brown has obtained a card for you for the ball, and I am here to solicit for the honour of standing up with you.

> [*For the moment* PHOEBE *is flattered. Here, she believes, is some one who does not think her too old for the dance. Then she perceives a meaning smile pass between* CHARLOTTE *and the* EN- SIGN.]

PHOEBE. [*Paling.*] Is it that you desire to make sport of me?

BLADES. [*Honestly distressed.*] Oh no, ma'am, I vow —but I—I am such a quiz, ma'am.

MISS SUSAN. Sister!

PHOEBE. I am sorry, sir, to have to deprive you of some entertainment, but I am not going to the ball.

MISS SUSAN. [*Haughtily.*] Ensign Blades, I bid you my adieux.

BLADES. [*Ashamed.*] If I have hurt Miss Phoebe's feelings I beg to apologise.

MISS SUSAN. *If* you have hurt them. Oh, sir, how is it possible for any one to be as silly as you seem to be.

BLADES. [*Who cannot find the answer.*] Charlotte— explain.

> [*But* CHARLOTTE *considers that their visit has not been sufficiently esteemed and departs with a cold curtsy, taking him with her.*]

[MISS SUSAN *turns sympathetically to* PHOEBE, *but* PHOEBE, *fighting with her pain, sits down at the spinet and plays at first excitedly a gay tune, then slowly, then comes to a stop with her head bowed. Soon she jumps up courageously, brushes away her distress, gets an algebra book from the desk and sits down to study it.* MISS SUSAN *is at the window, where ladies and gentlemen are now seen passing in ball attire.*]

MISS SUSAN. What book is it, Phoebe?

PHOEBE. It is an algebra.

MISS SUSAN. They are going by to the ball. [*In anger.*] My Phoebe should be going to the ball, too.

PHOEBE. You jest, Susan. [MISS SUSAN *watches her read.* PHOEBE *has to wipe away a tear; soon she rises and gives way to the emotion she has been suppressing ever since the entrance of* VALENTINE.] Susan, I hate him. Oh, Susan, I could hate him if it were not for his poor hand.

MISS SUSAN. My dear.

PHOEBE. He thought I was old, because I am weary, and he should not have forgotten. I am only thirty. Susan, why does thirty seem so much more than twenty-nine? [*As if* VALENTINE *were present.*] Oh, sir, how dare you look so pityingly at me? Because I have had to work so hard, —is it a crime when a woman works? Because I have tried to be courageous—have I been courageous, Susan?

MISS SUSAN. God knows you have.

PHOEBE. But it has given me the headache, it has tired my eyes. Alas, Miss Phoebe, all your charm has gone, for you have the headache, and your eyes are tired. He is dancing with Charlotte Parratt now, Susan. "I vow, Miss Charlotte, you are selfish and silly, but you are sweet eighteen." "Oh la, Captain Brown, what a quiz you are." That delights him, Susan; see how he waggles his silly head.

Miss Susan. Charlotte Parratt is a goose.

Phoebe. 'Tis what gentlemen prefer. If there were a sufficient number of geese to go round, Susan, no woman of sense would ever get a husband. "Charming Miss Charlotte, you are like a garden; Miss Phoebe was like a garden once, but 'tis a faded garden now."

Miss Susan. If to be ladylike——

Phoebe. Susan, I am tired of being ladylike. I am a young woman still, and to be ladylike is not enough. I wish to be bright and thoughtless and merry. It is every woman's birthright to be petted and admired; I wish to be petted and admired. Was I born to be confined within these four walls? Are they the world, Susan, or is there anything beyond them? I want to know. My eyes are tired because for ten years they have seen nothing but maps and desks. Ten years! Ten years ago I went to bed a young girl and I woke with this cap on my head. It is not fair. This is not me, Susan, this is some other person, I want to be myself.

Miss Susan. Phoebe, Phoebe, you who have always been so patient!

Phoebe. Oh no, not always. If you only knew how I have rebelled at times, you would turn from me in horror. Susan, I have a picture of myself as I used to be; I sometimes look at it. I sometimes kiss it, and say, "Poor girl, they have all forgotten you. But I remember."

Miss Susan. I cannot recall it.

Phoebe. I keep it locked away in my room. Would you like to see it? I shall bring it down. My room! Oh, Susan, it is there that the Phoebe you think so patient has the hardest fight with herself, for there I have seemed to hear and see the Phoebe of whom this [looking at herself] is but an image in a distorted glass. I have heard her singing as if she thought she was still a girl. I have heard her weeping; perhaps it was only I who was weeping; but she seemed to cry to me, "Let me out of this prison, give me back the years you have taken from me. Oh, where are my pretty curls?" she cried. "Where is my youth, my youth."

> [*She goes out, leaving* MISS SUSAN *woeful. Presently* SUSAN *takes up the algebra book and reads.*]

MISS SUSAN. "A stroke B multiplied by B stroke C equal AB stroke a little 2; stroke AC add BC." Poor Phoebe! "Multiply by C stroke A and we get"—Poor Phoebe! "C a B stroke a little 2 stroke AC little 2 add BC." Oh, I cannot believe it! "Stroke a little 2 again, add AB little 2 add a little 2 C stroke a BC." . . .

> [PATTY *comes in with the lamp.*]

PATTY. Hurting your poor eyes reading without a lamp. Think shame, Miss Susan.

MISS SUSAN. [*With spirit.*] Patty, I will not be dictated to. [PATTY *looks out at window.*] Draw the curtains at once. I cannot allow you to stand gazing at the foolish creatures who crowd to a ball.

PATTY. [*Closing curtains.*] I am not gazing at them, ma'am; I am gazing at my sweetheart.

MISS SUSAN. Your sweetheart? [*Softly.*] I did not know you had one.

PATTY. Nor have I, ma'am, as yet. But I looks out, and thinks I to myself, at any moment he may turn the corner. I ha' been looking out at windows waiting for him to oblige by turning the corner this fifteen years.

MISS SUSAN. Fifteen years, and still you are hopeful?

PATTY. There is not a more hopeful woman in all the king's dominions.

MISS SUSAN. You who are so much older than Miss Phoebe.

PATTY. Yes, ma'am, I ha' the advantage of her by ten years.

MISS SUSAN. It would be idle to pretend that you are specially comely.

PATTY. That may be, but my face is my own, and the more I see it in the glass the more it pleases me. I never look at it but I say to myself, "Who is to be the lucky man?"

MISS SUSAN. 'Tis wonderful.

PATTY. This will be a great year for females, ma'am. Think how many of the men that marched away strutting to the wars have come back limping. Who is to take off their wooden legs of an evening, Miss Susan? You, ma'am, or me?

MISS SUSAN. Patty!

PATTY. [*Doggedly.*] Or Miss Phoebe? [*With feeling.*] The pretty thing that she was, Miss Susan.

MISS SUSAN. Do you remember, Patty? I think there is no other person who remembers unless it be the Misses Willoughby and Miss Henrietta.

PATTY. [*Eagerly.*] Give her a chance, ma'am, and take her to the balls. There be three of them this week, and the last ball will be the best, for 'tis to be at the barracks, and you will need a carriage to take you there, and there will be the packing of you into it by gallant squires and the unpacking of you out, and other devilries.

MISS SUSAN. Patty!

PATTY. If Miss Phoebe were to dress young again and put candles in her eyes that used to be so bright, and coax back her curls——

> [PHOEBE *returns, and a great change has come*
> *over her. She is young and pretty again. She is*
> *wearing the wedding-gown of* ACT I, *her ringlets*
> *are glorious, her figure youthful, her face*
> *flushed and animated.* PATTY *is the first to see*

her, and is astonished. PHOEBE *signs to her to go.*]

PHOEBE. [*When* PATTY *has gone.*] Susan. [MISS SUSAN *sees and is speechless.*] Susan, this is the picture of my old self that I keep locked away in my room, and sometimes take out of its box to look at. This is the girl who kisses herself in the glass and sings and dances with glee until I put her away frightened lest you should hear her.

MISS SUSAN. How marvellous! Oh, Phoebe!

PHOEBE. Perhaps I should not do it, but it is so easy. I have but to put on the old wedding-gown and tumble my curls out of the cap. [*Passionately.*] Sister, am I as changed as he says I am?

MISS SUSAN. You almost frighten me.

[*The band is heard.*]

PHOEBE. The music is calling to us. Susan, I will celebrate Waterloo in a little ball of my own. See, my curls have begun to dance, they are so anxious to dance. One dance, Susan, to Phoebe of the ringlets, and then I will put her away in her box and never look at her again. Ma'am, may I have the honour? Nay, then I shall dance alone. [*She dances.*] Oh, Susan, I almost wish I were a goose.

[*Presently* PATTY *returns. She gazes at* MISS PHOEBE *dancing.*]

PATTY. Miss Phoebe!

PHOEBE. [*Still dancing.*] Not Miss Phoebe, Patty. I am not myself to-night, I am—let me see, I am my niece.

PATTY. [*In a whisper to* SUSAN.] But Miss Susan, 'tis Captain Brown.

MISS SUSAN. Oh, stop, Phoebe, stop!

PATTY. Nay, let him see her!

[MISS SUSAN *hurries scandalised into the other room as* VALENTINE *enters.*]

VALENTINE. I ventured to come back because——
[PHOEBE *turns to him—he stops abruptly, bewildered.*] I
beg your pardon, madam, I thought it was Miss Susan or
Miss Phoebe.

> [*His mistake surprises her, but she is in a wild
> mood and curtsies, then turns away and smiles.
> He stares as if half-convinced.*]

PATTY. [*With an inspiration.*] 'Tis my mistresses'
niece, sir; she is on a visit here.

> [*He is deceived. He bows gallantly, then re-
> members the object of his visit. He produces a
> bottle of medicine.*]

VALENTINE. Patty, I obtained this at the apothecary's
for Miss Phoebe's headache. It should be taken at once.

PATTY. Miss Phoebe is lying down, sir.

VALENTINE. Is she asleep?

PATTY. [*Demurely.*] No, sir, I think she be wide
awake.

VALENTINE. It may soothe her.

PHOEBE. Patty, take it to Aunt Phoebe at once.

> [PATTY *goes out sedately with the medicine.*]

VALENTINE. [*After a little awkwardness, which* PHOEBE
enjoys.] Perhaps I may venture to present myself, Miss—
Miss——?

PHOEBE. Miss—Livvy, sir.

VALENTINE. I am Captain Brown, Miss Livvy, an old
friend of both your aunts.

PHOEBE. [*Curtsying.*] I have heard them speak of a
dashing Mr. Brown. But I think it cannot be the same.

VALENTINE. [*A little chagrined.*] Why not, ma'am?

PHOEBE. I ask your pardon, sir.

VALENTINE. I was sure you must be related. Indeed,
for a moment the likeness—even the voice——

PHOEBE. [*Pouting.*] La, sir, you mean I am like Aunt Phoebe. Every one says so—and indeed 'tis no compliment.

VALENTINE. 'Twould have been a compliment once. You must be a daughter of the excellent Mr. James Throssel who used to reside at Great Buckland.

PHOEBE. He is still there.

VALENTINE. A tedious twenty miles from here, as I remember.

PHOEBE. La! I have found the journey a monstrous quick one, sir.

> [*The band is again heard. She runs to the window to peep between the curtains, and his eyes follow her admiringly.*]

VALENTINE. [*Eagerly.*] Miss Livvy, you go to the ball?

PHOEBE. Alas, sir, I have no card.

VALENTINE. I have two cards for your aunts. As Miss Phoebe has the headache, your Aunt Susan must take you to the ball.

PHOEBE. Oh, oh! [*Her feet move to the music.*] Sir, I cannot control my feet.

VALENTINE. They are already at the ball, ma'am; you must follow them.

PHOEBE. [*With all the pent-up mischief of ten years.*] Oh, sir, do you think some pretty gentleman might be partial to me at the ball?

VALENTINE. If that is your wish——

PHOEBE. I should love, sir, to inspire frenzy in the breast of the male. [*With sudden collapse.*] I dare not go —I dare not.

VALENTINE. Miss Livvy, I vow——

> [*He turns eagerly to* MISS SUSAN, *who enters.*]

I have ventured, Miss Susan, to introduce myself to your charming niece.

[MISS SUSAN *would like to run away again, but
the wicked* MISS PHOEBE *is determined to have
her help.*]

PHOEBE. Aunt Susan, do not be angry with your Livvy
—your Livvy, Aunt Susan. This gentleman says he is the
dashing Mr. Brown, he has cards for us for the ball, Auntie.
Of course we cannot go—we dare not go. Oh, Auntie, hasten
into your bombazine.

MISS SUSAN. [*Staggered.*] Phoebe——

PHOEBE. Aunt Phoebe wants me to go. If I say she
does you know she does!

MISS SUSAN. But my dear, my dear.

PHOEBE. Oh, Auntie, why do you talk so much. Come,
come.

VALENTINE. I shall see to it, Miss Susan, that your
niece has a charming ball.

PHOEBE. He means he will find me sweet partners.

VALENTINE. Nay, ma'am, I mean *I* shall be your
partner.

PHOEBE. [*Who is not an angel.*] Aunt Susan, he still
dances!

VALENTINE. *Still*, ma'am?

PHOEBE. Oh, sir, you are indeed dashing. Nay, sir,
please not to scowl, I could not avoid noticing them.

VALENTINE. Noticing what, Miss Livvy?

PHOEBE. The grey hairs, sir.

VALENTINE. I vow, ma'am, there is not one in my head.

PHOEBE. He is such a quiz. I so love a quiz.

VALENTINE. Then, ma'am, I shall do nothing but quiz
you at the ball. Miss Susan, I beg you——

MISS SUSAN. Oh, sir, dissuade her.

VALENTINE. Nay, I entreat.

PHOEBE. Auntie!

MISS SUSAN. Think, my dear, think, we dare not.

PHOEBE. [*Shuddering.*]   No, we dare not, I cannot go.

VALENTINE.   Indeed, ma'am.

PHOEBE.   'Tis impossible.

> [*She really means it, and had not the music here taken an unfair advantage of her it is certain that MISS PHOEBE would never have gone to the ball. In after years she and MISS SUSAN would have talked together of the monstrous evening when she nearly lost her head, but regained it before it could fall off. But suddenly the music swells so alluringly that it is a thousand fingers beckoning her to all the balls she has missed, and in a transport she whirls MISS SUSAN from the blue and white room to the bed-chamber where is the bombazine. VALENTINE awaits their return like a conqueror, until MISS LIVVY's words about his hair return to trouble him. He is stooping, gazing intently into a small mirror, extracting the grey hairs one by one, when PATTY ushers in the sisters WILLOUGHBY and MISS HENRIETTA. MISS HENRIETTA is wearing the new veil, which opens or closes like curtains when she pulls a string. She opens it now to see what he is doing, and the slight sound brings him to his feet.*]

MISS HENRIETTA.   'Tis but the new veil, sir; there is no cause for alarm.

> [*They have already learned from PATTY, we may be sure, that he is in the house, but they express genteel surprise.*]

MISS FANNY.   Mary, surely we are addressing the gallant Captain Brown!

VALENTINE.   It is the Misses Willoughby and Miss Henrietta. 'Tis indeed a gratification to renew acquaintance with such elegant and respectable females.

[*The greetings are elaborate.*]

MISS WILLOUGHBY. You have seen Miss Phoebe, sir?

VALENTINE. I have had the honour. Miss Phoebe, I regret to say, is now lying down with the headache. [*The ladies are too delicately minded to exchange glances before a man, but they are privately of opinion that this meeting after ten years with the dazzling* BROWN *has laid* MISS PHOEBE *low. They are in a twitter of sympathy with her, and yearning to see* MISS SUSAN *alone, so that they may draw from her an account of the exciting meeting.*] You do not favour the ball to-night?

MISS FANNY. I confess balls are distasteful to me.

MISS HENRIETTA. 'Twill be a mixed assembly. I am credibly informed that the woollen-draper's daughter has obtained a card.

VALENTINE. [*Gravely.*] Good God, ma'am, is it possible?

MISS WILLOUGHBY. We shall probably spend the evening here with Miss Susan at the card table.

VALENTINE. But Miss Susan goes with me to the ball, ma'am.

[*This is scarcely less exciting to them than the overthrow of the Corsican.*]

VALENTINE. Nay, I hope there be no impropriety. Miss Livvy will accompany her.

MISS WILLOUGHBY. [*Bewildered.*] Miss Livvy?

VALENTINE. Their charming niece.

[*The ladies repeat the word in a daze.*]

MISS FANNY. They had not apprised us that they have a visitor.

[*They think this reticence unfriendly, and are wondering whether they ought not to retire hurt,*

when Miss Susan *enters in her bombazine,
wraps, and bonnet. She starts at sight of them,
and has the bearing of a guilty person.*]

Miss Willoughby. [*Stiffly.*] We have but now been
advertised of your intention for this evening, Susan.

Miss Henrietta. We deeply regret our intrusion.

Miss Susan. [*Wistfully.*] Please not to be piqued,
Mary. 'Twas so—sudden.

Miss Willoughby. I cannot remember, Susan, that
your estimable brother had a daughter. I thought all the
three were sons.

Miss Susan. [*With deplorable readiness.*] Three sons
and a daughter. Surely you remember little Livvy, Mary?

Miss Willoughby. [*Bluntly.*] No, Susan, I do not.

Miss Susan. I—I must go. I hear Livvy calling.

Miss Fanny. [*Tartly.*] I hear nothing but the band.
We are not to see your niece?

Miss Susan. Another time—to-morrow. Pray rest a
little before you depart, Mary. I—I—Phoebe Livvy—the
headache——

[*But before she can go another lady enters gaily.*]

Valentine. Ah, here is Miss Livvy.

[*The true culprit is more cunning than* Miss
Susan, *and before they can see her she quickly
pulls the strings of her bonnet, which is like*
Miss Henrietta's, *and it obscures her face*]

Miss Susan. This—this is my niece, Livvy—Miss Willoughby, Miss Henrietta, Miss Fanny Willoughby.

Valentine. Ladies, excuse my impatience, but——

Miss Willoughby. One moment, sir. May I ask, Miss
Livvy, how many brothers you have?

Phoebe. Two.

Miss Willoughby. I thank you.

[*She looks strangely at* Miss Susan, *and* Miss
Phoebe *knows that she has blundered.*]

Phoebe. [*At a venture.*] Excluding the unhappy
Thomas.

Miss Susan. [*Clever for the only moment in her life.*]
We never mention him.

[*They are swept away on the arms of the impatient* Captain.]

Miss Willoughby, Miss Henreitta, and Miss Fanny.
What has Thomas done?

[*They have no suspicion as yet of what* Miss
Phoebe *has done; but they believe there is a
scandal in the Throssel family, and they will
not sleep happily until they know what it is.*]

End of Act II.

ACT III

THE BALL

A ball, but not the one to which we have seen Miss Susan
and Miss Phoebe *rush forth upon their career of
crime. This is the third of the series, the one of
which* Patty *has foretold with horrid relish that it
promises to be specially given over to deviltries. The
scene is a canvas pavilion, used as a retiring room and
for card play, and through an opening in the back we
have glimpses of gay uniforms and fair ladies intermingled in the bravery of the dance. There is coming
and going through this opening, and also through slits
in the canvas. The pavilion is fantastically decorated
in various tastes, and is lit with lanterns. A good-*

*natured moon, nevertheless, shines into it benignly.
Some of the card tables are neglected, but at one a game
of quadrille is in progress. There is much movement
and hilarity, but none from one side of the tent, where
sit several young ladies, all pretty, all appealing, and
all woeful, for no gallant comes to ask them if he may
have the felicity. The nervous woman chaperoning
them, and afraid to meet their gaze lest they scowl or
weep in reply, is no other than* MISS SUSAN, *the most
unhappy* MISS SUSAN *we have yet seen; she sits there
gripping her composure in both hands. Far less
susceptible to shame is the brazen* PHOEBE, *who may be
seen passing the opening on the arm of a cavalier, and
flinging her trembling sister a mischievous kiss. The
younger ladies note the incident; alas, they are probably meant to notice it, and they cower, as under a
blow.*

HARRIET. [*A sad-eyed, large girl, who we hope found
a romance at her next ball.*] Are we so disagreeable that
no one will dance with us? Miss Susan, 'tis infamous;
they have eyes for no one but your niece.

CHARLOTTE. Miss Livvy has taken Ensign Blades
from me.

HARRIET. If Miss Phoebe were here, I am sure she
would not allow her old pupils to be so neglected.

> [*The only possible reply for* MISS SUSAN *is to
> make herself look as small as possible. A lieu-
> tenant comes to them, once a scorner of woman,
> but now* SPICER *the bewitched.* HARRIET *has
> a moment's hope.*]

How do you do, sir?

SPICER. [*With dreadful indifference, though she is his*

dear cousin.] Nay, ma'am, how do *you* do? [*Wistfully.*] May I stand beside you, Miss Susan?

> [*He is a most melancholic young man, and he fidgets her.*]

MISS SUSAN. [*With spirit.*] You have been standing beside me, sir, nearly all the evening.

SPICER. [*Humbly. It is strange to think that he had been favourably mentioned in despatches.*] Indeed, I cannot but be cognisant of the sufferings I cause by attaching myself to you in this unseemly manner. Accept my assurances, ma'am, that you have my deepest sympathy.

MISS SUSAN. Then why do you do it?

SPICER. Because you are her aunt, ma'am. It is a scheme of mine by which I am in hopes to soften her heart. Her affection for you, ma'am, is beautiful to observe, and if she could be persuaded that I seek her hand from a passionate desire to have you for my Aunt Susan—do you perceive anything hopeful in my scheme, ma'am?

MISS SUSAN. No, sir, I do not.

> [SPICER *wanders away gloomily, takes too much to drink, and ultimately becomes a general.* ENSIGN BLADES *appears, frowning, and* CHARLOTTE *ventures to touch his sleeve.*]

CHARLOTTE. Ensign Blades, I have not danced with you once this evening.

BLADES. [*With the cold brutality of a lover to another she.*] Nor I with you, Charlotte. [*To* SUSAN.] May I solicit of you, Miss Susan, is Captain Brown Miss Livvy's guardian; is he affianced to her?

MISS SUSAN. No, sir.

BLADES. Then by what right, ma'am, does he interfere? Your elegant niece had consented to accompany me to the shrubbery—to look at the moon. And now Captain Brown forbids it. 'Tis unendurable.

CHARLOTTE. But you may see the moon from here, sir.

BLADES. [*Glancing at it contemptuously.*] I believe not, ma'am. [*The moon still shines on.*]

MISS SUSAN. [*Primly.*] I am happy Captain Brown forbade her.

BLADES. Miss Susan, 'twas but because he is to conduct her to the shrubbery himself.

> [*He flings out pettishly, and* MISS SUSAN *looks pityingly at the wall-flowers.*]

MISS SUSAN. My poor Charlotte! May I take you to some very agreeable ladies?

CHARLOTTE. [*Tartly.*] No, you may not. I am going to the shrubbery to watch Miss Livvy.

MISS SUSAN. Please not to do that.

CHARLOTTE. [*Implying that* MISS SUSAN *will be responsible for her early death.*] My chest is weak. I shall sit among the dew.

MISS SUSAN. Charlotte, you terrify me. At least, please to put this cloak about your shoulders. Nay, my dear, allow me.

> [*She puts a cloak around* CHARLOTTE, *who departs vindictively for the shrubbery. She will not find* LIVVY *there, however, for next moment* MISS PHOEBE *darts in from the back.*]

PHOEBE. [*In a gay whisper.*] Susan, another offer—Major Linkwater—rotund man, black whiskers, fierce expression; he has rushed away to destroy himself.

> [*We have been unable to find any record of the Major's tragic end.*]

AN OLD SOLDIER. [*Looking up from a card table, whence he has heard the raging of* BLADES.] Miss Livvy, ma'am, what is this about the moon?

> [PHOEBE *smiles roguishly.*]

PHOEBE. [*Looking about her.*]   I want my cloak, Aunt Susan.

MISS SUSAN. I have just lent it to poor Charlotte Parratt.

PHOEBE. Oh, auntie!

OLD SOLDIER. And now Miss Livvy cannot go into the shrubbery to see the moon; and she is so fond of the moon!

> [MISS PHOEBE *screws her nose at him merrily, and darts back to the dance, but she has left a defender behind her.*]   .

A GALLANT. [*Whose name we have not succeeded in discovering.*]   Am I to understand, sir, that you are intimating disparagement of the moon?   If a certain female has been graciously pleased to signify approval of that orb, any slight cast upon the moon, sir, I shall regard as a personal affront.

OLD SOLDIER. Hoity-toity.

> [*But he rises, and they face each other, as* MISS SUSAN *feels, for battle.   She is about to rush between their undrawn swords when there is a commotion outside; a crowd gathers and opens to allow some officers to assist a fainting woman into the tent.   It is* MISS PHOEBE, *and* MISS SUSAN *with a cry goes on her knees beside her. The tent has filled with the sympathetic and inquisitive, but* CAPTAIN BROWN, *as a physician, takes command, and by his order they retire.   He finds difficulty in bringing the sufferer to, and gets little help from* MISS SUSAN, *who can only call upon* MISS PHOEBE *by name.*]

VALENTINE. Nay, Miss Susan, 'tis useless calling for Miss Phoebe.   'Tis my fault; I should not have permitted Miss Livvy to dance so immoderately.   Why do they delay with the cordial?

[*He goes to the back to close the opening, and while he is doing so the incomprehensible* MISS PHOEBE *seizes the opportunity to sit up on her couch of chairs, waggle her finger at* MISS SUSAN, *and sign darkly that she is about to make a genteel recovery.*]

PHOEBE. Where am I? Is that you, Aunt Susan? What has happened?

VALENTINE. [*Returning.*] Nay, you must recline, Miss Livvy. You fainted. You have over-fatigued yourself.

PHOEBE. I remember.

[BLADES *enters with the cordial.*]

VALENTINE. You will sip this cordial.

BLADES. By your leave, sir.

[*He hands it to* PHOEBE *himself.*]

VALENTINE. She is in restored looks already, Miss Susan.

PHOEBE. I am quite recovered. Perhaps if you were to leave me now with my excellent aunt——

VALENTINE. Be off with you, apple cheeks.

BLADES. Sir, I will suffer no reference to my complexion; and, if I mistake not, this charming lady was addressing you.

PHOEBE. If you please, both of you. [*They retire together, and no sooner have they gone than* MISS PHOEBE *leaps from the couch, her eyes sparkling. She presses the cordial on* MISS SUSAN.] Nay, drink it, Susan. I left it for you on purpose. I have such awful information to impart. Drink. [MISS SUSAN *drinks tremblingly and then the bolt is fired.*] Susan, Miss Henrietta and Miss Fanny are here!

MISS SUSAN. Phoebe!

PHOEBE. Suddenly my eyes lighted on them. At once I slipped to the ground.

MISS SUSAN. You think they did not see you?

PHOEBE. I am sure of it. They talked for a moment to Ensign Blades, and then turned and seemed to be going towards the shrubbery.

MISS SUSAN. He had heard that you were there with Captain Brown. He must have told them.

PHOEBE. I was not. But oh, sister, I am sure they suspect, else why should they be here? They never frequent balls.

MISS SUSAN. They have suspected for a week, ever since they saw you in your veil, Phoebe, on the night of the first dance. How could they but suspect, when they have visited us every day since then and we have always pretended that Livvy was gone out.

PHOEBE. Should they see my face it will be idle to attempt to deceive them.

MISS SUSAN. Idle indeed; Phoebe, the scandal! You—a schoolmistress!

PHOEBE. That is it sister. A little happiness has gone to my head like strong waters.

[*She is very restless and troubled.*]

MISS SUSAN. My dear, stand still, and think.

PHOEBE. I dare not, I cannot. Oh, Susan, if they see me we need not open school again.

MISS SUSAN. We shall starve.

PHOEBE. [*Passionately.*] This horrid, forward, flirting, heartless, hateful little toad of a Livvy.

MISS SUSAN. Brother James's daughter, as we call her!

PHOEBE. 'Tis all James's fault.

MISS SUSAN. Sister, when you know that James has no daughter!

PHOEBE. If he had really had one, think you I could have been so wicked as to personate her? Susan, I know not what I am saying, but you know who it is that has turned me into this wild creature.

MISS SUSAN. Oh, Valentine Brown, how could you?

PHOEBE. To weary of Phoebe—patient, lady-like Phoebe—the Phoebe whom I have lost—to turn from her with a "Bah, you make me old," and become enamoured in a night of a thing like this!

MISS SUSAN. Yes, yes, indeed; yet he has been kind to us also. He has been to visit us several times.

PHOEBE. In the hope to see her. Was he not most silent and gloomy when we said she was gone out?

MISS SUSAN. He is infatuate— [*She hesitates.*] Sister, you are not partial to him still?

PHOEBE. No, Susan, no. I did love him all those years, though I never spoke of it to you. I put hope aside at once, I folded it up and kissed it and put it away like a pretty garment I could never wear again; I but loved to think of him as a noble man. But he is not a noble man, and Livvy found it out in an hour. The gallant! I flirted that I might enjoy his fury. Susan, there has been a declaration in his eyes all to-night, and when he cries "Adorable Miss Livvy, be mine," I mean to answer with an "Oh, la, how ridiculous you are. You are much too old—I have been but quizzing you, sir."

MISS SUSAN. Phoebe, how can you be so cruel?

PHOEBE. Because he has taken from me the one great glory that is in a woman's life. Not a man's love—she can do without that— but her own dear sweet love for him. He is unworthy of my love; that is why I can be so cruel.

MISS SUSAN. Oh, dear.

PHOEBE. And now my triumph is to be denied me, for we must steal away home before Henrietta and Fanny see us.

MISS SUSAN. Yes, yes.

PHOEBE. [*Dispirited.*] And to-morrow we must say

that Livvy has gone back to her father, for I dare keep up this deception no longer. Susan, let us go.

> [*They are going dejectedly, but are arrested by the apparition of* MISS HENRIETTA *and* MISS FANNY *peeping into the tent.* PHOEBE *has just time to signify to her sister that she will confess all and beg for mercy, when the intruders speak.*]

MISS HENRIETTA. [*Not triumphant but astounded.*] You, Miss Phoebe?

PHOEBE. [*With bowed head.*] Yes.

MISS FANNY. How amazing! You do not deny, ma'am, that you are Miss Phoebe?

PHOEBE. [*Making confession.*] Yes, Fanny, I am Miss Phoebe.

> [*To her bewilderment* HENRIETTA *and* FANNY *exchange ashamed glances.*]

MISS HENRIETTA. Miss Phoebe, we have done you a cruel wrong.

MISS FANNY. Phoebe, we apologise.

MISS HENRIETTA. To think how excitedly we have been following her about in the shrubbery.

MISS FANNY. She is wearing your cloak.

MISS HENRIETTA. Ensign Blades told us she was gone to the shrubbery.

MISS FANNY. And we were convinced there was no such person.

MISS HENRIETTA. So of course we thought it must be you.

MISS FANNY. [*Who has looked out.*] I can discern her in the shrubbery still. She is decidedly taller than Phoebe.

MISS HENRIETTA. I thought she looked taller. I meant

to say so. Phoebe, 'twas the cloak deceived us. We could
not see her face.

PHOEBE. *[Beginning to understand.]* Cloak? You
mean, Henrietta—you mean, Fanny——

MISS FANNY. 'Twas wicked of us, my dear, but we—
we thought that you and Miss Livvy were the same person.
[They have evidently been stalking CHARLOTTE *in* MISS
PHOEBE'S *cloak.* MISS SUSAN *shudders, but* MISS PHOEBE
*utters a cry of reproach, and it is some time before they
can persuade her to forgive them. It is of course also some
time before we can forgive* MISS PHOEBE.] Phoebe, you
look so pretty. Are they paying you no attentions, my
dear?

> [PHOEBE *is unable to resist these delightful open-
> ings. The imploring looks* MISS SUSAN *gives
> her but add to her enjoyment. It is as if the
> sense of fun she had caged a moment ago were
> broke loose again.*]

PHŒBE. Alas, they think of none but Livvy. They
come to me merely to say that they adore her.

MISS HENRIETTA. Surely not Captain Brown?

PHOEBE. He is infatuate about her.

MISS FANNY. Poor Phoebe!

> [*They make much of her, and she purrs naugh-
> tily to their stroking, with lightning peeps at*
> MISS SUSAN. *Affronted Providence seeks to pay
> her out by sending* ENSIGN BLADES *into the tent.
> Then the close observer may see* MISS PHOEBE'S
> *heart sink like a bucket in a well.* MISS SUSAN
> *steals from the tent.*]

MISS HENRIETTA. Mr. Blades, I have been saying that
if I were a gentleman I would pay my addresses to Miss
Phoebe much rather than to her niece.

BLADES. Ma'am, excuse me.

MISS HENRIETTA. [*Indignant that* MISS PHOEBE *should be slighted so publicly.*] Sir, you are a most ungallant and deficient young man.

BLADES. Really, ma'am, I assure you——

MISS HENRIETTA. Not another word, sir.

PHOEBE. [*In her most old-maidish manner.*] Miss Fanny, Miss Henrietta, it is time I spoke plainly to this gentleman. Please leave him to me. Surely 'twill come best from me.

MISS HENRIETTA. Indeed, yes, if it be not too painful to you.

PHOEBE. I must do my duty.

MISS FANNY. [*Wistfully.*] If we could remain——

PHOEBE. Would it be seemly, Miss Fanny?

MISS HENRIETTA. Come, Fanny. [*To* BLADES.] Sir, you bring your punishment upon yourself.

> [*They press* PHOEBE's *hand, and go. Her heart returns to its usual abode.*]

BLADES. [*Bewildered.*] Are you angry with me, Miss Livvy?

PHOEBE. Oh, no.

BLADES. Miss Livvy, I have something to say to you of supreme importance to me. With regard to my complexion, I am aware, Miss Livvy, that it has retained a too youthful bloom. My brother officers comment on it with a certain lack of generosity. [*Anxiously.*] Might I inquire, ma'am, whether you regard my complexion as a subject for light talk.

PHOEBE. No indeed, sir, I only wish I had it.

BLADES. [*Who has had no intention of offering, but is suddenly carried off his feet by the excellence of the opportunity, which is no doubt responsible for many proposals.*] Miss Livvy, ma'am, you may have it.

> [*She has a great and humorous longing that she*

*could turn before his affrighted eyes into the
schoolmistress she really is. She would endure
much to be able at this moment so say, "I have
listened to you, ENSIGN BLADES, with attention,
but I am really MISS PHOEBE, and I must now
request you to fetch me the implement."
Under the shock, would he have surrendered his
palm for punishment? It can never be known,
for as she looks at him longingly, LIEUTENANT
SPICER enters, and he mistakes the meaning of
that longing look.*]

SPICER. 'Tis my dance, ma'am—'tis not Ensign Blades'.

BLADES. Leave us, sir. We have matter of moment
to discuss.

SPICER. [*Fearing the worst.*] His affection, Miss Livvy,
is not so deep as mine. He is a light and shallow nature.

PHOEBE. Pooh! You are both light and shallow
natures.

BLADES. Both, ma'am? [*But he is not sure that he
has not had a miraculous escape.*]

PHOEBE. [*Severely.*] 'Tis such as you, with your foolish flirting ways, that confuse the minds of women and
make us try to be as silly as yourselves.

SPICER. [*Crushed.*] Ma'am.

PHOEBE. I did not mean to hurt you. [*She takes a
hand of each and tries to advise them as if her curls were
once more hidden under a cap.*] You are so like little
boys in a school. Do be good. Sit here beside me. I
know you are very brave——

BLADES. Ha!

PHOEBE. And when you come back from the wars it
must be so delightful to you to flirt with the ladies again.

SPICER. Oh, ma'am.

PHOEBE. As soon as you see a lady with a pretty nose you cannot help saying that you adore her.

BLADES. [*In an ecstasy.*] Nay, I swear.

PHOEBE. And you offer to her, not from love, but because you are so deficient in conversation.

SPICER. Charming, Miss Livvy.

PHOEBE. [*With sudden irritation.*] Oh, sir, go away; go away, both of you, and read improving books.

> [*They are cast down. She has not been quite fair to these gallants, for it is not really of them she has grown weary so much as of the lady they temporarily adore. If MISS PHOEBE were to analyse her feelings she would find that her remark is addressed to LIVVY, and that it means, "I have enjoyed for a little pretending to be you, but I am not you and I do not wish to be you. Your glitter and the airs of you and the racket of you tire me, I want to be done with you, and to be back in quiet Quality Street, of which I am a part; it is really pleasant to me to know that I shall wake up to-morrow slightly middle-aged." With the entrance of CAPTAIN BROWN, however, she is at once a frivol again. He frowns at sight of her cavaliers.*]

VALENTINE. Gentlemen, I instructed this lady to rest, and I am surprised to find you in attendance. Miss Livvy, you must be weary of their fatuities, and I have taken the liberty to order your chaise.

PHOEBE. It is indeed a liberty.

BLADES. An outrage.

PHOEBE. I prefer to remain.

VALENTINE. Nay.

PHOEBE. I promised this dance to Ensign Blades.

SPICER. To me, ma'am.

PHOEBE. And the following one to Lieutenant Spicer. Mr. Blades, your arm.

VALENTINE. I forbid any further dancing.

PHOEBE. Forbid. La!

BLADES. Sir, by what right——

VALENTINE. By a right which I hope to make clear to Miss Livvy as soon as you gentlemen have retired.

> [PHOEBE *sees that the declaration is coming. She steels herself.*]

PHOEBE. I am curious to know what Captain Brown can have to say to me. In a few minutes, Mr. Blades, Lieutenant Spicer, I shall be at your service.

VALENTINE. I trust not.

PHOEBE. I give them my word.

> [*The young gentlemen retire, treading air once more.* BROWN *surveys her rather grimly.*]

VALENTINE. You are an amazing pretty girl, ma'am, but you are a shocking flirt.

PHOEBE. La!

VALENTINE. It has somewhat diverted me to watch them go down before you. But I know you have a kind heart, and that if there be a rapier in your one hand there is a handkerchief in the other ready to staunch their wounds.

PHOEBE. I have not observed that they bled much.

VALENTINE. The Blades and the like, no. But one may, perhaps.

PHOEBE. [*Obviously the reference is to himself.*] Perhaps I may wish to see him bleed.

VALENTINE. [*Grown stern.*] For shame, Miss Livvy. [*Anger rises in her, but she wishes him to proceed.*] I speak, ma'am, in the interests of the man to whom I hope to see you affianced.

> [*No, she does not wish him to proceed. She had*

*esteemed him for so long, she cannot have him
debase himself before her now.*]

PHOEBE.   Shall we—I have changed my mind, I consent to go home.   Please to say nothing.

VALENTINE.   Nay——

PHOEBE.   I beg you.

VALENTINE.   No.   We must have it out.

PHOEBE.   Then if you must go on, do so.   But remember I begged you to desist.   Who is this happy man?

[*His next words are a great shock to her.*]

VALENTINE.   As to who he is, ma'am, of course I have
no notion.   Nor, I am sure, have you, else you would be
more guarded in your conduct.   But some day, Miss Livvy,
the right man will come.   Not to be able to tell him all,
would it not be hard?   And how could you acquaint him
with this poor sport?   His face would change, ma'am, as
you told him of it, and yours would be a false face until
it was told.   This is what I have been so desirous to say
to you—by the right of a friend.

PHOEBE.   [*In a low voice but bravely.*]   I see.

VALENTINE.   [*Afraid that he has hurt her.*]   It has been
hard to say and I have done it bunglingly.   Ah, but believe
me, Miss Livvy, it is not the flaunting flower men love; it
is the modest violet.

PHOEBE.   The modest violet!   *You* dare to say that.

VALENTINE.   Yes, indeed, and when you are acquaint
with what love really is——

PHOEBE.   Love!   What do you know of love?

VALENTINE.   [*A little complacently.*]   Why, ma'am, I
know all about it.   I am in love, Miss Livvy.

PHOEBE.   [*With a disdainful inclination of the head.*]
I wish you happy.

VALENTINE.   With a lady who was once very like you,
ma'am.

[*At first* PHOEBE *does not understand, then a suspicion of his meaning comes to her.*]

PHOEBE. Not—not—oh no.

VALENTINE. I had not meant to speak of it, but why should not I? It will be a fine lesson to you, Miss Livvy. Ma'am, it is your Aunt Phoebe whom I love.

PHOEBE. [*Rigid.*] You do not mean that.

VALENTINE. Most ardently.

PHOEBE. It is not true; how dare you make sport of her.

VALENTINE. Is it sport to wish she may be my wife?

PHOEBE. Your wife!

VALENTINE. If I could win her.

PHOEBE. [*Bewildered.*] May I solicit, sir, for how long you have been attached to Miss Phoebe?

VALENTINE. For nine years, I think.

PHOEBE. You think!

VALENTINE. I want to be honest. Never in all that time had I thought myself in love. Your aunts were my dear friends, and while I was at the wars we sometimes wrote to each other, but they were only friendly letters. I presume the affection was too placid to be love.

PHOEBE. I think that would be Aunt Phoebe's opinion.

VALENTINE. Yet I remember, before we went into action for the first time—I suppose the fear of death was upon me—some of them were making their wills—I have no near relative—I left everything to these two ladies.

PHOEBE. [*Softly.*] Did you?

[*What is it that* MISS PHOEBE *begins to see as she sits there so quietly, with her hands pressed together as if upon some treasure? It is* PHOEBE *of the ringlets with the stain taken out of her.*]

VALENTINE. And when I returned a week ago and saw Miss Phoebe, grown so tired-looking and so poor——

PHOEBE. The shock made you feel old, I know.

VALENTINE. No, Miss Livvy, but it filled me with a sudden passionate regret that I had not gone down in that first engagement. They would have been very comfortably left.

PHOEBE. Oh, sir!

VALENTINE. I am not calling it love.

PHOEBE. It was sweet and kind, but it was not love.

VALENTINE. It is love now.

PHOEBE. No, it is only pity.

VALENTINE. It is love.

PHOEBE. [*She smiles tremulously.*] You really mean Phoebe—tired, unattractive Phoebe, that woman whose girlhood is gone. Nay, impossible.

VALENTINE. [*Stoutly.*] Phoebe of the fascinating playful ways, whose ringlets were once as pretty as yours, ma'am. I have visited her in her home several times this week—you were always out—I thank you for that! I was alone with her, and with fragrant memories of her.

PHOEBE. Memories! Yes, that is the Phoebe you love, the bright girl of the past—not the schoolmistress in her old-maid's cap.

VALENTINE. There you wrong me, for I have discovered for myself that the schoolmistress in her old-maid's cap is the noblest Miss Phoebe of them all. [*If only he would go away, and let* MISS PHOEBE *cry.*] When I enlisted, I remember I compared her to a garden. I have often thought of that.

PHOEBE. 'Tis an old garden now.

VALENTINE. The paths, ma'am, are better shaded.

PHOEBE. The flowers have grown old-fashioned.

VALENTINE. They smell the sweeter. Miss Livvy, do you think there is any hope for me?

PHOEBE. There was a man whom Miss Phoebe loved—long ago. He did not love her.

VALENTINE. Now here was a fool!

PHOEBE. He kissed her once.

VALENTINE. If Miss Phoebe suffered him to do that she thought he loved her.

PHOEBE. Yes, yes. [*She has to ask him the ten years' old question.*] Do you opinion that this makes her action in allowing it less reprehensible? It has been such a pain to her ever since.

VALENTINE. How like Miss Phoebe! [*Sternly.*] But that man was a knave.

PHOEBE. No, he was a good man—only a little—inconsiderate. She knows now that he has even forgotten that he did it. I suppose men are like that?

VALENTINE. No, Miss Livvy, men are not like that. I am a very average man, but I thank God I am not like that.

PHOEBE. It was you.

VALENTINE. [*After a pause.*] Did Miss Phoebe say that?

PHOEBE. Yes.

VALENTINE. Then it is true.

[*He is very grave and quiet.*]

PHOEBE. It was raining and her face was wet. You said you did it because her face was wet.

VALENTINE. I had quite forgotten.

PHOEBE. But she remembers, and how often do you think the shameful memory has made her face wet since? The face you love, Captain Brown, you were the first to give it pain. The tired eyes—how much less tired they might be if they had never known you. You who are torturing me with every word, what have you done to Miss Phoebe? You who think you can bring back the bloom to that faded garden, and all the pretty airs and graces that fluttered round it once like little birds before the nest is torn down—bring them back to her if you can, sir; it was you who took them away.

VALENTINE. I vow I shall do my best to bring them back. [MISS PHOEBE *shakes her head*.] Miss Livvy, with your help——

PHOEBE. My help! I have not helped. I tried to spoil it all.

VALENTINE. [*Smiling*.] To spoil it? You mean that you sought to flirt even with me. Ah, I knew you did. But that is nothing.

PHOEBE. Oh, sir, if you could overlook it.

VALENTINE. I do.

PHOEBE. And forget these hateful balls.

VALENTINE. Hateful! Nay, I shall never call them that. They have done me too great a service. It was at the balls that I fell in love with Miss Phoebe.

PHOEBE. What can you mean?

VALENTINE. She who was never at a ball! [*Checking himself humorously*.] But I must not tell you, it might hurt you.

PHOEBE. Tell me.

VALENTINE. [*Gaily*.] Then on your own head be the blame. It is you who have made me love her, Miss Livvy.

PHOEBE. Sir?

VALENTINE. Yes, it is odd, and yet very simple. You who so resembled her as she was! for an hour, ma'am, you bewitched me; yes, I confess it, but 'twas only for an hour. How like, I cried at first, but soon it was, how unlike. There was almost nothing she would have said that you said; you did so much that she would have scorned to do. But I must not say these things to you!

PHOEBE. I ask it of you, Captain Brown.

VALENTINE. Well! Miss Phoebe's "lady-likeness," on

which she set such store that I used to make merry of the word—I gradually perceived that it is a wo·nan's most beautiful garment, and the casket which contains all the adorable qualities that go to the making of a perfect female. When Miss Livvy rolled her eyes—ah!

[*He stops apologetically.*]

PHOEBE. Proceed, sir.

VALENTINE. It but made me the more complacent that never in her life had Miss Phoebe been guilty of the slightest deviation from the strictest propriety. [*She shudders.*] I was always conceiving her in your place. Oh, it was monstrous unfair to you. I stood looking at you, Miss Livvy, and seeing in my mind her and the pretty things she did, and you did not do; why, ma'am, that is how I fell in love with Miss Phoebe at the balls.

PHOEBE. I thank you.

VALENTINE. Ma'am, tell me, do you think there is any hope for me?

PHOEBE. Hope!

VALENTINE. I shall go to her. "Miss Phoebe," I will say—oh, ma'am, so reverently—"Miss Phoebe, my beautiful, most estimable of women, let me take care of you for ever more."

[MISS PHOEBE *presses the words to her heart and then drops them.*]

PHOEBE. Beautiful. La, Aunt Phoebe!

VALENTINE. Ah, ma'am, you may laugh at a rough soldier so much enamoured, but 'tis true. "Marry me, Miss Phoebe," I will say, "and I will take you back through those years of hardships that have made your sweet eyes too patient. Instead of growing older you shall grow younger. We will travel back together to pick up the many little joys and pleasures you had to pass by when you trod that thorny path alone."

PHOEBE. Can't be—can't be.

VALENTINE. Nay, Miss Phoebe has loved me. 'Tis you have said it.

PHOEBE. I did not mean to tell you.

VALENTINE. She will be my wife yet.

PHOEBE. Never.

VALENTINE. You are severe, Miss Livvy. But it is because you are partial to her, and I am happy of that.

PHOEBE. [*In growing horror of herself.*] I partial to her! I am laughing at both of you. Miss Phoebe. La, that old thing.

VALENTINE. [*Sternly.*] Silence!

PHOEBE. I hate her and despise her. If you knew what she is——

[*He stops her with a gesture.*]

VALENTINE. I know what you are.

PHOEBE. That paragon who has never been guilty of the slightest deviation from the strictest propriety.

VALENTINE. Never.

PHOEBE. That garden——

VALENTINE. Miss Livvy, for shame.

PHOEBE. Your garden has been destroyed, sir; the weeds have entered it, and all the flowers are choked.

VALENTINE. You false woman, what do you mean?

PHOEBE. I will tell you. [*But his confidence awes her.*] What faith you have in her.

VALENTINE. As in my God. Speak.

PHOEBE. I cannot tell you.

VALENTINE. No, you cannot.

PHOEBE. It is too horrible.

VALENTINE. You are too horrible. Is not that it?

PHOEBE. Yes, that is it.

[MISS SUSAN *has entered and caught the last words.*]

Miss Susan. [*Shrinking as from a coming blow.*] What is too horrible?

Valentine. Ma'am, I leave the telling of it to her, if she dare. And I devoutly hope those are the last words I shall ever address to this lady.

> [*He bows and goes out in dudgeon.* Miss Susan *believes all is discovered and that* Miss Phoebe *is for ever shamed.*]

Miss Susan. [*Taking* Phoebe *in her arms.*] My love, my dear, what terrible thing has he said to you?

Phoebe. [*Forgetting everything but that she is loved.*] Not terrible—glorious! Susan, 'tis Phoebe he loves, 'tis me, not Livvy! He loves me, he loves me! Me—Phoebe!

> [Miss Susan's *bosom swells. It is her great hour as much as* Phoebe's.]

End of Act III.

ACT IV

THE BLUE AND WHITE ROOM

If we could shut our eyes to the two sisters sitting here in woe, this would be, to the male eye at least, the identical blue and white room of ten years ago; the same sun shining into it and playing familiarly with Miss Susan's *treasures. But the ladies are changed. It is not merely that* Miss Phoebe *has again donned her schoolmistress' gown and hidden her curls under the cap. To see her thus once more, her real self, after the escapade of the ball, is not unpleasant, and the cap and gown do not ill become the quiet room. But she now turns guiltily from the sun that used to be her intimate, her face is drawn, her form condensed into the smallest space, and her hands lie trembling in her lap. It is disquieting to note that any life there is in the room comes not from her but from* MISS SUSAN. *If the house were to go on fire now it would be she who would have to carry out* MISS PHOEBE.

Whatever of import has happened since the ball, PATTY *knows it, and is enjoying it. We see this as she ushers in* MISS WILLOUGHBY. *Note also, with concern, that at mention of the visitor's name the eyes of the sisters turn affrightedly, not to the door by which their old friend enters, but to the closed door of the spare bed-chamber.* PATTY *also gives it a meaning glance; then the three look at each other, and two of them blanch.*

MISS WILLOUGHBY. [*The fourth to look at the door.*] I am just run across, Susan, to inquire how Miss Livvy does now.

MISS SUSAN. She is still very poorly, Mary.

MISS WILLOUGHBY. I am so unhappy of that. I conceive it to be a nervous disorder?

MISS SUSAN. [*Almost too glibly.*] Accompanied by trembling, flutterings, and spasms.

MISS WILLOUGHBY. The excitements of the ball. You have summoned the apothecary at last, I trust, Phoebe?

[MISS PHOEBE, *once so ready of defence, can say nothing.*]

MISS SUSAN. [*To the rescue.*] It is Livvy's own wish that he should not be consulted.

MISS WILLOUGHBY. [*Looking longingly at the door.*] May I go in to see her?

MISS SUSAN. I fear not, Mary. She is almost asleep,

and it is best not to disturb her. [*Peeping into the bed-room.*] Lie quite still, Livvy, my love, quite still.

> [*Somehow this makes* PATTY *smile so broadly that she finds it advisable to retire.* MISS WIL-LOUGHBY *sighs, and produces a small bowl from the folds of her cloak.*]

MISS WILLOUGHBY. This is a little arrowroot, of which I hope Miss Livvy will be so obliging as to partake.

MISS SUSAN. [*Taking the bowl.*] I thank you, Mary.

PHOEBE. [*Ashamed.*] Susan, we ought not——

MISS SUSAN. [*Shameless.*] I will take it to her while it is still warm.

> [*She goes into the bedroom.* MISS WILLOUGHBY *gazes at* MISS PHOEBE, *who certainly shrinks. It has not escaped the notice of the visitor that* MISS PHOEBE *has become the more timid of the sisters, and she has evolved an explanation.*]

MISS WILLOUGHBY. Phoebe, has Captain Brown been apprised of Miss Livvy's illness?

PHOEBE. [*Uncomfortably.*] I think not, Miss Wil-loughby.

MISS WILLOUGHBY. [*Sorry for* PHOEBE, *and speaking very kindly.*] Is this right, Phoebe? You informed Fanny and Henrietta at the ball of his partiality for Livvy. My dear, it is hard for you, but have you any right to keep them apart?

PHOEBE. [*Discovering only now what are the suspicions of her friends.*] Is that what you think I am doing, Miss Willoughby?

MISS WILLOUGHBY. Such a mysterious illness. [*Sweetly.*] Long ago, Phoebe, I once caused much unhappiness through foolish jealousy. That is why I venture to hope that you will not be as I was, my dear.

PHOEBE. I jealous of Livvy!

MISS WILLOUGHBY. [*With a sigh.*] I thought as little of the lady I refer to, but he thought otherwise.

PHOEBE. Indeed, Miss Willoughby, you wrong me.

> [*But* MISS WILLOUGHBY *does not entirely believe her, and there is a pause, so long a pause that unfortunately* MISS SUSAN *thinks she has left the house.*]

MISS SUSAN. [*Peeping in.*] Is she gone?

MISS WILLOUGHBY. [*Hurt.*] No, Susan, but I am going.

MISS SUSAN. [*Distressed.*] Mary!

> [*She follows her out, but* MISS WILLOUGHBY *will not be comforted, and there is a coldness between them for the rest of the day.* MISS SUSAN *is not so abashed as she ought to be. She returns, and partakes with avidity of the arrowroot.*]

MISS SUSAN. Phoebe, I am well aware that this is wrong of me, but Mary's arrowroot is so delicious. The ladies'-fingers and petticoat-tails those officers sent to Livvy, I ate them also! [*Once on a time this would have amused* MISS PHOEBE, *but her sense of humour has gone. She is crying.*] Phoebe, if you have such remorse you will weep yourself to death.

PHOEBE. Oh, sister, were it not for you, how gladly would I go into a decline.

MISS SUSAN. [*After she has soothed* PHOEBE *a little.*] My dear, what is to be done about her? We cannot have her supposed to be here for ever.

PHOEBE. We had to pretend that she was ill to keep her out of sight; and now we cannot say she has gone away, for the Misses Willoughbys' windows command our door, and they are always watching.

MISS SUSAN. [*Peeping from the window.*] I see Fanny watching now. I feel, Phoebe, as if Livvy really existed.

PHOEBE. [*Mournfully.*] We shall never be able to esteem ourselves again.

MISS SUSAN. [*Who has in her the makings of a desperate criminal.*] Phoebe, why not marry him? If only we could make him think that Livvy had gone home. Then he need never know.

PHOEBE. Susan, you pain me. She who marries without telling all—hers must ever be a false face. They are his own words.

[PATTY *enters importantly.*]

PATTY. Captain Brown.

PHOEBE. [*Starting up.*] I wrote to him, begging him not to come.

MISS SUSAN. [*Quickly.*] Patty, I am sorry we are out.

[*But* VALENTINE *has entered in time to hear her words.*]

VALENTINE. [*Not unmindful that this is the room in which he is esteemed a wit.*] I regret that they are out, Patty, but I will await their return. [*The astonishing man sits on the ottoman beside* MISS SUSAN, *but politely ignores her presence.*] It is not my wish to detain you, Patty.

[PATTY *goes reluctantly, and the sisters think how like him, and how delightful it would be if they were still the patterns of propriety he considers them.*]

PHOEBE. [*Bravely.*] Captain Brown.

VALENTINE. [*Rising.*] You, Miss Phoebe. I hear Miss Livvy is indisposed?

PHOEBE. She is—very poorly.

VALENTINE. But it is not that unpleasant girl I have come to see, it is you.

MISS SUSAN. [*Meekly.*] How do you do?

VALENTINE. [*Ignoring her.*] And I am happy, Miss Phoebe, to find you alone.

MISS SUSAN. [*Appealingly.*] How do you do, sir?

PHOEBE. You know quite well, sir, that Susan is here.

VALENTINE. Nay, ma'am, excuse me. I heard Miss Susan say she was gone out. Miss Susan is incapable of prevarication.

MISS SUSAN. [*Rising—helpless.*] What am I to do?

PHOEBE. Don't go, Susan—'tis what he wants.

VALENTINE. I have her word that she is not present.

MISS SUSAN. Oh dear.

VALENTINE. My faith in Miss Susan is absolute. [*At this she retires into the bedroom, and immediately his manner changes. He takes* MISS PHOEBE'S *hands into his own kind one.*] You coward, Miss Phoebe, to be afraid of Valentine Brown.

PHOEBE. I wrote and begged you not to come.

VALENTINE. You implied as a lover, Miss Phoebe, but surely always as a friend.

PHOEBE. Oh yes, yes.

VALENTINE. You told Miss Livvy that you loved me once. How carefully you hid it from me!

PHOEBE. [*More firmly.*] A woman must never tell. You went away to the great battles. I was left to fight in a little one. Women have a flag to fly, Mr. Brown, as well as men, and old maids have a flag as well as women. I tried to keep mine flying.

VALENTINE. But you ceased to care for me. [*Tenderly.*] I dare ask your love no more, but I still ask you to put yourself into my keeping. Miss Phoebe, let me take care of you.

PHOEBE. It cannot be.

VALENTINE. This weary teaching! Let me close your school.

PHOEBE. Please, sir.

VALENTINE. If not for your own sake, I ask you, Miss Phoebe, to do it for mine. In memory of the thoughtless recruit who went off laughing to the wars. They say ladies cannot quite forget the man who has used them ill; Miss Phoebe, do it for me because I used you ill.

PHOEBE. I beg you—no more.

VALENTINE. [*Manfully.*] There, it is all ended. Miss Phoebe, here is my hand on it.

PHOEBE. What will you do now?

VALENTINE. I also must work. I will become a physician again, with some drab old housekeeper to neglect me and the house. Do you foresee the cobwebs gathering and gathering, Miss Phoebe?

PHOEBE. Oh, sir!

VALENTINE. You shall yet see me in Quality Street, wearing my stock all awry.

PHOEBE. Oh, oh!

VALENTINE. And with snuff upon my sleeve.

PHOEBE. Sir, sir!

VALENTINE. No skulker, ma'am, I hope, but gradually turning into a grump, crusty, bottlenosed old bachelor.

PHOEBE. Oh, Mr. Brown!

VALENTINE. And all because you will not walk across the street with me.

PHOEBE. Indeed, sir, you must marry—and I hope it may be some one who is really like a garden.

VALENTINE. I know but one. That reminds me, Miss Phoebe, of something I had forgot. [*He produces a paper from his pocket.*] 'Tis a trifle I have wrote about you. But I fear to trouble you.

[PHOEBE'S *hands go out longingly for it.*]

PHOEBE. [*Reading.*] "Lines to a Certain Lady, who is

Modestly Unaware of her Resemblance to a Garden. Wrote by her servant, V. B."

[*The beauty of this makes her falter. She looks up.*]

VALENTINE. [*With a poet's pride.*] There is more of it, ma'am.

PHOEBE. [*Reading.*]

The lilies are her pretty thoughts,
　　Her shoulders are the may,
Her smiles are all forget-me-nots,
　　The path's her gracious way,

The roses that do line it are
　　·Her fancies walking round,
'Tis sweetly smelling lavender
　　In which my lady's gowned.

[MISS PHOEBE *has thought herself strong, but she is not able to read such exquisite lines without betraying herself to a lover's gaze.*]

VALENTINE. [*Excitedly.*] Miss Phoebe, when did you cease to care for me?

PHOEBE. [*Retreating from him but clinging to her poem.*] You promised not to ask.

VALENTINE. I know not why you should, Miss Phoebe, but I believe you love me still!

[MISS PHOEBE *has the terrified appearance of a detected felon.*]

[MISS SUSAN *returns.*]

MISS SUSAN. You are talking so loudly.

VALENTINE. Miss Susan, does she care for me still?

MISS SUSAN. [*Forgetting her pride of sex.*] Oh, sir, how could she help it.

VALENTINE. Then by Gad, Miss Phoebe, you shall marry me though I have to carry you in my arms to the church.

PHOEBE. Sir, how can you!

> [*But* MISS SUSAN *gives her a look which means that it must be done if only to avoid such a scandal. It is at this inopportune moment that* MISS HENRIETTA *and* MISS FANNY *are announced.*]

MISS HENRIETTA. I think Miss Willoughby has already popped in.

PHOEBE. [*With a little spirit.*] Yes, indeed.

MISS SUSAN. [*A mistress of sarcasm.*] How is Mary, Fanny? She has not been to see us for several minutes.

MISS FANNY. [*Somewhat daunted.*] Mary is so partial to you, Susan.

VALENTINE. Your servant, Miss Henrietta, Miss Fanny.

MISS FANNY. How do you do, sir?

MISS HENRIETTA. [*Wistfully.*] And how do you find Miss Livvy, sir?

VALENTINE. I have not seen her, Miss Henrietta.

MISS HENRIETTA. Indeed!

MISS FANNY. Not even you?

VALENTINE. You seem surprised?

MISS FANNY. Nay, sir, you must not say so; but really, Phoebe!

PHOEBE. Fanny, you presume!

VALENTINE. [*Puzzled.*] If one of you ladies would deign to enlighten me. To begin with, what is Miss Livvy's malady?

MISS HENRIETTA. He does not know? Oh, Phoebe.

VALENTINE. Ladies, have pity on a dull man, and explain.

MISS FANNY. [*Timidly.*] Please not to ask us to

explain. I fear we have already said more than was proper. Phoebe, forgive.

[*To* CAPTAIN BROWN *this but adds to the mystery, and he looks to* PHOEBE *for enlightenment.*]

PHOEBE. [*Desperate.*] I understand, sir, there is a belief that I keep Livvy in confinement because of your passion for her.

VALENTINE. My passion for Miss Livvy? Why, Miss Fanny, I cannot abide her—nor she me. [*Looking manfully at* MISS PHOEBE.] Furthermore, I am proud to tell you that this is the lady whom I adore.

MISS FANNY. Phoebe?

VALENTINE. Yes, ma'am.

[*The ladies are for a moment bereft of speech, and the uplifted* PHOEBE *cannot refrain from a movement which, if completed, would be a curtsy. Her punishment follows promptly.*]

MISS HENRIETTA. [*From her heart.*] Phoebe, I am so happy 'tis you.

MISS FANNY. Dear Phoebe, I give you joy. And you also, sir. [MISS PHOEBE *sends her sister a glance of unutterable woe, and escapes from the room. It is most illbred of her.*] Miss Susan, I do not understand!

MISS HENRIETTA. Is it that Miss Livvy is an obstacle?

MISS SUSAN. [*Who knows that there is no hope for her but in flight.*] I think I hear Phoebe calling me—a sudden indisposition. Pray excuse me, Henrietta. [*She goes.*]

MISS HENRIETTA. We know not, sir, whether to offer you our felicitations?

VALENTINE. [*Cogitating.*] May I ask, ma'am, what you mean by an obstacle? Is there some mystery about Miss Livvy?

MISS HENRIETTA. So much so, sir, that we at one time thought she and Miss Phoebe were the same person.

VALENTINE. Pshaw!

MISS FANNY. Why will they admit no physician into her presence?

MISS HENRIETTA. The blinds of her room are kept most artfully drawn.

MISS FANNY. [*Plaintively.*] We have never seen her, sir. Neither Miss Susan nor Miss Phoebe will present her to us.

VALENTINE. [*Impressed.*] Indeed.

> [MISS HENRIETTA *and* MISS FANNY, *encouraged by his sympathy, draw nearer the door of the interesting bedchamber. They falter. Any one who thinks, however, that they would so far forget themselves as to open the door and peep in, has no understanding of the ladies of Quality Street. They are, nevertheless, not perfect, for* MISS HENRIETTA *knocks on the door.*]

MISS HENRIETTA. How do you find yourself, dear Miss Livvy?

> [*There is no answer. It is our pride to record that they come away without even touching the handle. They look appealing at* CAPTAIN BROWN, *whose face has grown grave.*]

VALENTINE. I think, ladies, as a physician——

> [*He walks into the bedroom. They feel an ignoble drawing to follow him, but do not yield to it. When he returns his face is inscrutable.*]

MISS HENRIETTA. Is she very poorly, sir?

VALENTINE. Ha.

MISS FANNY. We did not hear you address her.

VALENTINE. She is not awake, ma'am.

MISS HENRIETTA. It is provoking.

MISS FANNY. [*Sternly just.*] They informed Mary that she was nigh asleep.

VALENTINE. It is not a serious illness I think, ma'am. With the permission of Miss Phoebe and Miss Susan I will make myself more acquaint with her disorder presently. [*He is desirous to be alone.*] But we must not talk lest we disturb her.

MISS FANNY. You suggest our retiring, sir?

VALENTINE. Nay, Miss Fanny——

MISS FANNY. You are very obliging; but I think, Henrietta——

MISS HENRIETTA. [*Rising.*] Yes, Fanny.

> [*No doubt they are the more ready to depart that they wish to inform* MISS WILLOUGHBY *at once of these strange doings. As they go,* MISS SUSAN *and* MISS PHOEBE *return, and the adieux are less elaborate than usual. Neither visitors nor hostesses quite know what to say.* MISS SUSAN *is merely relieved to see them leave, but* MISS PHOEBE *has read something in their manner that makes her uneasy.*]

PHOEBE. Why have they departed so hurriedly, sir? They—they did not go in to see Livvy?

VALENTINE. No.

[*She reads danger in his face.*]

PHOEBE. Why do you look at me so strangely?

VALENTINE. [*Somewhat stern.*] Miss Phoebe, I desire to see Miss Livvy.

PHOEBE. Impossible.

VALENTINE. Why impossible? They tell me strange stories about no one's seeing her. Miss Phoebe, I will not leave this house until I have seen her.

PHOEBE. You cannot. [*But he is very determined, and she is afraid of him.*] Will you excuse me, sir, while I talk with Susan behind the door?

[*The sisters go guiltily into the bedroom, and*

Captain Brown *after some hesitation rings for* Patty.]

VALENTINE. Patty, come here. Why is this trick being played upon me?

PATTY. [*With all her wits about her.*] Trick, sir! Who would dare?

VALENTINE. I know, Patty, that Miss Phoebe has been Miss Livvy all the time.

PATTY. I give in!

VALENTINE. Why has she done this?

PATTY. [*Beseechingly.*] Are you laughing, sir?

VALENTINE. I am very far from laughing.

PATTY. [*Turning on him.*] 'Twas you that began it all by not knowing her in the white gown.

VALENTINE. Why has this deception been kept up so long?

PATTY. Because you would not see through it. Oh, the wicked denseness. She thought you were infatuate with Miss Livvy because she was young and silly.

VALENTINE. It is infamous.

PATTY. I will not have you call her names. 'Twas all playful innocence at first, and now she is so feared of you she is weeping her soul to death, and all I do I cannot rouse her. "I ha' a follower in the kitchen, ma'am," says I, to infuriate her. "Give him a glass of cowslip wine," says she, like a gentle lamb. And ill she can afford it, you having lost their money for them.

VALENTINE. What is that? On the contrary, all the money they have, Patty, they owe to my having invested it for them.

PATTY. That is the money they lost.

VALENTINE. You are sure of that?

PATTY. I can swear to it.

VALENTINE. Deceived me about that also. Good God; but why?

PATTY. I think she was feared you would offer to her out of pity. She said something to Miss Susan about keeping a flag flying. What she meant I know not. [*But he knows, and he turns away his face.*] Are you laughing, sir?

VALENTINE. No, Patty, I am not laughing. Why do they not say Miss Livvy has gone home? It would save them a world of trouble.

PATTY. The Misses Willoughby and Miss Henrietta— they watch the house all day. They would say she cannot be gone, for we did not see her go.

VALENTINE. [*Enlightened at last.*] I see!

PATTY. And Miss Phoebe and Miss Susan wring their hands, for they are feared Miss Livvy is bedridden here for all time. [*Now his sense of humour asserts itself.*] Thank the Lord, you're laughing!

> [*At this he laughs the more, and it is a gay* CAPTAIN BROWN *on whom* MISS SUSAN *opens the bedroom door. This desperate woman is too full of plot to note the change in him.*]

MISS SUSAN. I am happy to inform you, sir, that Livvy finds herself much improved.

VALENTINE. [*Bowing.*] It is joy to me to hear it.

MISS SUSAN. She is coming in to see you.

PATTY. [*Aghast.*] Oh, ma'am!

VALENTINE. [*Frowning on* PATTY.] I shall be happy to see the poor invalid.

PATTY. Ma'am——!

> [*But* MISS SUSAN, *believing that so far all is well, has returned to the bedchamber.* CAPTAIN BROWN *bestows a quizzical glance upon the maid.*]

VALENTINE. Go away, Patty. Anon I may claim a service of you, but for the present, go.

PATTY. But—but——

VALENTINE. Retire, woman.

> [*She has to go, and he prepares his face for the reception of the invalid.* PHOEBE *comes in without her cap, the ringlets showing again. She wears a dressing jacket and is supported by* MISS SUSAN.]

VALENTINE. [*Gravely.*] Your servant, Miss Livvy.

PHOEBE. [*Weakly.*] How do you do?

VALENTINE. Allow me, Miss Susan.

> [*He takes* MISS SUSAN'S *place; but after an exquisite moment* MISS PHOEBE *breaks away from him, feeling that she is not worthy of such bliss.*]

PHOEBE. No, no, I—I can walk alone—see.

> [*She reclines upon the couch.*]

MISS SUSAN. How do you think she is looking?

> [*He makes a professional examination of the patient, and they are very ashamed to deceive him, but not so ashamed that they must confess.*]

What do you think?

VALENTINE. [*Solemnly.*] She will recover. May I say, ma'am, it surprises me that any one should see much resemblance between you and your Aunt Phoebe. Miss Phoebe is decidedly shorter and more thick-set.

PHOEBE. [*Sitting up.*] No, I am not.

VALENTINE. I said Miss Phoebe, ma'am. [*She reclines.*] But tell me, is not Miss Phoebe to join us?

PHOEBE. She hopes you will excuse her, sir.

MISS SUSAN. [*Vaguely.*] Taking the opportunity of airing the room.

VALENTINE. Ah, of course.

MISS SUSAN. [*Opening bedroom door and calling mendaciously.*] Captain Brown will excuse you, Phoebe.

VALENTINE. Certainly, Miss Susan. Well, ma'am, I think I could cure Miss Livvy if she is put unreservedly into my hands.

MISS SUSAN. [*With a sigh.*] I am sure you could.

VALENTINE. Then you are my patient, Miss Livvy.

PHOEBE. [*Nervously.*] 'Twas but a passing indisposition, I am almost quite recovered.

VALENTINE. Nay, you still require attention. Do you propose making a long stay in Quality Street, ma'am?

PHOEBE. I—I—I hope not. It—it depends.

MISS SUSAN. [*Forgetting herself.*] Mary is the worst.

VALENTINE. I ask your pardon?

PHOEBE. Aunt Susan, you are excited.

VALENTINE. But you are quite right, Miss Livvy; home is the place for you.

PHOEBE. Would that I could go!

VALENTINE. You are going.

PHOEBE. Yes—soon.

VALENTINE. Indeed, I have a delightful surprise for you, Miss Livvy, you are going to-day.

PHOEBE. To-day?

VALENTINE. Not merely to-day, but now. As it happens, my carriage is standing idle at your door, and I am to take you in it to your home—some twenty miles if I remember.

PHOEBE. You are to take me?

VALENTINE. Nay, 'tis no trouble at all, and as your physician my mind is made up. Some wraps for her, Miss Susan.

MISS SUSAN. But—but——

PHOEBE. [*In a panic.*] Sir, I decline to go.

VALENTINE. Come, Miss Livvy, you are in my hands.

PHOEBE. I decline. I am most determined.

VALENTINE. You admit yourself that you are recovered.

PHOEBE. I do not feel so well now. Aunt Susan!

MISS SUSAN. Sir——

VALENTINE. If you wish to consult Miss Phoebe——

MISS SUSAN. Oh, no.

VALENTINE. Then the wraps, Miss Susan.

PHOEBE. Auntie, don't leave me.

VALENTINE. What a refractory patient it is. But reason with her, Miss Susan, and I shall ask Miss Phoebe for some wraps.

PHOEBE. Sir!

> [*To their consternation he goes cheerily into the bedroom.* MISS PHOEBE *saves herself by instant flight, and nothing but mesmeric influence keeps* MISS SUSAN *rooted to the blue and white room. When he returns he is loaded with wraps, and still cheerfully animated, as if he had found nothing untoward in* LIVVY'S *bedchamber.*]

VALENTINE. I think these will do admirably, Miss Susan.

MISS SUSAN. But Phoebe——

VALENTINE. If I swathe Miss Livvy in these——

MISS SUSAN. Phoebe——

VALENTINE. She is still busy airing the room. [*The extraordinary man goes to the couch as if unable to perceive that its late occupant has gone, and* MISS SUSAN *watches him, fascinated.*] Come, Miss Livvy, put these over you. Allow me—this one over your shoulders, so. Be so obliging as to lean on me. Be brave ma'am, you cannot fall—my arm is round you; gently, gently, Miss Livvy; ah, that is better; we are doing famously; come, come. Good-bye, Miss Susan, I will take every care of her.

[*He has gone, with the bundle on his arm, but*
MISS SUSAN *does not wake up. Even the
banging of the outer door is unable to rouse
her. It is heard, however, by* MISS PHOEBE,
*who steals back into the room, her cap upon
her head to give her courage.*]

PHOEBE. *He is gone!* [MISS SUSAN'S *rapt face alarms
her.*] Oh, Susan, was he as dreadful as that?

MISS SUSAN. [*In tones unnatural.*] Phoebe, he knows
all.

PHOEBE. Yes, of course he knows all now. Sister, did
his face change? Oh, Susan, what did he say?

MISS SUSAN. He said "Good-bye, Miss Susan." That
was almost all he said.

PHOEBE. Did his eyes flash fire?

MISS SUSAN. Phoebe, it was what he did. He—he
took Livvy with him.

PHOEBE. Susan, dear, don't say that. You are not distraught, are you?

MISS SUSAN. [*Clinging to facts.*] He did; he wrapped
her up in a shawl.

PHOEBE. Susan! You are Susan Throssel, my love.
You remember me, don't you? Phoebe, your sister. I was
Livvy also, you know, Livvy.

MISS SUSAN. He took Livvy with him.

PHOEBE. [*In woe.*] Oh, oh! sister, who am I?

MISS SUSAN. You are Phoebe.

PHOEBE. And who was Livvy?

MISS SUSAN. You were.

PHOEBE. Thank heaven.

MISS SUSAN. But he took her away in the carriage.

PHOEBE. Oh, dear! [*She has quite forgotten her own
troubles now.*] Susan, you will soon be well again. Dear,

let us occupy our minds. Shall we draw up the advertisement for the reopening of the school?

MISS SUSAN. I do so hate the school.

PHOEBE. Come, dear, come, sit down. Write, Susan. [*Dictating.*] "The Misses Throssel have the pleasure to announce——"

MISS SUSAN. Pleasure! Oh, Phoebe.

PHOEBE. "That they will resume school on the 5th of next month. Music, embroidery, the backboard, and all the elegancies of the mind. Latin—shall we say algebra?"

MISS SUSAN. I refuse to write algebra.

PHOEBE. ——for beginners.

MISS SUSAN. I refuse. There is only one thing I can write; it writes itself in my head all day. "Miss Susan Throssel presents her compliments to the Misses Willoughby and Miss Henrietta Turnbull, and requests the honour of their presence at the nuptials of her sister Phoebe and Captain Valentine Brown."

PHOEBE. Susan!

MISS SUSAN. Phoebe! [*A door is heard banging.*] He has returned!

PHOEBE. Oh cruel, cruel. Susan, I am so alarmed.

MISS SUSAN. I will face him.

PHOEBE. Nay, if it must be, I will.

[*But when he enters he is not very terrible.*]

VALENTINE. Miss Phoebe, it is not raining, but your face is wet. I wish always to kiss you when your face is wet.

PHOEBE. Susan!

VALENTINE. Miss Livvy will never trouble you any more, Miss Susan. I have sent her home.

MISS SUSAN. Oh, sir, how can you invent such a story for us.

VALENTINE. I did not. I invented it for the Misses

Willoughby and Miss Henrietta, who from their windows watched me put her into my carriage. Patty accompanies her, and in a few hours Patty will return alone.

MISS SUSAN. Phoebe, he has got rid of Livvy!

PHOEBE. Susan, his face hasn't changed!

VALENTINE. Dear Phoebe Throssel, will you be Phoebe Brown?

PHOEBE. [*Quivering.*] You know everything? And that I am not a garden?

VALENTINE. I know everything, ma'am—except that.

PHOEBE. [*So very glad to be prim at the end.*] Sir, the dictates of my heart enjoin me to accept your too flattering offer. [*He puts her cap in his pocket. He kisses her.* MISS SUSAN *is about to steal away.*] Oh, sir, Susan also. [*He kisses* MISS SUSAN *also; and here we bid them good-bye.*]

The End.

THE ADMIRABLE CRICHTON

A COMEDY

ACT I

AT LOAM HOUSE, MAYFAIR

A moment before the curtain rises, the HON. ERNEST
WOOLLEY *drives up to the door of Loam House in May-
fair. There is a happy smile on his pleasant, insignificant face, and this presumably means that he is
thinking of himself. He is too busy over nothing, this
man about town, to be always thinking of himself, but,
on the other hand, he almost never thinks of any other
person. Probably* ERNEST'S *great moment is when he
wakes of a morning and realises that he really is*
ERNEST, *for we must all wish to be that which is our
ideal. We can conceive him springing out of bed
light-heartedly and waiting for his man to do the rest.
He is dressed in excellent taste, with just the little bit
more which shows that he is not without a sense of
humour: the dandiacal are often saved by carrying
a smile at the whole thing in their spats, let us say.*
ERNEST *left Cambridge the other day, a member of the
Athenæum (which he would be sorry to have you con-
found with a club in London of the same name). He
is a bachelor, but not of arts, no mean epigrammatist
(as you shall see), and a favourite of the ladies. He
is almost a celebrity in restaurants, where he dines
frequently, returning to sup; and during this last year
he has probably paid as much in them for the privilege
of handing his hat to an attendant as the rent of a
working-man's flat. He complains brightly that he*

87

is hard up, and that if somebody or other at Westminster does not look out the country will go to the
dogs. He is no fool. He has the shrewdness to float
with the current because it is a labour-saving process,
but he has sufficient pluck to fight, if fight he must
(a brief contest, for he would soon be toppled over).
He has a light nature, which would enable him to bob
up cheerily in new conditions and return unaltered to
the old ones. His selfishness is his most endearing
quality. If he has his way he will spend his life like
a cat in pushing his betters out of the soft places, and
until he is old he will be fondled in the process.

He gives his hat to one footman and his cane to another,
and mounts the great staircase unassisted and un-
directed. As a nephew of the house he need show no
credentials even to CRICHTON, who is guarding a door
above.

It would not be good taste to describe CRICHTON, who is only
a servant; if to the scandal of all good houses he is to
stand out as a figure in the play, he must do it on his
own, as they say in the pantry and the boudoir. We
are not going to help him. We have had misgivings
ever since we found his name in the title, and we shall
keep him out of his rights as long as we can. Even
though we softened to him he would not be a hero in
these clothes of servitude; and he loves his clothes.
How to get him out of them? It would require a
cataclysm. To be an indoor servant at all is to
CRICHTON a badge of honour; to be a butler at thirty
is the realisation of his proudest ambitions. He is
devotedly attached to his master, who, in his opinion,
has but one fault, he is not sufficiently contemptuous of
his inferiors. We are immediately to be introduced to
this solitary failing of a great English peer.

This perfect butler, then, opens a door, and ushers ERNEST
*into a certain room. At the same moment the curtain
rises on this room, and the play begins.*

*It is one of several reception-rooms in Loam House, not the
most magnificent but quite the softest; and of a warm
afternoon all that those who are anybody crave for is
the softest. The larger rooms are magnificent and bare,
carpetless, so that it is an accomplishment to keep one's
feet on them; they are sometimes lent for charitable
purposes; they are also all in use on the night of a
dinner-party, when you may find yourself alone in one,
having taken a wrong turning; or alone, save for two
others who are within hailing distance. This room,
however, is comparatively small and very soft. There
are so many cushions in it that you wonder why, if
you are an outsider and don't know that it needs six
cushions to make one fair head comfy. The couches
themselves are cushions as large as beds, and there is
an art of sinking into them and of waiting to be helped
out of them. There are several famous paintings on the
walls, of which you may say "Jolly thing that," without losing caste as knowing too much; and in cases
there are glorious miniatures, but the daughters of the
house cannot tell you of whom; "there is a catalogue
somewhere." There are a thousand or so of roses in
basins, several library novels, and a row of weekly
illustrated newspapers lying against each other like
fallen soldiers. If any one disturbs this row* CRICHTON
*seems to know of it from afar and appears noiselessly
and replaces the wanderer. One thing unexpected in
such a room is a great array of tea things.* ERNEST
*spots them with a twinkle, and has his epigram at once
unsheathed. He dallies, however, before delivering the
thrust.*

ERNEST. I perceive, from the tea cups, Crichton, that the great function is to take place here.

CRICHTON. [*With a respectful sigh.*] Yes, sir.

ERNEST. [*Chuckling heartlessly.*] The servants' hall coming up to have tea in the drawing-room! [*With terrible sarcasm.*] No wonder you look happy, Crichton.

CRICHTON. [*Under the knife.*] No, sir.

ERNEST. Do you know, Crichton, I think that with an effort you might look even happier. [CRICHTON *smiles wanly.*] You don't approve of his lordship's compelling his servants to be his equals—once a month?

CRICHTON. It is not for me, sir, to disapprove of his lordship's Radical views.

ERNEST. Certainly not. And, after all, it is only once a month that he is affable to you.

CRICHTON. On all other days of the month, sir, his lordship's treatment of us is everything that could be desired.

ERNEST. [*This is the epigram.*] Tea cups! Life, Crichton, is like a cup of tea; the more heartily we drink, the sooner we reach the dregs.

CRICHTON. [*Obediently.*] Thank you, sir.

ERNEST. [*Becoming confidential, as we do when we have need of an ally.*] Crichton, in case I should be asked to say a few words to the servants, I have strung together a little speech. [*His hand strays to his pocket.*] I was wondering where I should stand.

> [*He tries various places and postures, and comes to rest leaning over a high chair, whence, in dumb show, he addresses a gathering.* CRICHTON, *with the best intentions, gives him a footstool to stand on, and departs, happily unconscious that* ERNEST *in some dudgeon has kicked the footstool across the room.*]

ERNEST. [*Addressing an imaginary audience, and desirous of startling them at once.*] Suppose you were all little fishes at the bottom of the sea——

> [*He is not quite satisfied with his position, though sure that the fault must lie with the chair for being too high, not with him for being too short. CRICHTON'S suggestion was not perhaps a bad one after all. He lifts the stool, but hastily conceals it behind him on the entrance of the LADIES CATHERINE and AGATHA, two daughters of the house. CATHERINE is twenty, and AGATHA two years younger. They are very fashionable young women indeed, who might wake up for a dance, but they are very lazy, CATHERINE being two years lazier than AGATHA.*]

ERNEST. [*Uneasily jocular, because he is concealing the footstool.*] And how are my little friends to-day?

AGATHA. [*Contriving to reach a settee.*] Don't be silly, Ernest. If you want to know how we are, we are dead. Even to think of entertaining the servants is so exhausting.

CATHERINE. [*Subsiding nearer the door.*] Besides which, we have had to decide what frocks to take with us on the yacht, and that is such a mental strain.

ERNEST. You poor over-worked things. [*Evidently AGATHA is his favourite, for he helps her to put her feet on the settee, while CATHERINE has to dispose of her own feet.*] Rest your weary limbs.

CATHERINE. [*Perhaps in revenge.*] But why have you a footstool in your hand?

AGATHA. Yes?

ERNEST. Why? [*Brilliantly; but to be sure he has had time to think it out.*] You see, as the servants are to be the guests I must be butler. I was practising. This is a tray, observe.

[*Holding the footstool as a tray, he minces across the room like an accomplished footman. The gods favour him, for just here* LADY MARY *enters, and he holds out the footstool to her.*]

Tea, my lady?

[LADY MARY *is a beautiful creature of twenty-two, and is of a natural hauteur which is at once the fury and the envy of her sisters. If she chooses she can make you seem so insignificant that you feel you might be swept away with the crumb-brush. She seldom chooses, because of the trouble of preening herself as she does it; she is usually content to show that you merely tire her eyes. She often seems to be about to go to sleep in the middle of a remark: there is quite a long and anxious pause, and then she continues, like a clock that hesitates, bored in the middle of its strike.*]

LADY MARY. [*Arching her brows.*] It is only you, Ernest; I thought there was some one here [*and she also bestows herself on cushions.*]

ERNEST. [*A little piqued, and deserting the footstool.*] Had a very tiring day also, Mary?

LADY MARY. [*Yawning.*] Dreadfully. Been trying on engagement-rings all the morning.

ERNEST. [*Who is as fond of gossip as the oldest club member.*] What's that? [*To* AGATHA.] Is it Brocklehurst?

[*The energetic* AGATHA *nods.*]

You have given your warm young heart to Brocky?

[LADY MARY *is impervious to his humour, but he continues bravely.*]

I don't wish to fatigue you, Mary, by insisting on a verbal

answer, but if, without straining yourself, you can signify Yes or No, won't you make the effort?

> [*She indolently flashes a ring on her most important finger, and he starts back melodramatically.*]

The ring! Then I am too late, too late! [*Fixing* LADY MARY *sternly, like a prosecuting counsel.*] May I ask, Mary, does Brocky know? Of course, it was that terrible mother of his who pulled this through. Mother does everything for Brocky. Still, in the eyes of the law you will be, not her wife, but his, and, therefore, I hold that Brocky ought to be informed. Now——

> [*He discovers that their languorous eyes have closed.*]

If you girls are shamming sleep in the expectation that I shall awaken you in the manner beloved of ladies, abandon all such hopes.

> [CATHERINE *and* AGATHA *look up without speaking.*]

LADY MARY. [*Speaking without looking up.*] You impertinent boy.

ERNEST. [*Eagerly plucking another epigram from his quiver.*] I knew that was it, though I don't know everything. Agatha, I'm not young enough to know everything.

> [*He looks hopefully from one to another, but though they try to grasp this, his brilliance baffles them.*]

AGATHA. [*His secret admirer.*] *Young* enough?

ERNEST. [*Encouragingly.*] Don't you see? I'm not young enough to know everything.

AGATHA. I'm sure it's awfully clever, but it's so puzzling.

> [*Here* CRICHTON *ushers in an athletic, pleasant-faced young clergyman,* MR. TREHERNE, *who greets the company.*]

CATHERINE.   Ernest, say it to Mr. Treherne.

ERNEST.   Look here, Treherne, I'm not young enough to know everything.

TREHERNE.   How do you mean, Ernest?

ERNEST.   [*A little nettled.*]   I mean what I say.

LADY MARY.   Say it again; say it more slowly.

ERNEST.   I'm — not — young — enough — to — know— everything.

TREHERNE.   *I* see.   What you really mean, my boy, is that you are not old enough to know everything.

ERNEST.   No, I don't.

TREHERNE.   I assure you that's it.

LADY MARY.   Of course it is.

CATHERINE.   Yes, Ernest, that's it.

[ERNEST, *in desperation, appeals to* CRICHTON.]

ERNEST.   I am not young enough, Crichton, to know everything.

[*It is an anxious moment, but a smile is at length extorted from* CRICHTON *as with a corkscrew.*]

CRICHTON.   Thank you, sir.   [*He goes.*]

ERNEST.   [*Relieved.*]   Ah, if you had that fellow's head, Treherne, you would find something better to do with it than play cricket.   I hear you bowl with your head.

TREHERNE.   [*With proper humility.*]   I'm afraid cricket is all I'm good for, Ernest.

CATHERINE.   [*Who thinks he has a heavenly nose.*] Indeed, it isn't.   You are sure to get on, Mr. Treherne.

TREHERNE.   Thank you, Lady Catherine.

CATHERINE.   But it was the bishop who told me so.   He said a clergyman who breaks both ways is sure to get on in England.

TREHERNE.   I'm jolly glad.

[*The master of the house comes in, accompanied by* LORD BROCKLEHURST. *The* EARL OF LOAM

*is a widower, a philanthropist, and a peer of
advanced ideas. As a widower he is at least
able to interfere in the domestic concerns of his
house—to rummage in the drawers, so to speak,
for which he has felt an itching all his blameless
life; his philanthropy has opened quite a number
of other drawers to him; and his advanced ideas
have blown out his figure. He takes in all the
weightiest monthly reviews, and prefers those
that are uncut, because he perhaps never looks
better than when cutting them; but he does not
read them, and save for the cutting it would suit
him as well merely to take in the covers. He
writes letters to the papers, which are printed
in a type to scale with himself, and he is very
jealous of those other correspondents who get
his type. Let laws and learning, art and commerce die, but leave the big type to an intellectual aristocracy. He is really the reformed
House of Lords which will come some day.*

[*Young* LORD BROCKLEHURST *is nothing, save for
his rank. You could pick him up by the handful any day in Piccadilly or Holborn, buying
socks—or selling them.*]

LORD LOAM. [*Expansively.*] You are here, Ernest.
Feeling fit for the voyage, Treherne?

TREHERNE. Looking forward to it enormously.

LORD LOAM. That's right. [*He chases his children about
as if they were chickens.*] Now then, Mary, up and doing,
up and doing. Time we had the servants in. They enjoy
it so much.

LADY MARY. They hate it.

LORD LOAM. Mary, to your duties. [*And he points
severely to the tea-table.*]

ERNEST. [*Twinkling.*] Congratulations, Brocky.

LORD BROCKLEHURST. [*Who detests humour.*] Thanks.

ERNEST. Mother pleased?

LORD BROCKLEHURST. [*With dignity.*] Mother is very pleased.

ERNEST. That's good. Do you go on the yacht with us?

LORD BROCKLEHURST. Sorry I can't. And look here, Ernest, I will *not* be called Brocky.

ERNEST. Mother don't like it?

LORD BROCKLEHURST. She does not. [*He leaves* ERNEST, *who forgives him and begins to think about his speech.* CRICHTON *enters.*]

LORD LOAM. [*Speaking as one man to another.*] We are quite ready, Crichton. [CRICHTON *is distressed.*]

LADY MARY. [*Sarcastically.*] How Crichton enjoys it!

LORD LOAM. [*Frowning.*] He is the only one who doesn't; pitiful creature.

CRICHTON. [*Shuddering under his lord's displeasure.*] I can't help being a Conservative, my lord.

LORD LOAM. Be a man, Crichton. You are the same flesh and blood as myself.

CRICHTON. [*In pain.*] Oh, my lord!

LORD LOAM. [*Sharply.*] Show them in; and, by the way, they were not all here last time.

CRICHTON. All, my lord, except the merest trifles.

LORD LOAM. It must be every one. [*Lowering.*] And remember this, Crichton, for the time being you are my equal. [*Testily.*] I shall soon show you whether you are not my equal. Do as you are told.

[CRICHTON *departs to obey, and his lordship is now a general. He has no pity for his daughters, and uses a terrible threat.*]

And girls, remember, no condescension. The first who condescends recites. [*This sends them skurrying to their labours.*]

By the way, Brocklehurst, can you do anything?

LORD BROCKLEHURST. How do you mean?

LORD LOAM. Can you do anything—with a penny or a handkerchief, make them disappear, for instance?

LORD BROCKLEHURST. Good heavens, no.

LORD LOAM. It's a pity. Every one in our position ought to be able to do something. Ernest, I shall probably ask you to say a few words; something bright and sparkling.

ERNEST. But, my dear uncle, I have prepared nothing.

LORD LOAM. Anything impromptu will do.

ERNEST. Oh—well—if anything strikes me on the spur of the moment.

　　　　[*He unostentatiously gets the footstool into posi-
　　　　tion behind the chair.* CRICHTON *reappears to
　　　　announce the guests, of whom the first is the
　　　　housekeeper.*]

CRICHTON. [*Reluctantly.*] Mrs. Perkins.

LORD LOAM. [*Shaking hands.*] Very delighted, Mrs. Perkins. Mary, our friend, Mrs. Perkins.

LADY MARY. How do you do, Mrs. Perkins? Won't you sit here?

LORD LOAM. [*Threateningly.*] Agatha!

AGATHA. [*Hastily.*] How do you do? Won't you sit down?

LORD LOAM. [*Introducing.*] Lord Brocklehurst—my valued friend, Mrs. Perkins.

　　　　[LORD BROCKLEHURST *bows and escapes. He has
　　　　to fall back on* ERNEST.]

LORD BROCKLEHURST. For heaven's sake, Ernest, don't leave me for a moment; this sort of thing is utterly opposed to all my principles.

ERNEST. [*Airily.*] You stick to me, Brocky, and I'll pull you through.

CRICHTON. Monsieur Fleury.

ERNEST. The chef.

LORD LOAM. [*Shaking hands with the chef.*] Very charmed to see you, Monsieur Fleury.

FLEURY. Thank you very much.

> [FLEURY *bows to* AGATHA, *who is not effusive.*]

LORD LOAM. [*Warningly.*] Agatha—recitation!

> [*She tosses her head, but immediately finds a seat and tea for* M. FLEURY. TREHERNE *and* ERNEST *move about, making themselves amiable.* LADY MARY *is presiding at the tea-tray.*]

CRICHTON. Mr. Rolleston.

LORD LOAM. [*Shaking hands with his valet.*] How do you do, Rolleston?

> [CATHERINE *looks after the wants of* ROLLESTON.]

CRICHTON. Mr. Tompsett.

> [TOMPSETT, *the coachman, is received with honours, from which he shrinks.*]

CRICHTON. Miss Fisher.

> [*This superb creature is no less than* LADY MARY'S *maid, and even* LORD LOAM *is a little nervous.*]

LORD LOAM. This is a pleasure, Miss Fisher.

ERNEST. [*Unabashed.*] If I might venture, Miss Fisher [*and he takes her unto himself.*]

CRICHTON. Miss Simmons.

LORD LOAM. [*To* CATHERINE'S *maid.*] You are always welcome, Miss Simmons.

ERNEST. [*Perhaps to kindle jealousy in* MISS FISHER.] At last we meet. Won't you sit down?

CRICHTON. Mademoiselle Jeanne.

LORD LOAM. Charmed to see you, Mademoiselle Jeanne.

> [*A place is found for* AGATHA'S *maid, and the*

*scene is now an animated one; but still our host
thinks his girls are not sufficiently sociable. He
frowns on* LADY MARY.]

LADY MARY. [*In alarm.*] Mr. Treherne, this is Fisher,
my maid.

LORD LOAM. [*Sharply.*] Your what, Mary?

LADY MARY. My friend.

CRICHTON. Thomas.

LORD LOAM. How do you do, Thomas?

[*The first footman gives him a reluctant hand.*]

CRICHTON. John.

LORD LOAM. How do you do, John?

[ERNEST *signs to* LORD BROCKLEHURST, *who
hastens to him.*]

ERNEST. [*Introducing.*] Brocklehurst, this is John. I
think you have already met on the door-step.

CRICHTON. Jane.

[*She comes, wrapping her hands miserably in her
apron.*]

LORD LOAM. [*Doggedly.*] Give me your hand, Jane.

CRICHTON. Gladys.

ERNEST. How do you do, Gladys. You know my
uncle?

LORD LOAM. Your hand, Gladys.

[*He bestows her on* AGATHA.]

CRICHTON. Tweeny.

[*She is a very humble and frightened kitchenmaid, of whom we are to see more.*]

LORD LOAM. So happy to see you.

FISHER. John, I saw you talking to Lord Brocklehurst
just now; introduce me.

LORD BROCKLEHURST. [*At the same moment to*
ERNEST.] That's an uncommon pretty girl; if I must
feed one of them, Ernest, that's the one.

[*But* ERNEST *tries to part him and* FISHER *as they
are about to shake hands.*]

ERNEST.   No you don't, it won't do, Brocky. [*To* MISS
FISHER.]   You are too pretty, my dear.   Mother wouldn't
like it.   [*Discovering* TWEENY.]   Here's something safer.
Charming girl, Brocky, dying to know you; let me introduce
you.   Tweeny, Lord Brocklehurst—Lord Brocklehurst,
Tweeny.

[BROCKLEHURST *accepts his fate; but he still has
an eye for* FISHER, *and something may come of
this.*]

LORD LOAM.   [*Severely.*]   They   are   not   all   here,
Crichton.

CRICHTON.   [*With a sigh.*]   Odds and ends.

[*A* STABLE-BOY *and a* PAGE *are shown in, and for
a moment no daughter of the house advances to
them.*]

LORD LOAM.   [*With a roving eye on his children.*]
Which is to recite?

[*The   last   of   the   company   are,   so   to   say,
embraced.*]

LORD LOAM.   [*to* TOMPSETT, *as they partake of tea together.*]   And how are all at home?

TOMPSETT.   Fairish, my lord, if 'tis the horses you are
inquiring for?

LORD LOAM.   No, no, the family.   How's the baby?

TOMPSETT.   Blooming, your lordship.

LORD LOAM.   A very fine boy.   I remember saying so
when I saw him; nice little fellow.

TOMPSETT.   [*Not quite knowing whether to let it pass.*]
Beg pardon, my lord, it's a girl.

LORD LOAM.   A girl?   Aha!   ha!   ha!   exactly what I
said.   I distinctly remember saying, If it's spared it will be
a girl.

[CRICHTON *now comes down.*]

LORD LOAM. Very delighted to see you, Crichton.

[CRICHTON *has to shake hands.*]

Mary, you know Mr. Crichton?

[*He wanders off in search of other prey.*]

LADY MARY. Milk and sugar, Crichton?

CRICHTON. I'm ashamed to be seen talking to you, my lady.

LADY MARY. To such a perfect servant as you all this must be most distasteful. [CRICHTON *is too respectful to answer.*] Oh, please to speak, or I shall have to recite. You do hate it, don't you?

CRICHTON. It pains me, your ladyship. It disturbs the etiquette of the servants' hall. After last month's meeting the pageboy, in a burst of equality, called me Crichton. He was dismissed.

LADY MARY. I wonder—I really do—how you can remain with us.

CRICHTON. I should have felt compelled to give notice, my lady, if the master had not had a seat in the Upper House. I cling to that.

LADY MARY. Do go on speaking. Tell me, what did Mr. Ernest mean by saying he was not young enough to know everything?

CRICHTON. I have no idea, my lady.

LADY MARY. But you laughed.

CRICHTON. My lady, he is the second son of a peer.

LADY MARY. Very proper sentiments. You are a good soul, Crichton.

LORD BROCKLEHURST. [*Desperately to* TWEENY.] And now tell me, have you been to the Opera? What sort of weather have you been having in the kitchen? [TWEENY *gurgles.*] For Heaven's sake, woman, be articulate.

CRICHTON. [*Still talking to* LADY MARY.] No, my

lady; his lordship may compel us to be equal upstairs, but there will never be equality in the servants' hall.

LORD LOAM. [*Overhearing this.*] What's that? No equality? Can't you see, Crichton, that our divisions into classes are artificial, that if we were to return to Nature, which is the aspiration of my life, all would be equal?

CRICHTON. If I may make so bold as to contradict your lordship——

LORD LOAM. [*With an effort.*] Go on.

CRICHTON. The divisions into classes, my lord, are not artificial. They are the natural outcome of a civilised society. [*To* LADY MARY.] There must always be a master and servants in all civilised communities, my lady, for it is natural, and whatever is natural is right.

LORD LOAM. [*Wincing.*] It is very unnatural for me to stand here and allow you to talk such nonsense.

CRICHTON. [*Eagerly.*] Yes, my lord, it is. That is what I have been striving to point out to your lordship.

AGATHA. [*To* CATHERINE.] What is the matter with Fisher? She is looking daggers.

CATHERINE. The tedious creature; some question of etiquette, I suppose.

[*She sails across to* FISHER.]
How are you, Fisher?

FISHER. [*With a toss of her head.*] I am nothing, my lady, I am nothing at all.

AGATHA. Oh dear, who says so?

FISHER. [*Affronted.*] His lordship has asked that kitchen wench to have a second cup of tea.

CATHERINE. But why not?

FISHER. If it pleases his lordship to offer it to *her* before offering it to *me*——

AGATHA. So that is it. Do you want another cup of tea, Fisher?

FISHER. No, my lady—but my position—I should have been asked first.

AGATHA. Oh dear.

> [*All this has taken some time, and by now the feeble appetites of the uncomfortable guests have been satiated. But they know there is still another ordeal to face—his lordship's monthly speech. Every one awaits it with misgiving—the servants lest they should applaud, as last time, in the wrong place, and the daughters because he may be personal about them, as the time before.* ERNEST *is annoyed that there should be this speech at all when there is such a much better one coming, and* BROCKLEHURST *foresees the degradation of the peerage. All are thinking of themselves alone save* CRICHTON, *who knows his master's weakness, and fears he may stick in the middle.* LORD LOAM, *however, advances cheerfully to his doom. He sees* ERNEST'S *stool, and artfully stands on it, to his nephew's natural indignation. The three ladies knit their lips, the servants look down their noses, and the address begins.*]

LORD LOAM. My friends, I am glad to see you all looking so happy. It used to be predicted by the scoffer that these meetings would prove distasteful to you. Are they distasteful? I hear you laughing at the question.

> [*He has not heard them, but he hears them now, the watchful* CRICHTON *giving them a lead.*]

No harm in saying that among us to-day is one who was formerly hostile to the movement, but who to-day has been won over. I refer to Lord Brocklehurst, who, I am sure, will presently say to me that if the charming lady now by his side has derived as much pleasure from his company as he has derived from hers, he will be more than satisfied.

> [*All look at* TWEENY, *who trembles.*]

For the time being the artificial and unnatural—I say unnatural [*glaring at* CRICHTON, *who bows slightly*]—barriers of society are swept away. Would that they could be swept away for ever.

> [*The* PAGEBOY *cheers, and has the one moment of
> prominence in his life. He grows up, marries
> and has children, but is never really heard of
> again.*]

But that is entirely and utterly out of the question. And now for a few months we are to be separated. As you know, my daughters and Mr. Ernest and Mr. Treherne are to accompany me on my yacht, on a voyage to distant parts of the earth. In less than forty-eight hours we shall be under weigh.

> [*But for* CRICHTON'S *eye the reckless* PAGEBOY
> *would repeat his success.*]

Do not think our life on the yacht is to be one long idle holiday. My views on the excessive luxury of the day are well known, and what I preach I am resolved to practise. I have therefore decided that my daughters, instead of having one maid each as at present, shall on this voyage have but one maid between them.

> [*Three maids rise; also three mistresses.*]

CRICHTON.   My lord!

LORD LOAM.   My mind is made up.

ERNEST.   I cordially agree.

LORD LOAM.   And now, my friends, I should like to think that there is some piece of advice I might give you, some thought, some noble saying over which you might ponder in my absence. In this connection I remember a proverb, which has had a great effect on my own life. I first heard it many years ago. I have never forgotten it. It constantly cheers and guides me. That proverb is—that proverb was—the proverb I speak of——

[*He grows pale and taps his forehead.*]

LADY MARY. Oh dear, I believe he has forgotten it.

LORD LOAM. [*Desperately.*] The proverb—that proverb to which I refer——

[*Alas, it has gone. The distress is general. He has not even the sense to sit down. He gropes for the proverb in the air. They try applause, but it is no help.*]

I have it now—[*not he.*]

LADY MARY. [*With confidence.*] Crichton.

[*He does not fail her. As quietly as if he were in goloshes, mind as well as feet, he dismisses the domestics; they go according to precedence as they entered, yet, in a moment, they are gone. Then he signs to MR. TREHERNE, and they conduct LORD LOAM with dignity from the room. His hands are still catching flies; he still mutters, "The proverb—that proverb"; but he continues, owing to CRICHTON's skilful treatment, to look every inch a peer. The ladies have now an opportunity to air their indignation.*]

LADY MARY. One maid among three grown women!

LORD BROCKLEHURST. Mary, I think I had better go. That dreadful kitchenmaid——

LADY MARY. I can't blame you, George.

[*He salutes her.*]

LORD BROCKLEHURST. Your father's views are shocking to me, and I am glad I am not to be one of the party on the yacht. My respect for myself, Mary, my natural anxiety as to what mother will say. I shall see you, darling, before you sail.

[*He bows to the others and goes.*]

ERNEST. Selfish brute, only thinking of himself. What about my speech?

LADY MARY. One maid among three of us. What's to be done?

ERNEST. Pooh! You must do for yourselves, that's all.

LADY MARY. Do for ourselves. How can we know where our things are kept?

AGATHA. Are you aware that dresses button up the back?

CATHERINE. How are we to get into our shoes and be prepared for the carriage?

LADY MARY. Who is to put us to bed, and who is to get us up, and how shall we ever know it's morning if there is no one to pull up the blinds?

[CRICHTON *crosses on his way out.*]

ERNEST. How is his lordship now?

CRICHTON. A little easier, sir.

LADY MARY. Crichton, send Fisher to me.

[*He goes.*]

ERNEST. I have no pity for you girls, I——

LADY MARY. Ernest, go away, and don't insult the broken-hearted.

ERNEST. And uncommon glad I am to go. Ta-ta, all of you. He asked me to say a few words. I came here to say a few words, and I'm not at all sure that I couldn't bring an action against him.

[*He departs, feeling that he has left a dart behind him. The girls are alone with their tragic thoughts.*]

LADY MARY. [*Become a mother to the younger ones at last.*] My poor sisters, come here. [*They go to her doubtfully.*] We must make this draw us closer together. I shall do my best to help you in every way. Just now I cannot think of myself at all.

AGATHA. But how unlike you, Mary.

LADY MARY. It is my duty to protect my sisters.

CATHERINE. I never knew her so sweet before, Agatha. [*Cautiously.*] What do you propose to do, Mary?

LADY MARY. I propose when we are on the yacht to lend Fisher to you when I don't need her myself.

AGATHA. Fisher?

LADY MARY. [*Who has the most character of the three.*] Of course, as the eldest, I have decided that it is *my* maid we shall take with us.

CATHERINE. [*Speaking also for* AGATHA.] Mary, you toad.

AGATHA. Nothing on earth would induce Fisher to lift her hand for either me or Catherine.

LADY MARY. I was afraid of it, Agatha. That is why I am so sorry for you.

> [*The further exchange of pleasantries is interrupted by the arrival of* FISHER.]

LADY MARY. Fisher, you heard what his lordship said?

FISHER. Yes, my lady.

LADY MARY. [*Coldly, though the others would have tried blandishment.*] You have given me some satisfaction of late, Fisher, and to mark my approval I have decided that you shall be the maid who accompanies us.

FISHER. [*Acidly.*] I thank you, my lady.

LADY MARY. That is all; you may go.

FISHER. [*Rapping it out.*] If you please, my lady, I wish to give notice.

> [CATHERINE *and* AGATHA *gleam, but* LADY MARY *is of sterner stuff.*]

LADY MARY. [*Taking up a book.*] Oh, certainly—you may go.

CATHERINE. But why, Fisher?

FISHER. I could not undertake, my lady, to wait upon three. *We* don't do it. [*In an indignant outburst to* LADY MARY.] Oh, my lady, to think that this affront——

LADY MARY. [*Looking up.*] I thought I told you to go, Fisher.

> [FISHER *stands for a moment irresolute; then goes. As soon as she has gone* LADY MARY *puts down her book and weeps. She is a pretty woman, but this is the only pretty thing we have seen her do yet.*]

AGATHA. [*Succinctly.*] Serves you right.

> [CRICHTON *comes.*]

CATHERINE. It will be Simmons after all. Send Simmons to me.

CRICHTON. [*After hesitating.*] My lady, might I venture to speak?

CATHERINE. What is it?

CRICHTON. I happen to know, your ladyship, that Simmons desires to give notice for the same reason as Fisher.

CATHERINE. Oh!

AGATHA. [*Triumphant*]. Then, Catherine, we take Jeanne.

CRICHTON. And Jeanne also, my lady.

> [LADY MARY *is reading, indifferent though the heavens fall, but her sisters are not ashamed to show their despair to* CRICHTON.]

AGATHA. We can't blame them. Could any maid who respected herself be got to wait upon three?

LADY MARY. [*With languid interest.*] I suppose there are such persons, Crichton?

CRICHTON. [*Guardedly.*] I have heard, my lady, that there are such.

LADY MARY. [*A little desperate.*] Crichton, what's to

be done? We sail in two days; could one be discovered in the time?

AGATHA. [*Frankly a supplicant.*] Surely you can think of some one?

CRICHTON. [*After hesitating.*] There is in this establishment, your ladyship, a young woman——

LADY MARY. Yes?

CRICHTON. A young woman, on whom I have for some time cast an eye.

CATHERINE. [*Eagerly.*] Do you mean as a possible lady's-maid?

CRICHTON. I had thought of her, my lady, in another connection.

LADY MARY. Ah!

CRICHTON. But I believe she is quite the young person you require. Perhaps if you could see her, my lady——

LADY MARY. I shall certainly see her. Bring her to me. [*He goes.*] You two needn't wait.

CATHERINE. Needn't we? We see your little game, Mary.

AGATHA. We shall certainly remain and have our two-thirds of her.

> [*They sit there doggedly until* CRICHTON *returns with* TWEENY, *who looks scared.*]

CRICHTON. This, my lady, is the young person.

CATHERINE. [*Frankly.*] Oh dear!

> [*It is evident that all three consider her quite unsuitable.*]

LADY MARY. Come here, girl. Don't be afraid.

> [TWEENY *looks imploringly at her idol.*]

CRICHTON. Her appearance, my lady, is homely, and her manners, as you may have observed, deplorable, but she has a heart of gold.

LADY MARY. What is your position downstairs?

TWEENY. [*Bobbing.*] I'm a tweeny, your ladyship.

CATHERINE. A what?

CRICHTON. A tweeny; that is to say, my lady, she is not at present, strictly speaking, anything; a *between* maid; she helps the vegetable maid. It is she, my lady, who conveys the dishes from the one end of the kitchen table where they are placed by the cook, to the other end, where they enter into the charge of Thomas and John.

LADY MARY. I see. And you and Crichton are—ah—keeping company?

[CRICHTON *draws himself up.*]

TWEENY. [*Aghast.*] A butler don't keep company, my lady.

LADY MARY. [*Indifferently.*] Does he not?

CRICHTON. No, your ladyship, we butlers may—[*he makes a gesture with his arms*]—but we do not keep company.

AGATHA. I know what it is; you are engaged?

[TWEENY *looks longingly at* CRICHTON.]

CRICHTON. Certainly not, my lady. The utmost I can say at present is that I have cast a favourable eye.

[*Even this is much to* TWEENY.]

LADY MARY. As you choose. But I am afraid, Crichton, she will not suit us.

CRICHTON. My lady, beneath this simple exterior are concealed a very sweet nature and rare womanly gifts.

AGATHA. Unfortunately, that is not what we want.

CRICHTON. And it is she, my lady, who dresses the hair of the ladies'-maids for our evening meals.

[*The ladies are interested at last.*]

LADY MARY. She dresses Fisher's hair?

TWEENY. Yes, my lady, and I does them up when they goes to parties.

CRICHTON. [*Pained, but not scolding.*] Does!

TWEENY. Doos. And it's me what alters your gowns to fit them.

CRICHTON. *What* alters!

TWEENY. Which alters.

AGATHA. Mary?

LADY MARY. I shall certainly have her.

CATHERINE. *We* shall certainly have her. Tweeny, we have decided to make a lady's-maid of you.

TWEENY. Oh lawks!

AGATHA. We are doing this for you so that your position socially may be more nearly akin to that of Crichton.

CRICHTON. [*Gravely.*] It will undoubtedly increase the young person's chances.

LADY MARY. Then if I get a good character for you from Mrs. Perkins, she will make the necessary arrangements.

[*She resumes reading.*]

TWEENY. [*Elated.*] My lady!

LADY MARY. By the way, I hope you are a good sailor.

TWEENY. [*Startled.*] You don't mean, my lady, I'm to go on the ship?

LADY MARY. Certainly.

TWEENY. But—— [*To* CRICHTON.] You ain't going, sir?

CRICHTON. No.

TWEENY. [*Firm at last.*] Then neither ain't I.

AGATHA. You must.

TWEENY. Leave him! Not me.

LADY MARY. Girl, don't be silly. Crichton will be— considered in your wages.

TWEENY. I ain't going.

CRICHTON. I feared this, my lady.

TWEENY. Nothing 'll budge me.

LADY MARY. Leave the room.

[CRICHTON *shows* TWEENY *out with marked politeness.*]

AGATHA.   Crichton, I think you might have shown more displeasure with her.

CRICHTON.   [*Contrite.*]   I was touched, my lady.   I see, my lady, that to part from her would be a wrench to me, though I could not well say so in her presence, not having yet decided how far I shall go with her.

[*He is about to go when* LORD LOAM *returns, fuming.*]

LORD LOAM.   The ingrate!   The smug!   The fop!

CATHERINE.   What is it now, father?

LORD LOAM.   That man of mine, Rolleston, refuses to accompany us because you are to have but one maid.

AGATHA.   Hurrah!

LADY MARY.   [*In better taste.*]   Darling father, rather than you should lose Rolleston, we will consent to take all the three of them.

LORD LOAM.   Pooh, nonsense!   Crichton, find me a valet who can do without three maids.

CRICHTON.   Yes, my lord.   [*Troubled.*]   In the time— the more suitable the party, my lord, the less willing will he be to come without the—the usual perquisites.

LORD LOAM.   Any one will do.

CRICHTON.   [*Shocked.*]   My lord!

LORD LOAM.   The ingrate!   The puppy!

[AGATHA *has an idea, and whispers to* LADY MARY.]

LADY MARY.   I ask a favour of a servant?—never!

AGATHA.   Then I will.   Crichton, would it not be very distressing to you to let his lordship go, attended by a valet who might prove unworthy?   It is only for three months; don't you think that you—you yourself—you——

[*As* CRICHTON *sees what she wants he pulls*

*himself up with noble, offended dignity, and she
is appalled.*]

I beg your pardon.

[*He bows stiffly.*]

CATHERINE. [*To* CRICHTON.] But think of the joy
to Tweeny.

[CRICHTON *is moved, but he shakes his head.*]

LADY MARY. [*So much the cleverest.*] Crichton, do
you think it safe to let the master you love go so far away
without you while he has these dangerous views about
equality?

[CRICHTON *is profoundly stirred. After a struggle
he goes to his master, who has been pacing the
room.*]

CRICHTON. My lord, I have found a man.

LORD LOAM. Already? Who is he?

[CRICHTON *presents himself with a gesture.*]

Yourself?

CATHERINE. Father, how good of him.

LORD LOAM. [*Pleased, but thinking it a small thing.*]
Uncommon good. Thank you, Crichton. This helps me
nicely out of a hole; and how it will annoy Rolleston!
Come with me, and we shall tell him. Not that I think
you have lowered yourself in any way. Come along.

[*He goes, and* CRICHTON *is to follow him, but is
stopped by* AGATHA *impulsively offering him
her hand.*]

CRICHTON. [*Who is much shaken.*] My lady—a
valet's hand!

AGATHA. I had no idea you would feel it so deeply; why
did you do it?

[CRICHTON *is too respectful to reply.*]

LADY MARY. [*Regarding him.*] Crichton, I am curious.
I insist upon an answer.

CRICHTON. My lady, I am the son of a butler and a lady's-maid—perhaps the happiest of all combinations, and to me the most beautiful thing in the world is a haughty, aristocratic English house, with every one kept in his place. Though I were equal to your ladyship, where would be the pleasure to me? It would be counterbalanced by the pain of feeling that Thomas and John were equal to me.

CATHERINE. But father says if we were to return to Nature——

CRICHTON. If we did, my lady, the first thing we should do would be to elect a head. Circumstances might alter cases; the same person might not be master; the same persons might not be servants. I can't say as to that, nor should we have the deciding of it. Nature would decide for us.

LADY MARY. You seem to have thought it all out carefully, Crichton.

CRICHTON. Yes, my lady.

CATHERINE. And you have done this for us, Crichton, because you thought that—that father needed to be kept in his place?

CRICHTON. I should prefer you to say, my lady, that I have done it for the house.

AGATHA. Thank you, Crichton. Mary, be nicer to him. [*But* LADY MARY *has begun to read again.*] If there was any way in which we could show our gratitude.

CRICHTON. If I might venture, my lady, would you kindly show it by becoming more like Lady Mary? That disdain is what we like from our superiors. Even so do we, the upper servants, disdain the lower servants, while they take it out of the odds and ends.

[*He goes, and they bury themselves in cushions.*]

AGATHA. Oh dear, what a tiring day.

CATHERINE. I feel dead. Tuck in your feet, you selfish thing.

[LADY MARY *is lying reading on another couch.*]

LADY MARY. I wonder what he meant by circumstances might alter cases.

AGATHA. [*Yawning.*] Don't talk, Mary, I was nearly asleep.

LADY MARY. I wonder what he meant by the same person might not be master, and the same persons might not be servants.

CATHERINE. Do be quiet, Mary, and leave it to Nature; he said Nature would decide.

LADY MARY. I wonder——

> [*But she does not wonder very much. She would wonder more if she knew what was coming. Her book slips unregarded to the floor. The ladies are at rest until it is time to dress.*]

End of Act I.

ACT II

THE ISLAND

Two months have elapsed, and the scene is a desert island in the Pacific, on which our adventurers have been wrecked.

The curtain rises on a sea of bamboo, which shuts out all view save the foliage of palm trees and some gaunt rocks. Occasionally CRICHTON *and* TREHERNE *come momentarily into sight, hacking and hewing the bamboo, through which they are making a clearing between the ladies and the shore; and by and by, owing to their efforts, we shall have an unrestricted outlook on* to a sullen sea that is at present hidden. Then we shall also be able to note a mast standing out of the water—all that is left, saving floating wreckage, of the ill-fated yacht the Bluebell. The beginnings of a hut will also be seen, with CRICHTON driving its walls into the ground or astride its roof of saplings, for at present he is doing more than one thing at a time. In a red shirt, with the ends of his sailor's breeches thrust into wading-boots, he looks a man for the moment; we suddenly remember some one's saying—perhaps it was ourselves—that a cataclysm would be needed to get him out of his servant's clothes, and apparently it has been forthcoming. It is no longer beneath our dignity to cast an inquiring eye on his appearance. His features are not distinguished, but he has a strong jaw and green eyes, in which a yellow light burns that we have not seen before. His dark hair, hitherto so decorously sleek, has been ruffled this way and that by wind and weather, as if they were part of the cataclysm and wanted to help his chance. His muscles must be soft and flabby still, but though they shriek aloud to him to desist, he rains lusty blows with his axe, like one who has come upon the open for the first time in his life, and likes it. He is as yet far from being an expert woodsman—mark the blood on his hands at places where he has hit them instead of the tree; but note also that he does not waste time in bandaging them—he rubs them in the earth and goes on. His face is still of the discreet pallor that befits a butler, and he carries the smaller logs as if they were a salver; not in a day or a month will he shake off the badge of servitude, but without knowing it he has begun.

But for the hatchets at work, and an occasional something

*horrible falling from a tree into the ladies' laps, they
hear nothing save the mournful surf breaking on a coral
shore.*

*They sit or recline huddled together against a rock, and
they are farther from home, in every sense of the word,
than ever before.   Thirty-six hours ago, they were
given three minutes in which to dress, without a maid,
and reach the boats, and they have not made the best
of that valuable time.   None of them has boots, and
had they known this prickly island they would have
thought first of boots.   They have a sufficiency of
garments, but some of them were gifts dropped into
the boat—LADY MARY'S tarpaulin coat and hat, for
instance, and CATHERINE'S blue jersey and red cap,
which certify that the two ladies were lately before
the mast.   AGATHA is too gay in ERNEST'S dressing-
gown, and clutches it to her person with both hands
as if afraid that it may be claimed by its rightful
owner.   There are two pairs of bath slippers between
the three of them, and their hair cries aloud and in
vain for hairpins.*

*By their side, on an inverted bucket, sits ERNEST, clothed
neatly in the garments of day and night, but, alas,
bare-footed.   He is the only cheerful member of this
company of four, but his brightness is due less to a
manly desire to succour the helpless than to his having
been lately in the throes of composition, and to his
modest satisfaction with the result.   He reads to the
ladies, and they listen, each with one scared eye to
the things that fall from trees.*

ERNEST.   [*Who has written on the fly-leaf of the only
book saved from the wreck.*]   This is what I have written.

"Wrecked, wrecked, wrecked! on an island in the Tropics, the following: the Hon. Ernest Woolley, the Rev. John Treherne, the Ladies Mary, Catherine, and Agatha Lasenby, with two servants. We are the sole survivors of Lord Loam's steam yacht *Bluebell,* which encountered a fearful gale in these seas, and soon became a total wreck. The crew behaved gallantly, putting us all into the first boat. What became of them I cannot tell, but we, after dreadful sufferings, and insufficiently clad, in whatever garments we could lay hold of in the dark——"

LADY MARY. Please don't describe our garments.

ERNEST.—"succeeded in reaching this island, with the loss of only one of our party, namely, Lord Loam, who flung away his life in a gallant attempt to save a servant who had fallen overboard."

> [*The ladies have wept long and sore for their father, but there is something in this last utterance that makes them look up.*]

AGATHA. But, Ernest, it was Crichton who jumped overboard trying to save father.

ERNEST. [*With the candour that is one of his most engaging qualities.*] Well, you know, it was rather silly of uncle to fling away his life by trying to get into the boat first; and as this document may be printed in the English papers, it struck me, an English peer, you know——

LADY MARY. [*Every inch an English peer's daughter.*] Ernest, that is very thoughtful of you.

ERNEST. [*Continuing, well pleased.*] —"By night the cries of wild cats and the hissing of snakes terrify us extremely"—[*this does not satisfy him so well, and he makes a correction*]—"terrify the ladies extremely. Against these we have no weapons except one cutlass and a hatchet. A bucket washed ashore is at present our only comfortable seat——"

LADY MARY. [*With some spirit.*] And Ernest is sitting on it.

ERNEST. H'sh! Oh, do be quiet. —"To add to our horrors, night falls suddenly in these parts, and it is then that savage animals begin to prowl and roar."

LADY MARY. Have you said that vampire bats suck the blood from our toes as we sleep?

ERNEST. No, that's all. I end up, "Rescue us or we perish. Rich reward. Signed Ernest Woolley, in command of our little party." This is written on a leaf taken out of a book of poems that Crichton found in his pocket. Fancy Crichton being a reader of poetry. Now I shall put it into the bottle and fling it into the sea.

> [*He pushes the precious document into a soda-water bottle, and rams the cork home. At the same moment, and without effort, he gives birth to one of his most characteristic epigrams.*]

The tide is going out, we mustn't miss the post.

> [*They are so unhappy that they fail to grasp it, and a little petulantly he calls for* CRICHTON, *ever his stand-by in the hour of epigram.* CRICHTON *breaks through the undergrowth quickly, thinking the ladies are in danger.*]

CRICHTON. Anything wrong, sir?

ERNEST. [*With fine confidence.*] The tide, Crichton, is a postman who calls at our island twice a day for letters.

CRICHTON. [*After a pause.*] Thank you, sir.

> [*He returns to his labours, however, without giving the smile which is the epigrammatist's right, and* ERNEST *is a little disappointed in him.*]

ERNEST. Poor Crichton! I sometimes think he is losing his sense of humour. Come along, Agatha.

[*He helps his favourite up the rocks, and they disappear gingerly from view.*]

CATHERINE. How horribly still it is.

LADY MARY. [*Remembering some recent sounds.*] It is best when it is still.

CATHERINE. [*Drawing closer to her.*] Mary, I have heard that they are always very still just before they jump.

LADY MARY. Don't. [*A distinct chopping is heard, and they are startled.*]

LADY MARY. [*Controlling herself.*] It is only Crichton knocking down trees.

CATHERINE. [*Almost imploringly.*] Mary, let us go and stand beside him.

LADY MARY. [*Coldly.*] Let a servant see that I am afraid!

CATHERINE. Don't, then; but remember this, dear, they often drop on one from above.

[*She moves away, nearer to the friendly sound of the axe, and* LADY MARY *is left alone. She is the most courageous of them as well as the haughtiest, but when something she had thought to be a stick glides toward her, she forgets her dignity and screams.*]

LADY MARY. [*Calling.*] Crichton, Crichton!

[*It must have been* TREHERNE *who was tree-felling, for* CRICHTON *comes to her from the hut, drawing his cutlass.*]

CRICHTON. [*Anxious.*] Did you call, my lady?

LADY MARY. [*Herself again, now that he is there.*] I! Why should I?

CRICHTON. I made a mistake, your ladyship. [*Hesitating.*] If you are afraid of being alone, my lady——

LADY MARY. Afraid! Certainly not. [*Doggedly.*] You may go.

[But she does not complain when he remains within eyesight cutting the bamboo. It is heavy work, and she watches him silently.]

LADY MARY. I wish, Crichton, you could work without getting so hot.

CRICHTON. *[Mopping his face.]* I wish I could, my lady. *[He continues his labours.]*

LADY MARY. *[Taking off her oilskins.]* It makes me hot to look at you.

CRICHTON. It almost makes me cool to look at your ladyship.

LADY MARY. *[Who perhaps thinks he is presuming.]* Anything I can do for you in that way, Crichton, I shall do with pleasure.

CRICHTON. *[Quite humbly.]* Thank you, my lady.
[By this time most of the bamboo has been cut, and the shore and sea are visible, except where they are hidden by the half completed hut. The mast rising solitary from the water adds to the desolation of the scene, and at last tears run down LADY MARY's face.]

CRICHTON. Don't give way, my lady, things might be worse.

LADY MARY. My poor father.

CRICHTON. If I could have given my life for his.

LADY MARY. You did all a man could do. Indeed I thank you, Crichton. *[With some admiration and more wonder.]* You are a man.

CRICHTON. Thank you, my lady.

LADY MARY. But it is all so awful. Crichton, is there any hope of a ship coming?

CRICHTON. *[After hesitation.]* Of course there is, my lady.

LADY MARY. *[Facing him bravely.]* Don't treat me as

a child. I have got to know the worst, and to face it. Crichton, the truth.

CRICHTON. [*Reluctantly.*] We were driven out of our course, my lady; I fear far from the track of commerce.

LADY MARY. Thank you; I understand.

> [*For a moment, however, she breaks down. Then she clenches her hands and stands erect.*]

CRICHTON. [*Watching her, and forgetting perhaps for the moment that they are not just a man and woman.*] You're a good pluckt 'un, my lady.

LADY MARY. [*Falling into the same error.*] I shall try to be. [*Extricating herself.*] Crichton, how dare you?

CRICHTON. I beg your ladyship's pardon; but you are.

> [*She smiles, as if it were a comfort to be told this even by* CRICHTON.]

And until a ship comes we are three men who are going to do our best for you ladies.

LADY MARY. [*With a curl of the lip.*] Mr. Ernest does no work.

CRICHTON. [*Cheerily.*] But he will, my lady.

LADY MARY. I doubt it.

CRICHTON. [*Confidently, but perhaps thoughtlessly.*] No work—no dinner—will make a great change in Mr. Ernest.

LADY MARY. No work—no dinner. When did you invent that rule, Crichton?

CRICHTON. [*Loaded with bamboo.*] I didn't invent it, my lady. I seem to see it growing all over the island.

LADY MARY. [*Disquieted.*] Crichton, your manner strikes me as curious.

CRICHTON. [*Pained.*] I hope not, your ladyship.

LADY MARY. [*Determined to have it out with him.*] You are not implying anything so unnatural, I presume, as that if I and my sisters don't work there will be no dinner for *us*?

CRICHTON. [*Brightly.*] If it is unnatural, my lady, that is the end of it.

LADY MARY. If? Now I understand. The perfect servant at home holds that we are all equal now. I see.

CRICHTON. [*Wounded to the quick.*] My lady, can you think me so inconsistent?

LADY MARY. That is it.

CRICHTON. [*Earnestly.*] My lady, I disbelieved in equality at home because it was against nature, and for that same reason I as utterly disbelieve in it on an island.

LADY MARY. [*Relieved by his obvious sincerity.*] I apologise.

CRICHTON. [*Continuing unfortunately.*] There must always, my lady, be one to command and others to obey.

LADY MARY. [*Satisfied.*] One to command, others to obey. Yes. [*Then suddenly she realises that there may be a dire meaning in his confident words.*] Crichton!

CRICHTON. [*Who has intended no dire meaning.*] What is it, my lady?

[*But she only stares into his face and then hurries from him. Left alone he is puzzled, but being a practical man he busies himself gathering firewood, until* TWEENY *appears excitedly carrying cocoa-nuts in her skirt. She has made better use than the ladies of her three minutes' grace for dressing.*]

TWEENY. [*Who can be happy even on an island if* CRICHTON *is with her.*] Look what I found.

CRICHTON. Cocoa-nuts. Bravo!

TWEENY. They grows on trees.

CRICHTON. Where did you think they grew?

TWEENY. I thought as how they grew in rows on top of little sticks.

CRICHTON. [*Wrinkling his brows.*] Oh Tweeny, Tweeny!

TWEENY. [*Anxiously.*] Have I offended of your feelings again, sir?

CRICHTON. A little.

TWEENY. [*In a despairing outburst.*] I'm full o' vulgar words and ways; and though I may keep them in their holes when you are by, as soon as I'm by myself out they comes in a rush like beetles when the house is dark. I says them gloating-like, in my head—"Blooming" I says, and "All my eye," and "Ginger," and "Nothink"; and all the time we was being wrecked I was praying to myself, "Please the Lord it may be an island as it's natural to be vulgar on."

> [*A shudder passes through* CRICHTON, *and she is abject.*]

That's the kind I am, sir. I'm 'opeless. You'd better give me up.

> [*She is a pathetic, forlorn creature, and his manhood is stirred.*]

CRICHTON. [*Wondering a little at himself for saying it.*] I won't give you up. It is strange that one so common should attract one so fastidious; but so it is. [*Thoughtfully.*] There is something about you, Tweeny, there is a *je ne sais quoi* about you.

TWEENY. [*Knowing only that he has found something in her to commend.*] Is there, is there? Oh, I am glad.

CRICHTON. [*Putting his hand on her shoulder like a protector.*] We shall fight your vulgarity together. [*All this time he has been arranging sticks for his fire.*] Now get some dry grass.

> [*She brings him grass, and he puts it under the*

sticks. He produces an odd lens from his pocket, and tries to focus the sun's rays.]

TWEENY. Why, what's that?

CRICHTON. [*The ingenious creature.*] That's the glass from my watch and one from Mr. Treherne's, with a little water between them. I'm hoping to kindle a fire with it.

TWEENY. [*Properly impressed.*] Oh sir!

> [*After one failure the grass takes fire, and they are blowing on it when excited cries near by bring them sharply to their feet.* AGATHA *runs to them, white of face, followed by* ERNEST.]

ERNEST. Danger! Crichton, a tiger-cat!

CRICHTON. [*Getting his cutlass.*] Where?

AGATHA. It is at our heels.

ERNEST. Look out, Crichton.

CRICHTON. H'sh!

> [TREHERNE *comes to his assistance, while* LADY MARY *and* CATHERINE *join* AGATHA *in the hut.*]

ERNEST. It will be on us in a moment.

> [*He seizes the hatchet and guards the hut. It is pleasing to see that* ERNEST *is no coward.*]

TREHERNE. Listen!

ERNEST. The grass is moving. It's coming

> [*It comes. But it is no tiger-cat; it is* LORD LOAM *crawling on his hands and knees, a very exhausted and dishevelled peer, wondrously attired in rags. The girls see him, and with glad cries rush into his arms.*]

LADY MARY. Father.

LORD LOAM. Mary—Catherine—Agatha. Oh dear, my dears, my dears, oh dear!

LADY MARY. Darling.

AGATHA. Sweetest.

CATHERINE. Love.

TREHERNE. Glad to see you, sir.

ERNEST. Uncle, uncle, dear old uncle.

> [*For a time such happy cries fill the air, but presently* TREHERNE *is thoughtless.*]

TREHERNE. Ernest thought you were a tiger-cat.

LORD LOAM. [*Stung somehow to the quick.*] Oh, did you? I knew you at once, Ernest; I knew you by the way you ran.

> [ERNEST *smiles forgivingly.*]

CRICHTON. [*Venturing forward at last.*] My lord, I am glad.

ERNEST. [*With upraised finger.*] But you are also idling, Crichton. [*Making himself comfortable on the ground.*] We mustn't waste time. To work, to work.

CRICHTON. [*After contemplating him without rancour.*] Yes, sir.

> [*He gets a pot from the hut and hangs it on a tripod over the fire, which is now burning brightly.*]

TREHERNE. Ernest, you be a little more civil. Crichton, let me help.

> [*He is soon busy helping* CRICHTON *to add to the strength of the hut.*]

LORD LOAM. [*Gazing at the pot as ladies are said to gaze on precious stones.*] Is that—but I suppose I'm dreaming again. [*Timidly.*] It isn't by any chance a pot on top of a fire, is it?

LADY MARY. Indeed, it is, dearest. It is our supper.

LORD LOAM. I have been dreaming of a pot on a fire for two days. [*Quivering.*] There's nothing in it, is there?

ERNEST. Sniff, uncle. [LORD LOAM *sniffs.*]

LORD LOAM. [*Reverently.*] It smells of onions!

> [*There is a sudden diversion.*]

CATHERINE. Father, you have boots!

LADY MARY. So he has.

LORD LOAM. Of course I have.

ERNEST. [*With greedy cunning.*] You are actually wearing boots, uncle. It's very unsafe, you know, in this climate.

LORD LOAM. Is it?

ERNEST. We have all abandoned them, you observe. The blood, the arteries, you know.

LORD LOAM. I hadn't a notion.

[*He holds out his feet, and* ERNEST *kneels.*]

ERNEST. O Lord, yes.

[*In another moment those boots will be his.*]

LADY MARY. [*Quickly.*] Father, he is trying to get your boots from you. There is nothing in the world we wouldn't give for boots.

ERNEST. [*Rising haughtily, a proud spirit misunderstood.*] I only wanted the loan of them.

AGATHA. [*Running her fingers along them lovingly.*] If you lend them to any one, it will be to us, won't it, father?

LORD LOAM. Certainly, my child.

ERNEST. Oh, very well. [*He is leaving these selfish ones.*] I don't want your old boots. [*He gives his uncle a last chance.*] You don't think you could spare me *one* boot?

LORD LOAM. [*Tartly.*] I do not.

ERNEST. Quite so. Well, all I can say is I'm sorry for you. [*He departs to recline elsewhere.*]

LADY MARY. Father, we thought we should never see you again.

LORD LOAM. I was washed ashore, my dear, clinging to a hencoop. How awful that first night was!

LADY MARY. Poor father.

LORD LOAM. When I woke, I wept. Then I began to feel extremely hungry. There was a large turtle on the beach. I remembered from the *Swiss Family Robinson* that if you turn a turtle over he is helpless. My dears, I crawled towards him, I flung myself upon him—[*here he pauses to rub his leg*]—the nasty, spiteful brute.

LADY MARY. You didn't turn him over?

LORD LOAM. [*Vindictively, though he is a kindly man.*] Mary, the senseless thing wouldn't wait; I found that none of them would wait.

CATHERINE. We should have been as badly off if Crichton hadn't——

LADY MARY. [*Quickly.*] Don't praise Crichton.

LORD LOAM. And then those beastly monkeys. I always understood that if you flung stones at them they would retaliate by flinging cocoa-nuts at you. Would you believe it, I flung a hundred stones, and not one monkey had sufficient intelligence to grasp my meaning. How I longed for Crichton.

LADY MARY. [*Wincing.*] For us also, father?

LORD LOAM. For you also. I tried for hours to make a fire. The authors say that when wrecked on an island you can obtain a light by rubbing two pieces of stick together. [*With feeling.*] The liars!

LADY MARY. And all this time you thought there was no one on the island but yourself?

LORD LOAM. I thought so until this morning. I was searching the pools for little fishes, which I caught in my hat, when suddenly I saw before me—on the sand——

CATHERINE. What?

LORD LOAM. A hairpin.

LADY MARY. A hairpin! It must be one of ours. Give it me, father.

AGATHA. No, it's mine.

LORD LOAM. I didn't keep it.

LADY MARY. [*Speaking for all three*.] Didn't keep it? Found a hairpin on an island, and didn't keep it?

LORD LOAM. [*Humbly*.]   My dears.

AGATHA. [*Scarcely to be placated*.] Oh father, we have returned to nature more than you bargained for.

LADY MARY. For shame, Agatha. [*She has something on her mind*.] Father, there is something I want you to do at once—I mean to assert your position as the chief person on the island.

[*They are all surprised*.]

LORD LOAM. But who would presume to question it?

CATHERINE. She must mean Ernest.

LADY MARY. Must I?

AGATHA. It's cruel to say anything against Ernest.

LORD LOAM. [*Firmly*.] If any one presumes to challenge my position, I shall make short work of him.

AGATHA. Here comes Ernest; now see if you can say these horrid things to his face.

LORD LOAM. I shall teach him his place at once.

LADY MARY. [*Anxiously*.] But how?

LORD LOAM. [*Chuckling*.] I have just thought of an extremely amusing way of doing it. [*As* ERNEST *approaches*.] Ernest.

ERNEST. [*Loftily*.] Excuse me, uncle, I'm thinking. I'm planning out the building of this hut.

LORD LOAM. I also have been thinking.

ERNEST. That don't matter.

LORD LOAM. Eh?

ERNEST. Please, please, this is important.

LORD LOAM. I have been thinking that I ought to give you my boots.

ERNEST. What!

LADY MARY. Father.

LORD LOAM. [*Genially.*] Take them, my boy. [*With a rapidity we had not thought him capable of,* ERNEST *becomes the wearer of the boots.*] And now I dare say you want to know why I give them to you, Ernest?

ERNEST. [*Moving up and down in them deliciously.*] Not at all. The great thing is, "I've got 'em, I've got 'em."

LORD LOAM. [*Majestically, but with a knowing look at his daughters.*] My reason is that, as head of our little party, you, Ernest, shall be our hunter, you shall clear the forests of those savage beasts that make them so dangerous. [*Pleasantly.*] And now you know, my dear nephew, why I have given you my boots.

ERNEST. This is my answer.

[*He kicks off the boots.*]

LADY MARY. [*Still anxious.*] Father, assert yourself.

LORD LOAM. I shall now assert myself. [*But how to do it? He has a happy thought.*] Call Crichton.

LADY MARY. Oh father.

[CRICHTON *comes in answer to a summons and is followed by* TREHERNE.]

ERNEST. [*Wondering a little at* LADY MARY'S *grave face.*] Crichton, look here.

LORD LOAM. [*Sturdily*] Silence! Crichton, I want your advice as to what I ought to do with Mr. Ernest. He has defied me.

ERNEST. Pooh!

CRICHTON. [*After considering.*] May I speak openly, my lord?

LADY MARY. [*Keeping her eyes fixed on him.*] That is what we desire.

CRICHTON. [*Quite humbly.*] Then I may say, your lordship, that I have been considering Mr. Ernest's case at odd moments ever since we were wrecked.

ERNEST. My case?

LORD LOAM. [*Sternly.*] Hush.

CRICHTON. Since we landed on the island, my lord, it seems to me that Mr. Ernest's epigrams have been particularly brilliant.

ERNEST. [*Gratified.*] Thank you, Crichton.

CRICHTON. But I find—I seem to find it growing wild, my lord, in the woods, that sayings which would be justly admired in England are not much use on an island. I would therefore most respectfully propose that henceforth every time Mr. Ernest favours us with an epigram his head should be immersed in a bucket of cold spring water.

[*There is a terrible silence.*]

LORD LOAM. [*Uneasily.*] Serve him right.

ERNEST. I should like to see you try to do it, uncle.

CRICHTON. [*Ever ready to come to the succour of his lordship.*] My feeling, my lord, is that at the next offence I should convey him to a retired spot, where I shall carry out the undertaking in as respectful a manner as is consistent with a thorough immersion.

[*Though his manner is most respectful, he is firm; he evidently means what he says.*]

LADY MARY. [*A ramrod.*] Father, you must not permit this; Ernest is your nephew.

LORD LOAM. [*With his hand to his brow.*] After all, he is my nephew, Crichton; and, as I am sure, he now sees that I am a strong man——

ERNEST. [*Foolishly in the circumstances.*] A strong man. You mean a stout man. You are one of mind to two of matter.

[*He looks round in the old way for approval. No one has smiled, and to his consternation he sees that CRICHTON is quietly turning up his sleeves. ERNEST makes an appealing gesture to his uncle; then he turns defiantly to* CRICHTON.]

CRICHTON. Is it to be before the ladies, Mr. Ernest, or in the privacy of the wood? [*He fixes* ERNEST *with his eye.* ERNEST *is cowed.*] Come.

ERNEST. [*Affecting bravado.*] Oh, all right.

CRICHTON. [*Succinctly.*] Bring the bucket.

[ERNEST *hesitates. He then lifts the bucket and follows* CRICHTON *to the nearest spring.*]

LORD LOAM. [*Rather white.*] I'm sorry for him, but I had to be firm.

LADY MARY. Oh, father, it wasn't you who was firm. Crichton did it himself.

LORD LOAM. Bless me, so he did.

LADY MARY. Father, be strong.

LORD LOAM. [*Bewildered.*] You can't mean that my faithful Crichton——

LADY MARY. Yes, I do.

TREHERNE. Lady Mary, I stake my word that Crichton is incapable of acting dishonourably.

LADY MARY. I know that; I know it as well as you. Don't you see that that is what makes him so dangerous?

TREHERNE. By Jove, I—I believe I catch your meaning.

CATHERINE. He is coming back.

LORD LOAM. [*Who has always known himself to be a man of ideas.*] Let us all go into the hut, just to show him at once that it is *our* hut.

LADY MARY. [*As they go.*] Father, I implore you, assert yourself now and for ever.

LORD LOAM. I will.

LADY MARY. And, please, don't ask him how you are to do it.

[CRICHTON *returns with sticks to mend the fire.*]

LORD LOAM. [*Loftily, from the door of the hut.*] Have you carried out my instructions, Crichton?

CRICHTON. [*Deferentially.*] Yes, my lord.

> [ERNEST *appears, mopping his hair, which has become very wet since we last saw him. He is not bearing malice, he is too busy drying, but* AGATHA *is specially his champion.*]

AGATHA. It's infamous, infamous.

LORD LOAM. [*Strongly.*] *My* orders, Agatha.

LADY MARY. Now, father, please.

LORD LOAM. [*Striking an attitude.*] Before I give you any further orders, Crichton——

CRICHTON. Yes, my lord.

LORD LOAM. [*Delighted.*] Pooh! It's all right.

LADY MARY. No. Please go on.

LORD LOAM. Well, well. This question of the leadership; what do you think now, Crichton?

CRICHTON. My lord, I feel it is a matter with which *I* have nothing to do.

LORD LOAM. Excellent. Ha, Mary? That settles it, I think.

LADY MARY. It seems to, but—I'm not sure.

CRICHTON. It will settle itself naturally, my lord, without any interference from us.

> [*The reference to Nature gives general dissatisfaction.*]

LADY MARY. Father.

LORD LOAM. [*A little severely.*] It settled itself long ago, Crichton, when I was born a peer, and you, for instance, were born a servant.

CRICHTON. [*Acquiescing.*] Yes, my lord, that was how it all came about quite naturally in England. We had nothing to do with it there, and we shall have as little to do with it here.

TREHERNE. [*Relieved.*] That's all right.

LADY MARY. [*Determined to clinch the matter.*] One moment. In short, Crichton, his lordship will continue to be our natural head.

CRICHTON. I dare say, my lady, I dare say.

CATHERINE. But you must *know*.

CRICHTON. Asking your pardon, my lady, one can't be sure—on an island.

[*They look at each other uneasily.*]

LORD LOAM. [*Warningly.*] Crichton, I don't like this.

CRICHTON. [*Harassed.*] The more I think of it, your lordship, the more uneasy I become myself. When I heard, my lord, that you had left that hairpin behind——

[*He is pained.*]

LORD LOAM. [*Feebly.*] One hairpin among so many would only have caused dissension.

CRICHTON. [*Very sorry to have to contradict him.*] Not so, my lord. From that hairpin we could have made a needle; with that needle we could, out of skins, have sewn trousers—of which your lordship is in need; indeed, we are all in need of them.

LADY MARY. [*Suddenly self-conscious.*] All?

CRICHTON. On an island, my lady.

LADY MARY. Father.

CRICHTON. [*Really more distressed by the prospect than she.*] My lady, if Nature does not think them necessary, you may be sure she will not ask you to wear them. [*Shaking his head.*] But among all this undergrowth——

LADY MARY. Now you see this man in his true colours.

LORD LOAM. [*Violently.*] Crichton, you will either this moment say, "Down with Nature," or——

CRICHTON. [*Scandalised.*] My lord!

LORD LOAM. [*Loftily.*] Then this is my last word to you; take a month's notice.

[*If the hut had a door he would now shut it to indicate that the interview is closed.*]

CRICHTON. [*In great distress.*]   Your lordship, the disgrace——

LORD LOAM. [*Swelling.*]   Not another word: you may go.

LADY MARY. [*Adamant.*]   And don't come to me, Crichton, for a character.

ERNEST. [*Whose immersion has cleared his brain.*] Aren't you all forgetting that this is an island?

[*This brings them to earth with a bump.* LORD LOAM *looks to his eldest daughter for the fitting response.*]

LADY MARY. [*Equal to the occasion.*]   It makes only this difference—that you may go at once, Crichton, to some other part of the island.

[*The faithful servant has been true to his superiors ever since he was created, and never more true than at this moment; but his fidelity is founded on trust in Nature, and to be untrue to it would be to be untrue to them. He lets the wood he has been gathering slip to the ground, and bows his sorrowful head. He turns to obey. Then affection for these great ones wells up in him.*]

CRICHTON.   My lady, let me work for you.

LADY MARY.   Go.

CRICHTON.   You need me so sorely; I can't desert you; I won't.

LADY MARY. [*In alarm, lest the others may yield.*] Then, father, there is but one alternative, *we* must leave him. [LORD LOAM *is looking yearningly at* CRICHTON.]

TREHERNE.   It seems a pity.

CATHERINE. [*Forlornly.*]   *You* will work for us?

TREHERNE. Most willingly. But I must warn you all that, so far, Crichton has done nine-tenths of the scoring.

LADY MARY. The question is, are we to leave this man?

LORD LOAM. [*Wrapping himself in his dignity.*] Come, my dears.

CRICHTON. My lord!

LORD LOAM. Treherne—Ernest—get our things.

ERNEST. We don't have any, uncle. They all belong to Crichton.

TREHERNE. Everything we have he brought from the wreck—he went back to it before it sank. He risked his life.

CRICHTON. My lord, anything you would care to take is yours.

LADY MARY. [*Quickly.*] Nothing.

ERNEST. Rot! If I could have your socks, Crichton——

LADY MARY. Come, father; we are ready.

> [*Followed by the others, she and* LORD LOAM *pick their way up the rocks. In their indignation they scarcely notice that daylight is coming to a sudden end.*]

CRICHTON. My lord, I implore you—*I* am not desirous of being head. Do you have a try at it, my lord?

LORD LOAM. [*Outraged.*] A try at it!

CRICHTON. [*Eagerly.*] It may be that you will prove to be the best man.

LORD LOAM. *May* be! My children, come.

> [*They disappear proudly in single file.*]

TREHERNE. Crichton, I'm sorry; but of course I must go with them.

CRICHTON. Certainly, sir.

> [*He calls to* TWEENY, *and she comes from behind the hut, where she has been watching breathlessly.*]

Will you be so kind, sir, as to take her to the others?

TREHERNE.   Assuredly.

TWEENY.   But what do it all mean?

CRICHTON.   Does, Tweeney, does. [*He passes her up the rocks to* TREHERNE.] We shall meet again soon, Tweeny. Good night, sir.

TREHERNE.   Good night. I dare say they are not far away.

CRICHTON.   [*Thoughtfully.*] They went westward, sir, and the wind is blowing in that direction. That may mean, sir, that Nature is already taking the matter into her own hands. They are all hungry, sir, and the pot has come a-boil. [*He takes off the lid.*] The smell will be borne westward. That pot is full of Nature, Mr. Treherne. Good night, sir.

TREHERNE.   Good night.

> [*He mounts the rocks with* TWEENY, *and they are heard for a little time after their figures are swallowed up in the fast growing darkness.* CRICHTON *stands motionless, the lid in his hand, though he has forgotten it, and his reason for taking it off the pot. He is deeply stirred, but presently is ashamed of his dejection, for it is as if he doubted his principles. Bravely true to his faith that Nature will decide now as ever before, he proceeds manfully with his preparations for the night. He lights a ship's lantern, one of several treasures he has brought ashore, and is filling his pipe with crumbs of tobacco from various pockets, when the stealthy movements of some animal in the grass startles him. With the lantern in one hand and his cutlass in the other, he searches the ground around the hut. He returns, lights*

his pipe, and sits down by the fire, which casts weird moving shadows. There is a red gleam on his face; in the darkness he is a strong and perhaps rather sinister figure. In the great stillness that has fallen over the land, the wash of the surf seems to have increased in volume. The sound is indescribably mournful. Except where the fire is, desolation has fallen on the island like a pall.]

[Once or twice, as Nature dictates, CRICHTON leans forward to stir the pot, and the smell is borne westward. He then resumes his silent vigil.]

[Shadows other than those cast by the fire begin to descend the rocks. They are the adventurers returning. One by one they steal nearer to the pot until they are squatted around it, with their hands out to the blaze. LADY MARY only is absent. Presently she comes within sight of the others, then stands against a tree with her teeth clenched. One wonders, perhaps, what Nature is to make of her.]

End of Act II.

ACT III

THE HAPPY HOME

The scene is the hall of their island home two years later. This sturdy log-house is no mere extension of the hut we have seen in process of erection, but has been built a mile or less to the west of it, on higher ground and near a stream. When the master chose this site, the others thought that all he expected from the stream was a sufficiency of drinking water. They know better now every time they go down to the mill or turn on the electric light.

This hall is the living-room of the house, and walls and roof are of stout logs. Across the joists supporting the roof are laid many home-made implements, such as spades, saws, fishing-rods, and from hooks in the joists are suspended cured foods, of which hams are specially in evidence. Deep recesses half way up the walls contain various provender in barrels and sacks. There are some skins, trophies of the chase, on the floor, which is otherwise bare. The chairs and tables are in some cases hewn out of the solid wood, and in others the result of rough but efficient carpentering. Various pieces of wreckage from the yacht have been turned to novel uses; thus the steering-wheel now hangs from the centre of the roof, with electric lights attached to it encased in bladders. A lifebuoy has become the back of a chair. Two barrels have been halved and turn coyly from each other as a settee.

The farther end of the room is more strictly the kitchen, and is a great recess, which can be shut off from the hall by folding doors. There is a large open fire in it. The chimney is half of one of the boats of the yacht. On the walls of the kitchen proper are many plate-racks, containing shells; there are rows of these of one size and shape, which mark them off as dinner plates or bowls; others are as obviously tureens. They are arranged primly as in a well-conducted kitchen; in-deed, neatness and cleanliness are the note struck *everywhere, yet the effect of the whole is romantic and barbaric.*

The outer door into this hall is a little peculiar on an island. It is covered with skins and is in four leaves, like the swing doors of fashionable restaurants, which allow you to enter without allowing the hot air to escape. During the winter season our castaways have found the contrivance useful, but CRICHTON'S *brain was perhaps a little lordly when he conceived it. Another door leads by a passage to the sleeping-rooms of the house, which are all on the ground-floor, and to* CRICHTON'S *work-room, where he is at this moment, and whither we should like to follow him, but in a play we may not, as it is out of sight. There is a large window space without a window, which, however, can be shuttered, and through this we have a view of cattle-sheds, fowl-pens, and a field of grain. It is a fine summer evening.*

TWEENY *is sitting there, very busy plucking the feathers off a bird and dropping them on a sheet placed for that purpose on the floor. She is trilling to herself in the lightness of her heart. We may remember that* TWEENY, *alone among the women, had dressed wisely for an island when they fled the yacht, and her going-away gown still adheres to her, though in fragments. A score of pieces have been added here and there as necessity compelled, and these have been patched and repatched in incongruous colours; but, when all is said and done, it can still be maintained that* TWEENY *wears a skirt. She is deservedly proud of her skirt, and sometimes lends it on important occasions when approached in the proper spirit.*

Some one outside has been whistling to TWEENY; *the guarded whistle which, on a less savage island, is some-*

times assumed to be an indication to cook that the con-
stable is willing, if the coast be clear. TWEENY, *how-*
ever, is engrossed, or perhaps she is not in the mood for
a follower, so he climbs in at the window undaunted,
to take her willy-nilly. He is a jolly-looking labouring
man, who answers to the name of DADDY, *and——*
But though that may be his island name, we recognize
his at once. He is LORD LOAM, *settled down to the*
new conditions, and enjoying life heartily as handy-
man about the happy home. He is comfortably at-
tired in skins. He is still stout, but all the flabbiness
has dropped from him; gone too is his pomposity; his
eye is clear, brown his skin; he could leap a gate.
In his hands he carries an island-made concertina, and such
is the exuberance of his spirits that, as he lights on the
floor, he bursts into music and song, something about
his being a chickety chickety chick chick, and will
TWEENY *please to tell him whose chickety chick is she.*
Retribution follows sharp. We hear a whir, as if from
insufficiently oiled machinery, and over the passage
door appears a placard showing the one word "Silence."
His lordship stops, and steals to TWEENY *on his tiptoes.*

LORD LOAM. I thought the Gov. was out.

TWEENY. Well, you see he ain't. And if he were to
catch you here idling——

> [LORD LOAM *pales. He lays aside his musical*
> *instrument and hurriedly dons an apron.*
> TWEENY *gives him the bird to pluck, and busies*
> *herself laying the table for dinner.*]

LORD LOAM. [*Softly.*] What is he doing now?

TWEENY. I think he's working out that plan for laying
on hot and cold.

LORD LOAM. [*Proud of his master.*] And he'll manage it too. The man who could build a blacksmith's forge without tools——

TWEENY. [*Not less proud.*] He made the tools.

LORD LOAM. Out of half a dozen rusty nails. The saw-mill, Tweeny; the speaking-tube; the electric lighting; and look at the use he has made of the bits of the yacht that were washed ashore. And all in two years. He's a master I'm proud to pluck for.

> [*He chirps happily at his work, and she regards him curiously.*]

TWEENY. Daddy, you're of little use, but you're a bright, cheerful creature to have about the house. [*He beams at this commendation.*] Do you ever think of old times now? We was a bit different.

LORD LOAM. [*Pausing.*] Circumstances alter cases.

> [*He resumes his plucking contentedly.*]

TWEENY. But, Daddy, if the chance was to come of getting back?

LORD LOAM. I have given up bothering about it.

TWEENY. You bothered that day long ago when we saw a ship passing the island. How we all ran like crazy folk into the water, Daddy, and screamed and held out our arms. [*They are both a little agitated.*] But it sailed away, and we've never seen another.

LORD LOAM. If we had had the electrical contrivance we have now we could have attracted that ship's notice. [*Their eyes rest on a mysterious apparatus that fills a corner of the hall.*] A touch on that lever, Tweeny, and in a few moments bonfires would be blazing all round the shore.

TWEENY. [*Backing from the lever as if it might spring at her.*] It's the most wonderful thing he has done.

LORD LOAM. [*In a reverie.*[And then—England—home!

TWEENY. [*Also seeing visions.*]   London of a Saturday night!

LORD LOAM.   My lords, in rising once more to address this historic chamber——

TWEENY.   There was a little ham and beef shop off the Edgware Road——

[*The visions fade; they return to the practical.*]

LORD LOAM.   Tweeny, do you think I could have an egg to my tea?

[*At this moment a wiry, athletic figure in skins darkens the window.   He is carrying two pails, which are suspended from a pole on his shoulder, and he is* ERNEST.   *We should say that he is* ERNEST *completely changed if we were of those who hold that people change.   As he enters by the window he has heard* LORD LOAM'S *appeal, and is perhaps justifiably indignant.*]

ERNEST.   What is that about an egg?   Why should you have an egg?

LORD LOAM.   [*With hauteur.*]   That is my affair, sir. [*With a Parthian shot as he withdraws stiffly from the room.*]   The Gov. has never put *my* head in a bucket.

ERNEST.   [*Coming to rest on one of his buckets, and speaking with excusable pride.   To* TWEENY.]   Nor mine for nearly three months.   It was only last week, Tweeny, that he said to me, "Ernest, the water cure has worked marvels in you, and I question whether I shall require to dip you any more."   [*Complacently.*]   Of course that sort of thing encourages a fellow.

TWEENY.   [*Who has now arranged the dinner table to her satisfaction.*]   I will say, Erny, I never seen a young chap more improved.

ERNEST.   [*Gratified.*]   Thank you, Tweeny, that's very precious to me.

[*She retires to the fire to work the great bellows with her foot, and* ERNEST *turns to* TREHERNE, *who has come in looking more like a cow-boy than a clergyman. He has a small box in his hand which he tries to conceal.*]

What have you got there, John?

TREHERNE. Don't tell anybody. It is a little present for the Gov.; a set of razors. One for each day in the week.

ERNEST. [*Opening the box and examining its contents.*] Shells! He'll like that. He likes sets of things.

TREHERNE. [*In a guarded voice.*] Have you noticed that?

ERNEST. Rather.

TREHERNE. He's becoming a bit magnificent in his ideas.

ERNEST. [*Huskily.*] John, it sometimes gives me the creeps.

TREHERNE. [*Making sure that* TWEENY *is out of hearing.*] What do you think of that brilliant robe he got the girls to make for him.

ERNEST. [*Uncomfortably.*] I think he looks too regal in it.

TREHERNE. Regal! I sometimes fancy that that's why he's so fond of wearing it. [*Practically.*] Well, I must take these down to the grindstone and put an edge on them.

ERNEST. [*Button-holing him.*] I say, John, I want a word with you.

TREHERNE. Well?

ERNEST. [*Become suddenly diffident.*] Dash it all, you know, you're a clergyman.

TREHERNE. One of the best things the Gov. has done is to insist that none of you forget it.

ERNEST. [*Taking his courage in his hands.*] Then—
would you, John?

TREHERNE. What?

ERNEST. [*Wistfully.*] Officiate at a marriage ceremony, John?

TREHERNE. [*Slowly.*] Now, that's really odd.

ERNEST. Odd? Seems to me it's natural. And whatever is natural, John, is right.

TREHERNE. I mean that same question has been put
to me to-day already.

ERNEST. [*Eagerly.*] By one of the women?

TREHERNE. Oh, no; they all put it to me long ago.
This was by the Gov. himself.

ERNEST. By Jove! [*Admiringly.*] I say, John, what
an observant beggar he is.

TREHERNE. Ah! You fancy he was thinking of you?

ERNEST. I do not hesitate to affirm, John, that he has
seen the love-light in my eyes. You answered——

TREHERNE. I said Yes, I thought it would be my duty
to officiate if called upon.

ERNEST. You're a brick.

TREHERNE. [*Still pondering.*] But I wonder whether
he *was* thinking of you?

ERNEST. Make your mind easy about that.

TREHERNE. Well, my best wishes. Agatha is a very
fine girl.

ERNEST. Agatha? What made you think it was Agatha?

TREHERNE. Man alive, you told me all about it soon
after we were wrecked.

ERNEST. Pooh! Agatha's all very well in her way,
John, but I'm flying at bigger game.

TREHERNE. Ernest, which is it?

ERNEST. Tweeny, of course.

TREHERNE. Tweeny? [*Reprovingly.*] Ernest, I hope her cooking has nothing to do with this.

ERNEST. [*With dignity.*] Her cooking has very little to do with it.

TREHERNE. But does she return your affection?

ERNEST. [*Simply.*] Yes, John, I believe I may say so. I am unworthy of her, but I think I have touched her heart.

TREHERNE. [*With a sigh.*] Some people seem to have all the luck. As you know, Catherine won't look at me.

ERNEST. I'm sorry, John.

TREHERNE. It's my deserts; I'm a second eleven sort of chap. Well, my heartiest good wishes, Ernest.

ERNEST. Thank you, John. How's the little black pig to-day?

TREHERNE. [*Departing.*] He has begun to eat again.

   [*After a moment's reflection* ERNEST *calls to* TWEENY.]

ERNEST. Are you very busy, Tweeny?

TWEENY. [*Coming to him good-naturedly.*] There's always work to do; but if you want me, Ernest——

ERNEST. There's something I should like to say to you if you could spare me a moment.

TWEENY. Willingly. What is it?

ERNEST. What an ass I used to be, Tweeny.

TWEENY. [*Tolerantly.*] Oh, let bygones be bygones.

ERNEST. [*Sincerely, and at his very best.*] I'm no great shakes even now. But listen to this, Tweeny; I have known many women, but until I knew you I never knew any woman.

TWEENY. [*To whose uneducated ears this sounds dangerously like an epigram.*] Take care—the bucket.

ERNEST. [*Hurriedly.*] I didn't mean it in that way. [*He goes chivalrously on his knees.*] Ah, Tweeny, I don't undervalue the bucket, but what I want to say now is that the sweet refinement of a dear girl has done more for me than any bucket could do.

TWEENY. [*With large eyes.*] Are you offering to walk out with me, Erny?

ERNEST. [*Passionately.*] More than that. I want to build a little house for you—in the sunny glade down by Porcupine Creek. I want to make chairs for you and tables; and knives and forks, and a sideboard for you.

TWEENY. [*Who is fond of language.*] I like to hear you. [*Eyeing him.*] Would there be any one in the house except myself, Ernest?

ERNEST. [*Humbly.*] Not often; but just occasionally there would be your adoring husband.

TWEENY. [*Decisively.*] It won't do, Ernest.

ERNEST. [*Pleading.*] It isn't as if I should be much there.

TWEENY. I know, I know; but I don't love you, Ernest. I'm that sorry.

ERNEST. [*Putting his case cleverly.*] Twice a week I should be away altogether—at the dam. On the other days you would never see me from breakfast time to supper.

[*With the self-abnegation of the true lover.*] If you like I'll even go fishing on Sundays.

TWEENY. It's no use, Erny.

ERNEST. [*Rising manfully.*] Thank you, Tweeny; it can't be helped. [*Then he remembers.*] Tweeny, we shall be disappointing the Gov.

TWEENY. [*With a sinking.*] What's that?

ERNEST. He wanted us to marry.

TWEENY. [*Blankly.*] You and me? the Gov.! [*Her head droops woefully. From without is heard the whistling of a happier spirit, and TWEENY draws herself up fiercely.*]

That's her; that's the thing what has stole his heart from me.

> [*A stalwart youth appears at the window, so handsome and tingling with vitality that, glad to depose* CRICHTON, *we cry thankfully, "The hero at last." But it is not the hero; it is the heroine. This splendid boy, clad in skins, is what Nature has done for* LADY MARY. *She carries bow and arrows and a blow-pipe, and over her shoulder is a fat buck, which she drops with a cry of triumph. Forgetting to enter demurely, she leaps through the window.*]

[*Sourly.*] Drat you, Polly, why don't you wipe your feet?

LADY MARY. [*Good-naturedly.*] Come, Tweeny, be nice to me. It's a splendid buck.

> [*But* TWEENY *shakes her off, and retires to the kitchen fire.*]

ERNEST. Where did you get it?

LADY MARY. [*Gaily.*] I sighted a herd near Penguin's Creek, but had to creep round Silver Lake to get to windward of them. However, they spotted me and then the fun began. There was nothing for it but to try and run them down, so I singled out a fat buck and away we went down the shore of the lake, up the valley of rolling stones; he doubled into Brawling River and took to the water, but I swam after him; the river is only half a mile broad there, but it runs strong. He went spinning down the rapids, down I went in pursuit; he clambered ashore, I clambered ashore; away we tore helter-skelter up the hill and down again. I lost him in the marshes, got on his track again near Bread Fruit Wood, and brought him down with an arrow in Firefly Grove.

TWEENY. [*Staring at her.*] Aren't you tired?

LADY MARY. Tired! It was gorgeous.

> [*She runs up a ladder and deposits her weapons on the joists. She is whistling again.*]

TWEENY. [*Snapping.*] I can't abide a woman whistling.

LADY MARY. [*Indifferently.*] I like it.

TWEENY. [*Stamping her foot.*] Drop it, Polly, I tell you.

LADY MARY. [*Stung.*] I won't. I'm as good as you are. [*They are facing each other defiantly.*]

ERNEST. [*Shocked.*] Is this necessary? Think how it would pain *him*.

> [LADY MARY'S *eyes take a new expression. We see them soft for the first time.*]

LADY MARY. [*Contritely.*] Tweeny, I beg your pardon. If my whistling annoys you, I shall try to cure myself of it.

> [*Instead of calming* TWEENY, *this floods her face in tears.*]

Why, how can that hurt you, Tweeny dear?

TWEENY. Because I can't make you lose your temper.

LADY MARY. [*Divinely.*] Indeed, I often do. Would that I were nicer to everybody.

TWEENY. There you are again. [*Wistfully.*] What makes you want to be so nice, Polly?

LADY MARY. [*With fervour.*] Only thankfulness, Tweeny. [*She exults.*] It is such fun to be alive.

> [*So also seem to think* CATHERINE *and* AGATHA, *who bounce in with fishing-rods and creel. They, too, are in manly attire.*]

CATHERINE. We've got some ripping fish for the Gov.'s dinner. Are we in time? We ran all the way.

TWEENY. [*Tartly.*] You'll please to cook them yourself, Kitty, and look sharp about it.

[*She retires to her hearth, where* AGATHA *follows her.*]

AGATHA. [*Yearning.*] Has the Gov. decided who is to wait upon him to-day?

CATHERINE. [*Who is cleaning her fish.*] It's my turn.

AGATHA. [*Hotly.*] I don't see that.

TWEENY. [*With bitterness.*] It's to be neither of you, Aggy; he wants Polly again.

[LADY MARY *is unable to resist a joyous whistle.*]

AGATHA. [*Jealously.*] Polly, you toad.

[*But they cannot make* LADY MARY *angry.*]

TWEENY. [*Storming.*] How dare you look so happy?

LADY MARY. [*Willing to embrace her.*] I wish Tweeny, there was anything I could do to make you happy also.

TWEENY. Me! Oh, I'm happy. [*She remembers* ERNEST, *whom it is easy to forget on an island.*] I've just had a proposal, I tell you.

[LADY MARY *is shaken at last, and her sisters with her.*]

AGATHA. A proposal?

CATHERINE. [*Going white.*] Not—not——

[*She dare not say his name.*]

ERNEST. [*With singular modesty.*] You needn't be alarmed; it's only me.

LADY MARY. [*Relieved.*] Oh, you!

AGATHA. [*Happy again.*] Ernest, you dear, I got such a shock.

CATHERINE. It was only Ernest. [*Showing him her fish in thankfulness.*] They are beautifully fresh; come and help me to cook them.

ERNEST. [*With simple dignity.*] Do you mind if I don't cook fish to-night? [*She does not mind in the least. They have all forgotten him. A lark is singing in three hearts.*] I think you might all be a little sorry for a chap. [*But they are not even sorry, and he addresses* AGATHA *in these winged words:*] I'm particularly disappointed in you, Aggy; seeing that I was half engaged to you, I think you might have had the good feeling to be a little more hurt.

AGATHA. Oh, bother.

ERNEST. [*Summing up the situation in so far as it affects himself.*] I shall now go and lie down for a bit.

> [*He retires coldly but unregretted.* LADY MARY *approaches* TWEENY *with her most insinuating smile.*]

LADY MARY. Tweeny, as the Gov. has chosen me to wait on him, please may I have the loan of *it* again?

> [*The reference made with such charming delicacy is evidently to* TWEENY'S *skirt.*]

TWEENY. [*Doggedly.*] No, you mayn't.

AGATHA. [*Supporting* TWEENY.] Don't you give it to her.

LADY MARY. [*Still trying sweet persuasion.*] You know quite well that he prefers to be waited on in a skirt.

TWEENY. I don't care. Get one for yourself.

LADY MARY. It is the only one on the island.

TWEENY. And it's mine.

LADY MARY. [*An aristocrat after all.*] Tweeny, give me that skirt directly.

CATHERINE. Don't.

TWEENY. I won't.

LADY MARY. [*Clearing for action.*] I shall make you.

TWEENY. I should like to see you try.

> [*An unseemly fracas appears to be inevitable, but something happens. The whir is again heard, and the notice is displayed "Dogs delight to bark and bite." Its effect is instantaneous and*

*cheering. The ladies look at each other guiltily
and immediately proceed on tiptoe to their
duties. These are all concerned with the
master's dinner.* CATHERINE *attends to his
fish.* AGATHA *fills a quaint toast-rack and
brings the menu, which is written on a shell.*
LADY MARY *twists a wreath of green leaves
around her head, and places a flower beside the
master's plate.* TWEENY *signs that all is ready,
and she and the younger sisters retire into the
kitchen, drawing the screen that separates it
from the rest of the room.* LADY MARY *beats
a tom-tom, which is the dinner bell. She then
gently works a punkah, which we have not
hitherto observed, and stands at attention.
No doubt she is in hopes that the Gov. will
enter into conversation with her, but she is too
good a parlour-maid to let her hopes appear in
her face. We may watch her manner with complete approval. There is not one of us who
would not give her £26 a year.*

*The master comes in quietly, a book in his hand,
still the only book on the island, for he has not
thought it worth while to build a printing-press.
His dress is not noticeably different from that
of the others, the skins are similar, but perhaps
these are a trifle more carefully cut or he carries
them better. One sees somehow that he has
changed for his evening meal. There is an odd
suggestion of a dinner jacket about his doeskin
coat. It is, perhaps, too grave a face for a man
of thirty-two, as if he were over much immersed in affairs, yet there is a sunny smile
left to lighten it at times and bring back its*

*youth; perhaps too intellectual a face to pass
as strictly handsome, not sufficiently suggestive
of oats. His tall figure is very straight, slight
rather than thick-set, but nobly muscular. His
big hands, firm and hard with labour though
they be, are finely shaped—note the fingers so
much more tapered, the nails better tended than
those of his domestics; they are one of many
indications that he is of a superior breed. Such
signs, as has often been pointed out, are infallible. A romantic figure, too. One can easily
see why the women-folks of this strong man's
house both adore and fear him.*

*He does not seem to notice who is waiting on
him to-night, but inclines his head slightly to
whoever it is, as she takes her place at the back
of his chair. LADY MARY respectfully places
the menu-shell before him, and he glances at it.*]

CRICHTON. Clear, please.

[*LADY MARY knocks on the screen, and a serv-
ing hutch in it opens, through which TWEENY
offers two soup plates. LADY MARY selects the
clear, and the aperture is closed. She works
the punkah while the master partakes of the
soup.*]

CRICHTON. [*Who always gives praise where it is due.*]
An excellent soup, Polly, but still a trifle too rich.

LADY MARY. Thank you.

[*The next course is the fish, and while it is being
passed through the hutch we have a glimpse of
three jealous women. LADY MARY'S movements
are so deft and noiseless that any observant
spectator can see that she was born to wait at
table.*]

CRICHTON. [*Unbending as he eats.*]   Polly, you are a very smart girl.

LADY MARY. [*Brindling, but naturally gratified.*]   La!

CRICHTON. [*Smiling.*]   And I'm not the first you've heard it from, I'll swear.

LADY MARY. [*Wriggling.*]   Oh Gov.!

CRICHTON.   Got any followers on the island, Polly?

LADY MARY. [*Tossing her head.*]   Certainly not.

CRICHTON.   I thought that perhaps John or Ernest——

LADY MARY. [*Tilting her nose.*]   I don't say that it's for want of asking.

CRICHTON. [*Emphatically.*]   I'm sure it isn't.

[*Perhaps he thinks he has gone too far.*]
You may clear.

> [*Flushed with pleasure, she puts before him a bird and vegetables, sees that his beaker is filled with wine, and returns to the punkah. She would love to continue their conversation, but it is for him to decide. For a time he seems to have forgotten her.*]

CRICHTON.   Did you lose any arrows to-day?

LADY MARY.   Only one in Firefly Grove.

CRICHTON.   You were as far as that? How did you get across the Black Gorge?

LADY MARY.   I went across on the rope.

CRICHTON.   Hand over hand?

LADY MARY. [*Swelling at the implied praise.*]   I wasn't in the least dizzy.

CRICHTON. [*Moved.*]   You brave girl! [*He sits back in his chair a little agitated.*]   But never do that again.

LADY MARY. [*Pouting.*]   It is such fun, Gov.

CRICHTON. [*Decisively.*]   I forbid it.

LADY MARY. [*The little rebel.*]   I shall.

CRICHTON. [*Surprised.*]   Polly!

[*He signs to her sharply to step forward, but for
a moment she holds back petulantly, and even
when she does come it is less obediently than
like a naughty, sulky child. Nevertheless, with
the forbearance that is characteristic of the man,
he addresses her with grave gentleness rather
than severely.*]

You must do as I tell you, you know.

LADY MARY. [*Strangely passionate.*] I shan't.

CRICHTON. [*Smiling at her fury.*] We shall see. Frown
at me, Polly; there, you do it at once. Clench your little
fists, stamp your feet, bite your ribbons——

[*A student of women, or at least of this woman,
he knows that she is about to do those things,
and thus she seems to do them to order. LADY
MARY screws up her face like a baby and cries.
He is immediately kind.*]

You child of Nature; was it cruel of me to wish to save
you from harm?

LADY MARY. [*Drying her eyes.*] I'm an ungracious
wretch. Oh Gov., I don't try half hard enough to please
you. I'm even wearing—[*she looks down sadly*]—when
I know you prefer *it*.

CRICHTON. [*Thoughtfully.*] I admit I do prefer *it*.
Perhaps I am a little old-fashioned in these matters.

[*Her tears again threaten.*]

Ah, don't, Polly; that's nothing.

LADY MARY. If I could only please you, Gov.

CRICHTON. [*Slowly.*] You do please me, child, very
much—[*he half rises*]—very much indeed. [*If he meant to
say more he checks himself. He looks at his plate.*] No
more, thank you.

[*The simple island meal is ended, save for the
walnuts and the wine, and CRICHTON is too*]

busy a man to linger long over them. But he is a stickler for etiquette, and the table is cleared charmingly, though with dispatch, before they are placed before him. LADY MARY is an artist with the crumb-brush, and there are few arts more delightful to watch. Dusk has come sharply, and she turns on the electric light. It awakens CRICHTON from a reverie in which he has been regarding her.]

CRICHTON. Polly, there is only one thing about you that I don't quite like.

[She looks up, making a moue, *if that can be said of one who so well knows her place. He explains.]*

That action of the hands.

LADY MARY. What do I do?

CRICHTON. So—like one washing them. I have noticed that the others tend to do it also. It seems odd.

LADY MARY. [*Archly.*] Oh Gov., have you forgotten?

CRICHTON. What?

LADY MARY. That once upon a time a certain other person did that.

CRICHTON. [*Groping.*] You mean myself? [*She nods, and he shudders.*] Horrible!

LADY MARY. [*Afraid she has hurt him.*] You haven't for a very long time. Perhaps it is natural to servants.

CRICHTON. That must be it. [*He rises.*] Polly! [*She looks up expectantly, but he only sighs and turns away.*]

LADY MARY. [*Gently*] You sighed, Gov.

CRICHTON. Did I? I was thinking. [*He paces the room and then turns to her agitatedly, yet with control over his agitation. There is some mournfulness in his voice.*] I have always tried to do the right thing on this island. Above all, Polly, I want to do the right thing by you.

LADY MARY. [*With shining eyes.*] How we all trust you. That is your reward, Gov.

CRICHTON. [*Who is having a fight with himself.*] And now I want a greater reward. Is it fair to you? Am I playing the game? Bill Crichton would like always to play the game. If we were in England——

[*He pauses so long that she breaks in softly.*]

LADY MARY. We know now that we shall never see England again.

CRICHTON. I am thinking of two people whom neither of us has seen for a long time—Lady Mary Lasenby, and one Crichton, a butler.

[*He says the last word bravely, a word he once loved, though it is the most horrible of all words to him now.*]

LADY MARY. That cold, haughty, insolent girl. Gov., look around you and forget them both.

CRICHTON. I had nigh forgotten them. He has had a chance, Polly—that butler—in these two years of becoming a man, and he has tried to take it. There have been many failures, but there has been some success, and with it I have let the past drop off me, and turned my back on it. That butler seems a far-away figure to me now, and not myself. I hail him, but we scarce know each other. If I am to bring him back it can only be done by force, for in my soul he is now abhorrent to me. But if I thought it best for you I'd haul him back; I swear as an honest man, I would bring him back with all his obsequious ways and deferential airs, and let you see the man you call your Gov. melt for ever into him who was your servant.

LADY MARY. [*Shivering.*] You hurt me. You say

these things, but you say them like a king. To me it is the past that was not real.

CRICHTON. [*Too grandly.*] A king!   I sometimes feel——

> [*For a moment the yellow light gleams in his green eyes. We remember suddenly what* TREHERNE *and* ERNEST *said about his regal look. He checks himself.*]

I say it harshly, it is so hard to say, and all the time there is another voice within me crying—— [*He stops.*]

LADY MARY. [*Trembling but not afraid.*] If it is the voice of Nature——

CRICHTON. [*Strongly.*]   I know it to be the voice of Nature.

LADY MARY. [*In a whisper.*]   Then, if you want to say it very much, Gov., please say it to Polly Lasenby.

CRICHTON. [*Again in the grip of an idea.*]   A king! Polly, some people hold that the soul but leaves one human tenement for another, and so lives on through all the ages. I have occasionally thought of late that, in some past existence, I may have been a king.   It has all come to me so naturally, not as if I had had to work it out, but—as—if —I—remembered.

> "Or ever the knightly years were gone,
>   With the old world to the grave,
>   I was a *king* in Babylon,
>   And you were a Christian slave."

It may have been; you hear me, it may have been.

LADY MARY. [*Who is as one fascinated.*]   It may have been.

CRICHTON. I am lord over all. They are but hewers of wood and drawers of water for me. These shores are mine. Why should I hesitate; I have no longer any doubt.

I do believe I am doing the right thing. Dear Polly, I have grown to love you; are you afraid to mate with me? [*She rocks her arms; no words will come from her.*]

> "I was a king in Babylon,
> And you were a Christian slave."

LADY MARY. [*Bewitched.*] You are the most wonderful man I have ever known, and I am not afraid.

> [*He takes her to him reverently. Presently he is seated, and she is at his feet looking up adoringly in his face. As the tension relaxes she speaks with a smile.*]

I want you to tell me—every woman likes to know—when was the first time you thought me nicer than the others?

CRICHTON. [*Who, like all big men, is simple.*] I think a year ago. We were chasing goats on the Big Slopes, and you out-distanced us all; you were the first of our party to run a goat down; I was proud of you that day.

LADY MARY. [*Blushing with pleasure.*] Oh Gov., I only did it to please you. Everything I have done has been out of the desire to please you. [*Suddenly anxious.*] If I thought that in taking a wife from among us you were imperilling your dignity——

CRICHTON. [*Perhaps a little masterful.*] Have no fear of that, dear. I have thought it all out. The wife, Polly, always takes the same position as the husband.

LADY MARY. But I am so unworthy. It was sufficient to me that I should be allowed to wait on you at that table.

CRICHTON. You shall wait on me no longer. At whatever table I sit, Polly, you shall soon sit there also. [*Boyishly.*] Come, let us try what it will be like.

LADY MARY. As your servant at your feet.

CRICHTON. No, as my consort by my side.

[*They are sitting thus when the hatch is again opened and coffee offered. But* LADY MARY *is no longer there to receive it. Her sisters peep through in consternation. In vain they rattle the cup and saucer.* AGATHA *brings the coffee to* CRICHTON.]

CRICHTON. [*Forgetting for the moment that it is not a month hence.*] Help your mistress first, girl. [*Three women are bereft of speech, but he does not notice it. He addresses* CATHERINE *vaguely.*] Are you a good girl, Kitty?

CATHERINE. [*When she finds her tongue.*] I try to be, Gov.

CRICHTON. [*Still more vaguely.*] That's right.

[*He takes command of himself again, and signs to them to sit down.* ERNEST *comes in cheerily, but finding* CRICHTON *here is suddenly weak. He subsides on a chair, wondering what has happened.*]

CRICHTON. [*Surveying him.*] Ernest. [ERNEST *rises.*] You are becoming a little slovenly in your dress, Ernest; I don't like it.

ERNEST. [*Respectfully.*] Thank you. [ERNEST *sits again.* DADDY *and* TREHERNE *arrive.*]

CRICHTON. Daddy, I want you.

LORD LOAM. [*With a sinking.*] Is it because I forgot to clean out the dam?

CRICHTON. [*Encouragingly.*] No, no. [*He pours some wine into a goblet.*] A glass of wine with you, Daddy.

LORD LOAM. [*Hastily.*] Your health, Gov.

[*He is about to drink, but the master checks him.*]

CRICHTON. And hers. Daddy, this lady has done me the honour to promise to be my wife.

LORD LOAM. [*Astounded.*] Polly!

CRICHTON. [*A little perturbed.*] I ought first to have asked your consent. I deeply regret—but Nature; may I hope I have your approval?

LORD LOAM. May you, Gov.? [*Delighted.*] Rather! Polly!

> [*He puts his proud arms around her.*]

TREHERNE. We all congratulate you, Gov., most heartily.

ERNEST. Long life to you both, sir.

> [*There is much shaking of hands, all of which is sincere.*]

TREHERNE. When will it be, Gov.?

CRICHTON. [*After turning to* LADY MARY, *who whispers to him.*] As soon as the bridal skirt can be prepared. [*His manner has been most indulgent, and without the slighest suggestion of patronage. But he knows it is best for all that he should keep his place, and that his presence hampers them.*] My friends, I thank you for your good wishes, I thank you all. And now, perhaps you would like me to leave you to yourselves. Be joyous. Let there be song and dance to-night. Polly, I shall take my coffee in the parlour—you understand.

> [*He retires with pleasant dignity. Immediately there is a rush of two girls at* LADY MARY.]

LADY MARY. Oh, oh! Father, they are pinching me.

LORD LOAM. [*Taking her under his protection.*] Agatha, Catherine, never presume to pinch your sister again. On the other hand, she may pinch you henceforth as much as ever she chooses.

> [*In the meantime* TWEENY *is weeping softly, and the two are not above using her as a weapon.*]

CATHERINE. Poor Tweeny, it's a shame.

AGATHA. After he had almost promised *you.*

TWEENY. [*Loyally turning on them.*] No, he never did. He was always honourable as could be. 'Twas me as was too vulgar. Don't you dare say a word agin that man.

ERNEST. [*To* LORD LOAM.] You'll get a lot of tit-bits out of this, Daddy.

LORD LOAM. That's what I was thinking.

ERNEST. [*Plunged in thought.*] I dare say *I* shall have to clean out the dam now.

LORD LOAM. [*Heartlessly.*] I dare say.

> [*His gay old heart makes him again proclaim that he is a chickety chick. He seizes the concertina.*]

TREHERNE. [*Eagerly.*] That's the proper spirit.

> [*He puts his arm round* CATHERINE, *and in another moment they are all dancing to Daddy's music. Never were people happier on an island. A moment's pause is presently created by the return of* CRICHTON *wearing the wonderful robe of which we have already had dark mention. Never has he looked more regal, never perhaps felt so regal. We need not grudge him the one foible of his rule, for it is all coming to an end.*]

CRICHTON. [*Graciously, seeing them hesitate.*] No, no; I am delighted to see you all so happy. Go on.

TREHERNE. We don't like to before you, Gov.

CRICHTON. [*His last order.*] It is my wish.

> [*The merrymaking is resumed, and soon* CRICHTON *himself joins in the dance. It is when the fun is at its fastest and most furious that all stop abruptly as if turned to stone. They have heard the boom of a gun. Presently they are alive again.* ERNEST *leaps to the window.*]

TREHERNE. [Huskily.] It was a ship's gun. [*They turn to* CRICHTON *for confirmation; even in that hour they turn to* CRICHTON.] Gov.?

CRICHTON. Yes.

[*In another moment* LADY MARY *and* LORD LOAM *are alone.*]

LADY MARY. [*Seeing that her father is unconcerned.*] Father, you heard.

LORD LOAM. [*Placidly.*] Yes, my child.

LADY MARY. [*Alarmed by his unnatural calmness.*] But it was a gun, father.

LORD LOAM. [*Looking an old man now, and shuddering a little.*] Yes—a gun—I have often heard it. It's only a dream, you know; why don't we go on dancing?

[*She takes his hands, which have gone cold.*]

LADY MARY Father. Don't you see, they have all rushed down to the beach? Come.

LORD LOAM. Rushed down to the beach; yes, always that—I often dream it.

LADY MARY. Come, father, come.

LORD LOAM. Only a dream, my poor girl.

[CRICHTON *returns. He is pale but firm.*]

CRICHTON. We can see lights within a mile of the shore—a great ship.

LORD LOAM. A ship—always a ship.

LADY MARY. Father, this is no dream.

LORD LOAM. [*Looking timidly at* CRICHTON.] It's a dream, isn't it? There's no ship?

CRICHTON. [*Soothing him with a touch.*] You are awake, Daddy, and there is a ship.

LORD LOAM. [*Clutching him.*] You are not deceiving me?

CRICHTON. It is the truth.

LORD LOAM. [*Reeling.*] True?—a ship—at last!

[*He goes after the others pitifully.*]

CRICHTON. [*Quietly.*] There is a small boat between it and the island; they must have sent it ashore for water.

LADY MARY. Coming in?

CRICHTON. No. That gun must have been a signal to recall it. It is going back. They can't hear our cries.

LADY MARY. [*Pressing her temples.*] Going away. So near—so near. [*Almost to herself.*] I think I'm glad.

CRICHTON. [*Cheerily.*] Have no fear. I shall bring them back.

[*He goes towards the table on which is the electrical apparatus.*]

LADY MARY. [*Standing on guard as it were between him and the table.*] What are you going to do?

CRICHTON. To fire the beacons.

LADY MARY. Stop! [*She faces him.*] Don't you see what it means?

CRICHTON. [*Firmly.*] It means that our life on the island has come to a natural end.

LADY MARY. [*Huskily.*] Gov., let the ship go.

CRICHTON. The old man—you saw what it means to him.

LADY MARY. But I am afraid.

CRICHTON. [*Adoringly.*] Dear Polly.

LADY MARY. Gov., let the ship go.

CRICHTON. [*She clings to him, but though it is his death sentence he loosens her hold.*] Bill Crichton has got to play the game.

[*He pulls the levers. Soon through the window one of the beacons is seen flaring red. There is a long pause. Shouting is heard.* [ERNEST *is the first to arrive.*]

ERNEST. Polly, Gov., the boat has turned back. They

are English sailors; they have landed! We are rescued, I tell you, rescued!

LADY MARY. [*Wanly.*] Is it anything to make so great a to-do about?

ERNEST. [*Staring.*] Eh?

LADY MARY. Have we not been happy here?

ERNEST. Happy? lord, yes.

LADY MARY. [*Catching hold of his sleeve.*] Ernest, we must never forget all that the Gov. has done for us.

ERNEST. [*Stoutly.*] Forget it? The man who could forget it would be a selfish wretch and a—— But I say, this makes a difference!

LADY MARY. [*Quickly.*] No, it doesn't.

ERNEST. [*His mind tottering.*] A mighty difference!
> [*The others come running in, some weeping with joy, others boisterous. We see blue-jackets gazing through the window at the curious scene.* LORD LOAM *comes accompanied by a naval officer, whom he is continually shaking by the hand.*]

LORD LOAM. And here, sir, is our little home. Let me thank you in the name of us all, again and again and again.

OFFICER. Very proud, my lord. It is indeed an honour to have been able to assist so distinguished a gentleman as Lord Loam.

LORD LOAM. A glorious, glorious day. I shall show you our other room. Come, my pets. Come, Crichton.
> [*He has not meant to be cruel. He does not know he has said it. It is the old life that has come back to him. They all go. All leave* CRICHTON *except* LADY MARY.]

LADY MARY. [*Stretching out her arms to him.*] Dear Gov., I will never give you up.
> [*There is a salt smile on his face as he shakes his*

*head to her. He lets the cloak slip to the
ground. She will not take this for an answer;
again her arms go out to him. Then comes
the great renunciation. By an effort of will he
ceases to be an erect figure; he has the humble
bearing of a servant. His hands come together
as if he were washing them.*]

CRICHTON. [*It is the speech of his life.*]   My lady.
  [*She goes away. There is none to salute him
  now, unless we do it.*]

End of Act III.

ACT IV

THE OTHER ISLAND

*Some months have elapsed, and we have again the honour
of waiting upon* LORD LOAM *in his London home. It
is the room of the first act, but with a new scheme of
decoration, for on the walls are exhibited many interesting trophies from the island, such as skins, stuffed
birds, and weapons of the chase, labelled "Shot by*
LORD LOAM," "HON. ERNEST WOOLLEY'S *Blowpipe,"
etc. There are also two large glass cases containing
other odds and ends, including, curiously enough, the
bucket in which* ERNEST *was first dipped, but there is
no label calling attention to the incident.*

*It is not yet time to dress for dinner, and his lordship is on
a couch, hastily yet furtively cutting the pages of a new
book. With him are his two younger daughters and
his nephew, and they also are engaged in literary pur-
suits; that is to say, the ladies are eagerly but furtively*

*reading the evening papers, of which Ernest is sitting
complacently but furtively on an endless number, and
doling them out as called for. Note the frequent use
of the word "furtive." It implies that they do not
wish to be discovered by their butler, say, at their
otherwise delightful task.*

AGATHA. [*Reading aloud, with emphasis on the wrong
words.*] "In conclusion, we most heartily congratulate
the Hon. Ernest Woolley. This book of his, regarding the
adventures of himself and his brave companions on a desert
isle, stirs the heart like a trumpet."

> [*Evidently the book referred to is the one in* LORD
> LOAM'S *hands.*]

ERNEST. [*Handing her a pink paper.*] Here is another.

CATHERINE. [*Reading.*] "From the first to the last
of Mr. Woolley's engrossing pages it is evident that he was
an ideal man to be wrecked with, and a true hero." [*Large-
eyed.*] Ernest!

ERNEST. [*Calmly.*] That's how it strikes *them*, you
know. Here's another one.

AGATHA. [*Reading.*] "There are many kindly refer-
ences to the two servants who were wrecked with the family,
and Mr. Woolley pays the butler a glowing tribute in a
footnote."

> [*Some one coughs uncomfortably.*]

LORD LOAM. [*Who has been searching the index for
the letter L.*] Excellent, excellent. At the same time I
must say, Ernest, that the whole book is about yourself.

ERNEST. [*Genially.*] As the author——

LORD LOAM. Certainly, certainly. Still, you know, as

a peer of the realm——[*with dignity*]——I think, Ernest, you might have given me one of your adventures.

ERNEST.   I say it was you who taught us how to obtain a fire by rubbing two pieces of stick together.

LORD LOAM.   [*Beaming.*]   Do you, do you?   I call that very handsome.   What page?

> [*Here the door opens, and the well-bred* CRICHTON *enters with the evening papers as subscribed for by the house. Those we have already seen have perhaps been introduced by* ERNEST *up his waistcoat. Every one except the intruder is immediately self-conscious, and when he with-draws there is a general sigh of relief. They pounce on the new papers.* ERNEST *evidently gets a shock from one, which he casts contemptuously on the floor.*]

AGATHA.   [*More fortunate.*]   Father, see page 81.   "It was a tiger-cat," says Mr. Woolley, "of the largest size. Death stared Lord Loam in the face, but he never flinched."

LORD LOAM.   [*Searching his book eagerly.*]   Page 81.

AGATHA.   "With presence of mind only equalled by his courage, he fixed an arrow in his bow."

LORD LOAM.   Thank you, Ernest; thank you my boy.

AGATHA.   "Unfortunately he missed."

LORD LOAM.   Eh?

AGATHA.   "But by great good luck I heard his cries——"

LORD LOAM.   My cries?

AGATHA.   "——and rushing forward with drawn knife, I stabbed the monster to the heart."

> [LORD LOAM *shuts his book with a pettish slam. There might be a scene here were it not that* CRICHTON *reappears and goes to one of the glass cases. All are at once on the alert, and his lordship is particularly sly.*]

LORD LOAM. Anything in the papers, Catherine?

CATHERINE. No, father, nothing——nothing at all.

ERNEST. [*It pops out as of yore.*] The papers! The papers are guides that tell us what we ought to do, and then we don't do it.

> [CRICHTON *having opened the glass case has taken out the bucket, and* ERNEST, *looking round for applause, sees him carrying it off and is undone. For a moment of time he forgets that he is no longer on the island, and with a sigh he is about to follow* CRICHTON *and the bucket to a retired spot. The door closes, and* ERNEST *comes to himself.*]

LORD LOAM. [*Uncomfortably.*] I told him to take it away.

ERNEST. I thought——[*he wipes his brow*]——I shall go and dress.

> [*He goes.*]

CATHERINE. Father, it's awful having Crichton here. It's like living on tiptoe.

LORD LOAM. [*Gloomily.*] While he is here we are sitting on a volcano.

AGATHA. How mean of you! I am sure he has only stayed on with us to——to help us through. It would have looked so suspicious if he had gone at once.

CATHERINE. [*Revelling in the worst.*] But suppose Lady Brocklehurst were to get at him and pump him. She's the most terrifying, suspicious old creature in England; and Crichton simply can't tell a lie.

LORD LOAM. My dear, that is the volcano to which I was referring. [*He has evidently something to communicate.*] It's all Mary's fault. She said to me yesterday that she would break her engagement with Brocklehurst unless I told him about——you know what.

[*All conjure up the vision of* CRICHTON.]

AGATHA. Is she mad?

LORD LOAM. She calls it common honesty.

CATHERINE. Father, have you told him?

LORD LOAM. [*Heavily.*] She thinks I have, but I couldn't. She's sure to find out to-night.

> [*Unconsciously he leans on the island concertina, which he has perhaps been lately showing to an interviewer as something he made for* TWEENY. *It squeaks, and they all jump.*]

CATHERINE. It's like a bird of ill-omen.

LORD LOAM. [*Vindictively.*] I must have it taken away; it has done that twice.

> [LADY MARY *comes in. She is in evening dress. Undoubtedly she meant to sail in, but she forgets, and despite her garments it is a manly entrance. She is properly ashamed of herself. She tries again, and has an encouraging success. She indicates to her sisters that she wishes to be alone with papa.*]

AGATHA.   All right, but we know what it's about. Come along, Kit.

> [*They go.* LADY MARY *thoughtlessly sits like a boy, and again corrects herself. She addresses her father, but he is in a brown study, and she seeks to draw his attention by whistling. This troubles them both.*]

LADY MARY. How horrid of me!

LORD LOAM. [*Depressed.*] If you would try to remember——

LADY MARY. [*Sighing.*] I do; but there are so many things to remember.

LORD LOAM. [*Sympathetically.*] There are——[*in a*

whisper.] Do you know, Mary, I constantly find myself secreting hairpins.

LADY MARY. I find it so difficult to go up steps one at a time.

LORD LOAM. I was dining with half a dozen members of our party last Thursday, Mary, and they were so eloquent that I couldn't help wondering all the time how many of their heads *he* would have put in the bucket.

LADY MARY. I use so many of his phrases. And my appetite is so scandalous. Father, I usually have a chop before we sit down to dinner.

LORD LOAM. As for my clothes——[*wriggling.*] My dear, you can't think how irksome collars are to me nowadays.

LADY MARY. They can't be half such an annoyance, father, as——

[*She looks dolefully at her skirt.*]

LORD LOAM. [*Hurriedly.*] Quite so——quite so. You have dressed early to-night, Mary.

LADY MARY. That reminds me; I had a note from Brocklehurst saying that he would come a few minutes before his mother as——as he wanted to have a talk with me. He didn't say what about, but of course we know.

[*His lordship fidgets.*]

[*With feeling.*] It was good of you to tell him, father. Oh, it is horrible to me——[*covering her face.*] It seemed so natural at the time.

LORD LOAM. [*Petulantly.*] Never again make use of that word in this house, Mary.

LADY MARY. [*With an effort.*] Father, Brocklehurst has been so loyal to me for these two years that I should despise myself were I to keep my——my extraordinary lapse from him. Had Brocklehurst been a little less good, then you need not have told him my strange little secret.

LORD LOAM. [*Weakly.*] Polly——I mean Mary——it was all Crichton's fault, he——

LADY MARY. [*With decision.*] No, father, no; not a word against him though. I haven't the pluck to go on with it; I can't even understand how it ever was. Father, do you not still hear the surf? Do you see the curve of the beach?

LORD LOAM. I have begun to forget——[*in a low voice.*] But they were happy days; there was something magical about them.

LADY MARY. It was glamour. Father, I have lived Arabian nights. I have sat out a dance with the evening star. But it was all in a past existence, in the days of Babylon, and I am myself again. But he has been chivalrous always. If the slothful, indolent creature I used to be has improved in any way, I owe it all to him. I am slipping back in many ways, but I am determined not to slip back altogether——in memory of him and his island. That is why I insisted on your telling Brocklehurst. He can break .our engagement if he chooses. [*Proudly.*] Mary Lasenby is going to play the game.

LORD LOAM. But my dear——

[LORD BROCKLEHURST *is announced.*]

LADY MARY. [*Meaningly.*] Father, dear, oughtn't you to be dressing?

LORD LOAM. [*Very unhappy.*] The fact is——before I go——I want to say——

LORD BROCKLEHURST. Loam, if you don't mind, I wish very specially to have a word with Mary before dinner.

LORD LOAM. But——

LADY MARY. Yes, father.

[*She induces him to go, and thus courageously faces* LORD BROCKLEHURST *to hear her fate.*]

I am ready, George.

LORD BROCKLEHURST. [*Who is so agitated that she ought to see he is thinking not of her but of himself.*] It is a painful matter——I wish I could have spared you this, Mary.

LADY MARY. Please go on.

LORD BROCKLEHURST. In common fairness, of course, this should be remembered, that two years had elapsed. You and I had no reason to believe that we should ever meet again.

[*This is more considerate than she had expected.*]

LADY MARY. [*Softening.*] I was so lost to the world, George.

LORD BROCKLEHURST. [*With a groan.*] At the same time, the thing is utterly and absolutely inexcusable——

LADY MARY. [*Recovering her hauteur.*] Oh!

LORD BROCKLEHURST. And so I have already said to mother.

LADY MARY. [*Disdaining him.*] You have told her?

LORD BROCKLEHURST. Certainly, Mary, certainly; I tell mother everything.

LADY MARY. [*Curling her lips.*] And what did she say?

LORD BROCKLEHURST. To tell the truth, mother rather pooh-poohed the whole affair.

LADY MARY. [*Incredulous.*] Lady Brocklehurst pooh-poohed the whole affair!

LORD BROCKLEHURST. She said, "Mary and I will have a good laugh over this."

LADY MARY. [*Outraged.*] George, your mother is a hateful, depraved old woman.

LORD BROCKLEHURST. Mary!

LADY MARY. [*Turning away.*] Laugh indeed, when it will always be such a pain to me.

LORD BROCKLEHURST. [*With strange humility.*] If only you would let me bear all the pain, Mary.

LADY MARY. [*Who is taken aback.*] George, I think you are the noblest man——

> [*She is touched, and gives him both her hands. Unfortunately he simpers.*]

LORD BROCKLEHURST. She was a pretty little thing.

> [*She stares, but he marches to his doom.*]

Ah, not beautiful like you. I assure you it was the merest flirtation; there were a few letters, but we have got them back. It was all owing to the boat being so late at Calais. You see she had such large, helpless eyes.

LADY MARY. [*Fixing him.*] George, when you lunched with father to-day at the club——

LORD BROCKLEHURST. I didn't. He wired me that he couldn't come.

LADY MARY. [*With a tremor.*] But he wrote you?

LORD BROCKLEHURST. No.

LADY MARY. [*A bird singing in her breast.*] You haven't seen him since?

LORD BROCKLEHURST. No.

> [*She is saved. Is he to be let off also? Not at all. She bears down on him like a ship of war.*]

LADY MARY. George, who and what is this woman?

LORD BROCKLEHURST. [*Cowering.*] She was——she is——the shame of it——a lady's-maid.

LADY MARY. [*Properly horrified.*] A what?

LORD BROCKLEHURST. A lady's-maid. A mere servant, Mary. [LADY MARY *whirls round so that he shall not see her face.*] I first met her at this house when you were entertaining the servants; so you see it was largely your father's fault.

LADY MARY. [*Looking him up and down.*] A lady's-maid?

LORD BROCKLEHURST. [*Degraded.*] Her name was Fisher.

LADY MARY. My maid!

LORD BROCKLEHURST. [*With open hands.*] Can you forgive me, Mary?

LADY MARY. Oh George, George!

LORD BROCKLEHURST. Mother urged me not to tell you anything about it; but——

LADY MARY. [*From her heart.*] I am so glad you told me.

LORD BROCKLEHURST. You see there was nothing wrong in it.

LADY MARY. [*Thinking perhaps of another incident.*] No, indeed.

LORD BROCKLEHURST. [*Inclined to simper again.*] And she behaved awfully well. She quite saw that it was because the boat was late. I suppose the glamour to a girl in service of a man in high position——

LADY MARY. Glamour!——yes, yes, that was it.

LORD BROCKLEHURST. Mother says that a girl in such circumstances is to be excused if she loses her head.

LADY MARY. [*Impulsively.*] George, I am so sorry if I said anything against your mother. I am sure she is the dearest old thing.

LORD BROCKLEHURST. [*In calm waters at last.*] Of course for women of our class she has a very different standard.

LADY MARY. [*Grown tiny.*] Of course.

LORD BROCKLEHURST. You see, knowing how good a woman she is herself, she was naturally anxious that I should marry some one like her. That is what has made her watch your conduct so jealously, Mary.

LADY MARY. [*Hurriedly thinking things out.*] I know.

I——I think, George, that before your mother comes I should like to say a word to father.

LORD BROCKLEHURST. [*Nervously.*] About this?

LADY MARY. Oh no; I shan't tell him of this. About something else.

LORD BROCKLEHURST. And you do forgive me, Mary?

LADY MARY. [*Smiling on him.*] Yes, yes. I——I am sure the boat was *very* late, George.

LORD BROCKLEHURST. [*Earnestly.*] It really was.

LADY MARY. I am even relieved to know that you are not quite perfect, dear. [*She rests her hands on his shoulders. She has a moment of contrition.*] George, when we are married, we shall try to be not an entirely frivolous couple, won't we? We must endeavour to be of some little use, dear.

LORD BROCKLEHURST. [*The ass.*] Noblesse oblige.

LADY MARY. [*Haunted by the phrases of a better man.*] Mary Lasenby is determined to play the game, George.

> [*Perhaps she adds to herself, "Except just this once." A kiss closes this episode of the two lovers; and soon after the departure of* LADY MARY *the* COUNTESS OF BROCKLEHURST *is announced. She is a very formidable old lady.*]

LADY BROCKLEHURST. Alone, George?

LORD BROCKLEHURST. Mother, I told her all; she has behaved magnificently.

LADY BROCKLEHURST. [*Who has not shared his fears.*] Silly boy. [*She casts a supercilious eye on the island trophies.*] So these are the wonders they brought back with them. Gone away to dry her eyes, I suppose?

LORD BROCKLEHURST. [*Proud of his mate.*] She didn't cry, mother.

LADY BROCKLEHURST. No? [*She reflects.*] You're

quite right. I wouldn't have cried. Cold, icy. Yes, that was it.

LORD BROCKLEHURST. [*Who has not often contradicted her.*] I assure you, mother, that wasn't it at all. She forgave me at once.

LADY BROCKLEHURST. [*Opening her eyes sharply to the full.*] Oh!

LORD BROCKLEHURST. She was awfully nice about the boat being late; she even said she was relieved to find that I wasn't quite perfect.

LADY BROCKLEHURST. [*Pouncing.*] She said that?

LORD BROCKLEHURST. She really did.

LADY BROCKLEHURST. I mean *I* wouldn't. Now if *I* had said that, what would have made me say it? [*Suspiciously.*] George, is Mary all we think her?

LORD BROCKLEHURST. [*With unexpected spirit.*] If she wasn't, mother, you would know it.

LADY BROCKLEHURST. Hold your tongue, boy. We don't really know what happened on that island.

LORD BROCKLEHURST. You were reading the book all the morning.

LADY BROCKLEHURST. How can I be sure that the book is true?

LORD BROCKLEHURST. They all talk of it as true.

LADY BROCKLEHURST. How do I know that they are not lying?

LORD BROCKLEHURST. Why should they lie?

LADY BROCKLEHURST. Why shouldn't they? [*She reflects again.*] If I had been wrecked on an island, I think it highly probable that I should have lied when I came back. Weren't some servants with them?

LORD BROCKLEHURST. Crichton, the butler.

[*He is surprised to see her ring the bell.*]

Why, mother, you are not going to——

LADY BROCKLEHURST. Yes, I am. [*Pointedly.*] George, watch whether Crichton begins any of his answers to my questions with "The fact is."

LORD BROCKLEHURST. Why?

LADY BROCKLEHURST. Because that is usually the beginning of a lie.

LORD BROCKLEHURST. [*As* CRICHTON *opens the door.*] Mother, you can't do these things in other people's houses.

LADY BROCKLEHURST. [*Coolly, to* CRICHTON.] It was I who rang. [*Surveying him through her eyeglass.*] So you were one of the castaways, Crichton?

CRICHTON. Yes, my lady.

LADY BROCKLEHURST. Delightful book Mr. Woolley has written about your adventures. [CRICHTON *bows.*] Don't you think so?

CRICHTON. I have not read it, my lady.

LADY BROCKLEHURST. Odd that they should not have presented you with a copy.

LORD BROCKLEHURST. Presumably Crichton is no reader.

LADY BROCKLEHURST. By the way, Crichton, were there any books on the island?

CRICHTON. I had one, my lady——Henley's poems.

LORD BROCKLEHURST. Never heard of him.

[CRICHTON *again bows.*]

LADY BROCKLEHURST. [*Who has not heard of him either.*] I think you were not the only servant wrecked?

CRICHTON. There was a young woman, my lady.

LADY BROCKLEHURST. I want to see her. [CRICHTON *bows, but remains.*] Fetch her up.

[*He goes.*]

LORD BROCKLEHURST. [*Almost standing up to his mother.*] This is scandalous.

LADY BROCKLEHURST. [*Defining her position.*] I am
a mother.

> [CATHERINE *and* AGATHA *enter in dazzling con-*
> *fections, and quake in secret to find themselves*
> *practically alone with* LADY BROCKLEHURST.]

[*Even as she greets them.*] How d'you do, Catherine
——Agatha? You didn't dress like this on the island, I
expect! By the way, how did you dress?

> [*They have thought themselves prepared,*
> *but——*]

AGATHA. Not——not so well, of course, but quite the
same idea.

> [*They are relieved by the arrival of* TREHERNE,
> *who is in clerical dress.*]

LADY BROCKLEHURST. How do you do, Mr. Treherne?
There is not so much of you in the book as I had hoped.

TREHERNE. [*Modestly.*] There wasn't very much of
me on the island, Lady Brocklehurst.

LADY BROCKLEHURST. How d'ye mean?

> [*He shrugs his honest shoulders.*]

LORD BROCKLEHURST. I hear you have got a living
Treherne. Congratulations.

TREHERNE. Thanks.

LORD BROCKLEHURST. Is it a good one?

TREHERNE. So-so. They are rather weak in bowling,
but it's a good bit of turf.

> [*Confidence is restored by the entrance of* ERNEST,
> *who takes in the situation promptly, and, of*
> *course, knows he is a match for any old lady.*]

ERNEST. [*With ease.*] How do you do, Lady Brocklehurst.

LADY BROCKLEHURST. Our brilliant author!

ERNEST. [*Impervious to satire.*] Oh, I don't know.

LADY BROCKLEHURST. It is as engrossing, Mr. Woolley, as if it were a work of fiction.

ERNEST. [*Suddenly uncomfortable.*] Thanks, awfully. [*Recovering.*] The fact is——

> [*He is puzzled by seeing the Brocklehurst family exchange meaning looks.*]

CATHERINE. [*To the rescue.*] Lady Brocklehurst, Mr. Treherne and I——we are engaged.

AGATHA. And Ernest and I.

LADY BROCKLEHURST. [*Grimly.*] I see, my dears; thought it wise to keep the island in the family.

> [*An awkward moment this for the entrance of LORD LOAM and LADY MARY, who, after a private talk upstairs, are feeling happy and secure.*]

LORD LOAM. [*With two hands for his distinguished guest.*] Aha! ha, ha! younger than any of them, Emily.

LADY BROCKLEHURST. Flatterer. [*To LADY MARY.*] You seem in high spirits, Mary.

LADY MARY. [*Gaily.*] I am.

LADY BROCKLEHURST. [*With a significant glance at LORD BROCKLEHURST.*] After——

LADY MARY. I——I mean. The fact is——

> [*Again that disconcerting glance between the Countess and her son.*]

LORD LOAM. [*Humorously.*] She hears wedding bells. Emily, ha, ha!

LADY BROCKLEHURST. [*Coldly.*] Do you, Mary? Can't say I do; but I'm hard of hearing.

LADY MARY. [*Instantly her match.*] If you don't Lady Brocklehurst, I'm sure I don't.

LORD LOAM. [*Nervously.*] Tut, tut. Seen our curios from the island, Emily; I should like you to examine them.

LADY BROCKLEHURST. Thank you, Henry. I am glad

you say that, for I have just taken the liberty of asking two of them to step upstairs.

> [*There is an uncomfortable silence, which the entrance of* CRICHTON *with* TWEENY *does not seem to dissipate.* CRICHTON *is impenetrable, but* TWEENY *hangs back in fear.*]

LORD BROCKLEHURST. [*Stoutly.*] Loam, I have no hand in this.

LADY BROCKLEHURST. [*Undisturbed.*] Pooh, what have I done? You always begged me to speak to the servants, Henry, and I merely wanted to discover whether the views you used to hold about equality were adopted on the island; it seemed a splendid opportunity, but Mr. Woolley has not a word on the subject.

> [*All eyes turn to* ERNEST.]

ERNEST. [*With confidence.*] The fact is——

> [*The fatal words again.*]

LORD LOAM. [*Not quite certain what he is to assure her of.*] I assure you, Emily——

LADY MARY. [*As cold as steel.*] Father, nothing whatever happened on the island of which I, for one, am ashamed, and I hope Crichton will be allowed to answer Lady Brocklehurst's questions.

LADY BROCKLEHURST. To be sure. There's nothing to make a fuss about, and we're a family party. [*To* CRICHTON.] Now, truthfully, my man.

CRICHTON. [*Calmly.*] I promise that, my lady.

> [*Some hearts sink, the hearts that could never understand a* CRICHTON.]

LADY BROCKLEHURST. [*Sharply.*] Well, were you all equal on the island?

CRICHTON. No, my lady. I think I may say there was as little equality there as elsewhere.

LADY BROCKLEHURST. All the social distinctions were preserved?

CRICHTON. As at home, my lady.

LADY BROCKLEHURST. The servants?

CRICHTON. They had to keep their place.

LADY BROCKLEHURST. Wonderful. How was it managed? [*With an inspiration.*] You, girl, tell me that?

[*Can there be a more critical moment?*]

TWEENY. [*In agony.*] If you please, my lady, it was all the Gov.'s doing.

[*They give themselves up for lost.* LORD LOAM *tries to sink out of sight.*]

CRICHTON. In the regrettable slang of the servants' hall, my lady, the master is usually referred to as the Gov.

LADY BROCKLEHURST. I see. [*She turns to* LORD LOAM.] You——

LORD LOAM. [*Reappearing.*] Yes, I understand that is what they call me.

LADY BROCKLEHURST. [*To* CRICHTON.] You didn't even take your meals with the family?

CRICHTON. No, my lady, I dined apart.

[*Is all safe?*]

LADY BROCKLEHURST. [*Alas.*] You, girl, also? Did you dine with Crichton?

TWEENY. [*Scared.*] No, your ladyship.

LADY BROCKLEHURST. [*Fastening on her.*] With whom?

TWEENY. I took my bit of supper with——with Daddy and Polly and the rest.

[*Væ victis.*]

ERNEST. [*Leaping into the breach.*] Dear old Daddy ——he was our monkey. You remember our monkey, Agatha?

AGATHA. Rather! What a funny old darling he was.

CATHERINE. [*Thus encouraged.*] And don't you think Polly was the sweetest little parrot, Mary?

LADY BROCKLEHURST. Ah! I understand; animals you had domesticated?

LORD LOAM. [*Heavily.*] Quite so——quite so.

LADY BROCKLEHURST. The servants' teas that used to take place here once a month——

CRICHTON. They did not seem natural on the island, my lady, and were discontinued by the Gov.'s orders.

LORD BROCKLEHURST. A clear proof, Loam, that they were a mistake here.

LORD LOAM. [*Seeing the opportunity for a diversion.*] I admit it frankly. I abandon them. Emily, as the result of our experiences on the island, I think of going over to the Tories.

LADY BROCKLEHURST. I am delighted to hear it.

LORD LOAM. [*Expanding.*] Thank you, Crichton, thank you; that is all.

> [*He motions to them to go, but the time is not yet.*]

LADY BROCKLEHURST. One moment. [*There is a universal but stifled groan.*] Young people, Crichton, will be young poeple, even on an island; now, I suppose there was a certain amount of——shall we say sentimentalising, going on?

CRICHTON. Yes, my lady, there was.

LORD BROCKLEHURST. [*Ashamed.*] Mother!

LADY BROCKLEHURST. [*Disregarding him.*] Which gentleman? [*To* TWEENY.] You, girl, tell me.

TWEENY. [*Confused.*] If you please, my lady——

ERNEST. [*Hurriedly.*] The fact is——

> [*He is checked as before, and probably says "D—n" to himself, but he has saved the situation.*]

TWEENY. [*Gasping.*] It was him——Mr. Ernest, your ladyship.

LADY BROCKLEHURST. [*Counsel for the prosecution.*] With which lady?

AGATHA. I have already told you, Lady Brocklehurst, that Ernest and I——

LADY BROCKLEHURST. Yes, *now;* but you were two years on the island. [*Looking at* LADY MARY.] Was it this lady?

TWEENY. No, your ladyship.

LADY BROCKLEHURST. Then I don't care which of the others it was. [TWEENY *gurgles.*] Well, I suppose that will do.

LORD BROCKLEHURST. Do! I hope you are ashamed of yourself, mother. [*To* CRICHTON, *who is going.*] You are an excellent fellow, Crichton; and if, after we are married, you ever wish to change your place, come to us.

LADY MARY. [*Losing her head for the only time.*] Oh no, impossible.

LADY BROCKLEHURST. [*At once suspicious.*] Why impossible? [LADY MARY *cannot answer, or perhaps she is too proud.*] Do you see why it should be impossible, my man?

> [*He can make or mar his unworthy* MARY *now. Have you any doubt of him?*]

CRICHTON. Yes, my lady. I had not told you, my lord, but as soon as your lordship is suited I wish to leave service.

> [*They are all immensely relieved, except poor* TWEENY.]

TREHERNE. [*The only curious one.*] What will you do, Crichton?

> [CRICHTON *shrugs his shoulders; "God knows," it may mean.*]

CRICHTON. Shall I withdraw, my lord?

[*He withdraws without a tremor,* TWEENY *accompanying him. They can all breathe again, the thunderstorm is over.*]

LADY BROCKLEHURST. [*Thankful to have made herself unpleasant.*] Horrid of me, wasn't it? But if one wasn't disagreeable now and again, it would be horribly tedious to be an old woman. He will soon be yours, Mary, and then ——think of the opportunities you will have of being disagreeable to me. On that understanding, my dear, don't you think we might——?

[*Their cold lips meet.*]

LORD LOAM. [*Vaguely.*] Quite so—quite so.

[CRICHTON *announces dinner, and they file out.* LADY MARY *stays behind a moment and impulsively holds out her hand.*]

LADY MARY. To wish you every dear happiness.

CRICHTON. [*An enigma to the last.*] The same to you, my lady.

LADY MARY. Do you despise me, Crichton? [*The man who could never tell a lie makes no answer.*] You are the best man among us.

CRICHTON. On an island, my lady, perhaps; but in England, no.

LADY MARY. Then there's something wrong with England.

CRICHTON. My lady, not even from you can I listen to a word against England.

LADY MARY. Tell me one thing: you have not lost your courage?

CRICHTON. No, my lady.

[*She goes. He turns out the lights.*]

The End.

WHAT EVERY WOMAN KNOWS

A COMEDY

ACT I

JAMES WYLIE *is about to make a move on the dambrod, and in the little Scotch room there is an awful silence befitting the occasion.* JAMES *with his hand poised—for if he touches a piece he has to play it,* ALICK *will see to that—raises his red head suddenly to read* ALICK'S *face. His father, who is* ALICK, *is pretending to be in a panic lest* JAMES *should make this move.* JAMES *grins heartlessly, and his fingers are about to close on the "man" when some instinct of self-preservation makes him peep once more. This time* ALICK *is caught: the unholy ecstasy on his face tells as plain as porridge that he has been luring* JAMES *to destruction.* JAMES *glares; and, too late, his opponent is a simple old father again.* JAMES *mops his head, sprawls in the manner most conducive to thought in the* WYLIE *family, and, protruding his underlip, settles down to a reconsideration of the board.* ALICK *blows out his cheeks, and a drop of water settles on the point of his nose.*

You will find them thus any Saturday night (after family worship, which sends the servant to bed); and sometimes the pauses are so long that in the end they forget whose move it is.

It is not the room you would be shown into if you were calling socially on MISS WYLIE. *The drawing-room for you, and* MISS WYLIE *in a coloured merino to receive you; very likely she would exclaim, "This is a pleasant surprise!" though she has seen you coming up the*

189

avenue and has just had time to whip the dustcloths off the chairs, and to warn ALICK, DAVID, *and* JAMES, *that they had better not dare come in to see you before they have put on a dickey. Nor is this the room in which you would dine in solemn grandeur if invited to drop in and take pot-luck, which is how the* WYLIES *invite, it being a family weakness to pretend that they sit down in the dining-room daily. It is the real living room of the house, where* ALICK, *who will never get used to fashionable ways, can take off his collar and sit happily in his stocking soles, and* JAMES *at times would do so also; but catch* MAGGIE *letting him.*

There is one very fine chair, but, heavens, not for sitting on; just to give the room a social standing in an emergency. It sneers at the other chairs with an air of insolent superiority, like a haughty bride who has married into the house for money. Otherwise the furniture is homely; most of it has come from that smaller house where the WYLIES *began. There is the large and shiny chair which can be turned into a bed if you look the other way for a moment.* JAMES *cannot sit on this chair without gradually sliding down it till he is lying luxuriously on the small of his back, his legs indicating, like the hands of a clock, that it is ten past twelve; a position in which* MAGGIE *shudders to see him receiving company.*

The other chairs are horse-hair, than which nothing is more comfortable if there be a good slit down the seat. The seats are heavily dented, because all the WYLIE *family sit down with a dump. The draughtboard is on the edge of a large centre table, which also displays four books placed at equal distances from each other, one of them a Bible, and another the family album. If these were the only books they would not justify* MAGGIE *in calling* this chamber the library, her dogged name for it; while DAVID and JAMES call it the west-room and ALICK calls it "the room," which is to him the natural name for any apartment without a bed in it. There is a bookcase of pitch pine, which contains six hundred books, with glass doors to prevent your getting at them. No one does try to get at the books, for the WYLIES are not a reading family. They like you to gasp when you see so much literature gathered together in one prison-house, but they gasp themselves at the thought that there are persons, chiefly clergymen, who, having finished one book, coolly begin another. Nevertheless it was not all vainglory that made DAVID buy this library: it was rather a mighty respect for education, as something that he has missed. This same feeling makes him take in the Contemporary Review and stand up to it like a man. ALICK, who also has a respect for education, tries to read the Contemporary, but becomes dispirited, and may be heard muttering over its pages, "No, no use, no use, no," and sometimes even "Oh hell." JAMES has no respect for education; and MAGGIE is at present of an open mind.

They are WYLIE AND SONS of the local granite quarry, in which ALICK was throughout his working days a mason. It is DAVID who has raised them to this position; he climbed up himself step by step (and hewed the steps), and drew the others up after him. "WYLIE BROTHERS," ALICK would have had the firm called, but DAVID said No, and JAMES said No, and MAGGIE said No; first honour must be to their father; and ALICK now likes it on the whole, though he often sighs at having to shave every day; and on some snell mornings he still creeps from his couch at four and even at two (thinking that his mallet and chisel *are calling him), and begins to pull on his trousers, until the grandeur of them reminds him that he can go to bed again. Sometimes he cries a little, because there is no more work for him to do for ever and ever; and then MAGGIE gives him a spade (without telling DAVID) or DAVID gives him the logs to saw (without telling MAGGIE).*

We have given JAMES a longer time to make his move than our kind friends in front will give him, but in the meantime something has been happening. DAVID has come in, wearing a black coat and his Sabbath boots, for he has been to a public meeting. David is nigh forty years of age, whiskered like his father and brother (ALICK'S whiskers being worn as a sort of cravat round the neck), and he has the too brisk manner of one who must arrive anywhere a little before any one else. The painter who did the three of them for fifteen pounds (you may observe the canvases on the walls) has caught this characteristic, perhaps accidentally, for DAVID is almost stepping out of his frame, as if to hurry off somewhere; while ALICK and JAMES look as if they were pinned to the wall for life. All the six of them, men and pictures, however, have a family resemblance, like granite blocks from their own quarry. They are as Scotch as peat for instance, and they might exchange eyes without any neighbour noticing the difference, inquisitive little blue eyes that seem to be always totting up the price of things.

The dambrod players pay no attention to DAVID, nor does he regard them. Dumping down on the sofa he removes his 'lastic sides, as his Sabbath boots are called, by pushing one foot against the other, gets into a pair of hand-sewn slippers, deposits the boots as according to rule in the ottoman, and crosses to the fire. There must be something on DAVID'S *mind to-night, for he pays no attention to the game, neither gives advice (than which nothing is more maddening) nor exchanges a wink with* ALICK *over the parlous condition of* JAMES'S *crown. You can hear the wag-at-the-wall clock in the lobby ticking. Then* DAVID *lets himself go; it runs out of him like a hymn:*

DAVID. Oh, let the solid ground
        Not fail beneath my feet,
        Before my life has found
        What some have found so sweet.
    [*This is not a soliloquy, but is offered as a definite statement. The players emerge from their game with difficulty.*]

ALICK. [*With* JAMES'S *crown in his hand.*] What's that you're saying, David?

DAVID. [*Like a public speaker explaining the situation in a few well chosen words.*] The thing I'm speaking about is Love.

JAMES. [*Keeping control of himself.*] Do you stand there and say you're in love, David Wylie?

DAVID. Me; what would I do with the thing?

JAMES. [*Who is by no means without pluck.*] I see no necessity for calling it a thing.

    [*They are two bachelors who all their lives have been afraid of nothing but Woman.* DAVID *in his sportive days—which continue—has done roguish things with his arm when conducting a lady home under an umbrella from a soiree, and has both chuckled and been scared on thinking of it afterwards.* JAMES, *a commoner fellow altogether, has discussed the sex over a glass, but is too canny to be in the company of less than two young women at a time.*]

DAVID.   [*Derisively.*] Oho, has she got you, James?

JAMES.   [*Feeling the sting of it.*] Nobody has got me.

DAVID.   They'll catch you yet, lad.

JAMES.   They'll never catch me. You've been nearer catched yourself.

ALICK.   Yes, Kitty Menzies, David.

DAVID.   [*Feeling himself under the umbrella.*] It was a kind of a shave that.

ALICK.   [*Who knows all that is to be known about women and can speak of them without a tremor.*] It's a curious thing, but a man cannot help winking when he hears that one of his friends has been catched.

DAVID.   That's so.

JAMES.   [*Clinging to his manhood.*] And fear of that wink is what has kept the two of us single men. And yet what's the glory of being single?

DAVID.   There's no particular glory in it, but it's safe.

JAMES.   [*Putting away his aspirations.*] Yes, it's lonely, but it's safe. But who did you mean the poetry for, then?

DAVID.   For Maggie, of course.

[*You don't know* DAVID *and* JAMES *till you know how they love their sister* MAGGIE.]

ALICK.   I thought that.

DAVID.   [*Coming to the second point of his statement about Love.*] I saw her reading poetry and saying those words over to herself.

JAMES.   She has such a poetical mind.

DAVID.   Love. There's no doubt as that's what Maggie has set her heart on. And not merely love, but one of those grand noble loves; for though Maggie is undersized she has a passion for romance.

JAMES.   [*Wandering miserably about the room.*] It's

terrible not to be able to give Maggie what her heart is set on.

> [*The others never pay much attention to* JAMES, *though he is quite a smart figure in less important houses.*]

ALICK. [*Violently.*] Those idiots of men.

DAVID. Father, did you tell her who had got the minister of Galashiels?

ALICK. [*Wagging his head sadly.*] I had to tell her. And then I—I—bought her a sealskin muff, and I just slipped it into her hands and came away.

JAMES. [*Illustrating the sense of justice in the Wylie family.*] Of course, to be fair to the man, he never pretended he wanted her.

DAVID. None of them wants her; that's what depresses her. I was thinking, father, I would buy her that gold watch and chain in Snibby's window. She hankers after it.

JAMES. [*Slapping his pocket.*] You're too late, David; I've got them for her.

DAVID. It's ill done of the minister. Many a pound of steak has that man had in this house.

ALICK. You mind the slippers she worked for him?

JAMES. I mind them fine; she began them for William Cathro. She's getting on in years, too, though she looks so young.

ALICK. I never can make up my mind, David, whether her curls make her look younger or older.

DAVID. [*Determinedly.*] Younger. Whisht! I hear her winding the clock. Mind, not a word about the minister to her, James. Don't even mention religion this day.

JAMES. Would it be like me to do such a thing?

DAVID. It would be very like you. And there's that other matter: say not a syllable about our having a reason for sitting up late to-night. When she says it's bed-time, just all pretend we're not sleepy.

ALICK.   Exactly, and when——

[*Here* MAGGIE *enters, and all three are suddenly engrossed in the dambrod. We could describe* MAGGIE *at great length. But what is the use? What you really want to know is whether she was good-looking. No, she was not. Enter* MAGGIE, *who is not good-looking. When this is said, all is said. Enter* MAGGIE, *as it were, with her throat cut from ear to ear. She has a soft Scotch voice and a more resolute manner than is perhaps fitting to her plainness; and she stops short at sight of* JAMES *sprawling unconsciously in the company chair.*]

MAGGIE.   James, I wouldn't sit on the fine chair.

JAMES.   I forgot again.

[*But he wishes she had spoken more sharply. Even profanation of the fine chair has not roused her. She takes up her knitting, and they all suspect that she knows what they have been talking about.*]

MAGGIE.   You're late, David, it's nearly bed-time.

DAVID.   [*Finding the subject a safe one.*]   I was kept late at the public meeting.

ALICK.   [*Glad to get so far away from Galashiels.*]   Was it a good meeting?

DAVID.   Fairish.   [*With some heat.*]   That young John Shand *would* make a speech.

MAGGIE.   John Shand? Is that the student Shand?

DAVID.   The same. It's true he's a student at Glasgow University in the winter months, but in summer he's just the railway porter here; and I think it's very presumptuous

of a young lad like that to make a speech when he hasn't
a penny to bless himself with.

ALICK. The Shands were always an impudent family,
and jealous. I suppose that's the reason they haven't been
on speaking terms with us this six years. Was it a good
speech?

DAVID. [*Illustrating the family's generosity.*] It was
very fine; but he needn't have made fun of *me*.

MAGGIE. [*Losing a stitch.*] He dared?

DAVID. [*Depressed.*] You see I can *not* get started
on a speech without saying things like "In rising *for* to
make a few remarks."

JAMES. What's wrong with it?

DAVID. He mimicked me, and said "Will our worthy
chairman come for to go for to answer my questions?" and
so on; and they roared.

JAMES. [*Slapping his money pocket.*] The sacket.

DAVID. I did feel bitterly, father, the want of education.
[*Without knowing it, he has a beautiful way of pronounc-
ing this noble word.*]

MAGGIE. [*Holding out a kind hand to him.*] David.

ALICK. I've missed it sore, David. Even now I feel
the want of it in the very marrow of me. I'm shamed to
think I never gave you your chance. But when you were
young I was so desperate poor, how could I do it, Maggie?

MAGGIE. It wasn't possible, father.

ALICK. [*Gazing at the book-shelves.*] To be able to
understand these books! To up with them one at a time
and scrape them as clean as though they were a bowl of
brose. Lads, it's not to riches, it's to scholarship that I make
my humble bow.

JAMES. [*Who is good at bathos.*] There's ten yards of
them. And they were selected by the minister of Galashiels.
He said——

DAVID.   [*Quickly.*]   James.

JAMES.   I mean—I mean——

MAGGIE.   [*Calmly.*]   I suppose you mean what you say,
James.   I hear, David, that the minister of Galashiels is
to be married on that Miss Turnbull.

DAVID.   [*On guard.*]   So they were saying.

ALICK.   All I can say is she has made a poor bargain.

MAGGIE.   [*The damned.*]   I wonder at you, father.
He's a very nice gentleman.   I'm sure I hope he has chosen
wisely.

JAMES.   Not him.

MAGGIE.   [*Getting near her tragedy.*]   How can you
say that when you don't know her?   I expect she is full
of charm.

ALICK.   Charm?   It's the very word he used.

DAVID.   Havering idiot.

ALICK.   What *is* charm, exactly, Maggie?

MAGGIE.   Oh, it's—it's a sort of bloom on a woman.
If you have it, you don't need to have anything else; and
if you don't have it, it doesn't much matter what else you
have.   Some women, the few, have charm for all; and
most have charm for one.   But some have charm for none.

> [*Somehow she has stopped knitting.   Her men-*
> *folk are very depressed.*   JAMES *brings his fist*
> *down on the table with a bang.*]

JAMES.   [*Shouting.*]   I have a sister that has charm.

MAGGIE.   No, James, you haven't.

JAMES.   [*Rushing at her with the watch and chain.*]
Ha'e, Maggie.

> [*She lets them lie in her lap.*]

DAVID.   Maggie, would you like a silk?

MAGGIE.   What could I do with a silk?   [*With a gust*
of passion.]   You might as well dress up a little brown hen.

> [*They wriggle miserably.*]

JAMES. [*Stamping.*]   Bring him here to me.

MAGGIE.   Bring whom, James?

JAMES.   David, I would be obliged if you wouldn't kick me beneath the table.

MAGGIE. [*Rising.*]   Let's be practical; let's go to our beds.

> [*This reminds them that they have a job on hand in which she is not to share.*]

DAVID. [*Slily.*]   I don't feel very sleepy yet.

ALICK.   Nor me either.

JAMES.   You've just taken the very words out of my mouth.

DAVID. [*With unusual politeness.*]   Good-night to you, Maggie.

MAGGIE. [*Fixing the three of them.*]   *All* of you unsleepy, when, as is well known, ten o'clock is your regular bed-time?

JAMES.   Yes, it's common knowledge that we go to our beds at ten.   [*Chuckling.*]   That's what we're counting on.

MAGGIE.   Counting on?

DAVID.   You stupid whelp.

JAMES.   What have *I* done?

MAGGIE. [*Folding her arms.*]   There's something up. You've got to tell me, David.

DAVID. [*Who knows when he is beaten.*]   Go out and watch, James.

MAGGIE.   Watch?

> [JAMES *takes himself off, armed, as* MAGGIE *notices, with a stick.*]

DAVID. [*In his alert business way.*]   Maggie, there are burglars about.

MAGGIE.   Burglars?   [*She sits rigid, but she is not the kind to scream.*]

DAVID.   We hadn't meant for to tell you till we nabbed

them; but they've been in this room twice of late. We sat up last night waiting for them, and we're to sit up again to-night.

MAGGIE. The silver plate.

DAVID. It's all safe as yet. That makes us think that they were either frightened away these other times, or that they are coming back for to make a clean sweep.

MAGGIE. How did you get to know about this?

DAVID. It was on Tuesday that the polissman called at the quarry with a very queer story. He had seen a man climbing out at this window at ten past two.

MAGGIE. Did he chase him?

DAVID. It was so dark he lost sight of him at once.

ALICK. Tell her about the window.

DAVID. We've found out that the catch of the window has been pushed back by slipping the blade of a knife between the woodwork.

MAGGIE. David.

ALICK. The polissman said he was carrying a little carpet bag.

MAGGIE. The silver plate *is* gone.

DAVID. No, no. We were thinking that very likely he has bunches of keys in the bag.

MAGGIE. Or weapons.

DAVID. As for that, we have some pretty stout weapons ourselves in the umbrella stand. So, if you'll go to your bed, Maggie——

MAGGIE. Me? and my brothers in danger.

ALICK. There's just one of them.

MAGGIE. The polissman just saw one.

DAVID. [*Licking his palms.*] I would be very pleased if there were three of them.

MAGGIE. I watch with you. I would be very pleased if there were four of them.

DAVID. And they say she has no charm!

[JAMES *returns on tiptoe as if the burglars were beneath the table. He signs to every one to breathe no more, and then whispers his news.*]

JAMES. He's there. I had no sooner gone out than I saw him sliding down the garden wall, close to the rhubarbs.

ALICK. What's he like?

JAMES. He's an ugly customer. That's all I could see. There was a little carpet bag in his hand.

DAVID. That's him.

JAMES. He slunk into the rhodydendrons, and he's there now, watching the window.

DAVID. We have him. Out with the light.

[*The room is beautified by a chandelier fitted for three gas jets, but with the advance of progress one of these has been removed and the incandescent light put in its place. This alone is lit.* ALICK *climbs a chair, pulls a little chain, and the room is now but vaguely lit by the fire. It plays fitfully on four sparkling faces.*]

MAGGIE. Do you think he saw you, James?

JAMES. I couldn't say, but in any case I was too clever for him. I looked up at the stars, and yawned loud at them as if I was tremendous sleepy.

[*There is a long pause during which they are lurking in the shadows. At last they hear some movement, and they steal like ghosts from the room. We see* DAVID *turning out the lobby light; then the door closes and an empty room awaits the intruder with a shudder of expectancy. The window opens and shuts as softly as if this were a mother peering in to see whether her baby is asleep. Then the head of*

a man shows between the curtains. The re-
mainder of him follows. He is carrying a little
carpet bag. He stands irresolute; what puz-
zles him evidently is that the WYLIES *should*
have retired to rest without lifting that piece
of coal off the fire. He opens the door and
peeps into the lobby, listening to the wag-at-
the-wall clock. All seems serene, and he turns
on the light. We see him clearly now. He is
JOHN SHAND, *age twenty-one, boots muddy, as*
an indignant carpet can testify. He wears a
shabby topcoat and a cockerty bonnet; other-
wise he is in the wellworn corduroys of a rail-
way porter. His movements, at first stealthy,
become almost homely as he feels that he is
secure. He opens the bag and takes out a
bunch of keys, a small paper parcel, and a
black implement that may be a burglar's jemmy.
This cool customer examines the fire and piles
on more coal. With the keys he opens the
door of the bookcase, selects two large volumes,
and brings them to the table. He takes off his
topcoat and opens his parcel, which we now see
contains sheets of foolscap paper. His next
action shows that the "jemmy" is really a
ruler. He knows where the pen and ink are
kept. He pulls the fine chair nearer to the
table, sits on it, and proceeds to write, occa-
sionally dotting the carpet with ink as he stabs
the air with his pen. He is so occupied that
he does not see the door opening, and the WYLIE
family staring at him. They are armed with
sticks.]

ALICK. [*At last.*] When you're ready, John Shand.
[JOHN *hints back, and then has the grace to rise,
dogged and expressionless.*]

JAMES. [*Like a railway porter.*] Ticket, please.

DAVID. You can't think of anything clever for to go
for to say now, John.

MAGGIE. I hope you find that chair comfortable, young
man.

JOHN. I have no complaint to make against the chair.

ALICK. [*Who is really distressed.*] A native of the
town. The disgrace to your family. I feel pity for the
Shands this night.

JOHN. [*Glowering.*] I'll thank you, Mr. Wylie, not to
pity my family.

JAMES. Canny, canny.

MAGGIE. [*That sense of justice again.*] I think you
should let the young man explain. It mayn't be so bad as
we thought.

DAVID. Explain away, my billie.

JOHN. Only the uneducated would need an explanation.
I'm a student, [*with a little passion*] and I'm desperate for
want of books. You have all I want here; no use to you
but for display; well, I came here to study. I come twice
weekly. [*Amazement of his hosts.*]

DAVID. [*Who is the first to recover.*] By the window.

JOHN. Do you think a Shand would so far lower himself
as to enter your door? Well, is it a case for the police?

JAMES. It is.

MAGGIE. [*Not so much out of the goodness of her heart
as to patronise the Shands.*] It seems to me it's a case
for us all to go to our beds and leave the young man to
study; but not on that chair. [*And she wheels the chair
away from him.*]

JOHN. Thank you, Miss Maggie, but I couldn't be beholden to you.

JAMES. My opinion is that he's nobody, so out with him.

JOHN. Yes, out with me. And you'll be cheered to hear I'm likely to be a nobody for a long time to come.

DAVID. [*Who had been beginning to respect him.*] Are you a poor scholar?

JOHN. On the contrary, I'm a brilliant scholar.

DAVID. It's siller, then?

JOHN. [*Glorified by experiences he has shared with many a gallant soul.*] My first year at college I lived on a barrel of potatoes, and we had just a sofa-bed between two of us; when the one lay down the other had to get up. Do you think it was hardship? It was sublime. But this year I can't afford it. I'll have to stay on here, collecting the tickets of the illiterate, such as you, when I might be with Romulus and Remus among the stars.

JAMES. [*Summing up.*] Havers.

DAVID. [*In whose head some design is vaguely taking shape.*] Whisht, James. I must say, young lad, I like your spirit. Now tell me, what's your professors' opinion of your future.

JOHN. They think me a young man of extraordinary promise.

DAVID. You have a name here for high moral character.

JOHN. And justly.

DAVID. Are you serious-minded?

JOHN. I never laughed in my life.

DAVID. Who do you sit under in Glasgow?

JOHN. Mr. Flemister of the Sauchiehall High.

DAVID. Are you a Sabbath-school teacher?

JOHN. I am.

DAVID. One more question. Are you promised?

JOHN. To a lady?

DAVID. Yes.

JOHN. I've never given one of them a single word of encouragement. I'm too much occupied thinking about my career.

DAVID. So. [*He reflects, and finally indicates by a jerk of the head that he wishes to talk with his father behind the door.*]

JAMES. [*Longingly.*] Do you want me too?

[*But they go out without even answering him.*]

MAGGIE. I don't know what maggot they have in their heads, but sit down, young man, till they come back.

JOHN. My name's Mr. Shand, and till I'm called that I decline to sit down again in this house.

MAGGIE. Then I'm thinking, young sir, you'll have a weary wait.

[*While he waits you can see how pinched his face is. He is little more than a boy, and he seldom has enough to eat. DAVID and ALICK return presently, looking as sly as if they had been discussing some move on the dambrod, as indeed they have.*]

DAVID. [*Suddenly become genial.*] Sit down, Mr. Shand, and pull in your chair. You'll have a thimbleful of something to keep the cold out? [*Briskly.*] Glasses, Maggie.

[*She wonders, but gets glasses and decanter from the sideboard, which JAMES calls the chiffy. DAVID and ALICK, in the most friendly manner, also draw up to the table.*]

You're not a totaller, I hope?

JOHN. [*Guardedly.*] I'm practically a totaller.

DAVID. So are we. How do you take it? Is there any hot water, Maggie?

JOHN. If I take it at all, and I haven't made up my mind yet, I'll take it cold.

DAVID. You'll take it hot, James?

JAMES. *Also sitting at the table but completely befogged.*] No, I——

DAVID. [*Decisively.*] I think you'll take it hot, James.

JAMES. [*Sulking.*] I'll take it hot.

DAVID. The kettle, Maggie.

> [JAMES *has evidently to take it hot so that they can get at the business now on hand, while* MAGGIE *goes kitchenward for the kettle.*]

ALICK. Now, David, quick, before she comes back.

DAVID. Mr. Shand, we have an offer to make you.

JOHN. [*Warningly.*] No patronage.

ALICK. It's strictly a business affair.

DAVID. Leave it to me, father. It's this—— [*But to his annoyance the suspicious* MAGGIE *has already returned with the kettle.*] Maggie, don't you see that you're not wanted?

MAGGIE. [*Sitting down by the fire and resuming her knitting.*] I do, David.

DAVID. I have a proposition to put before Mr. Shand, and women are out of place in business transactions.

> [*The needles continue to click.*]

ALICK. [*Sighing.*] We'll have to let her bide, David.

DAVID. [*Sternly.*] Woman. [*But even this does not budge her.*] Very well then, sit there, but don't interfere, mind. Mr. Shand, we're willing, the three of us, to lay out £300 on your education if——

JOHN. Take care——

DAVID. [*Slowly, which is not his wont.*] On condition that five years from now, Maggie Wylie, if still unmarried, can claim to marry you, should such be her wish; the thing

to be perfectly open on her side, but you to be strictly
tied down.

JAMES. [*Enlightened.*] So, so.

DAVID. [*Resuming his smart manner.*] Now, what have
you to say? Decide.

JOHN. [*After a pause.*] I regret to say——

MAGGIE. It doesn't matter what he regrets to say, because I decide against it. And I think it was very ill-done
of you to make any such proposal.

DAVID. [*Without looking at her.*] Quiet, Maggie.

JOHN. [*Looking at her.*] I must say, Miss Maggie, I
don't see what reasons *you* can have for being so set
against it.

MAGGIE. If you would grow a beard, Mr. Shand, the
reasons wouldn't be quite so obvious.

JOHN. I'll never grow a beard.

MAGGIE. Then you're done for at the start.

ALICK. Come, come.

MAGGIE. Seeing I have refused the young man——

JOHN. Refused!

DAVID. That's no reason why we shouldn't have his
friendly opinion. Your objections, Mr. Shand?

JOHN. Simply, it's a one-sided bargain. I admit I'm
no catch at present; but what could a man of my abilities
not soar to with three hundred pounds? Something far
above what she could aspire to.

MAGGIE. Oh, indeed.

DAVID. The position is that without the three hundred
you can't soar.

JOHN. You have me there.

MAGGIE. Yes, but——

ALICK. You see *you're* safe-guarded, Maggie; you don't
need to take him unless you like, but he has to take you.

JOHN. That's an unfair arrangement also.

MAGGIE.   I wouldn't dream of it without that condition.

JOHN.   Then you *are* thinking of it?

MAGGIE.   Poof.

DAVID.   It's a good arrangement for you, Mr. Shand. The chances are you'll never have to go on with it, for in all probability she'll marry soon.

JAMES.   She's tremendous run after.

JOHN.   Even if that's true, it's just keeping me in reserve in case she misses doing better.

DAVID.   [*Relieved.*]   That's the situation in a nutshell.

JOHN.   Another thing.   Supposing I was to get fond of her?

ALICK.   [*Wistfully.*]   It's very likely.

JOHN.   Yes, and then suppose she was to give me the go-by?

DAVID.   You have to risk that.

JOHN.   Or take it the other way.   Supposing as I got to know her I *could not* endure her?

DAVID.   [*Suavely.*]   You have both to take risks.

JAMES.   [*Less suavely.*]   What you need, John Shand, is a clout on the head.

JOHN.   Three hundred pounds is no great sum.

DAVID.   You can take it or leave it.

ALICK.   No great sum for a student studying for the ministry!

JOHN.   Do you think that with that amount of money I would stop short at being a minister?

DAVID.   That's how I like to hear you speak.   A young Scotsman of your ability let loose upon the world with £300, what could he not do?   It's almost appalling to think of; especially if he went among the English.

JOHN.   What do you think, Miss Maggie?

MAGGIE.   [*Who is knitting.*]   I have no thoughts on the subject either way.

JOHN. [*After looking her over.*] What's her age? She looks young, but they say it's the curls that does it.

DAVID. [*Rather happily.*] She's one of those women who are eternally young.

JOHN. I can't take that for an answer.

DAVID. She's twenty-five.

JOHN. I'm just twenty-one.

JAMES. I read in a book that about four years' difference in the ages is the ideal thing. [*As usual he is disregarded.*]

DAVID. Well, Mr. Shand?

JOHN. [*Where is his mother!*] I'm willing if she's willing.

DAVID. Maggie?

MAGGIE. There can be no "if" about it. It must be an offer.

JOHN. A Shand give a Wylie such a chance to humiliate him? Never.

MAGGIE. Then all is off.

DAVID. Come, come, Mr. Shand, it's just a form.

JOHN. [*Reluctantly.*] Miss Maggie, will you?

MAGGIE. [*Doggedly.*] Is it an offer?

JOHN. [*Dourly.*] Yes.

MAGGIE. [*Rising.*] Before I answer I want first to give you a chance of drawing back.

DAVID. Maggie.

MAGGIE. [*Bravely.*] When they said that I have been run after they were misleading you. I'm without charm; nobody has ever been after me.

JOHN. Oho!

ALICK. They will be yet.

JOHN. [*The innocent.*] It shows at least that you haven't been after them.

[*His hosts exchange a self-conscious glance.*]

MAGGIE. One thing more; David said I'm twenty-five, I'm twenty-six.

JOHN. Aha!

MAGGIE. Now be practical. Do you withdraw from the bargain, or do you not?

JOHN. [*On reflection.*] It's a bargain.

MAGGIE. Then so be it.

DAVID. [*Hurriedly.*] And that's settled. Did you say you would take it hot, Mr. Shand?

JOHN. I think I'll take it neat.

> [*The others decide to take it hot, and there is some careful business here with the toddy ladles.*]

ALICK. Here's to you, and your career.

JOHN. Thank you.   To you, Miss Maggie. Had we not better draw up a legal document? Lawyer Crosbie could do it on the quiet.

DAVID. Should we do that, or should we just trust to one another's honour?

ALICK. [*Gallantly.*] Let Maggie decide.

MAGGIE. I think we would better have a legal document.

DAVID. We'll have it drawn up to-morrow. I was thinking the best way would be for to pay the money in five yearly instalments.

JOHN. I was thinking, better bank the whole sum in my name at once.

ALICK. I think David's plan's the best.

JOHN. I think not. Of course if it's not convenient to you——

DAVID. [*Touched to the quick.*] It's perfectly convenient. What do you say, Maggie?

MAGGIE. I agree with John.

DAVID. [*With an odd feeling that* MAGGIE *is now on the other side.*] Very well.

JOHN. Then as that's settled I think I'll be stepping. [*He is putting his papers back in the bag.*]

ALICK. [*Politely.*] If you would like to sit on at your books——

JOHN. As I can come at any orra time now I think I'll be stepping. [MAGGIE *helps him into his topcoat.*]

MAGGIE. Have you a muffler, John?

JOHN. I have. [*He gets it from his pocket.*]

MAGGIE. You had better put it twice round. [*She does this for him.*]

DAVID. Well, good-night to you, Mr. Shand.

ALICK. And good luck.

JOHN. Thank you. The same to you. And I'll cry in at your office in the morning before the 6.20 is due.

DAVID. I'll have the document ready for you. [*There is the awkward pause that sometimes follows great events.*] I think, Maggie, you might see Mr. Shand to the door.

MAGGIE. Certainly. [JOHN *is going by the window.*] This way, John.

[*She takes him off by the more usual exit.*]

DAVID. He's a fine frank fellow; and you saw how cleverly he got the better of me about banking the money. [*As the heads of the conspirators come gleefully together.*] I tell you, father, he has a grand business head.

ALICK. Lads, he's canny. He's cannier than any of us.

JAMES. Except maybe Maggie. He has no idea what a remarkable woman Maggie is.

ALECK. Best he shouldn't know. Men are nervous of remarkable women.

JAMES. She's a long time in coming back.

DAVID. [*Not quite comfortable.*] It's a good sign. H'sh. What sort of a night is it, Maggie?

MAGGIE. It's a little blowy.

[*She gets a large dust-cloth which is lying folded*

*on a shelf, and proceeds to spread it over the
fine chair. The men exchange self-conscious
glances.*]

DAVID. [*Stretching himself.*] Yes—well, well, oh yes.
It's getting late. What is it with you, father?

ALICK. I'm ten forty-two.

JAMES. I'm ten forty.

DAVID. Ten forty-two.

[*They wind up their watches.*]

MAGGIE. It's high time we were bedded. [*She puts
her hands on their shoulders lovingly, which is the very
thing they have been trying to avoid.*] You're very kind
to me.

DAVID. Havers.

ALICK. Havers.

JAMES. [*But this does not matter.*] Havers.

MAGGIE. [*A little dolefully.*] I'm a sort of sorry for
the young man, David.

DAVID. Not at all. You'll be the making of him. [*She
lifts the two volumes.*] Are you taking the books to your
bed, Maggie?

MAGGIE. Yes. I don't want him to know things I don't
know myself.

[*She departs with the books; and* ALICK *and*
DAVID, *the villains, now want to get away from
each other.*]

ALICK. Yes—yes. Oh yes—ay, man—it is so—umpha.
You'll lift the big coals off, David.

[*He wanders away to his spring mattress.* DAVID
removes the coals.]

JAMES. [*Who would like to sit down and have an argy-
bargy.*] It's a most romantical affair. [*But he gets no
answer.*] I wonder how it'll turn out? [*No answer.*]
She's queer, Maggie. I wonder how some clever writer has

never noticed how queer women are. It's my belief you could write a whole book about them. [DAVID *remains obdurate*.] It was very noble of her to tell him she's twenty-six. [*Muttering as he too wanders away*.] But I thought she was twenty-seven.

[DAVID *turns out the light*.]

End of Act I.

ACT II

Six years have elapsed and JOHN SHAND'S *great hour has come. Perhaps his great hour really lies ahead of him, perhaps he had it six years ago; it often passes us by in the night with such a faint call that we don't even turn in our beds. But according to the trumpets this is* JOHN'S *great hour; it is the hour for which he has long been working with his coat off; and now the coat is on again (broadcloth but ill-fitting), for there is no more to do but await results. He is standing for Parliament, and this is election night.*

As the scene discloses itself you get, so to speak, one of JOHN SHAND'S *posters in the face. Vote for* SHAND, SHAND, SHAND, SHAND. *Civil and Religious Liberty, Faith, Hope, Freedom. They are all fly-blown names for* SHAND. *Have a placard about* SHAND, *have a hundred placards about him, it is snowing* SHAND *to-night in Glasgow; take the paste out of your eye, and you will see that we are in one of Shand's committee rooms. It has been a hairdresser's emporium, but* SHAND, SHAND, SHAND *has swept through it like a wind, leaving nothing but the fixtures; why shave, why have your head doused in those basins when you can be brushed*

*and scraped and washed up for ever by simply voting
for* SHAND?

There are a few hard chairs for yelling SHAND *from, and
then rushing away. There is an iron spiral staircase
that once led to the ladies' hairdressing apartments,
but now leads to more* SHAND, SHAND, SHAND. *A glass
door at the back opens on to the shop proper, scream-
ing Civil and Religious Liberty,* SHAND, *as it opens, and
beyond is the street crammed with still more* SHAND
*pro and con. Men in every sort of garb rush in and out,
up and down the stair, shouting the magic word. Then
there is a lull, and down the stair comes* MAGGIE WYLIE,
*decidedly over-dressed in blue velvet and (let us get
this over) less good-looking than ever. She raises her
hands to heaven, she spins round like a little teetotum.
To her from the street, suffering from a determination
of the word* SHAND *to the mouth, rush* ALICK *and*
DAVID. ALICK *is thinner (being older),* DAVID *is stouter
(being older), and they are both in tweeds and silk
hats.*

MAGGIE.   David—have they—is he? quick, quick!

DAVID.   There's no news yet, no news.   It's terrible.

   [*The teetotum revolves more quickly.*]

ALICK.   For God's sake, Maggie, sit down.

MAGGIE.   I can't, I can't.

DAVID.   Hold her down.

   [*They press her into a chair;* JAMES *darts in,
   stouter also. His necktie has gone; he will never
   again be able to attend a funeral in that hat.*]

JAMES.   [*Wildly.*]   John Shand's the man for you.
John Shand's the man for you.   John Shand's the man for
you.

DAVID. [*Clutching him.*] Have you heard anything?

JAMES. Not a word.

ALICK. Look at her.

DAVID. Maggie. [*He goes on his knees beside her, pressing her to him in affectionate anxiety.*] It was mad of him to dare.

MAGGIE. It was grand of him.

ALICK. [*Moving about distraught.*] Insane ambition.

MAGGIE. Glorious ambition.

DAVID. Maggie, Maggie, my lamb, best be prepared for the worst.

MAGGIE. [*Husky.*] I am prepared.

ALICK. Six weary years has she waited for this night.

MAGGIE. Six brave years has John toiled for this night.

JAMES. And you could have had him, Maggie, at the end of five. The document says five.

MAGGIE. Do you think I grudge not being married to him yet? Was I to hamper him till the fight was won?

DAVID. [*With wrinkled brows.*] But if it's lost?

   [*She can't answer.*]

ALICK. [*Starting.*] What's that?

   [*The three listen at the door; the shouting dies
     down.*]

DAVID. They're terrible still; what can make them so still?

   [JAMES *spirits himself away.* ALICK *and* DAVID
     blanch to hear MAGGIE *speaking softly as if to*
     JOHN.]

MAGGIE. Did you say you had lost, John? Of course you would lose the first time, dear John. Six years. Very well, we'll begin another six to-night. You'll win yet. [*Fiercely.*] Never give in, John, never give in!

   [*The roar of the multitude breaks out again and
     comes rolling nearer.*]

DAVID.   I think he's coming.

> [JAMES *is fired into the room like a squeezed onion.*]

JAMES.   He's coming!

> [*They may go on speaking, but through the clang outside none could hear. The populace seem to be trying to take the committee room by assault. Out of the scrimmage a man emerges dishevelled and bursts into the room, closing the door behind him. It is* JOHN SHAND *in a five guinea suit, including the hat. There are other changes in him also, for he has been delving his way through loamy ground all those years. His right shoulder, which he used to raise to pound a path through the crowd, now remains permanently in that position. His mouth tends to close like a box. His eyes are tired, they need some one to pull the lids over them and send him to sleep for a week. But they are honest eyes still, and faithful, and could even light up his face at times with a smile, if the mouth would give a little help.*]

JOHN.   [*Clinging to a chair that he may not fly straight to heaven.*]   I'm in; I'm elected.   Majority two hundred and forty-four; I'm John Shand, *M.P.*

> [*The crowd have the news by this time and their roar breaks the door open.* JAMES *is off at once to tell them that he is to be* SHAND'S *brother-in-law. A teardrop clings to* ALICK'S *nose;* DAVID *hits out playfully at* JOHN, *and* JOHN *in an ecstasy returns the blow.*]

DAVID.   Fling yourself at the door, father, and bar them out.   Maggie, what keeps you so quiet now?

MAGGIE. [*Weak in her limbs.*] You're sure you're in, John.

JOHN. Majority 244. I've beaten the baronet. I've done it, Maggie, and not a soul to help me; I've done it alone. [*His voice breaks; you could almost pick up the pieces.*] I'm as hoarse as a crow, and I have to address the Cowcaddens Club yet; David, pump some oxygen into me.

DAVID. Certainly, Mr. Shand. [*While he does it, MAGGIE is seeing visions.*]

ALICK. What are you doing, Maggie?

MAGGIE. This is the House of Commons, and I'm John, catching the Speaker's eye for the first time. Do you see a queer little old wifie sitting away up there in the Ladies' Gallery? That's me. Mr. Speaker, sir, I rise to make my historic maiden speech. I am no orator, sir; voice from Ladies' Gallery, "Are you not, John? you'll soon let them see that"; cries of "Silence, woman," and general indignation. Mr. Speaker, sir, I stand here diffidently with my eyes on the Treasury Bench; voice from the Ladies' Gallery, "And you'll soon have your coat-tails on it, John"; loud cries of "Remove that little old wifie," in which she is forcibly ejected, and the honourable gentleman resumes his seat in a torrent of admiring applause.

[ALICK *and* DAVID *waggle their proud heads.*]

JOHN. [*Tolerantly.*] Maggie, Maggie.

MAGGIE. You're not angry with me, John?

JOHN. No, no.

MAGGIE. But you glowered.

JOHN. I was thinking of Sir Peregrine. Just because I beat him at the poll he took a shabby revenge; he congratulated me in French, a language I haven't taken the trouble to master.

MAGGIE. [*Becoming a little taller.*] Would it help you,

John, if you were to marry a woman that could speak French?

DAVID. [*Quickly.*] Not at all.

MAGGIE. [*Gloriously.*] Mon cher Jean, laissez-moi parler le français, voulez-vous un interprète?

JOHN. Hullo!

MAGGIE. Je suis la sœur française de mes deux frères écossais.

DAVID. [*Worshipping her.*] She's been learning French.

JOHN. [*Lightly.*] Well done.

MAGGIE. [*Grandly.*] They're arriving.

ALICK. Who?

MAGGIE. Our guests. This is London, and Mrs. John Shand is giving her first reception. [*Airily.*] Have I told you, darling, who are coming to-night? There's that dear Sir Peregrine. [*To* ALICK.] Sir Peregrine, this *is* a pleasure. Avez-vous. . . . So sorry we beat you at the poll.

JOHN. I'm doubting the baronet would sit on you, Maggie.

MAGGIE. I've invited a lord to sit on the baronet. *Voilà!*

DAVID. [*Delighted.*] You thing! You'll find the lords expensive.

MAGGIE. Just a little cheap lord. [JAMES *enters importantly.*] My dear Lord Cheap, this is kind of you.

> [JAMES *hopes that* MAGGIE'S *reason is not unbalanced.*]

DAVID. [*Who really ought to have had education.*] How de doo, Cheap?

JAMES. [*Bewildered.*] Maggie——

MAGGIE. Yes, do call me Maggie.

ALICK. [*Grinning.*] She's practising her first party, James. The swells are at the door.

JAMES. [*Heavily.*] That's what I came to say. They *are* at the door.

JOHN. Who?

JAMES. The swells; a carriage and pair. [*He gives* JOHN *three cards.*]

JOHN. "Mr. Tenterden."

DAVID. Him that was speaking for you?

JOHN. The same. He's a whip and an Honourable. "Lady Sybil Tenterden." [*Frowns.*] Her! She's his sister.

MAGGIE. A married woman?

JOHN. No. "The Comtesse de la Brière."

MAGGIE. [*The scholar.*] She must be French.

JOHN. Yes; I think she's some relation. She's a widow.

JAMES. But what am I to say to them? [*"Mr. Shand's compliments, and he will be proud to receive them" is the very least that the Wylies expect.*]

JOHN. [*Who was evidently made for great ends.*] Say I'm very busy, but if they care to wait I hope presently to give them a few minutes.

JAMES. [*Thunderstruck.*] Good God, Mr. Shand!

    [*But it makes him* JOHN'S *more humble servant than ever, and he departs with the message.*]

JOHN. [*Not unaware of the sensation he has created.*] I'll go up and let the crowd see me from the window.

MAGGIE. But—but—what are we to do with these ladies?

JOHN. [*As he tramps upwards.*] It's your reception, Maggie; this will prove you.

MAGGIE. [*Growing smaller.*] Tell me what you know about this Lady Sybil?

JOHN. The only thing I know about her is that she thinks me vulgar.

MAGGIE. You?

JOHN. She has attended some of my meetings, and I'm told she said that.

MAGGIE. What could the woman mean?

JOHN. I wonder. When I come down I'll ask her.

> [*With his departure* MAGGIE'S *nervousness increases.*]

ALICK. [*Encouragingly.*] In at them, Maggie, with your French.

MAGGIE. It's all slipping from me, father.

DAVID. [*Gloomily.*] I'm sure to say "for to come for to go."

> [*The new-comers glorify the room, and* MAGGIE *feels that they have lifted her up with the tongs and deposited her in one of the basins. They are far from intending to be rude; it is not their fault that thus do swans scatter the ducks. They do not know that they are guests of the family, they think merely that they are waiting with other strangers in a public room; they undulate enquiringly, and if* MAGGIE *could undulate in return she would have no cause for offence. But she suddenly realises that this is an art as yet denied her, and that though* DAVID *might buy her evening gowns as fine as theirs (and is at this moment probably deciding to do so), she would look better carrying them in her arms than on her person. She also feels that to emerge from wraps as they are doing is more difficult than to plank your money on the counter for them. The* COMTESSE *she could forgive, for she is old; but* LADY SYBIL *is young and beautiful and comes lazily to rest like a stately ship of Tarsus.*]

COMTESSE. [*Smiling divinely, and speaking with such a pretty accent.*] I hope one is not in the way. We were told we might wait.

MAGGIE. [*Bravely climbing out of the basin.*] Certainly
—I am sure—if you will be so—it is——
   [*She knows that* DAVID *and her father are very
   sorry for her.*]
   [*A high voice is heard orating outside.*]

SYBIL. [*Screwing her nose deliciously.*] He is at it
again, Auntie.

COMTESSE. Mon Dieu! [*Like one begging pardon of
the universe.*] It is Mr. Tenterden, you understand, making one more of his delightful speeches to the crowd. *Would*
you be so charming as to shut the door?
   [*This to* DAVID *in such appeal that she is evidently
   making the petition of her life.* DAVID *saves
   her.*]

MAGGIE. [*Determined not to go under.*] J'espère que
vous—trouvez—cette—réunion—intéressante?

COMTESSE. Vous parlez français? Mais c'est charmant!
Voyons, causons un peu. Racontez-moi tout de ce grand
homme, toutes les choses merveilleuses qu'il a faites.

MAGGIE. I—I—Je connais—[*Alas!*]

COMTESSE. [*Naughtily.*] Forgive me, Mademoiselle, I
thought you spoke French.

SYBIL. [*Who knows that* DAVID *admires her shoulders.*]
How wicked of you, Auntie. [*To* MAGGIE.] I assure you
none of us can understand her when she gallops at that
pace.

MAGGIE. [*Crushed.*] It doesn't matter. I will tell Mr.
Shand that you are here.

SYBIL. [*Drawling.*] Please don't trouble him. We are
really only waiting till my brother recovers and can take us
back to our hotel.

MAGGIE. I'll tell him.
   [*She is glad to disappear up the stair.*]

COMTESSE. The lady seems distressed. Is she a relation of Mr. Shand?

DAVID. Not for to say a relation. She's my sister. Our name is Wylie.

[*But granite quarries are nothing to them.*]

COMTESSE. How do you do. You are the committee man of Mr. Shand?

DAVID. No, just friends.

COMTESSE. [*Gaily to the basins.*] Aha! I know you. Next, please! Sybil, do you weigh yourself, or are you asleep?

[LADY SYBIL *has sunk indolently into a weighing-chair.*]

SYBIL. Not quite, Auntie.

COMTESSE. [*The mirror of la politesse.*] Tell me all about Mr. Shand. Was it here that he—picked up the pin?

DAVID. The pin?

COMTESSE. As *I* have read, a self-made man always begins by picking up a pin. After that, as the memoirs say, his rise was rapid.

[DAVID, *however, is once more master of himself, and indeed has begun to tot up the cost of their garments.*]

DAVID. It wasn't a pin he picked up, my lady; it was £300.

ALICK. [*Who feels that* JOHN'S *greatness has been out-side the conversation quite long enough.*] And his rise wasn't so rapid, just at first, David!

DAVID. He had his fight. His original intention was to become a minister; he's university-educated, you know; he's not a workingman member.

ALICK. [*With reverence.*] He's an M.A. But while he was a student he got a place in an iron cementer's business.

COMTESSE. [*Now far out of her depths.*]   Iron cementer?

DAVID.   They scrape boilers.

COMTESSE.   I see.   The fun men have, Sybil!

DAVID. [*With some solemnity.*]   There have been millions made in scraping boilers.   They say, father, he went into business so as to be able to pay off the £300.

ALICK. [*Slily.*]   So I've heard.

COMTESSE.   Aha—it was a loan?

> [DAVID *and* ALICK *are astride their great subject now.*]

DAVID.   No, a gift—of a sort—from some well-wishers. But they wouldn't hear of his paying it off, father!

ALICK.   Not them!

COMTESSE. [*Restraining an impulse to think of other things.*]   That was kind, charming.

ALICK. [*With a look at* DAVID.]   Yes.   Well, my lady, he developed a perfect genius for the iron-cementing.

DAVID.   But his ambition wasn't satisfied.   Soon he had public life in his eye.   As a heckler he was something fearsome; they had to seat him on the platform for to keep him quiet.   Next they had to let him into the Chair.   After that he did all the speaking; he cleared all roads before him like a fire-engine; and when this vacancy occurred, you could hardly say it did occur, so quickly did he step into it.   My lady, there are few more impressive sights in the world than a Scotsman on the make.

COMTESSE.   I can well believe it.   And now he has said farewell to boilers?

DAVID. [*Impressively.*]   Not at all; the firm promised if he was elected for to make him their London manager at £800 a year.

COMTESSE.   There is a strong man for you, Sybil; but I believe you *are* asleep.

SYBIL. [*Stirring herself.*] Honestly I'm not. [*Sweetly to the others.*] But *would* you mind finding out whether my brother is drawing to a close?

[DAVID *goes out, leaving poor* ALICK *marooned. The* COMTESSE *is kind to him.*]

COMTESSE. Thank you very much. [*Which helps* ALICK *out.*] Don't you love a strong man, sleepy head?

SYBIL. [*Preening herself.*] I never met one.

COMTESSE. Neither have I. But if you *did* meet one, would he wake you up?

SYBIL. I dare say he would find there were two of us.

COMTESSE. [*Considering her.*] Yes, I think he would. Ever been in love, you cold thing?

SYBIL. [*Yawning.*] I have never shot up in flame, Auntie.

COMTESSE. Think you could manage it?

SYBIL. If Mr. Right came along.

COMTESSE. As a girl of to-day it would be your duty to tame him.

SYBIL. As a girl of to-day I would try to do my duty.

COMTESSE. And if it turned out that *he* tamed you instead?

SYBIL. He would have to do that if he were *my* Mr. Right.

COMTESSE. And then?

SYBIL. Then, of course, I should adore him. Auntie, I think if I ever really love it will be like Mary Queen of Scots, who said of her Bothwell that she could follow him round the world in her nighty.

COMTESSE. My petite!

SYBIL. I believe I mean it.

COMTESSE. Oh, it is quite my conception of your character. Do you know, I am rather sorry for this Mr. John Shand.

SYBIL. [*Opening her fine eyes.*] Why? He is quite a boor, is he not?

COMTESSE. For that very reason. Because his great hour is already nearly sped. That wild bull manner that moves the multitude—they will laugh at it in your House of Commons.

SYBIL. [*Indifferent.*] I suppose so.

COMTESSE. Yet if he had education——

SYBIL. Have we not been hearing how superbly he is educated?

COMTESSE. It is such as you or me that he needs to educate him now. *You* could do it almost too well.

SYBIL. [*With that pretty stretch of neck.*] I am not sufficiently interested. I retire in your favour. How would you begin?

COMTESSE. By asking him to drop in, about five, of course. By the way, I wonder is there a Mrs. Shand?

SYBIL. I have no idea. But they marry young.

COMTESSE. If there is not, there is probably a lady waiting for him, somewhere in a boiler.

SYBIL. I dare say.

[MAGGIE *descends.*]

MAGGIE. Mr. Shand will be down directly.

COMTESSE. Thank you. Your brother has been giving us such an interesting account of his career. I forget, Sybil, whether he said that he was married.

MAGGIE. No, he's not married; but he will be soon.

COMTESSE. Ah! [*She is merely making conversation.*] A friend of yours?

MAGGIE. [*Now a scorner of herself.*] I don't think much of her.

COMTESSE. In that case, tell me all about her.

MAGGIE. There's not much to tell. She's common, and stupid. One of those who go in for self-culture; and then when the test comes they break down. [*With sinister enjoyment.*] She'll be the ruin of him.

COMTESSE. But is not that sad! Figure to yourself how many men with greatness before them have been shipwrecked by marrying in the rank from which they sprang.

MAGGIE. I've told her that.

COMTESSE. But she will not give him up?

MAGGIE. No.

SYBIL. Why should she if he cares for her? What is her name?

MAGGIE. It's—Maggie.

COMTESSE. [*Still uninterested.*] Well, I am afraid that Maggie is to do for John. [JOHN *comes down.*] Ah, our hero!

JOHN. Sorry I have kept you waiting. The Comtesse?

COMTESSE. And my niece Lady Sybil Tenterden. [SYBIL'S *head inclines on its stem.*] She is not really all my niece; I mean I am only half of her aunt. What a triumph, Mr. Shand!

JOHN. Oh, pretty fair, pretty fair. Your brother has just finished addressing the crowd, Lady Sybil.

SYBIL. Then we must not detain Mr. Shand, Auntie.

COMTESSE. [*Who unless her heart is touched thinks insincerity charming.*] Only one word. I heard you speak last night. Sublime! Just the sort of impassioned eloquence that your House of Commons loves.

JOHN. It's very good of you to say so.

COMTESSE. But we must run. *Bon soir.*

[SYBIL *bows as to some one far away.*]

JOHN. Good-night, Lady Sybil. I hear you think I'm vulgar.

[*Eyebrows are raised.*]

COMTESSE. My dear Mr. Shand, what absurd——

John. I was told she said that after hearing me speak.

Comtesse. Quite a mistake, I——

John. [*Doggedly.*] Is it not true?

Sybil. [*"Waking up."*] You seem to know, Mr. Shand; and as you press me so unnecessarily—well, yes, that is how you struck me.

Comtesse. My child!

Sybil. [*Who is a little agitated.*] He would have it.

John. [*Perplexed.*] What's the matter? I just wanted to know, because if it's true I must alter it.

Comtesse. There, Sybil, see how he values your good opinion.

Sybil. [*Her svelte figure giving like a fly-rod.*] It is very nice of you to put it in that way, Mr. Shand. Forgive me.

John. But I don't quite understand yet. Of course, it can't matter to me, Lady Sybil, what you think of me; what I mean is, that I mustn't be vulgar if it would be injurious to my career.

[*The fly-rod regains its rigidity.*]

Sybil. I see. No, of course, I could not affect your career, Mr. Shand.

John. [*Who quite understands that he is being challenged.*] That's so, Lady Sybil, meaning no offence.

Sybil. [*Who has a naughty little impediment in her voice when she is most alluring.*] Of course not. And we are friends again?

John. Certainly.

Sybil. Then I hope you will come to see me in London as I present no terrors.

John. [*He is a man, is* John.] I'll be very pleased.

Sybil. Any afternoon about five.

John. Much obliged. And you can teach me the things I don't know yet, if you'll be so kind.

SYBIL. [*The impediment becoming more assertive.*] If you wish it, I shall do my best.

JOHN. Thank you, Lady Sybil. And who knows there may be one or two things I can teach you.

SYBIL. [*It has now become an angel's hiccough.*] Yes, we can help one another. Good-bye till then.

JOHN. Good-bye. Maggie, the ladies are going.

> [*During this skirmish* MAGGIE *has stood apart.
> At the mention of her name they glance at one
> another.* JOHN *escorts* SYBIL, *but the* COMTESSE
> *turns back. She says:*

"Are you, then, *the* Maggie? [MAGGIE *nods rather defiantly and the* COMTESSE *is distressed.*] But if I had known I would not have said those things. Please forgive an old woman."

"It doesn't matter."

"I—I dare say it will be all right. Mademoiselle, if I were you I would not encourage those tête-à-têtes with Lady Sybil. I am the rude one, but she is the dangerous one; and I am afraid his impudence has attracted her. *Bon voyage,* Miss Maggie."

"Good-bye—but I *can* speak French. Je parle français. Isn't that right?"

"But, yes, it is excellent. [*Making things easy for her.*] C'est très bien."

"Je me suis embrouillée—la dernière fois."

"Good! Shall I speak more slowly?"

"No, no. Non, non, faster, faster."

"J'admire votre courage!"

"Je comprends chaque mot."

"Parfait! Bravo!"

"Voilà!"

"Superbe!"

> [*The* COMTESSE *goes, applauding; and* MAGGIE

has a moment of elation, which however has passed before JOHN *returns for his hat.*]

"Have you more speaking to do, John?"

[*He is somehow in high good-humour.*]

"I must run across and address the Cowcaddens Club. [*He sprays his throat with a hand-spray.*] I wonder if I *am* vulgar, Maggie?"

"You are not, but *I* am."

"Not that *I* can see."

"Look how over-dressed I am, John! I knew it was too showy when I ordered it, and yet I could not resist the thing. But I will tone down, I will. What did you think of Lady Sybil?"

"That young woman had better be careful. She's a bit of a beson, Maggie."

"She's beautiful, John."

"She has a neat way of stretching herself. For playing with she would do as well as another."

[MAGGIE *looks at him wistfully.*]

"You couldn't stay and have a talk for a few minutes?"

"If you want me, Maggie. The longer you keep them waiting, the more they think of you."

"When are you to announce that we're to be married, John?"

"I won't be long. You've waited a year more than you need have done, so I think it's your due I should hurry things now."

"I think it's noble of you."

"Not at all, Maggie; the nobleness has been yours in waiting so patiently. And your brothers would insist on it at any rate. They're watching me like cats with a mouse."

"It's so little I've done to help."

"Three hundred pounds."

"I'm getting a thousand per cent. for it."

"And very pleased I am you should think so, Maggie."

"Is it terrible hard to you, John?"

"It's not hard at all. I can say truthfully, Maggie, that all, or nearly all, I've seen of you in these six years has gone to increase my respect for you."

"Respect!"

"And a bargain's a bargain."

"If it wasn't that you're so glorious to me, John, I would let you off."

[*There is a gleam in his eye, but he puts it out.*]

"In my opinion, Maggie, we'll be a very happy pair."

[*She accepts this eagerly.*]

"We know each other so well, John, don't we?"

"I'm an extraordinary queer character, and I suppose nobody knows me well except myself; but I know you, Maggie, to the very roots of you."

[*She magnanimously lets this remark alone.*]

"And it's not as if there was any other woman you—fancied more, John."

"There's none whatever."

"If there ever should be—oh, if there ever should be! Some woman with charm."

"Maggie, you forget yourself. There couldn't be another woman once I was a married man."

"One has heard of such things."

"Not in Scotsmen, Maggie; not in Scotsmen."

"I've sometimes thought, John, that the difference between us and the English is that the Scotch are hard in all other respects but soft with women, and the English are hard with women but soft in all other respects."

"You've forgotten the grandest moral attribute of a Scotsman, Maggie, that he'll do nothing which might damage his career."

"Ah, but John, whatever you do, you do it so tremendously; and if you were to love, what a passion it would be."

"There's something in that, I suppose."

"And then, what could I do? For the desire of my life now, John, is to help you to get everything you want, except just that I want you to have me, too."

"We'll get on fine, Maggie."

"You're just making the best of it. They say that love is sympathy, and if that's so mine must be a great love for you, for I see all you are feeling this night and bravely hiding; I feel for you as if I was John Shand myself." [JOHN *sighs.*]

"I had best go to the meeting, Maggie."

"Not yet. Can you look me in the face, John, and deny that there is surging within you a mighty desire to be free, to begin the new life untrammelled?"

"Leave such maggots alone, Maggie."

"It's a shame of me not to give you up."

"I would consider you a very foolish woman if you did."

"If I were John Shand I would no more want to take Maggie Wylie with me through the beautiful door that has opened wide for you than I would want to take an old pair of shoon. Why don't you bang the door in my face, John?" [*A tremor runs through* JOHN.]

"A bargain's a bargain, Maggie."

> [MAGGIE *moves about, an eerie figure, breaking into little cries. She flutters round him, threateningly.*]

"Say one word about wanting to get out of it, and I'll put the lawyers on you."

"Have I hinted at such a thing?"

"The document holds you hard and fast."

"It does."

> [*She gloats miserably.*]

"The woman never rises with the man. I'll drag you down, John. I'll drag you down."

"Have no fear of that, I won't let you. I'm too strong."

"You'll miss the prettiest thing in the world, and all owing to me."

"What's that?"

"Romance."

"Poof."

"All's cold and grey without it, John. They that have had it have slipped in and out of heaven."

"You're exaggerating, Maggie."

"You've worked so hard, you've had none of the fun that comes to most men long before they're your age."

"I never was one for fun. I cannot call to mind, Maggie, ever having laughed in my life."

"You have no sense of humor."

"Not a spark."

"I've sometimes thought that if you had, it might make you fonder of me. I think one needs a sense of humor to be fond of me."

"I remember reading of some one that said it needed a surgical operation to get a joke into a Scotsman's head."

"Yes, that's been said."

"What beats me, Maggie, is how you could insert a joke with an operation."

[*He considers this and gives it up.*]

"That's not the kind of fun I was thinking of. I mean fun with the lasses, John—gay, jolly, harmless fun. They could be impudent fashionable beauties now, stretching themselves to attract you, like that hiccoughing little devil, and running away from you, and crooking their fingers to you to run after them."

[JOHN *draws a big breath.*]

"No, I never had that."

"It's every man's birthright, and you would have it now but for me."

"I can do without, Maggie."

"It's like missing out all the Saturdays."

"You feel sure, I suppose, that an older man wouldn't suit you better, Maggie?"

"I couldn't feel surer of anything. You're just my ideal."

"Yes, yes. Well, that's as it should be."

[*She threatens him again.*]

"David has the document. It's carefully locked away."

"He would naturally take good care of it."

[*The pride of the Wylies deserts her.*]

"John, I make you a solemn promise that, in consideration of the circumstances of our marriage, if you should ever fall in love I'll act differently from other wives."

"There will be no occasion, Maggie."

[*Her voice becomes tremulous.*]

"John, David doesn't have the document. He thinks he has, but I have it here."

[*Somewhat heavily* JOHN *surveys the fatal paper.*]

"Well do I mind the look of it, Maggie. Yes, yes, that's it. Umpha."

"You don't ask why I've brought it."

"Why did you?"

"Because I thought I might perhaps have the courage and the womanliness to give it back to you. [JOHN *has a brief dream.*] Will you never hold it up against me in the future that I couldn't do that?"

"I promise you, Maggie, I never will."

"To go back to the Pans and take up my old life there, when all these six years my eyes have been centered on this night! I've been waiting for this night as long as you have been; and now to go back there, and wizen and dry up, when I might be married to John Shand!"

"And you will be, Maggie. You have my word."

"Never—never—never. [*She tears up the document. He remains seated immovable, but the gleam returns to his eye. She rages first at herself and then at him.*] I'm a fool, a fool, to let you go. I tell you, you'll rue this day, for you need me, you'll come to grief without me. There's nobody can help you as I could have helped you. I'm essential to your career, and you're blind not to see it."

"What's that, Maggie? In no circumstances would I allow any meddling with my career."

"You would never have known I was meddling with it. But that's over. Don't be in too great a hurry to marry, John. Have your fling with the beautiful dolls first. Get the whiphand of the haughty ones, John. Give them their licks. Every time they hiccough let them have an extra slap in memory of me. And be sure to remember this, my man, that the one who marries you will find you out."

"Find me out?"

"However careful a man is, his wife always finds out his failings."

"I don't know, Maggie, to what failings you refer.

> [*The Cowcaddens Club has burst its walls, and is pouring this way to raise the new Member on its crest. The first wave hurls itself against the barber's shop with cries of* "SHAND, SHAND, SHAND." *For a moment* JOHN *stems the torrent by planting his back against the door.*]

You are acting under an impulse, Maggie, and I can't take advantage of it. Think the matter over, and we'll speak about it in the morning."

"No, I can't go through it again. It ends to-night and now. Good luck, John."

[*She is immediately submerged in the sea that
surges through the door, bringing much wreckage with it. In a moment the place is so full that
another cupful could not find standing room.
Some slippery ones are squeezed upwards and remain aloft as warnings. JOHN has jumped on to
the stair, and harangues the flood vainly like another Canute. It is something about freedom
and noble minds, and, though unheard, goes
to all heads, including the speaker's. By the
time he is audible sentiment has him for her
own.*]

"But, gentlemen, one may have too much even of freedom. [*No, no.*] Yes, Mr. Adamson. One may want to
be tied. [*Never, never.*] I say yes, Willie Cameron; and
I have found a young lady who I am proud to say is willing
to be tied to me. I'm to be married. [*Uproar.*] Her
name's Miss Wylie. [*Transport.*] Quiet; she's here now.
[*Frenzy.*] She was here! Where are you, Maggie?" [*A
small voice*—"I'm here." *A hundred great voices*—"Where,
where—where?" *The small voice*—"I'm so little none of
you can see me."]

[*Three men, name of Wylie, buffet their way
forward. Anon is heard the voice of DAVID.*]

"James, father, have you grip of her?"

"We've got her."

"Then hoist her up."

[*The queer little elated figure is raised aloft.
With her fingers she can just touch the stars.
Not unconscious of the nobility of his behaviour, the hero of the evening points an impressive finger at her.*]

"Gentlemen, the future Mrs. John Shand!" ["*Speech,*

speech."] "No, no, being a lady she can't make a speech.
But——"

[*The heroine of the evening surprises him.*]
"I can make a speech, and I will make a speech, and it's
in two words, and they're these—[*holding out her arms to
enfold all the members of the Cowcaddens Club*]—My
Constituents!" [*Dementia.*]

End of Act II.

ACT III

A few minutes ago the COMTESSE DE LA BRIÈRE, *who has not
recently been in England, was shown into the London
home of the* SHANDS. *Though not sufficiently interested to express her surprise in words, she raised her
eyebrows on finding herself in a charming room; she
had presumed that the* SHAND *scheme of decoration
would be as impossible as themselves.*

*It is the little room behind the dining-room for which Eng-
lish architects have long been famous; "Make something of this, and you will indeed be a clever one,"
they seem to say to you as they unveil it. The* COM-
TESSE *finds that* JOHN *has undoubtedly made something
of it. It is his "study" [mon Dieu, the words these
English use!] and there is nothing in it that offends;
there is so much not in it too that might so easily
have been there. It is not in the least ornate; there
are no colours quarreling with each other [unseen,
unheard by the blissful occupant of the revolving
chair]; the* COMTESSE *has not even the gentle satisfaction of noting a "suite" in stained oak. Nature*

might have taken a share in the decorations, so restful
are they to the eyes; it is the working room of a man
of culture, probably lately down from Oxford; at a
first meeting there is nothing in it that pretends to be
what it is not. Our visitor is a little disappointed, but
being fair-minded blows her absent host a kiss for
disappointing her.

He has even, she observes with a twinkle, made something
of the most difficult of his possessions, the little wife.
For MAGGIE, *who is here receiving her, has been quite*
creditably toned down. He has put her into a little
grey frock that not only deals gently with her personal
defects, but is in harmony with the room. Evidently,
however, she has not "risen" with him, for she is as
stupid as ever; the COMTESSE, *who remembers having*
liked her the better of the two, could shake her for
being so stupid. For instance, why is she not asserting
herself in that other apartment?

The other apartment is really a correctly solemn dining-
room, of which we have a glimpse through partly open
folding-doors. At this moment it is harbouring MR.
SHAND'S *ladies' committee, who sit with pens and fools-*
cap round the large table, awaiting the advent of their
leader.   There are nobly wise ones and some foolish
ones among them, for we are back in the strange days
when it was considered "unwomanly" for women to
have minds. The COMTESSE *peeps at them with curi-*
osity, as they arrange their papers or are ushered into
the dining-room through a door which we cannot see.
To her frivolous ladyship they are a species of wild
fowl, and she is specially amused to find her niece
among them. She demands an explanation as soon
as the communicating doors close.

"Tell me since when has my dear Sybil become one of these ladies? It is not like her."

> [MAGGIE *is obviously not clever enough to under-*
> *stand the woman question. Her eye rests long-*
> *ingly on a half-finished stocking as she inno-*
> *cently but densely replies*:

"I think it was about the time that my husband took up their cause."

> [*The* COMTESSE *has been hearing tales of* LADY
> SYBIL *and the barbarian; and after having the*
> *grace to hesitate, she speaks with the directness*
> *for which she is famed in Mayfair.*]

"Mrs. Shand, excuse me for saying that if half of what I hear be true, your husband is seeing that lady a great deal too often. [MAGGIE *is expressionless; she reaches for her stocking, whereat her guest loses patience.*] Oh, mon Dieu, put that down; you can buy them at two francs the pair. Mrs. Shand, why do not you compel yourself to take an intelligent interest in your husband's work?"

"I typewrite his speeches."

"But do you know what they are about?"

"They are about various subjects."

"Oh!"

> [*Did* MAGGIE *give her an unseen quizzical glance*
> *before demurely resuming the knitting? One*
> *is not certain, as* JOHN *has come in, and this*
> *obliterates her. A "Scotsman on the make,"*
> *of whom* DAVID *has spoken reverently, is still*
> *to be read—in a somewhat better bound vol-*
> *ume—in* JOHN SHAND'S *person; but it is as dog-*
> *gedly honest a face as ever; and he champions*
> *women, not for personal ends, but because his*
> *blessed days of poverty gave him a light upon*

*their needs. His self-satisfaction, however, has
increased, and he has pleasantly forgotten some
things. For instance, he can now call out
"Porter" at railway stations without dropping
his hands for the barrow.* MAGGIE *introduces
the* COMTESSE, *and he is still undaunted.*]

"I remember you well—at Glasgow."

"It must be quite two years ago, Mr. Shand."

[JOHN *has no objection to showing that he has
had a classical education.*]

"Tempus fugit, Comtesse."

"I have not been much in this country since then, and
I return to find you a coming man."

[*Fortunately his learning is tempered with
modesty.*]

"Oh, I don't know, I don't know."

"The Ladies' Champion."

[*His modesty is tempered with a respect for
truth.*]

"Well, well."

"And you are about, as I understand, to introduce a bill
to give women an equal right with men to grow beards
[*which is all she knows about it.* JOHN *takes the remark
literally.*]

"There's nothing about beards in it, Comtesse. [*She
gives him time to cogitate, and is pleased to note that
there is no result.*] Have you typed my speech, Maggie?"

"Yes; twenty-six pages." [*She produces it from a
drawer.*]

[*Perhaps* JOHN *wishes to impress the visitor.*]

"I'm to give the ladies' committee a general idea of it.
Just see, Maggie, if I know the peroration. 'In conclusion,
Mr. Speaker, these are the reasonable demands of every

intelligent Englishwoman'—I had better say British woman—'and I am proud to nail them to my flag' "——

[*The visitor is properly impressed.*]

"Oho! defies his leaders!"

" 'So long as I can do so without embarrassing the Government.' "

"Ah, ah, Mr. Shand!"

" 'I call upon the Front Bench, sir, loyally but firmly' "——

"Firm again!"

". . . . 'either to accept my Bill, or to promise *without delay* to bring in one of their own; and if they decline to do so I solemnly warn them that though I will not press the matter to a division just now' "——

"Ahem!"

" 'I will bring it forward again in the near future.' And now, Comtesse, *you* know that I'm not going to divide—and not another soul knows it."

"I am indeed flattered by your confidence."

"I've only told you because I don't care who knows now."

"Oh!"

[*Somehow* MAGGIE *seems to be dissatisfied.*]

"But why is that, John?"

"I daren't keep the Government in doubt any longer about what I mean to do. I'll show the whips the speech privately to-night."

[*But still* MAGGIE *wants to know.*] "But not to go to a division is hedging, isn't it? Is that strong?"

"To make the speech at all, Maggie, is stronger than most would dare. They would *do* for me if I went to a division."

"Bark but not bite?"

"Now, now, Maggie, you're out of your depth."

"I suppose that's it."

[*The* COMTESSE *remains in the shallows.*]

"But what will the ladies say, Mr. Shand?"

"They won't like it, Comtesse, but they've got to lump it."

[*Here the* MAID *appears with a card for* MAGGIE, *who considers it quietly.*]

"Any one of importance?"

"No."

"Then I'm ready, Maggie."

[*This is evidently an intimation that she is to open the folding-doors, and he makes an effective entrance into the dining-room, his thumb in his waistcoat. There is a delicious clapping of hands from the committee, and the door closes. Not till then does* MAGGIE, *who has grown thoughtful, tell her maid to admit the visitor.*]

"Another lady, Mrs. Shand?"

"The card says, 'Mr. Charles Venables.' "

[*The* COMTESSE *is really interested at last.*]

"Charles Venables! Do *you* know him?"

"I think I call to mind meeting one of that name at the Foreign Office party."

"One of that name! He who is a Minister of your Cabinet. But as you know him so little why should he call on you?"

"I wonder."

[MAGGIE'S *glance wanders to the drawer in which she has replaced* JOHN'S *speech.*]

"Well, well, I shall take care of you, petite."

"Do *you* know him?"

"Do I know him! The last time I saw him he asked me to—to—hem!—ma chérie, it was thirty years ago."

"Thirty years!"

"I was a pretty woman then. I dare say I shall detest him now; but if I find I do not—let us have a little plot— I shall drop this book; and then perhaps you will be so charming as—as not to be here for a little while?"

> [MR. VENABLES, *who enters, is such a courtly seigneur that he seems to bring the eighteenth century with him; you feel that his sedan chair is at the door. He stoops over* MAGGIE'S *plebeian hand.*]

"I hope you will pardon my calling, Mrs. Shand; we had such a pleasant talk the other evening."

> [MAGGIE, *of course, is at once deceived by his gracious manner.*]

"I think it's kind of you. Do you know each other? The Comtesse de la Brière."

> [*He repeats the name with some emotion, and the* COMTESSE *half mischievously, half sadly, holds a hand before her face.*]

"Comtesse."

"Thirty years, Mr. Venables."

> [*He gallantly removes the hand that screens her face.*]

"It does not seem so much."

> [*She gives him a similar scrutiny.*]

"Mon Dieu, it seems all that."

> [*They smile rather ruefully.* MAGGIE *like a kind hostess relieves the tension.*]

"The Comtesse has taken a cottage in Surrey for the summer."

"I am overjoyed."

"No, Charles, you are not. You no longer care. Fickle one! And it is only thirty years."

> [*He sinks into a chair beside her.*]

"Those heavenly evenings, Comtesse, on the Bosphorus."

"I refuse to talk of them. I hate you."

> [*But she drops the book, and* MAGGIE *fades from the room. It is not a very clever departure, and the old diplomatist smiles. Then he sighs a beautiful sigh, for he does all things beautifully.*]

"It is moonlight, Comtesse, on the Golden Horn."

"Who are those two young things in a caïque?"

"Is he the brave Leander, Comtesse, and is she Hero of the Lamp?"

"No, she is the foolish wife of the French Ambassador, and he is a good-for-nothing British attaché trying to get her husband's secrets out of her."

"Is it possible! They part at a certain garden gate."

"Oh, Charles, Charles!"

"But you promised to come back; I waited there till dawn. Blanche, if you *had* come back——"

"How is Mrs. Venables?"

"She is rather poorly. *I* think it's gout."

"And you?"

"I creak a little in the mornings."

"So do I. There is such a good man at Wiesbaden."

"The Homburg fellow is better. The way he patched me up last summer—Oh, Lord, Lord!"

"Yes, Charles, the game is up; we are two old fogies. [*They groan in unison; then she raps him sharply on the knuckles*.] Tell me, sir, what are you doing here?"

"Merely a friendly call."

"I do not believe it."

"The same woman; the old delightful candour."

"The same man; the old fibs. [*She sees that the door is asking a question.*] Yes, come, Mrs. Shand, I have had quite enough of him; I warn you he is here for some crafty purpose."

MAGGIE. [*Drawing back timidly.*] Surely not?

VENABLES. Really, Comtesse, you make conversation difficult. To show that my intentions are innocent, Mrs. Shand, I propose that you choose the subject.

MAGGIE. [*Relieved.*] There, Comtesse.

VENABLES. I hope your husband is well?

MAGGIE. Yes, thank you. [*With a happy thought.*] I decide that we talk about him.

VENABLES. If you wish it.

COMTESSE. Be careful; *he* has chosen the subject.

MAGGIE. *I* chose it, didn't I?

VENABLES. You know you did.

MAGGIE. [*Appealingly.*] You admire John?

VENABLES. Very much. But he puzzles me a little. You Scots, Mrs. Shand, are such a mixture of the practical and the emotional that you escape out of an Englishman's hand like a trout.

MAGGIE. [*Open-eyed.*] Do we?

VENABLES. Well, not you, but your husband. I have known few men make a worse beginning in the House. He had the most atrocious bow-wow public park manner——

COMTESSE. I remember that manner!

MAGGIE. No, he hadn't.

VENABLES. [*Soothingly.*] At first. But by his second session he had shed all that, and he is now a pleasure to listen to. By the way, Comtesse, have you found any dark intention in that?

COMTESSE. You wanted to know whether he talks over these matters with his wife; and she has told you that he does not.

MAGGIE. [*Indignantly.*] I haven't said a word about it, have I?

VENABLES. Not a word. Then, again, I admire him for his impromptu speeches.

MAGGIE. What is impromptu?

VENABLES. Unprepared. They have contained some grave blunders, not so much of judgment as of taste——

MAGGIE. [*Hotly.*] I don't think so.

VENABLES. Pardon me. But he has righted himself subsequently in the neatest way. I have always found that the man whose second thoughts are good is worth watching. Well, Comtesse, I see you have something to say.

COMTESSE. You are wondering whether she can tell you who gives his second thoughts.

MAGGIE. Gives them to John? I would like to see anybody try to give thoughts to John.

VENABLES. Quite so.

COMTESSE. Is there anything more that has roused your admiration, Charles?

VENABLES. [*Purring.*] Let me see. Yes, we are all much edified by his humour.

COMTESSE. [*Surprised indeed.*] His humour? That man!

MAGGIE. [*With hauteur.*] Why not?

VENABLES. I assure you, Comtesse, some of the neat things in his speeches convulse the house. A word has even been coined for them—Shandisms.

COMTESSE. [*Slowly recovering from a blow.*] Humour!

VENABLES. In conversation, I admit, he strikes one as being—ah—somewhat lacking in humour.

COMTESSE. [*Pouncing.*] You are wondering who supplies his speeches with the humour.

MAGGIE. Supplies John?

VENABLES. Now that you mention it, some of his Shandisms do have a curiously feminine quality.

COMTESSE. You have thought it might be a woman.

VENABLES.   Really, Comtessé——

COMTESSE. I see it all. Charles, you thought it might be the wife!

VENABLES. [*Flinging up his hands.*] I own up.

MAGGIE. [*Bewildered.*] Me?

VENABLES. Forgive me, I see I was wrong.

MAGGIE. [*Alarmed.*] Have I been doing John any harm?

VENABLES. On the contrary, I am relieved to know that there are no hairpins in his speeches. If he is at home, Mrs. Shand, may I see him? I am going to be rather charming to him.

MAGGIE. [*Drawn in two directions.*] Yes, he is—oh yes—but——

VENABLES. That is to say, Comtesse, if he proves himself the man I believe him to be.

> [*This arrests* MAGGIE *almost as she has reached the dining-room door.*]

MAGGIE. [*Hesitating.*] He is very busy just now.

VENABLES. [*Smiling.*] I think he will see me.

MAGGIE. Is it something about his speech?

VENABLES. [*The smile hardening.*] Well, yes, it is.

MAGGIE. Then I dare say I could tell you what you want to know without troubling him, as I've been typing it.

VENABLES. [*With a sigh.*] I don't acquire information in that way.

COMTESSE. I trust not.

MAGGIE. There's no secret about it. He is to show it to the Whips to-night.

VENABLES. [*Sharply.*] You are sure of that?

COMTESSE. It is quite true, Charles. I heard him say so;

and indeed he repeated what he called the "peroration" before me.

MAGGIE.   I know it by heart.   [*She plays a bold game.*] "These are the demands of all intelligent British women, and I am proud to nail them to my flag——"

COMTESSE.   The very words, Mrs. Shand.

MAGGIE.   [*Looking at her imploringly.*]   "And I don't care how they may embarrass the Government."   [*The* COMTESSE *is bereft of speech, so suddenly has she been introduced to the real* MAGGIE SHAND.] "If the right honourable gentlemen will give us his pledge to introduce a similar bill this session I will willingly withdraw mine; but otherwise I solemnly warn him that I will press the matter now to a division."

> [*She turns her face from the great man; she has gone white.*]

VENABLES.   [*After a pause.*]   Capital.

> [*The blood returns to* MAGGIE'S *heart.*]

COMTESSE.   [*Who is beginning to enjoy herself very much.*]   Then you are pleased to know that he means to, as you say, go to a division?

VENABLES.   Delighted.   The courage of it will be the making of him.

COMTESSE.   I see.

VENABLES.   Had he been to hedge we should have known that he was a pasteboard knight and have disregarded him.

COMTESSE.   I see.

> [*She desires to catch the eye of* MAGGIE, *but it is carefully turned from her.*]

VENABLES.   Mrs. Shand, let us have him in at once.

COMTESSE.   Yes, yes, indeed.

> [MAGGIE'S *anxiety returns, but she has to call* . . JOHN *in.*]

JOHN. [*Impressed.*]   Mr. Venables! This is an honour.

VENABLES. ' How are you, Shand?

JOHN. Sit down, sit down.   [*Becoming himself again.*] I can guess what you have come about.

VENABLES. Ah, you Scotsmen.

JOHN. Of course I know I'm harassing the Government a good deal——

VENABLES. [*Blandly.*]   Not at all, Shand. The Government are very pleased.

JOHN. You don't expect me to believe that.

VENABLES. I called here to give you the proof of it. You may know that we are to have a big meeting at Leeds on the 24th, when two Ministers are to speak. There is room for a third speaker, and I am authorized to offer that place to you.

JOHN. To me!

VENABLES. Yes.

JOHN. [*Swelling.*]   It would be—the Government taking me up.

VENABLES. Don't make too much of it; it would be an acknowledgment that they look upon you as one of their likely young men.

MAGGIE. John!

JOHN. [*Not found wanting in a trying hour.*]   It's a bribe. You are offering me this on condition that I don't make my speech. How can you think so meanly of me as to believe that I would play the women's cause false for the sake of my own advancement. I refuse your bribe.

VENABLES. [*Liking him for the first time.*]   Good. But you are wrong. There are no conditions, and we want you to make your speech. Now do you accept?

JOHN. [*Still suspicious.*]   If you make me the same offer after you have read it. I insist on your reading it first.

VENABLES. [*Sighing.*]   By all means.

[MAGGIE *is in an agony as she sees* JOHN *hand the speech to his leader. On the other hand, the* COMTESSE *thrills.*]

But I assure you we look on the speech as a small matter. The important thing is your intention of going to a division; and we agree to that also.

JOHN. [*Losing his head.*] What's that?

VENABLES. Yes, we agree.

JOHN. But—but—why, you have been threatening to excommunicate me if I dared.

VENABLES. All done to test you, Shand.

JOHN. To test me?

VENABLES. We know that a division on your Bill can have no serious significance; we shall see to that. And so the test was to be whether you had the pluck to divide the House. Had you been intending to talk big in this speech, and then hedge, through fear of the Government, they would have had no further use for you.

JOHN. [*Heavily.*] I understand. [*But there is one thing he cannot understand, which is, why* VENABLES *should be so sure that he is not to hedge.*]

VENABLES. [*Turning over the pages carelessly.*] Any of your good things in this, Shand?

JOHN. [*Whose one desire is to get the pages back.*] No, I—no—it isn't necessary you should read it now.

VENABLES. [*From politeness only.*] Merely for my own pleasure. I shall look through it this evening. [*He rolls up the speech to put it in his pocket.* JOHN *turns despairingly to* MAGGIE, *though well aware that no help can come from her.*]

MAGGIE. That's the only copy there is, John. [*To* VENABLES.] Let me make a fresh one, and send it to you in an hour or two.

VENABLES. [*Good-naturedly.*]   I could not put you to that trouble, Mrs. Shand.   I will take good care of it.

MAGGIE.   If anything were to happen to you on the way home, wouldn't whatever is in your pocket be considered to be the property of your heirs?

VENABLES. [*Laughing.*]   Now there is forethought! Shand, I think that after that——!   [*He returns the speech to* JOHN, *whose hand swallows it greedily.*]   She is Scotch too, Comtesse.

COMTESSE.   [*Delighted.*]   Yes, she is Scotch too.

VENABLES.   Though the only persons likely to do for me in the street, Shand, are your ladies' committee.   Ever since they took the horse out of my brougham, I can scent them a mile away.

COMTESSE.   A mile?   Charles, peep in there.

> [*He softly turns the handle of the dining-room door, and realizes that his scent is not so good as he had thought it.   He bids his hostess and the* COMTESSE *good-bye in a burlesque whisper and tiptoes off to safer places.*   JOHN *having gone out with him,* MAGGIE *can no longer avoid the* COMTESSE'S *reproachful eye.   That much injured lady advances upon her with accusing finger.*]

"So, madam!"

> [MAGGIE *is prepared for her.*]

"I don't know what you mean."

"Yes, you do.   I mean that there *is* some one who 'helps' our Mr. Shand."

"There's not."

"And it *is* a woman, and it's you."

"I help in the little things."

"The little things!   You are the Pin he picked up and

that is to make his fortune. And now what I want to know
is whether your John is aware that you help at all."

> [JOHN *returns, and at once provides the answer.*]

"Maggie, Comtesse, I've done it again!"

"I'm so glad, John."

> [*The* COMTESSE *is in an ecstasy.*]

"And all because you were not to hedge, Mr. Shand."

> [*His appeal to her with the wistfulness of a school-*
> *boy makes him rather attractive.*]

"You won't tell on me, Comtesse! [*He thinks it out.*]
They had just guessed I would be firm because they know
I'm a strong man. You little saw, Maggie, what a good
turn you were doing me when you said you wanted to make
another copy of the speech."

> [*She is dense.*]

"How, John?"

"Because now I can alter the end."

> [*She is enlightened.*]

"So you can!"

"Here's another lucky thing, Maggie: I hadn't told the
ladies' committee that I was to hedge, and so they need
never know. Comtesse, I tell you there's a little cherub who
sits up aloft and looks after the career of John Shand."

> [*The* COMTESSE *looks not aloft but toward the*
> *chair at present occupied by* MAGGIE.]

"Where does she sit, Mr. Shand?"

> [*He knows that women are not well read.*]

"It's just a figure of speech."

> [*He returns airily to his committee room; and now*
> *again you may hear the click of* MAGGIE'S
> *needles. They no longer annoy the* COMTESSE;
> *she is setting them to music.*]

"It is not down here she sits, Mrs. Shand, knitting a
stocking."

"No, it isn't."

"And when I came in I gave him credit for everything; even for the prettiness of the room!"

"He has beautiful taste."

"Good-bye, Scotchy."

"Good-bye, Comtesse, and thank you for coming."

"Good-bye—Miss Pin."

[MAGGIE *rings genteelly.*]

"Good-bye."

[*The* COMTESSE *is now lost in admiration of her.*]

"You divine little wife. He can't be worthy of it, no man could be worthy of it. Why do you do it?"

[MAGGIE *shivers a little.*]

"He loves to think he does it all himself; that's the way of men. I'm six years older than he is. I'm plain, and I have no charm. I shouldn't have let him marry me. I'm trying to make up for it."

> [*The* COMTESSE *kisses her and goes away.* MAGGIE, *somewhat foolishly, resumes her knitting.*]

> [*Some days later this same room is listening—with the same inattention—to the outpouring of* JOHN SHAND'S *love for the lady of the hiccoughs. We arrive—by arrangement—rather late; and thus we miss some of the most delightful of the pangs.*]

> [*One can see that these two are playing no game, or, if they are, that they little know it. The wonders of the world [so strange are the instruments chosen by Love] have been revealed to* JOHN *in hiccoughs; he shakes in* SYBIL'S *presence; never were more swimming eyes; he who*

*has been of a wooden face till now, with ways
to match, has gone on flame like a piece of
paper; emotion is in flood in him. We may be
almost fond of JOHN for being so worshipful of
love. Much has come to him that we had almost despaired of his acquiring, including nearly
all the divine attributes except that sense of
humour. The beautiful SYBIL has always pos-
sessed but little of it also, and what she had has
been struck from her by Cupid's flail. Naked
of the saving grace, they face each other in
awful rapture.]*

"In a room, Sybil, I go to you as a cold man to a fire.
You fill me like a peal of bells in an empty house."

*[She is being brutally treated by the dear impedi-
ment, for which hiccough is such an inadequate
name that even to spell it is an abomination
though a sign of ability. How to describe a
sound that is noiseless? Let us put it thus, that
when SYBIL wants to say something very much
there are little obstacles in her way; she falters,
falls perhaps once, and then is over, the while
her appealing orbs beg you not to be angry
with her. We may express those sweet pauses in
precious dots, which some clever person can
afterwards string together and make a pearl
necklace of them.]*

"I should not . . . let you say it, . . . but . . . you
. . . say it so beautifully."

"You must have guessed."

"I dreamed . . . I feared . . . but you were . . .
Scotch, and I didn't know what to think."

"Do you know what first attracted me to you, Sybil? It

was your insolence. I thought, 'I'll break her insolence for her.' "

"And I thought . . . 'I'll break his str . . . ength!' "

"And now your cooing voice plays round me; the softness of you, Sybil, in your pretty clothes makes me think of young birds. [*The impediment is now insurmountable; she has to swim for it, she swims toward him.*] It is you who inspire my work."

[*He thrills to find that she can be touched without breaking.*]

"I am so glad . . . so proud . . ."

"And others know it, Sybil, as well as I. Only yesterday the Comtesse said to me, 'No man could get on so fast unaided. *Cherchez la femme,* Mr. Shand.' "

"Auntie said that!"

"I said 'Find her yourself, Comtesse.' "

"And she?"

"She said 'I have found her,' and I said in my blunt way, 'You mean Lady Sybil,' and she went away laughing."

"Laughing?"

"I seem to amuse the woman."

[Sybil *grows sad.*]

"If Mrs. Shand— It is so cruel to her. Whom did you say she had gone to the station to meet?"

"Her father and brothers."

"It is so cruel to them. We must think no more of this. It is mad . . . ness."

"It's fate. Sybil, let us declare our love openly."

"You can't ask that, now in the first moment that you tell me of it."

"The one thing I won't do even for you is to live a life of underhand."

"The . . . blow to her."

"Yes. But at least she has always known that I never loved her."

"It is asking me to give . . . up everything, every one, for you."

"It's too much."

[JOHN *is humble at last.*]

"To a woman who truly loves, even that is not too much. Oh! it is not I who matter—it is you."

"My dear, my dear."

"So gladly would I do it to save you; but, oh, if it were to bring you down!"

"Nothing can keep me down if I have you to help me."

"I am dazed, John, I . . ."

"My love, my love."

"I . . . oh . . . here . . ."

"Be brave, Sybil, be brave."

". . . . ."

> [*In this bewilderment of pearls she melts into his arms.* MAGGIE *happens to open the door just then; but neither fond heart hears her.*]

"I can't walk along the streets, Sybil, without looking in all the shop windows for what I think would become you best. [*As awkwardly as though his heart still beat against corduroy, he takes from his pocket a pendant and its chain. He is shy, and she drops pearls over the beauty of the ruby which is its only stone.*] It is a drop of my blood, Sybil."

> [*Her lovely neck is outstretched, and he puts the chain round it.* MAGGIE *withdraws as silently as she had come; but perhaps the door whispered "d—n," or* [*humorously*] *"d . . n" as it closed, for* SYBIL *wakes out of Paradise.*]

"I thought—— Did the door shut?"

"It was shut already."

> [*Perhaps it is only that* SYBIL *is bewildered to*

> *find herself once again in a world that has
> doors.*]

"It seemed to me——"

"There was nothing. But I think I hear voices; they
may have arrived."

> [*Some pretty instinct makes* SYBIL *go farther from
> him.* MAGGIE *kindly gives her time for this by
> speaking before opening the door.*]

"That will do perfectly, David. The maid knows where
to put them. [*She comes in.*] They've come, John; they
would help with the luggage. [JOHN *goes out.* MAGGIE *is
agreeably surprised to find a visitor.*] How do you do,
Lady Sybil? This is nice of you."

"I was so sorry not to find you in, Mrs. Shand."

> [*The impediment has run away. It is only for
> those who love it.*]

"Thank you. You'll sit down?"

"I think not; your relatives——"

"They will be so proud to see that you are my friend."

> [*If* MAGGIE *were less simple her guest would feel
> more comfortable. She tries to make conver-
> sation.*]

"It is their first visit to London?"

> [*Instead of relieving her anxiety on this point,*
> MAGGIE *has a long look at the gorgeous armful.*]

"I'm glad you are so beautiful, Lady Sybil."

> [*The beautiful one is somehow not flattered. She
> pursues her investigations with growing un-
> easiness.*]

"One of them is married now, isn't he? [*Still there is no
answer;* MAGGIE *continues looking at her, and shivers
slightly.*] Have they travelled from Scotland to-day? Mrs.
Shand, why do you look at me so? The door did open!
[MAGGIE *nods.*] What are you to do?"

"That would be telling. Sit down, my pretty."

> [*As* SYBIL *subsides into what the* WYLIES *with one glance would call the best chair,* MAGGIE'S *menfolk are brought in by* JOHN, *all carrying silk hats and looking very active after their long rest in the train. They are gazing about them. They would like this lady, they would like* JOHN, *they would even like* MAGGIE *to go away for a little and leave them to examine the room. Is that linen on the walls, for instance, or just paper? Is the carpet as thick as it feels, or is there brown paper beneath it? Had* MAGGIE *got anything off that bookcase on account of the wormholes?* DAVID *even discovers that we were simpletons when we said there was nothing in the room that pretended to be what it was not. He taps the marble mantelpiece, and is favourably impressed by the tinny sound.*]

DAVID. Very fine imitation. It's a capital house, Maggie.

MAGGIE. I'm so glad you like it. Do you know one another? This is my father and my brothers, Lady Sybil.

> [*The lovely form inclines toward them.* ALICK *and* JOHN *remain firm on their legs, but* JAMES *totters.*]

JAMES. A ladyship! Well done, Maggie.

ALICK. [*Sharply.*] James! I remember you, my lady.

MAGGIE. Sit down, father. This is the study.

> [JAMES *wanders round it inquisitively until called to order.*]

SYBIL. You must be tired after your long journey.

DAVID. [*Drawing the portraits of himself and partners in one lightning sketch.*] Tired, your ladyship? We sat on cushioned seats the whole way.

JAMES. [*Looking about him for the chair you sit on.*] Every seat in this room is cushioned.

MAGGIE. You may say all my life is cushioned now, James, by this dear man of mine.

> [*She gives* JOHN'S *shoulder a loving pressure, which* SYBIL *feels is a telegraphic communication to herself in a cypher that she cannot read.* ALICK *and the* BROTHERS *bask in the evidence of* MAGGIE'S *happiness.*]

JOHN. [*Uncomfortably.*] And is Elizabeth hearty, James?

JAMES. [*Looking down his nose in the manner proper to young husbands when addressed about their wives.*] She's very well, I thank you kindly.

MAGGIE. James is a married man now, Lady Sybil.

> [SYBIL *murmurs her congratulations.*]

JAMES. I thank you kindly. [*Courageously.*] Yes, I'm married. [*He looks at* DAVID *and* ALICK *to see if they are smiling; and they are.*] It wasn't a case of being catched; it was entirely of my own free will. [*He looks again; and the mean fellows are smiling still.*] Is your ladyship married?

SYBIL. Alas! no.

DAVID. James! [*Politely.*] You will be yet, my lady.

> [SYBIL *indicates that he is kind indeed.*]

JOHN. Perhaps they would like you to show them their rooms, Maggie?

DAVID. Fine would we like to see all the house as well as the sleeping accommodation. But first—— [*He gives his father the look with which chairmen call on the next speaker.*]

ALICK. *I take you, David.* [*He produces a paper par-*

cel from a roomy pocket.]   It wasn't likely, Mr. Shand, that we would forget the day.

JOHN.   The day?

DAVID.   The second anniversary of your marriage. We came purposely for the day.

JAMES.   [*His fingers itching to take the parcel from his father.*]   It's a lace shawl, Maggie, from the three of us, a pure Tobermory; you would never dare wear it if you knew the cost.

> [*The shawl in its beauty is revealed, and* MAGGIE
> *hails it with little cries of joy. She rushes at
> the donors and kisses each of them just as if
> she were a pretty woman. They are much
> pleased and give expression to their pleasure
> in a not very dissimilar manner.*]

ALICK.   Havers.

DAVID.   Havers.

JAMES.   Havers.

JOHN.   It's a very fine shawl.

> [*He should not have spoken, for he has set*
> JAMES's *volatile mind working.*]

JAMES.   You may say so. What did you give her, Mr. Shand?

JOHN.   [*Suddenly deserted by God and man.*]   Me?

ALICK.   Yes, yes, let's see it.

JOHN.   Oh—I——

> [*He is not deserted by* MAGGIE, *but she can think
> of no way out.*]

SYBIL.   [*Prompted by the impediment, which is in hiding quite close.*]   Did he . . . forget?

> [*There is more than a touch of malice in the question. It is a challenge, and the* WYLIES *as a
> family are almost too quick to accept a challenge.*]

MAGGIE.   [*Lifting the gage of battle.*]   John forget?
Never!   It's a pendant, father.

[*The impediment bolts.*   JOHN *rises.*]

ALICK.   A pendant?   One of those things on a chain?
[*He grins, remembering how once, about sixty
years ago, he and a lady and a pendant—but
we have no time for this.*]

MAGGIE.   Yes.

DAVID.   [*Who has felt the note of antagonism and is
troubled.*]   You were slow in speaking of it, Mr. Shand.

MAGGIE.   [*This is her fight.*]   He was shy, because he
thought you might blame him for extravagance.

DAVID.   [*Relieved.*]   Oh, that's it.

JAMES.   [*Licking his lips.*]   Let's see it.

MAGGIE.   [*A daughter of the devil.*]   Where did you
put it, John?

[JOHN'S *mouth opens but has nothing to con-
tribute.*]

SYBIL.   [*The impediment has stolen back again.*]   Perhaps it has been . . . mislaid.

[*The* BROTHERS *echo the word incredulously.*]

MAGGIE.   Not it.   I can't think where we laid it down,
John.   It's not on that table, is it, James?   [*The* WYLIES
turn to look, and MAGGIE'S *hand goes out to* LADY SYBIL:
JOHN SHAND, *witness.   It is a very determined hand, and
presently a pendant is placed in it.*]   Here it is!   [ALICK
and the BROTHERS *cluster round it, weigh it, and appraise
it.*]

ALICK.   Preserve me.   Is that stone real, Mr. Shand?

JOHN.   [*Who has begun to look his grimmest.*]   Yes.

MAGGIE.   [*Who is now ready, if he wishes it, to take
him on too.*]   John says it's a drop of his blood.

JOHN.   [*Wishing it.*]   And so it is.

DAVID.   Well said, Mr. Shand.

MAGGIE. [*Scared.*] And now, if you'll all come with me, I think John has something he wants to talk over with Lady Sybil. [*Recovering and taking him on.*] Or would you prefer, John, to say it before us all?

SYBIL. [*Gasping.*] No!

JOHN. [*Flinging back his head.*] Yes, I prefer to say it before you all.

MAGGIE. [*Flinging back hers.*] Then sit down again.

[*The* WYLIES *wonderingly obey.*]

SYBIL. Mr. Shand, Mr. Shand!——

JOHN. Maggie knows, and it was only for her I was troubled. Do you think I'm afraid of *them?* [*With mighty relief.*] Now we can be open.

DAVID. [*Lowering.*] What is it? What's wrong, John Shand?

JOHN. [*Facing him squarely.*] It was to Lady Sybil I gave the pendant, and all my love with it. [*Perhaps* JAMES *utters a cry, but the silence of* ALICK *and* DAVID *is more terrible.*]

SYBIL. [*Whose voice is smaller than we had thought.*] What are you to do?

[*It is to* MAGGIE *she is speaking.*]

DAVID. She'll leave it for us to do.

JOHN. That's what I want.

[*The lords of creation look at the ladies.*]

MAGGIE. [*Interpreting.*] You and I are expected to retire, Lady Sybil, while the men decide our fate. [*Sybil is ready to obey the law, but* MAGGIE *remains seated.*] Man's the oak, woman's the ivy. Which of us is it that's to cling to you, John?

[*With three stalwarts glaring at him,* JOHN *rather grandly takes* SYBIL's *hand. They are two against the world.*]

SYBIL. [*A heroine.*]   I hesitated, but I am afraid no longer; whatever he asks of me I will do.

> [*Evidently the first thing he asks of her is to await him in the dining-room.*]

It will mean surrendering everything for him.   I am glad it means all that.   [*She passes into the dining-room looking as pretty as a kiss.*]

MAGGIE.   So that settles it.

ALICK.   I'm thinking that doesn't settle it.

DAVID.   No, by God!   [*But his love for MAGGIE steadies him.   There is even a note of entreaty in his voice.*] Have you nothing to say to her, man?

JOHN.   I have things to say to her, but not before you.

DAVID.   [*Sternly.*]   Go away, Maggie.   Leave him to us.

JAMES.   [*Who thinks it is about time that he said something.*]   Yes, leave him to us.

MAGGIE.   No, David, I want to hear what is to become of me; I promise not to take any side.

> [*And sitting by the fire she resumes her knitting. The four regard her as on an evening at The Pans a good many years ago.*]

DAVID.   [*Barking.*]   How long has this been going on?

JOHN.   If you mean how long has that lady been the apple of my eye, I'm not sure; but I never told her of it until to-day.

MAGGIE.   [*Thoughtfully and without dropping a stitch.*] I think it wasn't till about six months ago, John, that she began to be very dear to you.   At first you liked to bring in her name when talking to me, so that I could tell you of any little things I might have heard she was doing.   But afterwards, as she became more and more to you, you avoided mentioning her name.

JOHN.   [*Surprised.*]   Did you notice that?

MAGGIE. [*In her old-fashioned way.*] Yes.

JOHN. I tried to be done with it for your sake. I've often had a sore heart for you, Maggie.

JAMES. You're proving it!

MAGGIE. Yes, James, he had. I've often seen him looking at me very sorrowfully of late because of what was in his mind; and many a kindly little thing he has done for me that he didn't used to do.

JOHN. You noticed that too!

MAGGIE. Yes.

DAVID. [*Controlling himself.*] Well, we won't go into that; the thing to be thankful for is that it's ended.

ALICK. [*Who is looking very old.*] Yes, yes, that's the great thing.

JOHN. All useless, sir, it's not ended; it's to go on.

DAVID. There's a devil in you, John Shand.

JOHN. [*Who is an unhappy man just now.*] I dare say there is. But do you think he had a walk over, Mr. David?

JAMES. Man, I could knock you down!

MAGGIE. There's not one of you could knock John down.

DAVID. [*Exasperated.*] Quiet, Maggie. One would think you were taking his part.

MAGGIE. Do you expect me to desert him at the very moment that he needs me most?

DAVID. It's him that's deserting you.

JOHN. Yes, Maggie, that's what it is.

ALICK. Where's your marriage vow? And your church attendances?

JAMES. [*With terrible irony.*] And your prize for moral philosophy?

JOHN. [*Recklessly.*] All gone whistling down the wind.

DAVID. I suppose you understand that you'll have to resign your seat.

JOHN. [*His underlip much in evidence.*] There are hundreds of seats, but there's only one John Shand.

MAGGIE. [*But we don't hear her.*] That's how I like to hear him speak.

DAVID. [*The ablest person in the room.*] Think, man, I'm old by you, and for long I've had a pride in you. It will be beginning the world again with more against you than there was eight years ago.

JOHN. I have a better head to begin it with than I had eight years ago.

ALICK. [*Hoping this will bite.*] She'll have her own money, David!

JOHN. She's as poor as a mouse.

JAMES. [*Thinking possibly of his* ELIZABETH's *mother.*] We'll go to her friends, and tell them all. They'll stop it.

JOHN. She's of age.

JAMES. They'll take her far away.

JOHN. I'll follow, and tear her from them.

ALICK. Your career——

JOHN. [*To his credit.*] To hell with my career. Do you think I don't know I'm on the rocks. What can you, or you, or you, understand of the passions of a man! I've fought, and I've given in. When a ship founders, as I suppose I'm foundering, it's not a thing to yelp at. Peace all of you. [*He strides into the dining-room, where we see him at times pacing the floor.*]

DAVID. [*To* JAMES, *who gives signs of a desire to take off his coat.*] Let him be. We can't budge him. [*With bitter wisdom.*] It's true what he says, true at any rate about me. What do I know of the passions of a man! I'm up against something I don't understand.

ALICK. It's something wicked.

DAVID. I dare say it is, but it's something big.

JAMES. It's that damned charm.

MAGGIE. [*Still by the fire.*] That's it. What was it that made you fancy Elizabeth, James?

JAMES. [*Sheepishly.*] I can scarcely say.

MAGGIE. It was her charm.

DAVID. *Her* charm!

JAMES. [*Pugnaciously.*] Yes, *her* charm.

MAGGIE. She had charm for James.

> [*This somehow breaks them up.* MAGGIE *goes from one to another with an odd little smile flickering on her face.*]

DAVID. Put on your things, Maggie, and we'll leave his house.

MAGGIE. [*Patting his kind head.*] Not me, David.

> [*This is a* MAGGIE *they have known but forgotten; all three brighten.*]

DAVID. You haven't given in!

> [*The smile flickers and expires.*]

MAGGIE. I want you all to go upstairs, and let me have my try now.

JAMES. Your try?

ALICK. Maggie, you put new life into me.

JAMES. And into me.

> [DAVID *says nothing; the way he grips her shoulder says it for him.*]

MAGGIE. I'll save him, David, if I can.

DAVID. Does he deserve to be saved after the way he has treated you?

MAGGIE. You stupid David. What has that to do with it.

> [*When they have gone,* JOHN *comes to the door of the dining-room. There is welling up in him a great pity for* MAGGIE, *but it has to subside*

*a little when he sees that the knitting is still
in her hand. No man likes to be so soon sup-
planted. SYBIL follows, and the two of them
gaze at the active needles.*]

MAGGIE. [*Perceiving that she has visitors.*]   Come in,
John. Sit down, Lady Sybil, and make yourself comfortable. I'm afraid we've put you about.

[*She is, after all, only a few years older than they
and scarcely looks her age; yet it must have
been in some such way as this that the little old
woman who lived in a shoe addressed her nu-
merous progeny.*]

JOHN. I'm mortal sorry, Maggie.

SYBIL. [*Who would be more courageous if she could
hold his hand.*]   And I also.

MAGGIE. [*Soothingly.*]   I'm sure you are. But as it
can't be helped I see no reason why we three shouldn't
talk the matter over in a practical way.

[*SYBIL looks doubtful, but JOHN hangs on desperately to the word practical.*]

JOHN. If you could understand, Maggie, what an inspiration she is to me and my work.

SYBIL. Indeed, Mrs. Shand, I think of nothing else.

MAGGIE. That's fine. That's as it should be.

SYBIL. [*Talking too much.*]   Mrs. Shand, I think you
are very kind to take it so reasonably.

MAGGIE. That's the Scotch way. When were you
thinking of leaving me, John?

[*Perhaps this is the Scotch way also; but SYBIL
is English, and from the manner in which she
starts you would say that something has fallen
on her toes.*]

JOHN. [*Who has heard nothing fall.*]   I think, now
that it has come to a breach, the sooner the better. [*His*

tone becomes that of JAMES *when asked after the health of his wife.*] So long as it is convenient to you, Maggie.

MAGGIE. [*Making a rapid calculation.*] It couldn't well be before Wednesday. That's the day the laundry comes home.

[SYBIL *has to draw in her toes again.*]

JOHN. And it's the day the House rises. [*Stifling a groan.*] It may be my last appearance in the House.

SYBIL. [*Her arms yearning for him.*] No, no, please don't say that.

MAGGIE. [*Surveying them sympathetically.*] You love the House, don't you, John, next to her? It's a pity you can't wait till after your speech at Leeds. Mr. Venables won't let you speak at Leeds, I fear, if you leave me.

JOHN. What a chance it would have been. But let it go.

MAGGIE. The meeting is in less than a month. Could you not make it such a speech that they would be very loth to lose you?

JOHN. [*Swelling.*] That's what was in my mind.

SYBIL. [*With noble confidence.*] And he could have done it.

MAGGIE. Then we've come to something practical.

JOHN. [*Exercising his imagination with powerful effect.*] No, it wouldn't be fair to you if I was to stay on now.

MAGGIE. Do you think I'll let myself be considered when your career is at stake. A month will soon pass for me; I'll have a lot of packing to do.

JOHN. It's noble of you, but I don't deserve it, and I can't take it from you.

MAGGIE. Now's the time, Lady Sybil, for you to have one of your inspiring ideas.

SYBIL. [*Ever ready.*] Yes, yes—but what?

[*It is odd that they should both turn to* MAGGIE *at this moment.*]

MAGGIE. [*Who has already been saying it to herself.*] What do you think of this: I can stay on here with my father and brothers; and you, John, can go away somewhere and devote yourself to your speech?

SYBIL. Yes.

JOHN. That might be. [*Considerately.*] Away from both of you. Where could I go?

SYBIL. [*Ever ready.*] Where?

MAGGIE. I know.

[*She has called up a number on the telephone before they have time to check her.*]

JOHN. [*On his dignity.*] Don't be in such a hurry, Maggie.

MAGGIE. Is this Lamb's Hotel? Put me on to the Comtesse de la Brière, please.

SYBIL. [*With a sinking.*] What do you want with Auntie?

MAGGIE. Her cottage in the country would be the very place. She invited John and me.

JOHN. Yes, but——

MAGGIE. [*Arguing.*] And Mr. Venables is to be there. Think of the impression you could make on *him*, seeing him daily for three weeks.

JOHN. There's something in that.

MAGGIE. Is it you, Comtesse? I'm Maggie Shand.

SYBIL. You are not to tell her that——

MAGGIE. No. [*To the* COMTESSE.] Oh, I'm very well, never was better. Yes, yes; you see I can't, because my folk have never been in London before, and I must take them about and show them the sights. But John could come to you alone; why not?

JOHN. [*With proper pride.*] If she's not keen to have me, I won't go.

MAGGIE. She's very keen. Comtesse, I could come for a day by and by to see how you are getting on. Yes— yes—certainly. [*To* JOHN.] She says she'll be delighted.

JOHN. [*Thoughtfully.*] You're not doing this, Maggie, thinking that my being absent from Sybil for a few weeks can make any difference? Of course it's natural you should want us to keep apart, but——

MAGGIE. [*Grimly.*] I'm founding no hope on keeping you apart, John.

JOHN. It's what other wives would do.

MAGGIE. I promised to be different.

JOHN. [*His position as a strong man assured.*] Then tell her I accept. [*He wanders back into the dining-room.*]

SYBIL. I think—[*She is not sure what she thinks*]—I think you are very wonderful.

MAGGIE. Was that John calling to you?

SYBIL. Was it? [*She is glad to join him in the dining-room.*]

MAGGIE. Comtesse, hold the line a minute—— [*She is alone, and she has nearly reached the end of her self-control. She shakes emotionally and utters painful little cries; there is something she wants to do, and she is loth to do it. But she does it.*] Are you there, Comtesse? There's one other thing, dear Comtesse; I want you to invite Lady Sybil also; yes, for the whole time that John is there. No, I'm not mad; as a great favour to me; yes, I have a very particular reason, but I won't tell you what it is; oh, call me Scotchy as much as you like, but consent; do, do, do. Thank you, thank you, good-bye.

> [*She has control of herself now, and is determined not to let it slip from her again. When they reappear the stubborn one is writing a letter.*]

JOHN. I thought I heard the telephone again.

MAGGIE. [*Looking up from her labours.*] It was the Comtesse; she says she's to invite Lady Sybil to the cottage at the same time.

SYBIL. Me!

JOHN. To invite Sybil? Then of course I won't go, Maggie.

MAGGIE. [*Wondering seemingly at these niceties.*] What does it matter? Is anything to be considered except the speech? [*It has been admitted that she was a little devil.*] And, with Sybil on the spot, John, *to help you and inspire you,* what a speech it will be!

JOHN. [*Carried away.*] Maggie, you really are a very generous woman.

SYBIL. [*Convinced at last.*] She is indeed.

JOHN. And you're queer too. How many women in the circumstances would sit down to write a letter.

MAGGIE. It's a letter to you, John.

JOHN. To me?

MAGGIE. I'll give it to you when it's finished, but I ask you not to open it till your visit to the Comtesse ends.

JOHN. What is it about?

MAGGIE. It's practical.

SYBIL. [*Rather faintly.*] Practical? [*She has heard the word so frequently to-day that it is beginning to have a Scotch sound. She feels she ought to like MAGGIE, but that she would like her better if they were farther apart. She indicates that the doctors are troubled about her heart, and murmuring her adieux she goes. JOHN, who is accompanying her, pauses at the door.*]

JOHN. [*With a queer sort of admiration for his wife.*] Maggie, I wish I was fond of you.

MAGGIE. [*Heartily.*] I wish you were, John.

[*He goes, and she resumes her letter. The stock-*

*ing is lying at hand, and she pushes it to the
floor. She is done for a time with knitting.]*

End of Act III.

ACT IV

*Man's greatest invention is the lawn-mower. All the birds
know this, and that is why, when it is at rest, there is
always at least one of them sitting on the handle with
his head cocked, wondering how the delicious whirring
sound is made. When they find out, they will change
their note. As it is, you must sometimes have thought
that you heard the mower very early in the morning,
and perhaps you peeped in négligé from your lattice
window to see who was up so early. It was really the
birds trying to get the note.*

*On this broiling morning, however, we are at noon, and
whoever looks will see that the whirring is done by
MR. VENABLES. He is in a linen suit with the coat
discarded [the bird is sitting on it], and he comes and
goes across the COMTESSE'S lawns, pleasantly mopping
his face. We see him through a crooked bowed window generously open, roses intruding into it as if to
prevent its ever being closed at night; there are other
roses in such armfuls on the tables that one could not
easily say where the room ends and the garden begins.*

*In the COMTESSE'S pretty comic drawing-room [for she likes
the comic touch when she is in England] sits JOHN
SHAND with his hostess, on chairs at a great distance
from each other. No linen garments for JOHN, nor
flannels, nor even knickerbockers; he envies the Eng-*

*lish way of dressing for trees and lawns, but is too
Scotch to be able to imitate it; he wears tweeds, just
as he would do in his native country where they would
be in kilts.   Like many another Scot, the first time he
ever saw a kilt was on a Sassenach; indeed kilts were
only invented, like golf, to draw the English north.
JOHN is doing nothing, which again is not a Scotch
accomplishment, and he looks rather miserable and
dour.   The COMTESSE is already at her Patience cards,
and occasionally she smiles on him as if not displeased
with his long silence.   At last she speaks:*

"I feel it rather a shame to detain you here on such a
lovely day, Mr. Shand, entertaining an old woman."

"I don't pretend to think I'm entertaining you, Comtesse."

"But you *are*, you know."

"I would be pleased to be told how?"

> [*She shrugs her impertinent shoulders, and pres-
> ently there is another heavy sigh from* JOHN.]

"Again!   Why do not you go out on the river?"

"Yes, I can do that."   [*He rises.*]

"And take Sybil with you."   [*He sits again.*]

"No?"

"I have been on the river with her twenty times."

"Then take her for a long walk through the Fairloe
woods."

"We were there twice last week."

"There is a romantically damp little arbour at the end
of what the villagers call the Lovers' Lane."

"One can't go there every day.   I see nothing to
laugh at."

"Did I laugh? I must have been translating the situation into French."

> [*Perhaps the music of the lawn-mower is not to
> JOHN's mood, for he betakes himself to another
> room. MR. VENABLES pauses in his labours
> to greet a lady who has appeared on the lawn,
> and who is MAGGIE. She is as neat as if she
> were one of the army of typists [who are quite
> the nicest kind of women], and carries a little
> bag. She comes in through the window, and
> puts her hands over the COMTESSE's eyes. The
> COMTESSE says:*

"They are a strong pair of hands, at any rate."

"And not very white, and biggish for my size. Now guess."

> [*The COMTESSE guesses, and takes both the hands
> in hers as if she valued them. She pulls off
> MAGGIE's hat as if to prevent her flying away.*]

"Dear abominable one, not to let me know you were coming."

"It is just a surprise visit, Comtesse. I walked up from the station. [*For a moment MAGGIE seems to have borrowed SYBIL's impediment.*] How is—everbody?"

"He is quite well. But, my child, he seems to me to be a most unhappy man."

> [*This sad news does not seem to make a most
> unhappy woman of the child. The COMTESSE
> is puzzled, as she knows nothing of the situa-
> tion save what she has discovered for herself.*]

"Why should that please you, O heartless one?"

"I won't tell you."

"I could take you and shake you, Maggie. Here have I put my house at your disposal for so many days for some sly Scotch purpose, and you will not tell me what it is."

"No."

"Very well then, but I have what you call a nasty one for you. [*The* Comtesse *lures* Mr. Venables *into the room by holding up what might be a foaming glass of lemon squash.*] Alas, Charles, it is but a flower vase. I want you to tell Mrs. Shand what you think of her husband's speech."

[Mr. Venables *gives his hostess a reproachful look.*]

"Eh—ah—Shand will prefer to do that himself. I promised the gardener—I must not disappoint him—excuse me——"

"You must tell her, Charles."

"Please, Mr. Venables, I should like to know."

[*He sits down with a sigh and obeys.*]

"Your husband has been writing the speech here, and by his own wish he read it to me three days ago. The occasion is to be an important one; and, well, there are a dozen young men in the party at present, all capable of filling a certain small ministerial post. [*He looks longingly at the mower, but it sends no message to his aid.*] And as he is one of them I was anxious that he should show in this speech of what he is capable."

"And hasn't he?"

[*Not for the first time* Mr. Venables *wishes that he was not in politics.*]

"I am afraid he has."

"What is wrong with the speech, Charles?"

"Nothing—and he can still deliver it. It is a powerful, well-thought-out piece of work, such as only a very able man could produce. But it has no *special quality* of its own—none of the little touches that used to make an old stager like myself want to pat Shand on the shoulder. [*The* Comtesse's *mouth twitches, but* Maggie *declines to notice it.*] He pounds on manfully enough, but, if I may say so, with a wooden leg. It is as good, I dare say, as the rest of them could have done; but they start with such inherited advantages, Mrs. Shand, that he had to do better."

"Yes, I can understand that."

"I am sorry, Mrs. Shand, for he interested me. His career has set me wondering whether if *I* had begun as a railway porter I might not still be calling out, 'By your leave.'"

[MAGGIE *thinks it probable but not important.*]

"Mr. Venables, now that I think of it, surely john wrote to me that you were dissatisfied with his first speech, and that he was writing another."

[*The* COMTESSE'S *eyes open very wide indeed.*]

"I have heard nothing of that, Mrs. Shand. [VENABLES *shakes his wise head.*] And in any case, I am afraid——"
[*He still hears the wooden leg.*]

"But you said yourself that his second thoughts were sometimes such an improvement on the first."

[*The* COMTESSE *comes to the help of the baggage.*]

"I remember your saying that, Charles."

"Yes, that has struck me. [*Politely.*] Well, if he has anything to show me—— In the meantime——"

[*He regains the lawn, like one glad to escape attendance at* JOHN'S *obsequies. The* COMTESSE *is brought back to speech by the sound of the mower—nothing wooden in it.*]

"What are you up to now, Miss Pin? You know as well as I do that there is no such speech."

[MAGGIE'S *mouth tightens.*]

"I do not."

"It is a duel, is it, my friend?"

[*The* COMTESSE *rings the bell and* MAGGIE'S *guilty mind is agitated.*]

"What are you ringing for?"

"As the challenged one, Miss Pin, I have the choice of weapons. I am going to send for your husband to ask him if he has written such a speech. After which, I suppose, *you* will ask me to leave you while you and he write it together."

[MAGGIE *wrings her hands*.]

"You are wrong, Comtesse; but please don't do that."

"You but make me more curious, and my doctor says that I must be told everything. [*The* COMTESSE *assumes the pose of her sex in melodrama*.] Put your cards on the table, Maggie Shand, *or*—— [*She indicates that she always pinks her man*. MAGGIE *dolefully produces a roll of paper from her bag*.] What precisely is that?"

[*The reply is little more than a squeak*.]

"John's speech."

"You have written it yourself!"

[MAGGIE *is naturally indignant*.]

"It's typed."

"You guessed that the speech he wrote unaided would not satisfy, and you prepared this to take its place!"

"Not at all, Comtesse. It is the draft of his speech that he left at home. That's all."

"With a few trivial alterations by yourself, I swear. Can you deny it?"

[*No wonder that* MAGGIE *is outraged. She replaces* JOHN'S *speech in the bag with becoming hauteur*.]

"Comtesse, these insinuations are unworthy of you. May I ask where is my husband?"

[*The* COMTESSE *drops her a curtsy*.]

"I believe your Haughtiness may find him in the Dutch garden. Oh, I see through you. You are not to show him your speech. But you are to get him to write another one,

and somehow all your additions will be in it. Think not,
creature, that you can deceive one so old in iniquity as the
Comtesse de la Brière."

> [*There can be but one reply from a good wife
> to such a charge, and at once the* COMTESSE
> *is left alone with her shame. Anon a foot-
> man appears. You know how they come and
> go.*]

"You rang, my lady?"

"Did I? Ah, yes, but why? [*He is but lately from the
ploughshare and cannot help her. In this quandary her eyes
alight upon the bag. She is unfortunately too abandoned
to feel her shame: she still thinks that she has the choice
of weapons. She takes the speech from the bag and bestows it on her servitor.*] Take this to Mr. Venables,
please, and say it is from Mr. Shand. [THOMAS—*but in
the end we shall probably call him* JOHN—*departs with the
little explosive; and when* MAGGIE *returns she finds that
the* COMTESSE *is once more engaged on her interrupted
game of Patience.*] You did not find him?"

> [*All the bravery has dropped from* MAGGIE's
> *face.*]

"I didn't see him, but I heard him. *She* is with him.
I think they are coming here."

> [*The* COMTESSE *is suddenly kind again.*]

"Sybil? Shall I get rid of her?"

"No, I want her to be here, too. Now I shall know."

> [*The* COMTESSE *twists the little thing round.*]

"Know what?"

"As soon as I look into his face I shall know."

> [*A delicious scent ushers in the fair* SYBIL, *who is
> .as sweet as a milking stool. She greets* MRS.
> SHAND *with some alarm.*]

MAGGIE. How do you do, Lady Sybil? How pretty

you look in that frock.   [SYBIL *rustles uncomfortably.*]
You are a feast to the eye.

SYBIL.   Please, I wish you would not.

> [*Shall we describe* SYBIL'S *frock, in which she
> looks like a great strawberry that knows it
> ought to be plucked; or would it be easier to
> watch the coming of* JOHN?   *Let us watch*
> JOHN.]

JOHN.   You, Maggie!   You never wrote that you were
coming.

> [*No, let us watch* MAGGIE.   *As soon as she looked
> into his face she was to know something of
> importance.*]

MAGGIE.   [*Not dissatisfied with what she sees.*]   No,
John, it's a surprise visit.   I just ran down to say good-bye.

> [*At this his face falls, which does not seem to
> pain her.*]

SYBIL.   [*Foreseeing another horrible Scotch scene.*]   To
say good-bye?

COMTESSE.   [*Thrilling with expectation.*]   To whom,
Maggie?

SYBIL.   [*Deserted by the impediment, which is probably
playing with rough boys in the Lovers' Lane.*]   Auntie, do
leave us, won't you?

COMTESSE.   Not I.   It is becoming far too interesting.

MAGGIE.   I suppose there's no reason the Comtesse
shouldn't be told, as she will know so soon at any rate?

JOHN.   That's so.   [SYBIL *sees with a sinking that he is
to be practical also.*]

MAGGIE.   It's so simple.   You see, Comtesse, John and
Lady Sybil have fallen in love with one another, and they
are to go off as soon as the meeting at Leeds has taken
place.

[*The* COMTESSE'S *breast is too suddenly introduced to Caledonia and its varied charms.*]

COMTESSE. Mon Dieu!

MAGGIE. I think that's putting it correctly, John.

JOHN. In a sense. But I'm not to attend the meeting
at Leeds. My speech doesn't find favour. [*With a strange
humility.*] There's something wrong with it.

COMTESSE. I never expected to hear you say that, Mr.
Shand.

JOHN. [*Wondering also.*] I never expected it myself.
I meant to make it the speech of my career. But somehow
my hand seems to have lost its cunning.

COMTESSE. And you don't know how?

JOHN. It's inexplicable. My brain was never clearer.

COMTESSE. You might have helped him, Sybil.

SYBIL. [*Quite sulkily.*] I did.

COMTESSE. But I thought she was such an inspiration
to you, Mr. Shand.

JOHN. [*Going bravely to* SYBIL'S *side.*] She slaved at
it with me.

COMTESSE. Strange. [*Wickedly becoming practical
also.*] So now there is nothing to detain you. Shall I
send for a fly, Sybil?

SYBIL. [*With a cry of the heart.*] Auntie, do leave us.

COMTESSE. I can understand your impatience to be
gone, Mr. Shand.

JOHN. [*Heavily.*] I promised Maggie to wait till the
24th, and I'm a man of my word.

MAGGIE. But I give you back your word, John. You
can go now.

[JOHN *looks at* SYBIL, *and* SYBIL *looks at* JOHN,
*and the impediment arrives in time to take a
peep at both of them.*]

SYBIL. [*Groping for the practical, to which we must all*

come in the end.]   He must make satisfactory arrangements about you first. I insist on that.

MAGGIE. [*With no more imagination than a hen*.]
Thank you, Lady Sybil, but I have made all my arrangements.

JOHN. [*Stung*.] Maggie, that was my part.

MAGGIE. [*The hens are saying it all the time*.] You
see, my brothers feel they can't be away from their business any longer; and so, if it would be convenient to you,
John, I could travel north with them by the night train on
Wednesday.

SYBIL. I—I— The way you put things——!

JOHN. This is just the 21st.

MAGGIE. My things are all packed. I think you'll
find the house in good order, Lady Sybil. I have had the
vacuum cleaners in. I'll give you the keys of the linen
and the silver plate; I have them in that bag. The carpet
on the upper landing is a good deal frayed, but——

SYBIL. Please, I don't want to hear any more.

MAGGIE. The ceiling of the dining-room would be the
better of a new lick of paint——

SYBIL. [*Stamping her foot, small fours*.] Can't you
stop her?

JOHN. [*Soothingly*.] She's meaning well. Maggie, I
know it's natural to you to value those things, because your
outlook on life is bounded by them; but all this jars on me.

MAGGIE. Does it?

JOHN. Why should you be so ready to go?

MAGGIE. I promised not to stand in your way.

JOHN. [*Stoutly*.] You needn't be in such a hurry.
There are three days to run yet. [*The French are so different from us that we shall probably never be able to
understand why the* COMTESSE *laughed aloud here*.] It's
just a joke to the Comtesse.

COMTESSE. It seems to be no joke to you, Mr. Shand. Sybil, my pet, are you to let him off?

SYBIL. [*Flashing.*] Let him off? If he wishes it. Do you?

JOHN. [*Manfully.*] I want it to go on. [*Something seems to have caught in his throat: perhaps it is the impediment trying a temporary home.*] It's the one wish of my heart. If you come with me, Sybil, I'll do all in a man's power to make you never regret it.

[*Triumph of the Vere de Veres.*]

MAGGIE. [*Bringing them back to earth with a dump.*] And I can make my arrangements for Wednesday?

SYBIL. [*Seeking the* COMTESSE'S *protection.*] No, you can't. Auntie, I am not going on with this. I'm very sorry for you, John, but I see now—I couldn't face it——

[*She can't face anything at this moment except the sofa pillows.*]

COMTESSE. [*Noticing* JOHN'S *big sigh of relief.*] So *that* is all right, Mr. Shand!

MAGGIE. Don't you love her any more, John? Be practical.

SYBIL. [*To the pillows.*] At any rate I have tired of him. Oh, best to tell the horrid truth. I am ashamed of myself. I have been crying my eyes out over it—I thought I was such a different kind of woman. But I am weary of him. I think him—oh, so dull.

JOHN. [*His face lighting up.*] Are you sure that is how you have come to think of me?

SYBIL. I'm sorry; [*With all her soul*] but yes—yes—yes.

JOHN. By God, it's more than I deserve.

COMTESSE. Congratulations to you both.

[SYBIL *runs away; and in the fulness of time she*

married successfully in Cloth of Silver, which was afterwards turned into a bed-spread.]

MAGGIE. You haven't read my letter yet, John, have you?

JOHN. No.

COMTESSE. [*Imploringly.*] May I know to what darling letter you refer?

MAGGIE. It's a letter I wrote to him before he left London. I gave it to him closed, not to be opened until his time here was ended.

JOHN. [*As his hand strays to his pocket.*] Am I to read it now?

MAGGIE. Not before her. Please go away, Comtesse.

COMTESSE. Every word you say makes me more determined to remain.

MAGGIE. It will hurt you. [*Distressed.*] Don't read it, John; tear it up.

JOHN. You make me very curious, Maggie. And yet I don't see what can be in it.

COMTESSE. But you feel a little nervous? Give *me* the dagger.

MAGGIE. [*Quickly.*] No. [*But the* COMTESSE *has already got it.*]

COMTESSE. May I? [*She must have thought they said Yes, for she opens the letter. She shares its contents with them.*] "Dearest John, It is at my request that the Comtesse is having Lady Sybil at the cottage at the same time as yourself."

JOHN. What?

COMTESSE. Yes, she begged me to invite you together.

JOHN. But why?

MAGGIE. I promised you not to behave as other wives would do.

JOHN. It's not understandable.

COMTESSE. "You may ask why I do this, John, and my reason is, I think that after a few weeks of Lady Sybil, every day, and all day, you will become sick to death of her. I am also giving her the chance to help you and inspire you with your work, so that you may both learn what her help and her inspiration amount to. Of course, if your love is the great strong passion you think it, then those weeks will make you love her more than ever and I can only say good-bye. But if, as I suspect, you don't even now know what true love is, then by the next time we meet, dear John, you will have had enough of her.—Your affectionate wife, MAGGIE." Oh, why was not Sybil present at the reading of the will! And now, if you two will kindly excuse me, I think I must go and get that poor sufferer the eau de Cologne.

JOHN. It's almost enough to make a man lose faith in himself.

COMTESSE. Oh, don't say that, Mr. Shand.

MAGGIE. [*Defending him.*] You mustn't hurt him. If you haven't loved deep and true, that's just because you have never met a woman yet, John, capable of inspiring it.

COMTESSE. [*Putting her hand on* MAGGIE's *shoulder.*] Have you not, Mr. Shand?

JOHN. I see what you mean. But Maggie wouldn't think better of me for any false pretences. She knows my feelings for her now are neither more nor less than what they have always been.

MAGGIE. [*Who sees that he is looking at her as solemnly as a volume of sermons printed by request.*] I think no one could be fond of me that can't laugh a little at me.

JOHN. How could that help?

COMTESSE. [*Exasperated.*] Mr. Shand, I give you up.

MAGGIE. I admire his honesty.

COMTESSE. Oh, I give you up also. Arcades ambo. Scotchies both.

JOHN. [*When she has gone.*] But this letter, it's not like you. By Gosh, Maggie, you're no fool.

[*She beams at this, as any wife would.*]

But how could I have made such a mistake? It's not like a strong man. [*Evidently he has an inspiration.*]

MAGGIE. What is it?

JOHN. [*The inspiration.*] Am I a strong man?

MAGGIE. You? Of course you are. And self made. Has anybody ever helped you in the smallest way?

JOHN. [*Thinking it out again.*] No, nobody.

MAGGIE. Not even Lady Sybil?

JOHN. I'm beginning to doubt it. It's very curious, though, Maggie, that this speech should be disappointing.

MAGGIE. It's just that Mr. Venables hasn't the brains to see how good it is.

JOHN. That must be it. [*But he is too good a man to rest satisfied with this.*] No, Maggie, it's not. Somehow I seem to have lost my neat way of saying things.

MAGGIE. [*Almost cooing.*] It will come back to you.

JOHN. [*Forlorn.*] If you knew how I've tried.

MAGGIE. [*Cautiously.*] Maybe if you were to try again; and I'll just come and sit beside you, and knit. I think the click of the needles sometimes put you in the mood.

JOHN. Hardly that; and yet many a Shandism have I knocked off while you were sitting beside me knitting. I suppose it was the quietness.

MAGGIE. Very likely.

JOHN. [*With another inspiration.*] Maggie!

MAGGIE. [*Again.*] What is it, John?

JOHN. What if it was you that put those queer ideas into my head!

MAGGIE. Me?

JOHN. Without your knowing it, I mean.

MAGGIE. But how?

JOHN. We used to talk bits over; and it may be that you dropped the seed, so to speak.

MAGGIE. John, could it be this, that I sometimes had the idea in a rough womanish sort of way and then you polished it up till it came out a Shandism?

JOHN. [*Slowly slapping his knee.*] I believe you've hit it, Maggie: to think that you may have been helping me all the time—and neither of us knew it.

> [*He has so nearly reached a smile that no one can say what might have happened within the next moment if the* COMTESSE *had not reappeared.*]

COMTESSE. Mr. Venables wishes to see you, Mr. Shand.

JOHN. [*Lost, stolen, or strayed a smile in the making.*] Hum.

COMTESSE. He is coming now.

JOHN. [*Grumpy.*] Indeed.

COMTESSE. [*Sweetly.*] It is about your speech.

JOHN. He has said all he need say on that subject, and more.

COMTESSE. [*Quaking a little.*] I think it is about the second speech.

JOHN. What second speech?

> [MAGGIE *runs to her bag and opens it.*]

MAGGIE. [*Horrified.*] Comtesse, you have given it to him.

COMTESSE. [*Impudently.*] Wasn't I meant to?

JOHN. What is it? What second speech?

MAGGIE.   Cruel, cruel.   [*Willing to go on her knees.*] You had left the first draft of your speech at home, John, and I brought it here with—with a few little things I've added myself.

JOHN.   [*A seven-footer.*]   What's that?

MAGGIE.   [*Four foot ten at most.*]   Just trifles—things I was to suggest to you—while I was knitting—and then, if you liked any of them you could have polished them—and turned them into something good. John, John—and now she has shown it to Mr. Venables.

JOHN.   [*Thundering.*]   As my work, Comtesse?

> [*But the* COMTESSE *is not of the women who are afraid of thunder.*]

MAGGIE.   It is your work—nine-tenths of it.

JOHN.   [*In the black cap.*]   You presumed, Maggie Shand! Very well, then, here he comes, and now we'll see to what extent you've helped me.

VENABLES.   My dear fellow. My dear Shand, I congratulate you. Give me your hand.

JOHN.   The speech?

VENABLES.   You have improved it out of knowledge. It is the same speech, but those new touches make all the difference.   [JOHN *sits down heavily.*]   Mrs. Shand, be proud of him.

MAGGIE.   I am. I am, John.

COMTESSE.   You always said that his second thoughts were best, Charles.

VENABLES.   [*Pleased to be reminded of it.*]   Didn't I? didn't I? Those delicious little touches! How good that is, Shand, about the flowing tide.

COMTESSE.   The flowing tide?

VENABLES.   In the first speech it was something like this —"Gentlemen, the Opposition are calling to you to vote for them and the flowing tide, but I solemnly warn you to beware lest the flowing tide does not engulf you." The second way is much better.

COMTESSE. What is the second way, Mr. Shand?

[JOHN *does not tell her.*]

VENABLES. This is how he puts it now. [JOHN *cannot help raising his head to listen.*] "Gentlemen, the Opposition are calling to you to vote for them and the flowing tide, but I ask you cheerfully to vote for us and *dam* the flowing tide."

[VENABLES *and his old friend the* COMTESSE *laugh heartily, but for different reasons.*]

COMTESSE. It *is* better, Mr. Shand.

MAGGIE. *I* don't think so.

VENABLES. Yes, yes, it's so virile. Excuse me, Comtesse, I'm off to read the whole thing again. [*For the first time he notices that* JOHN *is strangely quiet.*] I think this has rather bowled you over, Shand.

[JOHN's *head sinks lower.*]

Well, well, good news doesn't kill.

MAGGIE. [*Counsel for the defence.*] Surely the important thing about the speech is its strength and knowledge and eloquence, the things that were in the first speech as well as in the second.

VENABLES. That of course is largely true. The wit would not be enough without them, just as they were not enough without the wit. It is the combination that is irresistible. [JOHN's *head rises a little.*] Shand, you are our man, remember that, it is emphatically the best thing you have ever done. How this will go down at Leeds.

[*He returns gaily to his hammock; but lower sinks* JOHN's *head, and even the* COMTESSE *has the grace to take herself off.* MAGGIE's *arms flutter near her husband, not daring to alight.*]

"You heard what he said, John. It's the combination. Is

it so terrible to you to find that my love for you had made me able to help you in the little things?"

"The little things! It seems strange to me to hear you call me by my name, Maggie. It's as if I looked on you for the first time."

"Look at me, John, for the first time. What do you see?"

"I see a woman who has brought her husband low."

"Only that?"

"I see the tragedy of a man who has found himself out. Eh, I can't live with you again, Maggie."

[*He shivers.*]

"Why did you shiver, John?"

"It was at myself for saying that I couldn't live with you again, when I should have been wondering how for so long you have lived with me. And I suppose you have for-given me all the time. [*She nods.*]   And forgive me still? [*She nods again.*]   Dear God!"

"John, am I to go? or are you to keep me on? [*She is now a little bundle near his feet.*]   I'm willing to stay be-cause I'm useful to you, if it can't be for a better reason. [*His hand feels for her, and the bundle wriggles nearer.*] It's nothing unusual I've done, John. Every man who is high up loves to think that he has done it all himself; and the wife smiles, and let's it go at that. It's our only joke. Every woman knows that. [*He stares at her in hopeless perplexity.*]   Oh, John, if only you could laugh at me."

"I can't laugh, Maggie."

> [*But as he continues to stare at her a strange dis-order appears in his face.* MAGGIE *feels that it is to be now or never.*]

"Laugh, John, laugh. Watch me; see how easy it is."

> [*A terrible struggle is taking place within him. He creaks. Something that may be mirth forces a passage, at first painfully, no more joy in it*

than in the discoloured water from a spring that has long been dry. Soon, however, he laughs loud and long. The spring water is becoming clear. MAGGIE *claps her hands. He is saved.*]

The End.

DEAR BRUTUS

A COMEDY IN THREE ACTS

ACT I

*The scene is a darkened room, which the curtain reveals so
stealthily that if there was a mouse on the stage it is
there still.   Our object is to catch our two chief characters unawares; they are Darkness and Light.*

*The room is so obscure as as to be invisible, but at the back
of the obscurity are French windows, through which is
seen* LOB'S *garden bathed in moonshine.   The Darkness and Light, which this room and garden represent
are very still, but we should feel that it is only the
pause in which old enemies regard each other before
they come to the grip.   The moonshine stealing about
among the flowers, to give them their last instructions,
has left a smile upon them, but it is a smile with a
menace in it for the dwellers in darkness.   What we
expect to see next is the moonshine slowly pushing the
windows open, so that it may whisper to a confederate
in the house, whose name is* LOB.   *But though we may
be sure that this was about to happen it does not happen; a stir among the dwellers in darkness prevents it.*

*These unsuspecting ones are in the dining-room, and as a
communicating door opens we hear them at play.
Several tenebrious shades appear in the lighted door-
way and hesitate on the two steps that lead down into
the unlit room.   The fanciful among us may conceive
a rustle at the same moment among the flowers.   The
engagement has begun, though not in the way we had
intended.*

Voices.—

"Go on, Coady: lead the way."

"Oh dear, I don't see why I should go first."

"The nicest always goes first."

"It is a strange house if I am the nicest."

"It is a strange house."

"Don't close the door; I can't see where the switch is."

"Over here."

*They have been groping their way forward, blissfully un-
aware of how they shall be groping there again more
terribly before the night is out. Some one finds a
switch, and the room is illumined, with the effect
that the garden seems to have drawn back a step as if
worsted in the first encounter. But it is only waiting.*

*The apparently inoffensive chamber thus suddenly revealed
is, for a bachelor's home, creditably like a charming
country house drawing-room and abounds in the little
feminine touches that are so often best applied by the
hand of man. There is nothing in the room inimical
to the ladies, unless it be the cut flowers which are
from the garden and possibly in collusion with it. The
fireplace may also be a little dubious. It has been
hacked out of a thick wall which may have been
there when the other walls were not, and is presumably
the cavern where Lob, when alone, sits chatting to
himself among the blue smoke. He is as much at home
by this fire as any gnome that may be hiding among
its shadows; but he is less familiar with the rest of the
room, and when he sees it, as for instance on his lonely
way to bed, he often stares long and hard at it before
chuckling uncomfortably.*

There are five ladies, and one only of them is elderly, the

MRS. COADE *whom a voice in the darkness has already
proclaimed the nicest. She is the nicest, though the
voice was no good judge.* COADY, *as she is familiarly
called and as her husband also is called, each having
for many years been able to answer for the other, is
a rounded old lady with a beaming smile that has accompanied her from childhood. If she lives to be a
hundred she will pretend to the census man that she is
only ninety-nine. She has no other vice that has not
been smoothed out of existence by her placid life, and
she has but one complaint against the male* COADY, *the
rather odd one that he has long forgotten his first wife.
Our* MRS. COADY *never knew the first one, but it is
she alone who sometimes looks at the portrait of her
and preserves in their home certain mementoes of her,
such as a lock of brown hair, which the equally gentle
male* COADY *must have treasured once but has now
forgotten. The first wife had been slightly lame, and
in their brief married life he had carried solicitously
a rest for her foot, had got so accustomed to doing
this, that after a quarter of a century with our* MRS.
COADY *he still finds footstools for her as if she were
lame also. She has ceased to pucker her face over this,
taking it as a kind little thoughtless attention, and
indeed with the years has developed a friendly limp.*
*Of the other four ladies, all young and physically fair, two
are married.* MRS. DEARTH *is tall, of smouldering eye
and fierce desires, murky beasts lie in ambush in the
labyrinths of her mind, she is a white-faced gypsy with
a husky voice, most beautiful when she is sullen, and
therefore frequently at her best. The other ladies
when in conclave refer to her as The Dearth.* MRS.
PURDIE *is a safer companion for the toddling kind of
man. She is soft and pleading, and would seek what*

she wants by laying her head on the loved one's shoulder, while The Dearth might attain it with a pistol. A brighter spirit than either is JOANNA TROUT who, when her affections are not engaged, has a merry face and figure, but can dismiss them both at the important moment, which is at the word "love." Then JOANNA quivers, her sense of humour ceases to beat and the dullest man may go ahead. There remains LADY CAROLINE LANEY of the disdainful poise, lately from the enormously select school where they are taught to pronounce their r's as w's; nothing else seems to be taught, but for matrimonial success nothing else is necessary. Every woman who pronounces r as w will find a mate; it appeals to all that is chivalrous in man.

An old-fashioned gallantry induces us to accept from each of these ladies her own estimate of herself, and fortunately it is favourable in every case. This refers to their estimate of themselves up to the hour of ten on the evening on which we first meet them; the estimate may have changed temporarily by the time we part from them on the following morning. What their mirrors say to each of them is, A dear face, not classically perfect but abounding in that changing charm which is the best type of English womanhood; here is a woman who has seen and felt far more than her reticent nature readily betrays; she sometimes smiles, but behind that concession, controlling it in a manner hardly less than adorable, lurks the sigh called Knowledge; a strangely interesting face, mysterious; a line for her tombstone might be "If I had been a man what adventures I could have had with her who lies here."

Are these ladies then so very alike? They would all deny it, so we must take our own soundings. At this moment of their appearance in the drawing-room at *least they are alike in having a common interest. No sooner has the dining-room door closed than purpose leaps to their eyes; oddly enough, the men having been got rid of, the drama begins.*

ALICE DEARTH. [*The darkest spirit but the bravest.*] We must not waste a second. Our minds are made up, I think?

JOANNA. Now is the time.

MRS. COADE. [*At once delighted and appalled.*] Yes, now if at all; but should we?

ALICE. Certainly; and before the men come in.

MABEL PURDIE. You don't think we should wait for the men? They are as much in it as we are.

LADY CAROLINE. [*Unlucky, as her opening remark is without a single* r.] Lob would be with them. If the thing is to be done at all it should be done now.

MRS. COADE. Is it quite fair to Lob? After all, he is our host.

JOANNA. Of course it isn't fair to him, but let's do it, Coady.

MRS. COADE. Yes, let's do it!

MABEL. Mrs. Dearth *is* doing it.

ALICE. [*Who is writing out a telegram.*] Of course I am. The men are not coming, are they?

JOANNA. [*Reconnoitring.*] No; your husband is having another glass of port.

ALICE. I am sure he is. One of you ring, please.

[*The bold* JOANNA *rings.*]

MRS. COADE. Poor Matey!

LADY CAROLINE. He wichly desewves what he is about to get.

JOANNA. He is coming! Don't all stand huddled together like conspirators.

MRS. COADE. It is what we are!

> [*Swiftly they find seats, and are sunk thereon like ladies waiting languidly for their lords, when the doomed butler appears. He is a man of brawn, who would cast any one of them forth for a wager; but we are about to connive at the triumph of mind over matter.*]

ALICE. [*Always at her best before "the bright face of danger."*] Ah, Matey, I wish this telegram sent.

MATEY. [*A general favorite.*] Very good, ma'am. The village post office closed at eight, but if your message is important——

ALICE. It is; and you are so clever, Matey, I am sure that you can persuade them to oblige you.

MATEY. [*Taking the telegram.*] I will see to it myself, ma'am; you can depend on its going.

> [*There comes a little gasp from* COADY, *which is the equivalent to dropping a stitch in needlework.*]

ALICE. [*Who is* THE DEARTH *now.*] Thank you. Better read the telegram, Matey, to be sure that you can make it out. [MATEY *reads it to himself, and he has never quite the same faith in woman again.* THE DEARTH *continues in a purring voice.*] Read it aloud, Matey.

MATEY. Oh, ma'am!

ALICE. [*Without the purr.*] Aloud

> [*Thus encouraged, he reads the fatal missive.*]

MATEY. "To Police Station, Great Cumney. Send officer first thing to-morrow morning to arrest Matey, butler, for theft of rings."

ALICE. Yes, that is quite right.

MATEY. Ma'am! [*But seeing that she has taken up a book, he turns to* LADY CAROLINE.] My lady!

LADY CAROLINE. [*Whose voice strikes colder than* THE DEARTH'S.] Should we not say how many wings?

ALICE. Yes, put in the number of rings, Matey.

> [MATEY *does not put in the number, but he produces three rings from unostentatious parts of his person and returns them without noticeable dignity to their various owners.*]

MATEY. [*Hopeful that the incident is now closed.*] May I tear up the telegram, ma'am?

ALICE. Certainly not.

LADY CAROLINE. I always said that this man was the culpwit. I am nevaw mistaken in faces, and I see bwoad awwows all over youws, Matey.

> [*He might reply that he sees* w's *all over hers, but it is no moment for repartee.*]

MATEY. It is deeply regretted.

ALICE. [*Darkly.*] I am sure it is.

JOANNA. [*Who has seldom remained silent for so long.*] We may as well tell him now that it is not our rings we are worrying about. They have just been a means to an end, Matey.

> [*The stir among the ladies shows that they have arrived at the more interesting point.*]

ALICE. Precisely. In other words that telegram is sent unless——

> [MATEY'S *head rises.*]

JOANNA. Unless you can tell us instantly what peculiarity it is that all we ladies have in common.

MABEL. Not only the ladies; all the guests in this house.

ALICE. We have been here a week, and we find that when Lob invited us he knew us all so little that we begin to wonder why he asked us. And now from words he has

let drop we know that we were invited because of something he thinks we have in common.

MABEL. But he won't say what it is.

LADY CAROLINE. [*Drawing back a little from* JOANNA.]
One knows that no people could be more unlike.

JOANNA. [*Thankfully.*] One does.

MRS. COADE. And we can't sleep at night, Matey, for
wondering what this something is.

JOANNA. [*Summing up.*] But we are sure you know,
and if you don't tell us—quod.

MATEY. [*With growing uneasiness.*] I don't know
what you mean, ladies.

ALICE. Oh yes, you do.

MRS. COADE. You must admit that your master is a
very strange person.

MATEY. [*Wriggling.*] He is a little odd, ma'am.
That is why every one calls him Lob; not Mr. Lob.

JOANNA. He is so odd that it has got on my nerves that
we have been invited here for some sort of horrid experiment. [MATEY *shivers.*] You look as if you thought
so too!

MATEY. Oh no, miss, I—he—[*The words he would
keep back elude him.*] You shouldn't have come, ladies;
you didn't ought to have come.

> [*For the moment he is sorrier for them than for
> himself.*]

LADY CAROLINE. Shouldn't have come! Now, my man,
what do you mean by that?

MATEY. Nothing, my lady: I—I just mean, why did
you come if you are the kind he thinks?

MABEL. The kind he thinks?

ALICE. What kind does he think? Now we are getting
at it.

MATEY. [*Guardedly.*] I haven't a notion, ma'am.

LADY CAROLINE. [*Whose w's must henceforth be supplied by the judicious reader.*] Then it is not necessarily our virtue that makes Lob interested in us?

MATEY. [*Thoughtlessly.*] No, my lady; oh no, my lady. [*This makes an unfavourable impression.*]

MRS. COADE. And yet, you know, he is rather lovable.

MATEY. [*Carried away.*] He is, ma'am. He is the most lovable old devil—I beg pardon, ma'am.

JOANNA. You scarcely need to, for in a way it is true. I have seen him out there among his flowers, petting them, talking to them, coaxing them till they simply *had* to grow.

ALICE. [*Making use perhaps of the wrong adjective.*] It is certainly a divine garden.

[*They all look at the unblinking enemy.*]

MRS. COADE. [*Not more deceived than the others.*] How lovely it is in the moonlight! Roses, roses, all the way. [*Dreamily.*] It is like a hat I once had when I was young.

ALICE. Lob is such an amazing gardener that I believe he could even grow hats.

LADY CAROLINE. [*Who will catch it for this.*] He is a wonderful gardener; but is that quite nice at his age? What *is* his age, man?

MATEY. [*Shuffling.*] He won't tell, my lady. I think he is frightened that the police would step in if they knew how old he is. They do say in the village that they remember him seventy years ago, looking just as he does to-day.

ALICE. Absurd.

MATEY. Yes, ma'am; but there are his razors.

LADY CAROLINE. Razors?

MATEY. *You* won't know about razors, my lady, not being married—as yet—excuse me. But a married lady can tell a man's age by the number of his razors. [*A little scared.*] If you saw his razors—there is a little world of them, from patents of the present day back to implements so horrible, you can picture him with them in his hand scraping his way through the ages.

LADY CAROLINE. You amuse one to an extent. Was he ever married?

MATEY. [*Too lightly.*] He has quite forgotten, my lady. [*Reflecting.*] How long ago is it since Merry England?

LADY CAROLINE. Why do you ask?

MABEL. In Queen Elizabeth's time, wasn't it?

MATEY. He says he is all that is left of Merry England: that little man.

MABEL. [*Who has brothers.*] Lob? I think there is a famous cricketer called Lob.

MRS. COADE. Wasn't there a Lob in Shakespeare? No, of course I am thinking of Robin Goodfellow.

LADY CAROLINE. The names are so alike.

JOANNA. Robin Goodfellow was Puck.

MRS. COADE. [*With natural elation.*] That is what was in my head. Lob was another name for Puck.

JOANNA. Well, he is certainly rather like what Puck might have grown into if he had forgotten to die. And, by the way, I remember now he does call his flowers by the old Elizabethan names.

MATEY. He always calls the Nightingale Philomel, miss —if that is any help.

ALICE. [*Who is not omniscient.*] None whatever. Tell me this, did he specially ask you all for Midsummer week?

[*They assent.*]

MATEY. [*Who might more judiciously have remained silent.*] He would!

MRS. COADE. Now what do you mean?

MATEY. He always likes them to be here on Midsummer night, ma'am.

ALICE. Them? Whom?

MATEY. Them who have that in common.

MABEL. What can it be?

MATEY. I don't know.

LADY CAROLINE. [*Suddenly introspective.*] I hope we are all nice women? We don't know each other very well. [*Certain suspicions are reborn in various breasts.*] Does anything startling happen at those times?

MATEY. I don't know.

JOANNA. Why, I believe this is Midsummer Eve!

MATEY. Yes, miss, it is. The villagers know it. They are all inside their houses, to-night—with the doors barred.

LADY CAROLINE. Because of—of him?

MATEY. He frightens them. There are stories.

ALICE. What alarms them? Tell us—or—[*She brandishes the telegram.*]

MATEY. I know nothing for certain, ma'am. I have never done it myself. He has wanted me to, but I wouldn't.

MABEL. Done what?

MATEY. [*With fine appeal.*] Oh, ma'am, don't ask me. Be merciful to me, ma'am. I am not bad naturally. It was just going into domestic service that did for me; the accident of being flung among bad companions. It's touch and go how the poor turn out in this world; all depends on your taking the right or the wrong turning.

MRS. COADE. [*The lenient.*] I daresay that is true.

MATEY. [*Under this touch of sun.*] When I was young, ma'am, I was offered a clerkship in the city. If I had taken it there wouldn't be a more honest man alive to-day. I would give the world to be able to begin over again.

> [*He means every word of it, though the flowers would here, if they dared, burst into ironical applause.*]

MRS. COADE. It is very sad, Mrs. Dearth.

ALICE. I am sorry for him; but still——

MATEY. [*His eyes turning to* LADY CAROLINE.] What do you say, my lady?

LADY CAROLINE. [*Briefly.*] As you ask me, I should certainly say jail.

MATEY. [*Desperately.*] If you will say no more about this, ma'am—I'll give you a tip that is worth it.

ALICE. Ah, now you are talking.

LADY CAROLINE. Don't listen to him.

MATEY. [*Lowering.*] You are the one that is hardest on me.

LADY CAROLINE. Yes, I flatter myself I am.

MATEY. [*Forgetting himself.*] You might take a wrong turning yourself, my lady.

LADY CAROLINE. I? How dare you, man?

> [*But the flowers rather like him for this: it is possibly what gave them a certain idea.*]

JOANNA. [*Near the keyhole of the dining-room door.*] The men are rising.

ALICE. [*Hurriedly.*] Very well, Matey, we agree—if the "tip" is good enough.

LADY CAROLINE. You will regret this.

MATEY. I think not, my lady. It's this: I wouldn't go out to-night if he asks you. Go into the garden, if you like. The garden is all right. [*He really believes this.*] I wouldn't go farther—not to-night.

MRS. COADE. But he never proposes to us to go farther. Why should he to-night?

MATEY. I don't know, ma'am, but don't any of you go— [*Devilishly*] except you, my lady; I should like you to go.

LADY CAROLINE. Fellow!

> [*They consider this odd warning.*]

ALICE. Shall I? [*They nod and she tears up the telegram.*]

MATEY. [*With a gulp.*] Thank you, ma'am.

LADY CAROLINE. You should have sent that telegram off.

JOANNA. You are sure you have told us all you know, Matey?

MATEY. Yes, miss. [*But at the door he is more generous.*] Above all, ladies, I wouldn't go into the wood.

MABEL. The wood? Why, there is no wood within a dozen miles of here.

MATEY. No, ma'am. But all the same I wouldn't go into it, ladies—not if I was you.

> [*With this cryptic warning he leaves them, and any discussion of it is prevented by the arrival of their host. LOB is very small, and probably no one has ever looked so old except some newborn child. To such as watch him narrowly, as the ladies now do for the first time, he has the effect of seeming to be hollow, an attenuated piece of piping insufficiently inflated; one feels that if he were to strike against a solid object he might rebound feebly from it, which would be less disconcerting if he did not obviously know this and carefully avoid the furniture; he is so light that the subject must not be mentioned in his presence, but it is possible that, were the ladies to combine, they could blow him out of a chair. He enters portentously, his hands behind his back, as if every bit of him, from his domed head to his little feet, were the physical expressions of the deep thoughts within him, then suddenly he whirls round to make his guests jump. This amuses him vastly, and he regains his gravity with difficulty. He addresses MRS. COADE.*]

LOB. Standing, dear lady? Pray be seated.

[*He finds a chair for her and pulls it away as she is about to sit, or kindly pretends to be about to do so, for he has had this quaint conceit every evening since she arrived.*]

MRS. COADE. [*Who loves children.*] You naughty!

LOB. [*Eagerly.*] It is quite a flirtation, isn't it?

[*He rolls on a chair, kicking out his legs in an ecstasy of satisfaction. But the ladies are not certain that he is the little innocent they have hitherto thought him. The advent of* MR. COADE *and* MR. PURDIE *presently adds to their misgivings.* MR. COADE *is old, a sweet pippin of a man with a gentle smile for all; he must have suffered much, you conclude incorrectly, to acquire that tolerant smile. Sometimes, as when he sees other people at work, a wistful look takes the place of the smile, and* MR. COADE *fidgets like one who would be elsewhere. Then there rises before his eyes the room called the study in his house, whose walls are lined with boxes marked A. B. C. to Z. and A^2. B^2. C^2. to K^2. These contain dusty notes for his great work on the Feudal System, the notes many years old, the work, strictly speaking, not yet begun. He still speaks at times of finishing it but never of beginning it. He knows that in more favourable circumstances, for instance if he had been a poor man instead of pleasantly well to do, he could have flung himself avidly into that noble undertaking; but he does not allow his secret sorrow to embitter him or darken the house. Quickly the vision passes, and he is again his bright self. Idleness, he says in his game way, has its recompenses. It is charming now to see*] *how he at once crosses to his wife, solicitous for her comfort. He is bearing down on her with a footstool when* MR. PURDIE *comes from the dining-room. He is the most brilliant of our company, recently notable in debate at Oxford, where he was runner-up for the presidentship of the Union and only lost it because the other man was less brilliant. Since then he has gone to the bar on Monday, married on Tuesday, and had a brief on Wednesday. Beneath his brilliance, and making charming company for himself, he is aware of intellectual powers beyond his years. As we are about to see, he has made one mistake in his life which he is bravely facing.*]

ALICE. Is my husband still sampling the port, Mr. Purdie?

PURDIE. [*With a disarming smile for the absent* DEARTH.] Do you know, I believe he is. Do the ladies like our proposal, Coade?

COADE. I have not told them of it yet. The fact is, I am afraid that it might tire my wife too much. Do you feel equal to a little exertion to-night, Coady, or is your foot troubling you?

MRS. COADE. [*The kind creature.*] I have been resting it, Coady.

COADE. [*Propping it on the footstool.*] There! Is that more comfortable? Presently, dear, if you are agreeable we are all going out for a walk.

MRS. COADE. [*Quoting* MATEY.] The garden is all right.

PURDIE. [*With jocular solemnity.*] Ah, but it is not to be the garden. We are going farther afield. We have an adventure for to-night. Get thick shoes and a wrap, Mrs. Dearth; all of you.

LADY CAROLINE. [*With but languid interest.*] Where do you propose to take us?

PURDIE. To find a mysterious wood.

> [*With the word "wood" the ladies are blown up-right. Their eyes turn to* LOB, *who, however, has never looked more innocent.*]

JOANNA. Are you being funny, Mr. Purdie? You know quite well that there are not any trees for miles around. You have said yourself that it is the one blot on the landscape.

COADE. [*Almost as great a humorist as* PURDIE.] Ah, on ordinary occasions! But allow us to point out to you, Miss Joanna, that this is Midsummer Eve.

> [LOB *again comes sharply under female observation.*]

PURDIE. Tell them what you told us, Lob.

LOB. [*With a pout for the credulous.*] It is all nonsense, of course; just foolish talk of the villagers. They say that on Midsummer Eve there is a strange wood in this part of the country.

ALICE. [*Lowering.*] Where?

PURDIE. Ah, that is one of its most charming features. It is never twice in the same place apparently. It has been seen on different parts of the Downs and on More Common; once it was close to Radley village and another time about a mile from the sea. Oh, a sporting wood!

LADY CAROLINE. And Lob is anxious that we should all go and look for it?

COADE. Not he; Lob is the only sceptic in the house. Says it is all rubbish, and that we shall be sillies if we go. But we believe, eh, Purdie?

PURDIE. [*Waggishly.*] Rather!

LOB. [*The artful.*] Just wasting the evening. Let us have a round game at cards here instead.

PURDIE. [*Grandly.*] No, sir, I am going to find that wood.

JOANNA. What is the good of it when it is found?

PURDIE. We shall wander in it deliciously, listening to a new sort of bird called the Philomel.

> [LOB *is behaving in the most exemplary manner: making sweet little clucking sounds.*]

JOANNA. [*Doubtfully.*] Shall we keep together, Mr. Purdie?

PURDIE. No, we must hunt in pairs.

JOANNA. [*Converted.*] I think it would be rather fun. Come on, Coady, I'll lace your boots for you. I am sure your poor foot will carry you nicely.

ALICE. Miss Trout, wait a moment. Lob, has this wonderful wood any special properties?

LOB. Pooh! There's no wood.

LADY CAROLINE. You've never seen it?

LOB. Not I. I don't believe in it.

ALICE. Have any of the villagers ever been in it?

LOB. [*Dreamily.*] So it's said; so it's said.

ALICE. What did they say were their experiences?

LOB. That isn't known. They never came back.

JOANNA. [*Promptly resuming her seat.*] Never came back!

LOB. Absurd, of course. You see in the morning the wood was gone; and so they were gone, too. [*He clucks again.*]

JOANNA. I don't think I like this wood.

MRS. COADE. It certainly is Midsummer Eve.

COADE. [*Remembering that women are not yet civilised.*] Of course if you ladies are against it we will drop the idea. It was only a bit of fun.

ALICE. [*With a malicious eye on* LOB.] Yes, better
give it up—to please Lob.

PURDIE. Oh, all right, Lob. What about that round
game of cards?

[*The proposal meets with approval.*]

LOB. [*Bursting into tears.*] I wanted you to go. I had
set my heart on your going. It is the thing I wanted, and it
isn't good for me not to get the thing I want.

> [*He creeps under the table and threatens the
> hands that would draw him out.*]

MRS. COADE. Good gracious, he has wanted it all the
time. You wicked Lob!

ALICE. Now, you see there *is* something in it.

COADE. Nonsense, Mrs. Dearth, it was only a joke.

MABEL. [*Melting.*] Don't cry, Lobby.

LOB. Nobody cares for me—nobody loves me. And I
need to be loved.

> [*Several of them are on their knees to him.*]

JOANNA. Yes, we do, we all love you. Nice, nice Lobby.

MABEL. Dear Lob, I am so fond of you.

JOANNA. Dry his eyes with my own handkerchief. [*He
holds up his eyes but is otherwise inconsolable.*]

LADY CAROLINE. Don't pamper him.

LOB. [*Furiously.*] I need to be pampered.

MRS. COADE. You funny little man. Let us go at once
and look for his wood.

> [*All feel that thus alone can his tears be dried.*]

JOANNA. Boots and cloaks, hats forward. Come on,
Lady Caroline, just to show you are not afraid of Matey.

> [*There is a general exodus, and* LOB *left alone
> emerges from his temporary retirement. He
> clucks victoriously, but presently is on his knees
> again distressfully regarding some flowers that
> have fallen from their bowl.*]

LOB. Poor bruised one, it was I who hurt you. Lob is so sorry. Lie there! [*To another.*] Pretty, pretty, let me see where you have a pain? You fell on your head; is this the place? Now I make it better. Oh, little rascal, you are not hurt at all; you just pretend. Oh dear, oh dear! Sweetheart, don't cry, you are now prettier than ever. You were too tall. Oh, how beautifully you smell now that you are small. [*He replaces the wounded tenderly in their bowl.*] Drink, drink. Now, you are happy again. The little rascal smiles. All smile, please—nod heads—aha! aha! You love Lob—Lob loves you.

[*JOANNA and MR. PURDIE stroll in by the window.*]

JOANNA. What were you saying to them, Lob?

LOB. I was saying "Two's company, three's none."

[*He departs with a final cluck.*]

JOANNA. That man—he suspects!

> [*This is a very different JOANNA from the one who has so far flitted across our scene. It is also a different PURDIE. In company they seldom look at each other, though when the one does so the eyes of the other magnetically respond. We have seen them trivial, almost cynical, but now we are to greet them as they know they really are, the great strong-hearted man and his natural mate, in the grip of the master passion. For the moment LOB's words have unnerved JOANNA and it is JOHN PURDIE's dear privilege to soothe her.*]

PURDIE. No one minds Lob. My dear, oh my dear.

JOANNA. [*Faltering.*] Yes, but he saw you kiss my hand. Jack, if Mabel were to suspect!

PURDIE. [*Happily.*] There is nothing for her to suspect.

JOANNA. [*Eagerly.*] No, there isn't, is there? [*She is*

desirous ever to be without a flaw.] Jack, I am not doing anything wrong, am I?

PURDIE. You!

> [*With an adorable gesture she gives him one of her hands, and manlike he takes the other also.*]

JOANNA. Mabel is your wife, Jack. I should so hate myself if I did anything that was disloyal to her.

PURDIE. [*Pressing her hand to her eyes as if counting them, in the strange manner of lovers.*] Those eyes could never be disloyal—my lady of the nut-brown eyes. [*He holds her from him, surveying her, and is scorched in the flame of her femininity.*] Oh, the sveldtness of you. [*Almost with reproach.*] Joanna, why are you so sveldt!

> [*For his sake she would be less sveldt if she could, but she can't. She admits her failure with eyes grown still larger, and he envelops her so that he may not see her. Thus men seek safety.*]

JOANNA. [*While out of sight.*] All I want is to help her and you.

PURDIE. I know—how well I know—my dear brave love.

JOANNA. I am very fond of Mabel, Jack. I should like to be the best friend she has in the world.

PURDIE. You are, dearest. No woman ever had a better friend.

JOANNA. And yet I don't think she really likes me. I wonder why?

PURDIE. [*Who is the bigger brained of the two.*] It is just that Mabel doesn't understand. Nothing could make me say a word against my wife——

JOANNA. [*Sternly.*] I wouldn't listen to you if you did.

PURDIE. I love you all the more, dear, for saying that. But Mabel is a cold nature and she doesn't understand.

JOANNA. [*Thinking never of herself but only of him.*] She doesn't appreciate your finer qualities.

PURDIE. [*Ruminating.*] That's it. But of course I am difficult. I always was a strange, strange creature. I often think, Joanna, that I am rather like a flower that has never had the sun to shine on it nor the rain to water it.

JOANNA. You break my heart.

PURDIE. [*With considerable enjoyment.*] I suppose there is no more lonely man than I walking the earth to-day.

JOANNA. [*Beating her wings.*] It is so mournful.

PURDIE. It is the thought of you that sustains me, elevates me. You shine high above me like a star.

JOANNA. No, no. I wish I was wonderful, but I am not.

PURDIE. You have made me a better man, Joanna.

JOANNA. I am so proud to think that.

PURDIE. You have made me kinder to Mabel.

JOANNA. I am sure you are always kind to her.

PURDIE. Yes, I hope so. But I think now of special little ways of giving her pleasure. That never-to-be-forgotten day when we first met, you and I!

JOANNA. [*Fluttering nearer to him.*] That tragic, lovely day by the weir. Oh, Jack!

PURDIE. Do you know how in gratitude I spent the rest of that day?

JOANNA. [*Crooning.*] Tell me.

PURDIE. I read to Mabel aloud for an hour. I did it out of kindness to her, because I had met you.

JOANNA. It was dear of you.

PURDIE. Do you remember that first time my arms—your waist—you are so fluid, Joanna. [*Passionately.*] Why are you so fluid?

JOANNA. [*Downcast.*] I can't help it, Jack.

PURDIE. I gave her a ruby bracelet for that.

JOANNA.   It is a gem. You have given that lucky woman many lovely things.

PURDIE.   It is my invariable custom to go straight off and buy Mabel something whenever you have been sympathetic to me. Those new earrings of hers—they are in memory of the first day you called me Jack. Her Paquin gown—the one with the beads—was because you let me kiss you.

JOANNA.   I didn't exactly let you.

PURDIE.   No, but you have such a dear way of giving in.

JOANNA.   Jack, she hasn't worn that gown of late.

PURDIE.   No, nor the jewels. I think she has some sort of idea now that when I give her anything nice it means that you have been nice to me. She has rather a suspicious nature, Mabel; she never used to have it, but it seems to be growing on her. I wonder why, I wonder why?

> [*In this wonder which is shared by* JOANNA *their lips meet, and* MABEL, *who has been about to enter from the garden quietly retires.*]

JOANNA.   Was that any one in the garden?

PURDIE.   [*Returning from a quest.*]   There is no one there now.

JOANNA.   I am sure I heard some one. If it was Mabel! [*With a perspicacity that comes of knowledge of her sex.*] Jack, if she saw us she will think you were kissing me.

> [*These fears are confirmed by the rather odd bearing of* MABEL, *who now joins their select party.*]

MABEL.   [*Apologetically.*]   I am so sorry to interrupt you, Jack; but please wait a moment before you kiss her again. Excuse me, Joanna. [*She quietly draws the curtains, thus shutting out the garden and any possible onlooker.*]   I did not want the others to see you; they might not understand how noble you are, Jack. You can go on now.

[*Having thus passed the time of day with them
she withdraws by the door, leaving* JACK *bewildered and* JOANNA *knowing all about it.*]

JOANNA. How extraordinary! Of all the——! Oh, but
how contemptible! [*She sweeps to the door and calls to*
MABEL *by name.*]

MABEL. [*Returning with promptitude.*] Did you call
me, Joanna?

JOANNA. [*Guardedly.*] I insist on an explanation.
[*With creditable hauteur.*] What were you doing in the
garden, Mabel?

MABEL. [*Who has not been so quiet all day.*] I was
looking for something I have lost.

PURDIE. [*Hope springing eternal.*] Anything important?

MABEL. I used to fancy it, Jack. It is my husband's
love. You don't happen to have picked it up, Joanna? If
so and you don't set great store by it I should like it back—
the pieces, I mean.

[MR. PURDIE *is about to reply to this, when*
JOANNA *rather wisely fills the breach.*]

JOANNA. Mabel, I—I will not be talked to in that way.
To imply that I—that your husband—oh, shame!

PURDIE. [*Finely.*] I must say, Mabel, that I am a little
disappointed in you. I certainly understood that you had
gone up-stairs to put on your boots.

MABEL. Poor old Jack. [*She muses.*] A woman like
that!

JOANNA. [*Changing her comment in the moment of ut-
terance*]—I forgive you Mabel, you will be sorry for this
afterwards.

PURDIE. [*Warningly, but still reluctant to think less
well of his wife.*] Not a word against Joanna, Mabel.
If you knew how nobly she has spoken of you.

JOANNA. [*Imprudently.*] She does know. She has been listening.

> [*There is a moment's danger of the scene degenerating into something mid-Victorian. Fortunately a chivalrous man is present to lift it to a higher plane.* JOHN PURDIE *is one to whom subterfuge of any kind is abhorrent; if he has not spoken out before it is because of his reluctance to give* MABEL *pain. He speaks out now, and seldom probably has he proved himself more worthy.*]

PURDIE. This is a man's business. I must be open with you now, Mabel: it is the manlier way. If you wish it I shall always be true to you in word and deed; it is your right. But I cannot pretend that Joanna is not the one woman in the world for me. If I had met her before you—it's Kismet, I suppose. [*He swells.*]

JOANNA. [*From a chair.*] Too late, too late.

MABEL. [*Although the woman has seen him swell.*] I suppose you never knew what true love was till you met her, Jack?

PURDIE. You force me to say it. Joanna and I are as one person. We have not a thought at variance. We are one rather than two.

MABEL. [*Looking at* JOANNA.] Yes, and that's the one! [*With the cheapest sarcasm.*] I am so sorry to have marred your lives.

PURDIE. If any blame there is, it is all mine; she is as spotless as the driven snow. The moment I mentioned love to her she told me to desist.

MABEL. Not she.

JOANNA. So you *were* listening! [*The obtuseness of* MABEL *is very strange to her.*] Mabel, don't you see how splendid he is!

MABEL. Not quite, Joanna.

> [*She goes away. She is really a better woman than this, but never capable of scaling that higher plane to which he has, as it were, offered her a hand.*]

JOANNA. How lovely of you, Jack, to take it all upon yourself.

PURDIE. [*Simply.*] It is the man's privilege.

JOANNA. Mabel has such a horrid way of seeming to put people in the wrong.

PURDIE. Have you noticed that? Poor Mabel, it is not an enviable quality.

JOANNA. [*Despondently.*] I don't think I care to go out now. She has spoilt it all. She has taken the innocence out of it, Jack.

PURDIE. [*A rock.*] We must be brave and not mind her. Ah, Joanna, if we had met in time. If only I could begin again. To be battered for ever just because I once took the wrong turning, it isn't fair.

JOANNA. [*Emerging from his arms.*] The wrong turning! Now, who was saying that a moment ago—about himself? Why, it was Matey.

> [*A footstep is heard.*]

PURDIE. [*For the first time losing patience with his wife.*] Is that her coming back again? It's too bad.

> [*But the intruder is MRS. DEARTH, and he greets her with relief.*]

Ah, it is you, Mrs. Dearth.

ALICE. Yes, it is; but thank you for telling me, Mr. Purdie. I don't intrude, do I?

JOANNA. [*Descending to the lower plane, on which even goddesses snap.*] Why should you?

PURDIE. Rather not. We were—hoping it would be

you. We want to start on the walk. I can't think what has become of the others. We have been looking for them everywhere. [*He glances vaguely round the room, as if they might so far have escaped detection.*]

ALICE. [*Pleasantly.*] Well, do go on looking; under that flower-pot would be a good place. It is my husband I am in search of.

PURDIE. [*Who likes her best when they are in different rooms.*] Shall I rout him out for you?

ALICE. How too unutterably kind of you, Mr. Purdie. I hate to trouble you, but it would be the sort of service one never forgets.

PURDIE. You know, I believe you are chaffing me.

ALICE. No, no, I am incapable of that.

PURDIE. I won't be a moment.

ALICE. Miss Trout and I will await your return with ill-concealed impatience.

> [*They await it across a table, the newcomer in a reverie and* JOANNA *watching her. Presently* MRS. DEARTH *looks up, and we may notice that she has an attractive screw of the mouth which denotes humour.*]

Yes, I suppose you are right; I daresay I am.

JOANNA. [*Puzzled.*] I didn't say anything.

ALICE. I thought I heard you say "That hateful Dearth woman, coming butting in where she is not wanted."

> [JOANNA *draws up her sveldt figure, but a screw of one mouth often calls for a similar demonstration from another, and both ladies smile. They nearly become friends.*]

JOANNA. You certainly have good ears.

ALICE. [*Drawling.*] Yes, they have always been rather admired.

JOANNA. [*Snapping.*] By the painters for whom you sat when you were an artist's model?

ALICE. [*Measuring her.*] So that has leaked out, has it!

JOANNA. [*Ashamed.*] I shouldn't have said that.

ALICE. [*Their brief friendship over.*] Do you think I care whether you know or not?

JOANNA. [*Making an effort to be good.*] I'm sure you don't. Still, it was cattish of me.

ALICE. It was.

JOANNA. [*In flame.*] I don't see it.

> [MRS. DEARTH *laughs and forgets her, and with the entrance of a man from the dining-room* JOANNA *drifts elsewhere. Not so much a man, this newcomer, as the relic of what has been a good one; it is the most he would ever claim for himself. Sometimes, brandy in hand, he has visions of the* WILL DEARTH *he used to be, clear of eye, sees him but a field away, singing at his easel or, fishing-rod in hand, leaping a stile. Our* WILL *stares after the fellow for quite a long time, so long that the two melt into the one who finishes* LOB'S *brandy. He is scarcely intoxicated as he appears before the lady of his choice, but he is shaky and has watery eyes.*
>
> ALICE *has had a rather wild love for this man, or for that other one, and he for her, but somehow it has gone whistling down the wind. We may expect therefore to see them at their worst when in each other's company.*]

DEARTH. [*Who is not without a humorous outlook on his own degradation.*] I am uncommonly flattered, Alice, to hear that you have sent for me. It quite takes me aback.

ALICE. [*With cold distaste.*] It isn't your company I want, Will.

DEARTH. You know, I felt that Purdie must have delivered your message wrongly.

ALICE. I want you to come with us on this mysterious walk and keep an eye on Lob.

DEARTH. On poor little Lob? Oh, surely not.

ALICE. I can't make the man out. I want you to tell me something; when he invited us here, do you think it was you or me he specially wanted?

DEARTH. Oh, you. He made no bones about it; said there was something about you that made him want uncommonly to have you down here.

ALICE. Will, try to remember this: did he ask us for any particular time?

DEARTH. Yes, he was particular about its being Midsummer week.

ALICE. Ah! I thought so. Did he say what it was about me that made him want to have me here in Midsummer week?

DEARTH. No, but I presumed it must be your fascination, Alice.

ALICE. Just so. Well, I want you to come out with us to-night to watch him.

DEARTH. Crack-in-my-eye-Tommy, spy on my host! And such a harmless little chap, too. Excuse me, Alice. Besides I have an engagement.

ALICE. An engagement—with the port decanter, I presume.

DEARTH. A good guess, but wrong. The decanter is now but an empty shell. Still, how you know me! My engagement is with a quiet cigar in the garden.

ALICE. Your hand is so unsteady, you won't be able to light the match.

DEARTH. I shall just manage. [*He triumphantly proves the exact truth of his statement.*]

ALICE. A nice hand for an artist!

DEARTH. One would scarcely call me an artist now-a-days.

ALICE. Not so far as any work is concerned.

DEARTH. Not so far as having any more pretty dreams to paint is concerned. [*Grinning at himself.*] Wonder why I have been become such a waster, Alice?

ALICE. I suppose it was always in you.

DEARTH. [*With perhaps a glimpse of the fishing-rod.*] I suppose so; and yet I was rather a good sort in the days when I went courting you.

ALICE. Yes, I thought so. Unlucky days for me, as it has turned out.

DEARTH. [*Heartily.*] Yes, a bad job for you. [*Puzzling unsteadily over himself.*] I didn't know I was a wrong 'un at the time; thought quite well of myself, thought a vast deal more of you. Crack-in-my-eye-Tommy, how I used to leap out of bed at 6 a.m. all agog to be at my easel; blood ran through my veins in those days. And now I'm middle-aged and done for. Funny! Don't know how it has come about, nor what has made the music mute. [*Mildly curious.*] When did you begin to despise me, Alice?

ALICE. When I got to know you really, Will; a long time ago.

DEARTH. [*Bleary of eye.*] Yes, I think that is true. It was a long time ago, and before I had begun to despise myself. It wasn't till I knew you had no opinion of me that I began to go down hill. You will grant that, won't you; and that I did try for a bit to fight on? If you had cared for me I wouldn't have come to this, surely?

ALICE. Well, I found I didn't care for you, and I wasn't hypocrite enough to pretend I did. That's blunt, but you used to admire my bluntness.

DEARTH. The bluntness of you, the adorable wildness of you, you untamed thing! There were never any shades in you; kiss or kill was your motto, Alice. I felt from the first moment I saw you that you would love me or knife me.

[Memories of their shooting star flare in both of them for as long as a sheet of paper might take to burn.]

ALICE. I didn't knife you.

DEARTH. No. I suppose that was where you made the mistake. It is hard on you, old lady. *[Becoming watery.]* I suppose it's too late to try to patch things up?

ALICE. Let's be honest; it is too late, Will.

DEARTH. *[Whose tears would smell of brandy.]* Perhaps if we had had children—Pity!

ALICE. A blessing I should think, seeing what sort of a father they would have had.

DEARTH. *[Ever reasonable.]* I daresay you're right. Well, Alice, I know that somehow it's my fault. I'm sorry for you.

ALICE. I'm sorry for myself. If I hadn't married you what a different woman I should be. What a fool I was.

DEARTH. Ah! Three things they say come not back to men nor women—the spoken word, the past life, and the neglected opportunity. Wonder if we should make any more of them, Alice, if they did come back to us.

ALICE. You wouldn't.

DEARTH. *[Avoiding a hiccup.]* I guess you're right.

ALICE. But I——

DEARTH. [*Sincerely.*] Yes, what a boon for you. But I hope it's not Freddy Finch-Fallowe you would put in my place; I know he is following you about again. [*He is far from threatening her, he has too beery an opinion of himself for that.*]

ALICE. He followed me about, as you put it, before I knew you. I don't know why I quarreled with him.

DEARTH. Your heart told you that he was no good, Alice.

ALICE. My heart told me that you *were*. So it wasn't of much service to me, my heart!

DEARTH. The Honourable Freddy Finch-Fallowe is a rotter.

ALICE. [*Ever inflammable.*] You are certainly an authority on the subject.

DEARTH. [*With the sad smile of the disillusioned.*] You have me there. After which brief, but pleasant, little connubial chat, he pursued his dishonoured way into the garden.

> [*He is however prevented doing so for the moment by the return of the others. They are all still in their dinner clothes though wearing wraps. They crowd in through the door, chattering.*]

LOB. Here they are! Are you ready, dear lady?

MRS. COADE. [*Seeing that* DEARTH'S *hand is on the window curtains.*] Are you not coming with us to find the wood, Mr. Dearth.

DEARTH. Alas, I am unavoidably detained. You will find me in the garden when you come back.

JOANNA. [*Whose sense of humour has been restored.*] If we ever do come back!

DEARTH. Precisely. [*With a groggy bow.*] Should

we never meet again, Alice, fare thee well. Purdie, if you find the tree of knowledge in the wood bring me back an apple.

PURDIE. I promise.

LOB. Come quickly. Matey mustn't see me. [*He is turning out the lights.*]

LADY CAROLINE. [*Pouncing.*] Matey? What difference would that make, Lob?

LOB. He would take me off to bed; it's past my time.

COADE. [*Not the least gay of the company.*] You know, old fellow, you make it very difficult for us to embark upon this adventure in the proper eerie spirit.

DEARTH. Well, I'm for the garden.

> [*He walks to the window, and the others are going out by the door. But they do not go. There is a hitch somewhere—at the window apparently, for* DEARTH *having begun to draw the curtains apart lets them fall, like one who has had a shock. The others remember long afterwards his grave face as he came quietly back and put his cigar on the table. The room is in darkness save for the light from one lamp.*]

PURDIE. [*Wondering.*] How, now, Dearth?

DEARTH. What is it we get in that wood, Lob?

ALICE. Ah, he won't tell us that.

LOB. [*Shrinking.*] Come on!

ALICE. [*Impressed by the change that has come over her husband.*] Tell us first.

LOB. [*Forced to the disclosure.*] They say that in the wood you get what nearly everbody here is longing for— a second chance.

> [*The ladies are simultaneously enlightened.*]

JOANNA. [*Speaking for all.*] So that is what we have in common!

COADE. [*With gentle regret.*] I have often thought, Coady, that if I had a second chance I should be a useful man instead of just a nice lazy one.

ALICE. [*Morosely.*] A second chance!

LOB. Come on.

PURDIE. [*Gaily.*] Yes, to the wood—the wood!

DEARTH. [*As they are going out by the door.*] Stop, why not go this way?

> [*He pulls the curtains apart, and there comes a sudden indrawing of breath from all, for no garden is there now. In its place is an endless wood of great trees; the nearest of them has come close to the window. It is a sombre wood, with splashes of moonshine and of blackness standing very still in it.*
>
> *The party in the drawing-room are very still also, there is scarcely a cry or a movement. It is perhaps strange that the most obviously frightened is* LOB *who calls vainly for* MATEY. *The first articulate voice is* DEARTH'S.]

DEARTH. [*Very quietly.*] Any one ready to risk it?

PURDIE. [*After another silence.*] Of course there is nothing in it—just——

DEARTH. [*Grimly.*] Of course. Going out, Purdie?

> [PURDIE *draws back.*]

MRS. DEARTH. [*The only one who is undaunted.*] A second chance! [*She is looking at her husband. They all look at him as if he had been a leader once.*]

DEARTH. [*With his sweet mournful smile.*] I shall be back in a moment—probably.

> [*As he passes into the wood his hands rise, as if*

a hammer had tapped him on the forehead.
He is soon lost to view.]

LADY CAROLINE. [*After a long pause.*] He does not
come back.

MRS. COADE. It's horrible.

[*She steals off by the door to her room, calling to*
her husband to do likewise. He takes a step
after her, and stops in the grip of the last two
words that holds them all. The stillness con-
tinues. At last MRS. PURDIE *goes out into the*
wood, her hands raised, and is swallowed up
by it.]

PURDIE. Mabel!

ALICE. [*Sardonically.*] You will have to go now, Mr.
Purdie.

[*He looks at* JOANNA, *and they go out together,*
one tap of the hammer for each.]

LOB. That's enough. [*Warningly.*] Don't *you* go,
Mrs. Dearth. *You'll* catch it if you go.

ALICE. A second chance!

[*She goes out unflinching.*]

LADY CAROLINE. One would like to know.

[*She goes out.* MRS. COADE'S *voice is heard*
from the stair calling to her husband. He
hesitates but follows LADY CAROLINE. *To* LOB
now alone comes MATEY *with a tray of coffee*
cups.]

MATEY. [*As he places his tray on the table.*] It is
past your bed-time, sir. Say good-night to the ladies, and
come along.

LOB. Matey, look!

[MATEY *looks.*]

MATEY. [*Shrinking.*] Great heavens, then it's true!

LOB. Yes, but I—I wasn't sure.

[MATEY *approaches the window cautiously to
peer out, and his master gives him a sudden
push that propels him into the wood.* LOB'S
*back is toward us as he stands alone staring
out upon the unknown. He is terrified still;
yet quivers of rapture are running up and
down his little frame.*]

End of Act I.

ACT II

*We are translated to the depths of the wood in the enchant-
ment of a moonlight night. In some other glade a
nightingale is singing; in this one, in proud motoring
attire, recline two mortals whom we have known in different conditions; the second chance has converted
them into husband and wife. The man, of gross muddy
build, lies luxurious on his back exuding affluence, a
prominent part of him heaving playfully, like some little
wave that will not rest in a still sea. A handkerchief
over his face conceals from us what Colossus he may
be, but his mate is our Lady Caroline. The nightingale trills on, and Lady Caroline takes up its song.*

LADY CAROLINE. Is it not a lovely night, Jim. Listen,
my own, to Philomel; he is saying that he is lately married.
So are we, you ducky thing. I feel, Jim, that I am Rosa-
lind and that you are my Orlando.

　　　　[*The handkerchief being removed* MR. MATEY *is
revealed; and the nightingale seeks some farther tree.*]

MATEY. What do you say I am, Caroliny?

LADY CAROLINE. [*Clapping her hands.*] My own one, don't you think it would be fun if we were to write poems about each other and pin them on the tree trunks?

MATEY. [*Tolerantly.*] Poems? I never knew such a lass for high-flown language.

LADY CAROLINE. Your lass, dearest. Jim's lass.

MATEY. [*Pulling her ear.*] And don't you forget it.

LADY CAROLINE. [*With the curiosity of woman.*] What would you do if I were to forget it, great bear?

MATEY. Take a stick to you.

LADY CAROLINE. [*So proud of him.*] I love to hear you talk like that; it is so virile. I always knew that it was a master I needed.

MATEY. It's what you all need.

LADY CAROLINE. It is, it is, you knowing wretch.

MATEY. Listen, Caroliny. [*He touches his money pocket, which emits a crinkly sound—the squeak of angels.*] That is what gets the ladies.

LADY CAROLINE. How much have you made this week, you wonderful man?

MATEY. [*Blandly.*] Another two hundred or so. That's all, just two hundred or so.

LADY CAROLINE. [*Caressing her wedding ring.*] My dear golden fetter, listen to him. Kiss my fetter, Jim.

MATEY. Wait till I light this cigar.

LADY CAROLINE. Let me hold the darling match.

MATEY. Tidy-looking Petitey Corona, this. There was a time when one of that sort would have run away with two days of my screw.

LADY CAROLINE. How I should have loved, Jim, to know you when you were poor. Fancy your having once been a clerk.

MATEY. [*Remembering Napoleon and others.*] We

all have our beginnings. But it wouldn't have mattered how I began, Caroliny: I should have come to the top just the same. [*Becoming a poet himself.*] I am a climber, and there are nails in my boots for the parties beneath me. Boots! I tell you if I had been a bootmaker, I should have been the first bootmaker in London.

LADY CAROLINE. [*A humourist at last.*] I am sure you would, Jim; but should you have made the best boots?

MATEY. [*Uxoriously wishing that others could have heard this.*] Very good, Caroliny; that is the neatest thing I have heard you say. But it's late; we had best be strolling back to our Rolls-Royce.

LADY CAROLINE. [*As they rise.*] I do hope the ground wasn't damp.

MATEY. Don't matter if it was; I was lying on your rug.

> [*Indeed we notice now that he has had all the rug, and she the bare ground.* JOANNA *reaches the glade, now an unhappy lady who has got what she wanted. She is in country dress and is unknown to them as they are to her.*]

Who is the mournful party?

JOANNA. [*Hesitating.*] I wonder, sir, whether you happen to have seen my husband? I have lost him in the wood.

MATEY. We are strangers in these parts ourselves, missis. Have we passed any one, Caroliny?

LADY CAROLINE. [*Coyly.*] Should we have noticed, dear? Might it be that old gent over there? [*After the delightful manner of those happily wed she has already picked up many of her lover's favourite words and phrases.*]

JOANNA. Oh no, my husband is quite young.

> [*The woodlander referred to is* MR. COADE *in gala costume; at his mouth a whistle he has*

*made him from some friendly twig. To its
ravishing music he is seen pirouetting charmingly among the trees, his new occupation.]*

MATEY. [*Signing to the unknown that he is wanted.*]
Seems a merry old cock. Evening to you, sir. Do you
happen to have seen a young gentleman in the wood lately,
all by himself, and looking for his wife?

COADE. [*With a flourish of his legs.*] Can't say I have.

JOANNA. [*Dolefully.*] He isn't necessarily by himself; and I don't know that he is looking for me. There
may be a young lady with him.

[*The more happily married lady smiles, and
JOANNA is quick to take offense.*]

JOANNA. What do you mean by that?

LADY CAROLINE. [*Neatly.*] Oho—if you like that
better.

MATEY. Now, now, now—your manners, Caroliny.

COADE. Would he be singing or dancing?

JOANNA. Oh no—at least, I hope not.

COADE. [*An artist to the tips.*] Hope not? Odd! If
he is doing neither I am not likely to notice him, but if I
do, what name shall I say?

JOANNA. [*Gloating not.*] Purdie; I am Mrs. Purdie.

COADE. I will try to keep a look-out, and if I see him
——but I am rather occupied at present—— [*The reference is to his legs and a new step they are acquiring. He
sways this way and that, and, whistle to lips, minuets off in
the direction of Paradise.*]

JOANNA. [*Looking elsewhere.*] I am sorry I troubled
you. I see him now.

LADY CAROLINE. Is he alone?

[*JOANNA glares at her.*]
Ah, I see from your face that he isn't.

MATEY. [*Who has his wench in training.*] Caroliny,

no awkward questions. Evening, missis, and I hope you
will get him to go along with you quietly. [*Looking after*
COADE.] Watch the old codger dancing.

> [*Light-hearted as children they dance after him,*
> *while* JOANNA *behind a tree awaits her lord.*
> PURDIE *in knickerbockers approaches with mis-*
> *givings to make sure that his* JOANNA *is not in*
> *hiding, and then he gambols joyously with a*
> *charming confection whose name is* MABEL.
> *They chase each other from tree to tree, but*
> *fortunately not round* JOANNA'S *tree.*]

MABEL. [*As he catches her.*] No, and no, and no. I
don't know you nearly well enough for that. Besides,
what would your wife say! I shall begin to think you are
a very dreadful man, Mr. Purdie.

PURDIE. [*Whose sincerity is not to be questioned.*]
Surely you might call me Jack by this time.

MABEL. [*Heaving.*] Perhaps, if you are very good,
Jack.

PURDIE. [*Of noble thoughts compact.*] If only Joanna
were more like you.

MABEL. Like me? You mean her face? It is a—well,
if it is not precisely pretty, it is a good face. [*Handsomely.*]
I don't mind her face at all. I am glad you have got such
a dependable little wife, Jack.

PURDIE. [*Gloomily.*] Thanks.

MABEL. [*Seated with a moonbeam in her lap.*] What
would Joanna have said if she had seen you just now?

PURDIE. A wife should be incapable of jealousy.

MABEL. Joanna jealous? But has she any reason?
Jack, tell me, who is the woman?

PURDIE. [*Restraining himself by a mighty effort, for he
wishes always to be true to* JOANNA.] Shall I, Mabel,
shall I?

MABEL. [*Faltering, yet not wholly giving up the chase.*] I can't think who she is. Have I ever seen her?

PURDIE. Every time you look in a mirror.

MABEL. [*With her head on one side.*] How odd, Jack, that can't be; when I look in a mirror I see only myself.

PURDIE. [*Gloating.*] How adorably innocent you are, Mabel. Joanna would have guessed at once.

> [*Slowly his meaning comes to her, and she is appalled.*]

MABEL. Not that!

PURDIE. [*Aflame.*] Shall I tell you now?

MABEL. [*Palpitating exquisitely.*] I don't know, I am not sure. Jack, try not to say it, but if you feel you must, say it in such a way that it would not hurt the feelings of Joanna if she happened to be passing by, as she nearly always is.

> [*A little moan from* JOANNA'S *tree is unnoticed.*]

PURDIE. I would rather not say it at all than that way. [*He is touchingly anxious that she should know him as he really is.*] I don't know, Mabel, whether you have noticed that I am not like other men. [*He goes deeply into the very structure of his being.*] All my life I have been a soul that has had to walk alone. Even as a child I had no hope that it would be otherwise. I distinctly remember when I was six thinking how unlike other children I was. Before I was twelve I suffered from terrible self-depreciation; I do so still. I suppose there never was a man who had a more lowly opinion of himself.

MABEL. Jack, you who are so universally admired.

PURDIE. That doesn't help; I remain my own judge. I am afraid I am a dark spirit, Mabel. Yes, yes, my dear, let me leave nothing untold however it may damage me in your eyes. Your eyes! I cannot remember a time when I did not think of Love as a great consuming passion;

I visualised it, Mabel, as perhaps few have done, but always as the abounding joy that could come to others but never to me. I expected too much of women: I suppose I was touched to finer issues than most. That has been my tragedy.

MABEL. Then you met Joanna.

PURDIE. Then I met Joanna. Yes! Foolishly, as I now see, I thought she would understand that I was far too deep a nature really to mean the little things I sometimes said to her. I suppose a man was never placed in such a position before. What was I to do? Remember, I was always certain that the ideal love could never come to me. Whatever the circumstances, I was convinced that my soul must walk alone.

MABEL. Joanna, how could you?

PURDIE. [*Firmly.*] Not a word against her, Mabel; if blame there is the blame is mine.

MABEL. And so you married her.

PURDIE. And so I married her.

MABEL. Out of pity.

PURDIE. I felt it was a man's part. I was such a child in worldly matters that it was pleasant to me to have the right to pay a woman's bills; I enjoyed seeing her garments lying about on my chairs. In time that exultation wore off. But I was not unhappy, I didn't expect much, I was always so sure that no woman could ever plumb the well of my emotions.

MABEL. Then you met me.

PURDIE. Then I met you.

MABEL. Too late — never — forever — forever—never. They are the saddest words in the English tongue.

PURDIE. At the time I thought a still sadder word was Joanna.

MABEL. What was it you saw in me that made you love me?

PURDIE. [*Plumbing the well of his emotions.*] I think it was the feeling that you are so like myself.

MABEL. [*With great eyes.*] Have you noticed that, Jack? Sometimes it has almost terrified me.

PURDIE. We think the same thoughts; we are not two, Mabel; we are one. Your hair——

MABEL. Joanna knows you admire it, and for a week she did hers in the same way.

PURDIE. I never noticed.

MABEL. That was why she gave it up. And it didn't really suit her. [*Ruminating.*] I can't think of a good way of doing dear Joanna's hair. What is that you are muttering to yourself, Jack? Don't keep anything from me.

PURDIE. I was repeating a poem I have written: it is in two words, "Mabel Purdie." May I teach it to you, sweet: say "Mabel Purdie" to me.

MABEL. [*Timidly covering his mouth with her little hand.*] If I were to say it, Jack, I should be false to Joanna: never ask me to be that. Let us go on.

PURDIE. [*Merciless in his passion.*] Say it, Mabel, say it. See I write it on the ground with your sunshade.

MABEL. If it could be! Jack, I'll whisper it to you.

[*She is whispering it as they wander, not two but one, farther into the forest, ardently believing in themselves; they are not hypocrites. The somewhat bedraggled figure of JOANNA follows them, and the nightingale resumes his love-song. "That's all you know, you bird!" thinks JOANNA cynically. The nightingale, however, is not singing for them nor for her, but for another pair he has espied below. They are racing, the prize to be for the one who first finds*

the spot where the easel was put up last night.
The hobbledehoy is sure to be the winner, for
she is less laden, and the father loses time by
singing as he comes. Also she is all legs and
she started ahead. Brambles adhere to her,
one boot has been in the water and she has as
many freckles as there are stars in heaven. She
is as lovely as you think she is, and she is aged
the moment when you like your daughter best.
A hoot of triumph from her brings her father to
to the spot.]

MARGARET. Daddy, Daddy. I have won. Here is
the place. Crack-in-my-eye-Tommy!

[*He comes. Crack-in-my-eye-Tommy, this en-*
gaging fellow in tweeds, is MR. DEARTH, *ablaze*
in happiness and health and a daughter. He
finishes his song, picked up in the Latin
Quarter.]

DEARTH. Yes, that is the tree I stuck my easel under
last night, and behold the blessed moon behaving more
gorgeously than ever. I am sorry to have kept you waiting, old moon; but you ought to know by now how time
passes. Now, keep still, while I hand you down to
posterity.

[*The easel is erected,* MARGARET *helping by get-*
ting in the way.]

MARGARET. [*Critical, as an artist's daughter should*
be.] The moon is rather pale to-night, isn't she?

DEARTH. Comes of keeping late hours.

MARGARET. [*Showing off.*] Daddy, watch me, look
at me. Please, sweet moon, a pleasant expression. No, no,
not as if you were sitting for it; that is too professional.
That is better; thank you. Now keep it. That is the
sort of thing you say to them, Dad.

DEARTH. [*Quickly at work.*] I oughtn't to have brought you out so late; you should be tucked up in your cozy bed at home.

MARGARET. [*Pursuing a squirrel that isn't there.*] With the pillow anyhow.

DEARTH. Except in its proper place.

MARGARET. [*Wetting the other foot.*] And the sheet over my face.

DEARTH. Where it oughtn't to be.

MARGARET. [*More or less upside down.*] And Daddy tiptoeing in to take it off.

DEARTH. Which is more than you deserve.

MARGARET. [*In a tree.*] Then why does he stand so long at the door? And before he has gone she bursts out laughing, for she has been awake all the time.

DEARTH. That's about it. What a life! But I oughtn't to have brought you here. Best to have the sheet over you when the moon is about; moonlight is bad for little daughters.

MARGARET. [*Pelting him with nuts.*] I can't sleep when the moon's at the full; she keeps calling to me to get up. Perhaps I am *her* daughter too.

DEARTH. Gad, you look it to-night.

MARGARET. Do I? Then can't you paint me into the picture as well as Mamma? You could call it "A Mother and Daughter" or simply "Two ladies," if the moon thinks that calling me her daughter would make her seem too old.

DEARTH. O matre pulchra filia pulchrior. That means, "O Moon—more beautiful than any twopenny-halfpenny daughter."

MARGARET. [*Emerging in an unexpected place.*] Daddy do you really prefer her?

DEARTH. 'Sh! She's not a patch on you; it's the sort of thing we say to our sitters to keep them in good

humour. [*He surveys ruefully a great stain on her frock.*]
I wish to heaven, Margaret, we were not both so fond of
appletart. And what's this! [*Catching hold of her skirt.*]

MARGARET. [*Unnecessarily.*] It's a tear.

DEARTH. I should think it is a tear.

MARGARET. That boy at the farm did it. He kept calling Snubs after me, but I got him down and kicked him in
the stomach. He is rather a jolly boy.

DEARTH. He sounds it. Ye Gods, what a night!

MARGARET. [*Considering the picture.*] And what a
moon! Dad, she is not quite so fine as that.

DEARTH. 'Sh! I have touched her up.

MARGARET. Dad, Dad—what a funny man!

> [*She has seen* MR. COADE *with whistle, enlivening
> the wood. He pirouettes round them and de-
> parts to add to the happiness of others.* MAR-
> GARET *gives an excellent imitation of him at
> which her father shakes his head, then repre-
> hensibly joins in the dance. Her mood changes,
> she clings to him.*]

MARGARET. Hold me tight, Daddy, I'm frightened. I
think they want to take you away from me.

DEARTH. Who, gosling?

MARGARET. I don't know. It's too lovely, Daddy; I
won't be able to keep hold of it.

DEARTH. What is?

MARGARET. The world—everything—and you, Daddy,
most of all. Things that are too beautiful can't last.

DEARTH. [*Who knows it.*] Now, how did you find
that out?

MARGARET. [*Still in his arms.*] I don't know, Daddy,
am I sometimes stranger than other people's daughters?

DEARTH. More of a madcap, perhaps.

MARGARET. [*Solemnly.*] Do you think I am sometimes too full of gladness?

DEARTH. My sweetheart, you do sometimes run over with it. [*He is at his easel again.*]

MARGARET. [*Persisting.*] To be very gay, dearest dear, is so near to being very sad.

DEARTH. [*Who knows it.*] How did you find that out, child?

MARGARET. I don't know. From something in me that's afraid. [*Unexpectedly.*] Daddy, what is a "might-have-been?"

DEARTH. A might-have-been? They are ghosts, Margaret. I daresay I "might have been" a great swell of a painter, instead of just this uncommonly happy nobody. Or again, I might have been a worthless idle waster of a fellow.

MARGARET. [*Laughing.*] You!

DEARTH. Who knows? Some little kink in me might have set me off on the wrong road. And that poor soul I might so easily have been might have had no Margaret. My word, I'm sorry for him.

MARGARET. So am I. [*She conceives a funny picture.*] The poor old Daddy, wandering about the world without me!

DEARTH. And there are other "might-have-beens"— lovely ones, but intangible. Shades, Margaret, made of sad folk's thoughts.

MARGARET. [*Jigging about.*] I am so glad I am not a shade. How awful it would be, Daddy, to wake up and find one wasn't alive.

DEARTH. It would, dear.

MARGARET. Daddy, wouldn't it be awful! I think men need daughters.

DEARTH. They do.

MARGARET. Especially artists.

Dearth. Yes, especially artists.

Margaret. Especially artists.

Dearth. Especially artists.

Margaret. [*Covering herself with leaves and kicking them off.*] Fame is not everything.

Dearth. Fame is rot; daughters are the thing.

Margaret. Daughters are the thing.

Dearth. Daughters are the thing.

Margaret. I wonder if sons would be even nicer?

Dearth. Not a patch on daughters. The awful thing about a son is that never, never—at least, from the day he goes to school—can you tell him that you rather like him. By the time he is ten you can't even take him on your knee. Sons are not worth having, Margaret. Signed, W. Dearth.

Margaret. But if you were a mother, Dad, I daresay he would let you do it.

Dearth. Think so?

Margaret. I mean when no one was looking. Sons are not so bad. Signed, M. Dearth. But I'm glad you prefer daughters. [*She works her way toward him on her knees, making the tear larger.*] At what age are we nicest, Daddy? [*She has constantly to repeat her questions, he is so engaged with his moon.*] Hie, Daddy, at what age are we nicest? Daddy, hie, hie, at what age are we nicest?

Dearth. Eh? That's a poser. I think you were nicest when you were two and knew your alphabet up to G but fell over at H. No, you were best when you were half-past three; or just before you struck six; or in the mumps year, when I asked you in the early morning how you were and you said solemnly "I haven't tried yet."

Margaret. [*Awestruck.*] Did I?

Dearth. Such was your answer. [*Struggling with the momentous question.*] But I am not sure that chicken-pox doesn't beat mumps. Oh Lord, I'm all wrong. The nicest time in a father's life is the year before she puts up her hair.

MARGARET. [*Topheavy with pride in herself.*] I suppose that is a splendid time. But there's a nicer year coming to you. Daddy, there is a nicer year coming to you.

DEARTH. Is there, darling?

MARGARET. Daddy, the year she does put up her hair!

DEARTH. [*With arrested brush.*] Puts it up for ever? You know, I am afraid that when the day for that comes I shan't be able to stand it. It will be too exciting. My poor heart, Margaret.

MARGARET. [*Rushing at him.*] No, no, it will be lucky you, for it isn't to be a bit like that. I am to be a girl and woman day about for the first year. You will never know which I am till you look at my hair. And even then you won't know, for if it is down I shall put it up, and if it is up I shall put it down. And so my Daddy will gradually get used to the idea.

DEARTH. [*Wryly.*] I see you have been thinking it out.

MARGARET. [*Gleaming.*] I have been doing more than that. Shut your eyes, Dad, and I shall give you a glimpse into the future.

DEARTH. I don't know that I want that: the present is so good.

MARGARET. Shut your eyes, please.

DEARTH. No, Margaret.

MARGARET. Please, Daddy.

DEARTH. Oh, all right. They are shut.

MARGARET. Don't open them till I tell you. What finger is that?

DEARTH. The dirty one.

MARGARET. [*On her knees among the leaves.*] Daddy, now I am putting up my hair. I have got such a darling of a mirror. It is such a darling mirror I've got, Dad. Dad, don't look. I shall tell you about it. It is a little pool of water. I wish we could take it home and hang it up. Of course the moment my hair is up there will be other changes also; for instance, I shall talk quite differently.

DEARTH. Pooh. Where are my matches, dear?

MARGARET. Top pocket, waistcoat.

DEARTH. [*Trying to light his pipe in darkness.*] You were meaning to frighten me just now.

MARGARET. No. I am just preparing you. You see, darling, I can't call you Dad when my hair is up. I think I shall call you Parent.

[*He growls.*]

Parent dear, do you remember the days when your Margaret was a slip of a girl, and sat on your knee? How foolish we were, Parent, in those distant days.

DEARTH. Shut up, Margaret.

MARGARET. Now I must be more distant to you; more like a boy who could not sit on your knee any more.

DEARTH. See here, I want to go on painting. Shall I look now?

MARGARET. I am not quite sure whether I want you to. It makes such a difference. Perhaps you won't know me. Even the pool is looking a little scared. [*The change in her voice makes him open his eyes quickly. She confronts him shyly.*] What do you think? Will I do?

DEARTH. Stand still, dear, and let me look my fill. The Margaret that is to be.

MARGARET. [*The change in his voice falling clammy on her.*] You'll see me often enough, Daddy, like this, so you don't need to look your fill. You are looking as long as if this were to be the only time.

DEARTH. [*With an odd tremor.*] Was I? Surely it isn't to be that.

MARGARET. Be gay, Dad. [*Bumping into him and round him and over him.*] You will be sick of Margaret with her hair up before you are done with her.

DEARTH. I expect so.

MARGARET. Shut up, Daddy. [*She waggles her head, and down comes her hair.*] Daddy, I know what you are thinking of. You are thinking what a handful she is going to be.

DEARTH. Well, I guess she is.

MARGARET. [*Surveying him from another angle.*] Now you are thinking about—about my being in love some day.

DEARTH. [*With unnecessary warmth.*] Rot!

MARGARET. [*Reassuringly.*] I won't, you know; no, never. Oh, I have quite decided, so don't be afraid. [*Disordering his hair.*] Will you hate him at first, Daddy? Daddy, will you hate him? Will you hate him, Daddy?

DEARTH. [*At work.*] Whom?

MARGARET. Well, if there was?

DEARTH. If there was what, darling?

MARGARET. You know the kind of thing I mean, quite well. Would you hate him at first?

DEARTH. I hope not. I should want to strangle him, but I wouldn't hate him.

MARGARET. *I* would. That is to say, if I liked him.

DEARTH. If you liked him how could you hate him?

MARGARET. For daring!

DEARTH. Daring what?

MARGARET. You know. [*Sighing.*] But of course I shall have no say in the matter. You will do it all. You do everything for me.

DEARTH. [*With a groan.*] I can't help it.

MARGARET. You will even write my love-letters, if I ever have any to write, which I won't.

DEARTH. [*Ashamed.*] Surely to goodness, Margaret, I will leave you alone to do that!

MARGARET. Not you; you will try to, but you won't be able.

DEARTH. [*In a hopeless attempt at self-defense.*] I want you, you see, to do everything exquisitely. I do wish I could leave you to do things a little more for yourself. I suppose it's owing to my having had to be father and mother both. I knew nothing practically about the bringing up of children, and of course I couldn't trust you to a nurse.

MARGARET. [*Severely.*] Not you; so sure you could do it better yourself. That's you all over. Daddy, do you remember how you taught me to balance a biscuit on my nose, like a puppy?

DEARTH. [*Sadly.*] Did I?

MARGARET. You called me Rover.

DEARTH. I deny that.

MARGARET. And when you said "snap" I caught the biscuit in my mouth.

DEARTH. Horrible!

MARGARET. [*Gleaming.*] Daddy, I can do it still! [*Putting a biscuit on her nose.*] Here is the last of my supper. Say "snap," Daddy.

DEARTH. Not I.

MARGARET. Say "snap," please.

DEARTH. I refuse.

MARGARET. Daddy!

DEARTH. Snap.

[*She catches the biscuit in her mouth.*]

Let that be the last time, Margaret.

MARGARET. Except just once more. I don't mean now, but when my hair is really up. If I should ever have a— a Margaret of my own, come in and see me, Daddy, in my white bed, and say "snap"—and I'll have the biscuit ready.

DEARTH. [*Turning away his head.*] Right O.

MARGARET. Dad, if I ever should marry, not that I will but if I should—at the marriage ceremony will you let me be the one who says "I do?"

DEARTH. I suppose I deserve this.

MARGARET. [*Coaxingly.*] You think I'm pretty, don't you, Dad, whatever other people say?

DEARTH. Not so bad.

MARGARET. I *know* I have nice ears.

DEARTH. They are all right now, but I had to work on them for months.

MARGARET. You don't mean to say that you did my *ears?*

DEARTH. Rather!

MARGARET. [*Grown humble.*] My dimple is my own.

DEARTH. I am glad you think so. I wore out the point of my little finger over that dimple.

MARGARET. Even my dimple! Have I anything that is really mine? A bit of my nose or anything?

DEARTH. When you were a babe you had a laugh that was all your own.

MARGARET. Haven't I it now?

DEARTH. It's gone. [*He looks ruefully at her.*] I'll tell you how it went. We were fishing in a stream—that is to say, I was wading and you were sitting on my shoulders holding the rod. We didn't catch anything. Somehow or another—I can't think how I did it—you irritated me, and I answered you sharply.

MARGARET. [*Gasping.*] I can't believe that.

DEARTH. Yes, it sounds extraordinary, but I did. It gave you a shock, and, for the moment, the world no longer seemed a safe place to you; your faith in me had always made it safe till then. You were suddenly not even sure of your bread and butter, and a frightened tear came to your eyes. I was in a nice state about it I can tell you. [*He is in a nice state about it still.*]

MARGARET. Silly! [*Bewildered.*] But what has that to do with my laugh, Daddy?

DEARTH. The laugh that children are born with lasts just so long as they have perfect faith. To think that it was I who robbed you of yours!

MARGARET. Don't, dear. I am sure the laugh just went off with the tear to comfort it, and they have been playing about that stream ever since. They have quite forgotten us, so why should we remember them? Cheeky little beasts! Shall I tell you my farthest back recollection? [*In some awe.*] I remember the first time I saw the stars. I had never seen night, and then I saw it and the stars together. Crack-in-my-eye-Tommy, it isn't every one who can boast of such a lovely, lovely recollection for their earliest, is it?

DEARTH. I was determined your earliest should be a good one.

MARGARET. [*Blankly.*] Do you mean to say you planned it?

DEARTH. Rather! Most people's earliest recollection is of some trivial thing; how they cut their finger, or lost a piece of string. I was resolved my Margaret's should be something bigger. I was poor, but I could give her the stars.

MARGARET. [*Clutching him round the legs.*] Oh, how you love me, Daddikins.

DEARTH. Yes, I do, rather.

> [*A vagrant woman has wandered in their direction, one whom the shrill winds of life have lashed and bled; here and there ragged graces still cling to her, and unruly passion smoulders, but she, once a dear fierce rebel with eyes of storm,*

*is now first of all a whimperer. She and they
meet as strangers.*]

MARGARET. [*Nicely, as becomes an artist's daughter.*]
Good evening.

ALICE. Good evening, Missy; evening, Mister.

DEARTH. [*Seeing that her eyes search the ground.*] Lost
anything?

ALICE. Sometimes when the tourists have had their
sandwiches there are bits left over, and they squeeze them
between the roots to keep the place tidy. I am looking for
bits.

DEARTH. You don't tell me you are as hungry as that?

ALICE. [*With spirit.*] Try me. [*Strange that he should
not know that once loved husky voice.*]

MARGARET. [*Rushing at her father and feeling all his
pockets.*] Daddy, that was my last biscuit!

DEARTH. We must think of something else.

MARGARET. [*Taking her hand.*] Yes, wait a bit, we are
sure to think of something. Daddy, think of something.

ALICE. [*Sharply.*] Your father doesn't like you to
touch the likes of me.

MARGARET. Oh yes, he does. [*Defiantly.*] And if he
didn't, I'd do it all the same. This is a bit of *myself*, daddy.

DEARTH. That is all you know.

ALICE. [*Whining.*] You needn't be angry with her,
Mister; I'm all right.

DEARTH. I am not angry with her; I am very sorry for
you.

ALICE. [*Flaring.*] If I had my rights, I would be as
good as you—and better.

DEARTH. I daresay.

ALICE. I have had men-servants and a motorcar.

DEARTH. Margaret and I never rose to that.

MARGARET. [*Stung.*] I have been in a taxi several times, and Dad often gets telegrams.

DEARTH. Margaret!

MARGARET. I'm sorry I boasted.

ALICE. That's nothing. I have a town house—at least I had—— At any rate he said there was a town house.

MARGARET. [*Interested.*] Fancy his not knowing for certain.

ALICE. The Honourable Mrs. Finch-Fallowe—that's who I am.

MARGARET. [*Cordially.*] It's a lovely name.

ALICE. Curse him.

MARGARET. Don't you like him?

DEARTH. We won't go into that. I have nothing to do with your past, but I wish we had some food to offer you.

ALICE. You haven't a flask?

DEARTH. No, I don't take anything myself. But let me see——

MARGARET. [*Sparkling.*] I know! You said we had five pounds. [*To the needy one.*] Would you like five pounds?

DEARTH. Darling, don't be stupid; we haven't paid our bill at the inn.

ALICE. [*With bravado.*] All right; I never asked you for anything.

DEARTH. Don't take me up in that way: I have had my ups and downs myself. Here is ten bob and welcome.

> [*He surreptitiously slips a coin into* MARGARET'S *hand.*]

MARGARET. And I have half a crown. It is quite easy for us. Dad will be getting another fiver any day. You can't think how exciting it is when the fiver comes in; we dance and then we run out and buy chops.

DEARTH. Margaret!

ALICE. It's kind of you. I'm richer this minute than I have been for many a day.

DEARTH. It's nothing; I am sure you would do the same for us.

ALICE. I wish I was as sure.

DEARTH. Of course you would. Glad to be of any help. Get some victuals as quickly as you can. Best of wishes, ma'am, and may your luck change.

ALICE. Same to you, and may yours go on.

MARGARET. Good-night.

ALICE. What is her name, Mister?

DEARTH. [*Who has returned to his easel.*] Margaret.

ALICE. Margaret. You drew something good out of the lucky bag when you got her, Mister.

DEARTH. Yes.

ALICE. Take care of her; they are easily lost.

[*She shuffles away.*]

DEARTH. Poor soul. I expect she has had a rough time, and that some man is to blame for it—partly, at any rate. [*Restless.*] That woman rather affects me, Margaret; I don't know why. Didn't you like her husky voice? [*He goes on painting.*] I say, Margaret, we lucky ones, let's swear always to be kind to people who are down on their luck, and then when we are kind let's be a little kinder.

MARGARET. [*Gleefully.*] Yes, let's.

DEARTH. Margaret, always feel sorry for the failures, the ones who are always failures—especially in my sort of calling. Wouldn't it be lovely, to turn them on the thirty-ninth year of failure into glittering successes?

MARGARET. Topping.

DEARTH. Topping.

MARGARET. Oh, topping. How could we do it, Dad?

DEARTH. By letter. "To poor old Tom Broken Heart,

Top Attic, Garret Chambers, S.E.—DEAR SIR,—His Majesty has been graciously pleased to purchase your superb picture of Marlow Ferry."

MARGARET. "*P.S.*—I am sending the money in a sack so as you can hear it chink."

DEARTH. What could we do for our friend who passed just now? I can't get her out of my head.

MARGARET. You have made me forget her. [*Plaintively.*] Dad, I didn't like it.

DEARTH. Didn't like what, dear?

MARGARET. [*Shuddering.*] I didn't like her saying that about your losing me.

DEARTH. [*The one thing of which he is sure.*] I shan't lose you.

MARGARET. [*Hugging his arm.*] It would be hard for me if you lost me, but it would be worse for you. I don't know how I know that, but I do know it. What would you do without me?

DEARTH. [*Almost sharply.*] Don't talk like that, dear. It is wicked and stupid, and naughty. Somehow that poor woman—I won't paint any more to-night.

MARGARET. Let's get out of the wood; it frightens me.

DEARTH. And you loved it a moment ago. Hullo! [*He has seen a distant blurred light in the wood, apparently from a window.*] I hadn't noticed there was a house there.

MARGARET. [*Tingling.*] Daddy, I feel sure there wasn't a house there!

DEARTH. Goose. It is just that we didn't look: our old way of letting the world go hang; so interested in ourselves. Nice behaviour for people who have been boasting about what they would do for other people. Now I see what I ought to do.

MARGARET. Let's get out of the wood.

DEARTH. Yes, but my idea first. It is to rouse these people and get food from them for the husky one.

MARGARET. [*Clinging to him.*] She is too far away now.

DEARTH. I can overtake her.

MARGARET. [*In a frenzy.*] Don't go into that house, Daddy! I don't know why it is, but I am afraid of that house!

[*He waggles a reproving finger at her.*]

DEARTH. There is a kiss for each moment until I come back.

[*She wipes them from her face.*]

Oh, naughty, go and stand in the corner.

[*She stands against a tree but she stamps her foot.*]

Who has got a nasty temper!

[*She tries hard not to smile, but she smiles and he smiles, and they make comic faces at each other, as they have done in similar circumstances since she first opened her eyes.*]

I shall be back before you can count a hundred.

[*He goes off humming his song so that she may still hear him when he is lost to sight; all just as so often before. She tries dutifully to count her hundred, but the wood grows dark and soon she is afraid again. She runs from tree to tree calling to her* DADDY. *We begin to lose her among the shadows.*]

MARGARET. [*Out of the impalpable that is carrying her away.*] Daddy, come back; I don't want to be a might-have-been.

End of Act II.

ACT III

LOB'S *room has gone very dark as it sits up awaiting the possible return of the adventurers. The curtains are drawn, so that no light comes from outside. There is a tapping on the window, and anon two intruders are stealing about the floor, with muffled cries when they meet unexpectedly. They find the switch and are revealed as* PURDIE *and his* MABEL. *Something has happened to them as they emerged from the wood, but it is so superficial that neither notices it: they are again in the evening dress in which they had left the house. But they are still being led by that strange humour of the blood.*

MABEL. [*Looking around her curiously.*] A pretty little room; I wonder who is the owner?

PURDIE. It doesn't matter; the great thing is that we have escaped Joanna.

MABEL. Jack, look, a man!

[*The term may not be happily chosen, but the person indicated is* LOB *curled up on his chair by a dead fire. The last look on his face before he fell asleep having been a leery one it is still there.*]

PURDIE. He is asleep.

MABEL. Do you know him?

PURDIE. Not I. Excuse me, sir, Hi! [*No shaking, however, wakens the sleeper.*]

MABEL. Darling, how extraordinary.

PURDIE. [*Always considerate.*] After all, precious,

have we any right to wake up a stranger, just to tell him that we are runaways hiding in his house?

MABEL. [*Who comes of a good family.*] I think he would expect it of us.

PURDIE. [*After trying again.*] There is no budging him.

MABEL. [*Appeased.*] At any rate, we have done the civil thing.

> [*She has now time to regard the room more atten-tively, including the tray of coffee cups which* MATEY *had left on the table in a not unim-portant moment of his history.*]

There have evidently been people here, but they haven't drunk their coffee. Ugh! cold as a deserted egg in a bird's nest. Jack, if you were a clever detective you could con-struct those people out of their neglected coffee cups. I wonder who they are and what has spirited them away?

PURDIE. Perhaps they have only gone to bed. Ought we to knock them up?

MABEL. [*After considering what her mother would have done.*] I think not, dear. I suppose we have run away, Jack—meaning to?

PURDIE. [*With the sturdiness that weaker vessels adore.*] Irrevocably. Mabel, if the dog-like devotion of a lifetime. ——[*He becomes conscious that something has happened to* LOB's *leer. It has not left his face but it has shifted.*] He is not shamming, do you think?

MABEL. Shake him again.

PURDIE. [*After shaking him.*] It's all right. Mabel, if the dog-like devotion of a lifetime——

MABEL. Poor little Joanna! Still, if a woman insists on being a pendulum round a man's neck——

PURDIE. Do give me a chance, Mabel. If the dog-like devotion of a lifetime——

[JOANNA *comes through the curtains so inoppor-*
tunely that for the moment he is almost pettish.]

May I say, this is just a little too much, Joanna!

JOANNA. [*Unconscious as they of her return to her*
dinner gown.] So, sweet husband, your soul is still walking
alone, is it?

MABEL. [*Who hates coarseness of any kind.*] How can
you sneak about in this way, Joanna? Have you no pride?

JOANNA. [*Dashing away a tear.*] Please to address me
as Mrs. Purdie, madam. [*She sees* LOB.] Who is this
man?

PURDIE. We don't know; and there is no waking him.
You can try, if you like.

> [*Failing to rouse him* JOANNA *makes a third at*
> *table. They are all a little inconsequential, as*
> *if there were still some moonshine in their hair.*]

JOANNA. You were saying something about the devotion of a lifetime; please go on.

PURDIE. [*Diffidently.*] I don't like to before you,
Joanna.

JOANNA. [*Becoming coarse again.*] Oh, don't mind me.

PURDIE. [*Looking like a note of interrogation.*] I
should certainly like to say it.

MABEL. [*Loftily.*] And I shall be proud to hear it.

PURDIE. I should have liked to spare you this, Joanna;
you wouldn't put your hands over your ears?

JOANNA. [*Alas.*] No, sir.

MABEL. Fie, Joanna. Surely a wife's natural delicacy——

PURDIE. [*Severely.*] As you take it in that spirit,
Joanna, I can proceed with a clear conscience. If the dog-
like devotion of a lifetime—— [*He reels a little, staring at*
LOB, *over whose face the leer has been wandering like an*
insect.]

MABEL. Did he move?

PURDIE. It isn't that. I am feeling—very funny. Did one of you tap me just now on the forehead?

[*Their hands also have gone to their foreheads.*]

MABEL. I think I have been in this room before.

PURDIE. [*Flinching.*] There is something coming rushing back to me.

MABEL. I seem to know that coffee set. If I do, the lid of the milk jug is chipped. It is!

JOANNA. I can't remember this man's name; but I am sure it begins with L.

MABEL. Lob.

PURDIE. Lob.

JOANNA. Lob.

PURDIE. Mabel, your dress?

MABEL. [*Beholding it.*] How on earth——?

JOANNA. My dress! [*To* PURDIE.] You were in knickerbockers in the wood.

PURDIE. And so I am now. [*He sees he is not.*] Where did I change? The wood! Let me think. The wood——the wood, certainly. But the wood wasn't the wood.

JOANNA. [*Revolving like one in pursuit.*] My head is going round.

MABEL. Lob's wood! I remember it all. We were here. We did go.

PURDIE. So we did. But how could——? Where was——?

JOANNA. And who was——?

MABEL. And what was——?

PURDIE. [*Even in this supreme hour a man.*] Don't let go. Hold on to what we were doing, or we shall lose grip of ourselves. Devotion. Something about devotion. Hold on to devotion. "If the dog-like devotion of a lifetime——" Which of you was I saying that to?

MABEL. To me.

PURDIE. Are you sure?

MABEL. [*Shakily.*] I am not quite sure.

PURDIE. [*Anxiously.*] Joanna, what do you think? [*With a sudden increase of uneasiness.*] Which of you is my wife?

JOANNA. [*Without enthusiasm.*] I am. No, I am not. It is Mabel who is your wife!

MABEL. Me?

PURDIE. [*With a curious gulp.*] Why, of course you are, Mabel!

MABEL. I believe I am!

PURDIE. And yet how can it be? I was running away with you.

JOANNA. [*Solving that problem.*] You don't need to do it now.

PURDIE. The wood. Hold on to the wood. The wood is what explains it. Yes, I see the whole thing. [*He gazes at* LOB.] You infernal old rascal! Let us try to think it out. Don't any one speak for a moment. Think first. Love—— Hold on to love. [*He gets another tap.*] I say, I believe I am not a deeply passionate chap at all; I believe I am just——a philanderer!

MABEL. It is what you are,

JOANNA. [*More magnanimous.*] Mabel, what about ourselves?

PURDIE. [*To whom it is truly a nauseous draught.*] I didn't know. Just a philanderer! [*The soul of him would like at this instant to creep into another body.*] And if people don't change, I suppose we shall begin all over again now.

JOANNA. [*The practical.*] I daresay; but not with each other. I may philander again, but not with you.

[*They look on themselves without approval, al-*

ways a sorry occupation. The man feels it most because he has admired himself most, or perhaps partly for some better reason.]

PURDIE. [*Saying good-bye to an old friend.*] John Purdie, John Purdie, the fine fellow I used to think you! [*When he is able to look them in the face again.*] The wood has taught me one thing, at any rate.

MABEL. [*Dismally.*] What, Jack?

PURDIE. That it isn't accident that shapes our lives.

JOANNA. No, it's Fate.

PURDIE. [*The truth running through him, seeking for a permanent home in him, willing to give him still another chance, loth to desert him.*] It's not Fate, Joanna. Fate is something outside us. What really plays the dickens with us is something in ourselves. Something that makes us go on doing the same sort of fool things, however many chances we get.

MABEL. Something in ourselves?

PURDIE. [*Shivering.*] Something we are born with.

JOANNA. Can't we cut out the beastly thing?

PURDIE. Depends, I expect, on how long we have pampered him. We can at least control him if we try hard enough. But I have for the moment an abominably clear perception that the likes of me never really tries. Forgive me, Joanna—no, Mabel—both of you. [*He is a shamed man.*] It isn't very pleasant to discover that one is a rotter. I suppose I shall get used to it.

JOANNA. I could forgive anybody anything to-night. [*Candidly.*] It is so lovely not to be married to you, Jack.

PURDIE. [*Spiritless.*] I can understand that. I do feel small.

JOANNA. [*The true friend.*] You will soon swell up again.

PURDIE. [*For whom, alas, we need not weep.*] That is

the appalling thing. But at present, at any rate, I am a rag at your feet, Joanna—no, at yours, Mabel. Are you going to pick me up? I don't advise it.

MABEL. I don't know whether I want to, Jack. To begin with, which of us is it your lonely soul is in search of?

JOANNA. Which of us is the fluid one, or the fluider one?

MABEL. Are you and I one? Or are you and Joanna one? Or are the three of us two?

JOANNA. He wants you to whisper in his ear, Mabel, the entrancing poem, "Mabel Purdie." Do it, Jack; there will be nothing wrong in it now.

PURDIE. Rub it in.

MABEL. When I meet Joanna's successor——

PURDIE. [*Quailing.*] No, no, Mabel, none of that. At least credit me with having my eyes open at last. There will be no more of this. I swear it by all that is——

JOANNA. [*In her excellent imitation of a sheep.*] Baa-a, he is off again.

PURDIE. Oh Lord, so I am.

MABEL. Don't, Joanna.

PURDIE. [*His mind still illumined.*] She is quite right— I was. In my present state of depression—which won't last —I feel there is something in me that will make me go on being the same ass, however many chances I get. I haven't the stuff in me to take warning. My whole being is corroded. Shakespeare knew what he was talking about——
   "The fault, dear Brutus, is not in our stars,
      But in ourselves, that we are underlings."

JOANNA. For "dear Brutus" we are to read "dear audience" I suppose?

PURDIE. You have it.

JOANNA. Meaning that we have the power to shape ourselves?

PURDIE. We have the power right enough.

JOANNA.   But isn't that rather splendid?

PURDIE.   For those who have the grit in them, yes. [*Still seeing with a strange clearness through the chink the hammer has made.*]   And they are not the dismal chappies; they are the ones with the thin bright faces. [*He sits lugubriously by his wife and is sorry for the first time that she has not married a better man.*]   I am afraid there is not much fight in me, Mabel, but we shall see.   If you catch me at it again, have the goodness to whisper to me in passing, "Lob's Wood."   That may cure me for the time being.

MABEL.   [*Still certain that she loved him once but not so sure why.*]   Perhaps I will——as long as I care to bother, Jack.   It depends on you how long that is to be.

JOANNA.   [*To break an awkward pause.*]   I feel that there is hope in that as well as a warning.   Perhaps the wood may prove to have been useful after all. [*This brighter view of the situation meets with no immediate response. With her next suggestion she reaches harbour.*]   You know, we are not people worth being sorrowful about —so let us laugh.

> [*The ladies succeed in laughing though not prettily, but the man has been too much shaken.*]

JOANNA.   [*In the middle of her laugh.*]   We have forgotten the others!   I wonder what is happening to them?

PURDIE.   [*Reviving.*]   Yes, what about them?   Have *they* changed!

MABEL.   I didn't see any of them in the wood.

JOANNA.   Perhaps we did see them without knowing them; we didn't know Lob.

PURDIE.   [*Daunted.*]   That's true.

JOANNA.   Won't it be delicious to be here to watch them

when they come back, and see them waking up—or what-ever it was we did.

PURDIE. What was it we did? I think something tapped me on the forehead.

MABEL. [*Blanching.*] How do we know the others *will* come back?

JOANNA. [*Infected.*] We don't know. How awful!

MABEL. Listen!

PURDIE. I distinctly hear some one on the stairs.

MABEL. It will be Matey.

PURDIE. [*The chink beginning to close.*] Be cautious both of you; don't tell him we have had any——odd experiences.

> [*It is, however,* MRS. COADE *who comes down-stairs in a dressing-gown and carrying a candle and her husband's muffler.*]

MRS. COADE. So you are back at last. A nice house, I must say. Where is Coady?

PURDIE. [*Taken aback.*] Coady! Did he go into the wood, too?

MRS. COADE. [*Placidly.*] I suppose so. I have been down several times to look for him.

MABEL. Coady, too!

JOANNA. [*Seeing visions.*] I wonder——Oh, how dreadful!

MRS. COADE. What is dreadful, Joanna?

JOANNA. [*Airily.*] Nothing. I was just wondering what he is doing.

MRS. COADE. Doing? What should he be doing? Did anything odd happen to you in the wood?

PURDLE. [*Taking command.*] No, no, nothing.

JOANNA. We just strolled about, and came back. [*That subject being exhausted she points to* LOB.] Have you noticed him?

MRS. COADE. Oh, yes; he has been like that all the time. A sort of stupor, I think; and sometimes the strangest grin comes over his face.

PURDIE. [*Wincing.*] Grin?

MRS. COADE. Just as if he were seeing amusing things in his sleep.

PURDIE. [*Guardedly.*] I daresay he is. Oughtn't we to get Matey to him?

MRS. COADE. Matey has gone, too.

PURDIE. Wha-at!

MRS. COADE. At all events he is not in the house.

JOANNA. [*Unguardedly.*] Matey! I wonder who is with him.

MRS. COADE. Must somebody be with him?

JOANNA. Oh, no, not at all.

> [*They are simultaneously aware that some one outside has reached the window.*]

MRS. COADE. I hope it is Coady.

> [*The other ladies are too fond of her to share this wish.*]

MABEL. Oh, I hope not.

MRS. COADE. [*Blissfully.*] Why, Mrs. Purdie?

JOANNA. [*Coaxingly.*] Dear Mrs. Coade, whoever he is, and whatever he does, I beg you not to be surprised. We feel that though we had no unusual experiences in the wood, others may not have been so fortunate.

MABEL. And be cautious, you dear, what you say to them before they come to.

MRS. COADE. "Come to"? You puzzle me. And Coady didn't have his muffler.

> [*Let it be recorded that in their distress for this old lady they forget their own misadventures. PURDIE takes a step toward the curtains in a vague desire to shield her;—and gets a rich*

reward; he has seen the coming addition to their circle.]

PURDIE. [*Elated and pitiless.*] It is Matey!

[*A butler intrudes who still thinks he is wrapped in fur.*]

JOANNA. [*Encouragingly.*] Do come in.

MATEY. With apologies, ladies and gents——May I ask who is host?

PURDIE. [*Splashing in the temperature that suits him best.*] A very reasonable request. Third on the left.

MATEY. [*Advancing upon* LOB.] Merely to ask, sir, if you can direct me to my hotel?

[*The sleeper's only response is a slight quiver in one leg.*]

The gentleman seems to be reposing.

MRS. COADE. It is Lob.

MATEY. What is lob, ma'am?

MRS. COADE. [*Pleasantly curious.*] Surely you haven't forgotten?

PURDIE. [*Over-riding her.*] Anything we can do for you, sir? Just give it a name.

JOANNA. [*In the same friendly spirit.*] I hope you are not alone: do say you have some lady friends with you.

MATEY. [*With an emphasis on his leading word.*] My wife is with me.

JOANNA. His wife!——[*With commendation.*] You *have* been quick!

MRS. COADE. I didn't know you were married.

MATEY. Why should you, madam? You talk as if you knew me.

MRS. COADE. Good gracious, do you really think I don't?

PURDIE. [*Indicating delicately that she is subject to a*

certain softening.] Sit down, won't you, my dear sir, and make yourself comfy.

MATEY. [*Accustomed of late to such deferential treatment.*] Thank you. But my wife——

JOANNA. [*Hospitably.*] Yes, bring her in; we are simply dying to make her acquaintance.

MATEY. You are very good; I am much obliged.

MABEL. [*As he goes out.*] Who can she be?

JOANNA. [*Leaping.*] Who, who, who!

MRS. COADE. But what an extraordinary wood! He doesn't seem to know who he is at all.

MABEL. [*Soothingly.*] Don't worry about that, Coady, darling. He will know soon enough.

JOANNA. [*Again finding the bright side.*] And so will the little wife! By the way, whoever she is, I hope she is fond of butlers.

MABEL. [*Who has peeped.*] It is Lady Caroline!

JOANNA. [*Leaping again.*] Oh, joy, joy! And she was so sure she couldn't take the wrong turning!

[*Lady Caroline is evidently still sure of it.*]

MATEY. May I present my wife—Lady Caroline Matey?

MABEL. [*Glowing.*] How do you do!

PURDIE. Your servant, Lady Caroline.

MRS. COADE. Lady Caroline Matey! You?

LADY CAROLINE. [*Without an* r *in her.*] Charmed, I'm sure.

JOANNA. [*Neatly.*] Very pleased to meet any wife of Mr. Matey.

PURDIE. [*Taking the floor.*] Allow me. The Duchess of Candelabra. The Ladies Helena and Matilda M'Nab. I am the Lord Chancellor.

MABEL. I have wanted so long to make your acquaintance.

LADY CAROLINE. Charmed.

JOANNA. [*Gracefully.*] These informal meetings are so delightful, don't you think?

LADY CAROLINE. Yes, indeed.

MATEY. [*The introductions being thus pleasantly concluded.*] And your friend by the fire?

PURDIE. I will introduce you to him when you wake up—I mean when he wakes up.

MATEY. Perhaps I ought to have said that I am *James* Matey.

LADY CAROLINE. [*The happy creature.*] The James Matey.

MATEY. A name not, perhaps, unknown in the world of finance.

JOANNA. Finance? Oh, so you did take that clerkship in the City!

MATEY. [*A little stiffly.*] I began as a clerk in the City, certainly; and I am not ashamed to admit it.

MRS. COADE. [*Still groping.*] Fancy that, now. And did it save you?

MATEY. Save me, madam?

JOANNA. Excuse us—we ask odd questions in this house; we only mean, did that keep you honest? Or are you still a pilferer?

LADY CAROLINE. [*An outraged swan.*] Husband mine, what does she mean?

JOANNA. No offense; I mean a pilferer on a large scale.

MATEY. [*Remembering certain newspaper jealousy.*] If you are referring to that Labrador business—or the Working Women's Bank——

PURDIE. [*After the manner of one who has caught a fly.*] O-ho, got him!

JOANNA. [*Bowing.*] Yes, those are what I meant.

MATEY. [*Stoutly.*] There was nothing proved.

JOANNA. [*Like one calling a meeting.*] Mabel, Jack,

here is another of us! You have gone just the same way again, my friend. [*Ecstatically.*] There is more in it, you see, than taking the wrong turning; you would always take the wrong turning. [*The only fitting comment.*] Tra-la-la!

LADY CAROLINE. If you are casting any aspersions on my husband, allow me to say that a prouder wife than I does not to-day exist.

MRS. COADE. [*Who finds herself the only clear-headed one.*] My dear, do be careful.

MABEL. So long as you are satisfied, dear Lady Caroline. But I thought you shrank from all blood that was not blue.

LADY CAROLINE. You thought? Why should you think about me? I beg to assure you that I adore my Jim.

> [*She seeks his arm, but her JIM has encountered the tray containing coffee cups and a cake, and his hands close on it with a certain intimacy.*]

Whatever are you doing, Jim?

MATEY. I don't understand it, Caroliny; but somehow I feel at home with this in my hands.

MABEL. "Caroliny!"

MRS. COADE. Look at me well; don't you remember me?

MATEY. [*Musing.*] I don't remember you; but I seem to associate you with hard-boiled eggs. [*With conviction.*] You like your eggs hard-boiled.

PURDIE. Hold on to hard-boiled eggs! She used to tip you especially to see to them.

> [*MATEY's hand goes to his pocket.*]

Yes, that was the pocket.

LADY CAROLINE. [*With distaste.*] Tip!

MATEY. [*Without distaste.*] Tip!

PURDIE. Jolly word, isn't it?

MATEY. [*Raising the tray.*] It seems to set me thinking.

LADY CAROLINE. [*Feeling the tap of the hammer.*] Why is my work-basket in this house?

MRS. COADE. You are living here, you know.

LADY CAROLINE. That is what a person feels. But when did I come? It is very odd, but one feels one ought to say when did one go.

PURDIE. She is coming to with a wush!

MATEY. [*Under the hammer.*] Mr.—— Purdie!

LADY CAROLINE. Mrs. Coade!

MATEY. The Guv'nor! My clothes!

LADY CAROLINE. One is in evening dress!

JOANNA. [*Charmed to explain.*] You will understand clearly in a minute, Caroliny. You didn't really take that clerkship, Jim; you went into domestic service; but in the essentials you haven't altered.

PURDIE. [*Pleasantly.*] I'll have my shaving water at 7.30 sharp, Matey.

MATEY. [*Mechanically.*] Very good, sir.

LADY CAROLINE. Sir? Midsummer Eve! The wood!

PURDIE. Yes, hold on to the wood.

MATEY. You are——you are——you are Lady Caroline Laney!

LADY CAROLINE. It is Matey, the butler!

MABEL. You seemed quite happy with him, you know, Lady Caroline.

JOANNA. [*Nicely.*] We won't tell.

LADY CAROLINE. [*Subsiding.*] Caroline Matey! And I seemed to like it! How horrible!

MRS. COADE. [*Expressing a general sentiment.*] It is rather difficult to see what we should do next.

MATEY. [*Tentatively.*] Perhaps if I were to go downstairs?

PURDIE. It would be conferring a personal favour on us all.

> [*Thus encouraged* MATEY *and his tray resume friendly relations with the pantry.*]

LADY CAROLINE. [*With itching fingers as she glares at* LOB.] It is all that wretch's doing.

> [*A quiver from* LOB'S *right leg acknowledges the compliment. The gay music of a pipe is heard from outside.*]

JOANNA. [*Peeping.*] Coady!

MRS. COADE. Coady! Why is he so happy?

JOANNA. [*Troubled.*] Dear, hold my hand.

MRS. COADE. [*Suddenly trembling.*] Won't he know me?

PURDIE. [*Abashed by that soft face.*] Mrs. Coade, I'm sorry. It didn't so much matter about the likes of us, but for your sake I wish Coady hadn't gone out.

MRS. COADE. We that have been happily married this thirty years.

COADE. [*Popping in buoyantly.*] May I intrude? My name is Coade. The fact is I was playing about in the wood on a whistle, and I saw your light.

MRS. COADE. [*The only one with the nerve to answer.*] Playing about in the wood with a whistle!

COADE. [*With mild dignity.*] And why not, madam?

MRS. COADE. Madam! Don't you know me?

COADE. I don't know you—— [*Reflecting.*] But I wish I did.

MRS. COADE. Do you? Why?

COADE. If I may say so, you have a very soft, lovable face.

> [*Several persons breathe again.*]

MRS. COADE. [*Inquisitorially.*] Who was with you, playing whistles in the wood? [*The breathing ceases.*]

COADE. No one was with me.

[*And is resumed.*]

MRS. COADE. No——lady?

COADE. Certainly not. [*Then he spoils it.*] I am a bachelor.

MRS. COADE. A bachelor!

JOANNA. Don't give way, dear; it might be much worse.

MRS. COADE. A bachelor! And you are sure you never spoke to me before? Do think.

COADE. Not to my knowledge. Never——except in dreams.

MABEL. [*Taking a risk.*] What did you say to her in dreams?

COADE. I said, "My dear." [*This when uttered surprises him.*] Odd!

JOANNA. The darling man!

MRS. COADE. [*Wavering.*] How could you say such things to an old woman?

COADE. [*Thinking it out.*] Old? I didn't think of you as old. No, no, young—with the morning dew on your face—coming across a lawn—in a black and green dress—and carrying such a pretty parasol.

MRS. COADE. [*Thrilling.*] That was how he first met me! He used to love me in black and green; and it *was* a pretty parasol. Look, I am old—— So it can't be the same woman.

COADE. [*Blinking.*] Old? Yes, I suppose so. But it is the same soft, lovable face, and the same kind, beaming smile that children could warm their hands at.

MRS. COADE. He always liked my smile.

PURDIE. So do we all.

COADE. [*To himself.*] Emma!

MRS. COADE. He hasn't forgotten my name!

COADE. It is sad that we didn't meet long ago. I think I have been waiting for you. I suppose we have met too late? You couldn't overlook my being an old fellow, could you, eh?

JOANNA. How lovely; he is going to propose to her again. Coady, you happy thing, he is wanting the same soft face after thirty years!

MRS. COADE. [*Undoubtedly hopeful.*] We musn't be too sure, but I think that is it. [*Primly.*] What is it exactly that you want, Mr. Coade?

COADE. [*Under a lucky star.*] I want to have the right to hold the parasol over you. Won't you be my wife, my dear, and so give my long dream of you a happy ending?

MRS. COADE. [*Preening.*] Kisses are not called for at our age, Coady, but here is a muffler for your old neck.

COADE. My muffler; I have missed it. [*It is however to his forehead that his hand goes. Immediately thereafter he misses his sylvan attire.*] Why——why——what—— who——how is this?

PURDIE. [*Nervously.*] He is coming to.

COADE. [*Ruling and righting himself.*] Lob!
[*The leg indicates that he has got it.*]
Bless me, Coady, I went into that wood!

MRS. COADY. And without your muffler, you that are so subject to chills. What are you feeling for in your pocket?

COADE. The whistle. It is a whistle I—Gone! of course it is. It's rather a pity; but—— [*Anxious.*] Have I been saying awful things to you?

MABEL. You have been making her so proud. It is a compliment to our whole sex. You had a second chance, and it is her, again!

COADE. Of course it is. [*Crestfallen.*] But I see I was just the same nice old lazy Coady as before; and I had thought that if I had a second chance, I could do things.

I have often said to you, Coady, that it was owing to my being cursed with a competency that I didn't write my great book. But I had no competency this time, and I haven't written a word.

PURDIE. [*Bitterly enough.*] That needn't make you feel lonely in this house.

MRS. COADE. [*In a small voice.*] You seem to have been quite happy as an old bachelor, dear.

COADE. I am surprised at myself, Emma, but I fear I was.

MRS. COADE. [*With melancholy perspicacity.*] I wonder if what it means is that you don't especially need even me. I wonder if it means that you are just the sort of amiable creature that would be happy anyhere, and anyhow?

COADE. Oh dear, can it be as bad as that!

JOANNA. [*A ministering angel she.*] Certainly not. It is a romance, and I won't have it looked upon as anything else.

MRS. COADE. Thank you, Joanna. You will try not to miss that whistle, Coady?

COADE. [*Getting the footstool for her.*] You are all I need.

MRS. COADE. Yes; but I am not so sure as I used to be that it is a great compliment.

JOANNA. Coady, behave.

[*There is a knock on the window.*]

PURDIE. [*Peeping.*] Mrs. Dearth! [*His spirits revive.*] She is alone. Who would have expected that of *her!*

MABEL. She is a wild one, Jack, but I sometimes thought rather a dear; I do hope she has got off cheaply.

[ALICE *comes to them in her dinner gown.*]

PURDIE. [*The irrepressible.*] Pleased to see you, stranger.

ALICE. [*Prepared for ejection.*] I was afraid such an unceremonious entry might startle you.

PURDIE. Not a bit.

ALICE. [*Defiant.*] I usually enter a house by the front door.

PURDIE. I have heard that such is the swagger way.

ALICE. [*Simpering.*] So stupid of me. I lost myself in the wood——and——

JOANNA. [*Genially.*] Of course you did. But never mind that; do tell us your name.

LADY CAROLINE. [*Emerging again.*] Yes, yes, your name.

ALICE. Of course, I am the Honourable Mrs. Finch-Fallowe.

LADY CAROLINE. Of course, of course!

PURDIE. I hope Mr. Finch-Fallowe is very well? We don't know him personally, but may we have the pleasure of seeing him bob up presently?

ALICE. No, I am not sure where he is.

LADY CAROLINE. [*With point.*] I wonder if the dear clever police know?

ALICE. [*Imprudently.*] No, they don't.

> [*It is a very secondary matter to her. This woman of calamitous fires hears and sees her tormentors chiefly as the probable owners of the cake which is standing on that tray.*]

So awkward, I gave my sandwiches to a poor girl and her father whom I met in the wood, and now——isn't it a nuisance——I am quite hungry. [*So far with a mincing bravado.*] May I?

> [*Without waiting for consent she falls to upon the*

cake, looking over it like one ready to fight them for it.]

PURDIE. [*Sobered again.*] Poor soul.

LADY CAROLINE. We are so anxious to know whether you met a friend of ours in the wood—a Mr. Dearth. Perhaps you know him, too?

ALICE. Dearth? I don't know any Dearth.

MRS. COADE. Oh dear, what a wood!

LADY CAROLINE. He is quite a front door sort of man; knocks and rings, you know.

PURDIE. Don't worry her.

ALICE. [*Gnawing.*] I meet so many; you see I go out a great deal. I have visiting-cards—printed ones.

LADY CAROLINE. How very distingué. Perhaps Mr. Dearth has painted your portrait; he is an artist.

ALICE. Very likely; they all want to paint me. I daresay that is the man to whom I gave my sandwiches.

MRS. COADE. But I thought you said he had a daughter?

ALICE. Such a pretty girl; I gave her half a crown.

COADE. A daughter? That can't be Dearth.

PURDIE. [*Darkly.*] Don't be too sure. Was the man you speak of a rather chop-fallen, gone-to-seed sort of person.

ALICE. No, I thought him such a jolly, attractive man.

COADE. Dearth jolly, attractive! oh no. Did he say anything about his wife?

LADY CAROLINE. Yes, do try to remember if he mentioned her.

ALICE. [*Snapping.*] No, he didn't.

PURDIE. He was far from jolly in her time.

ALICE. [*With an archness for which the cake is responsible.*] Perhaps that was the lady's fault.

[*The last of the adventurers draws nigh, carolling a French song as he comes.*]

COADE. Dearth's voice. He sounds quite merry!

JOANNA. [*Protecting.*] Alice, you poor thing.

PURDIE. This is going to be horrible.

[*A clear-eyed man of lusty gait comes in.*]

DEARTH. I am sorry to bounce in on you in this way, but really I have an excuse. I am a painter of sorts, and——

[*He sees he has brought some strange discomfort here.*]

MRS. COADE. I must say, Mr. Dearth, I am delighted to see you looking so well. Like a new man, isn't he?

[*No one dares to answer.*]

DEARTH. I am certainly very well, if you care to know. But did I tell you my name?

JOANNA. [*For some one has to speak.*] No, but—but we have an instinct in this house.

DEARTH. Well, it doesn't matter. Here is the situation; my daughter and I have just met in the wood a poor woman famishing for want of food. We were as happy as grigs ourselves, and the sight of her distress rather cut us up. Can you give me something for her? Why are you looking so startled? [*Seeing the remains of the cake.*] May I have this?

[*A shrinking movement from one of them draws his attention, and he recognises in her the woman of whom he has been speaking. He sees her in fine clothing and he grows stern.*]

I feel I can't be mistaken; it was you I met in the wood? Have you been playing some trick on me? [*To the others.*] It was for her I wanted the food.

ALICE. [*Her hand guarding the place where his gift lies.*] Have you come to take back the money you gave me?

DEARTH. Your dress! You were almost in rags when I saw you outside.

ALICE. [*Frightened as she discovers how she is now attired.*] I don't——understand——

COADE. [*Gravely enough.*] For that matter, Dearth, I daresay you were different in the wood, too.

[DEARTH *sees his own clothing.*]

DEARTH. What——!

ALICE. [*Frightened.*] Where am I? [*To* MRS. COADE.] I seem to know you——do I?

MRS. COADE. [*Motherly.*] Yes, you do; hold my hand, and you will soon remember all about it.

JOANNA. I am afraid, Mr. Dearth, it is harder for you than for the rest of us.

PURDIE. [*Looking away.*] I wish I could help you, but I can't; I am a rotter.

MABEL. We are awfully sorry. Don't you remember ——Midsummer Eve?

DEARTH. [*Controlling himself.*] Midsummer Eve? This room. Yes, this room——You——was it you?—— were going out to look for something—— The tree of knowledge, wasn't it? Somebody wanted me to go, too. ——Who was that? A lady, I think—— Why did she ask me to go? What was I doing here? I was smoking a cigar—— I laid it down, there—— [*He finds the cigar.*] Who was the lady?

ALICE. [*Feebly.*] Something about a second chance.

MRS. COADE. Yes, you poor dear, you thought you could make so much of it.

DEARTH. A lady who didn't like me—[*With conviction.*] She had good reasons, too—but what were they——?

ALICE. A little old man! He did it. What did he do?

[*The hammer is raised.*]

DEARTH. I am——it is coming back—I am not the man I thought myself.

ALICE. I am not Mrs. Finch-Fallowe. Who am I?

DEARTH. [*Staring at her.*] You were that lady.

ALICE. It is you—my husband!

[*She is overcome.*]

MRS. COADE. My dear, you are much better off, so far as I can see, than if you were Mrs. Finch-Fallowe.

ALICE. [*With passionate knowledge.*] Yes, yes indeed! [*Generously.*] But he isn't.

DEARTH. Alice!—— I—[*He tries to smile.*] I didn't know you when I was in the wood with Margaret. She ——she——Margaret——

[*The hammer falls.*]

O my God!

[*He buries his face in his hands.*]

ALICE. I wish—I wish——

[*She presses his shoulder fiercely and then stalks out by the door.*]

PURDIE. [*To* LOB, *after a time.*] You old ruffian.

DEARTH. No, I am rather fond of him, our lonely, friendly little host. Lob, I thank thee for that hour.

[*The seedy-looking fellow passes from the scene.*]

COADE. Did you see that his hand is shaking again?

PURDIE. The watery eye has come back.

JOANNA. And yet they are both quite nice people.

PURDIE. [*Finding the tragedy of it.*] We are all quite nice people.

MABEL. If she were not such a savage!

PURDIE. I daresay there is nothing the matter with her except that she would always choose the wrong man, good man or bad man, but the wrong man for her.

COADE. We can't change.

MABEL. Jack says the brave ones can.

JOANNA. "The ones with the thin bright faces."

MABEL. Then there is hope for you and me, Jack.

PURDIE. [*Ignobly.*] I don't expect so.

JOANNA. [*Wandering about the room, like one renewing acquaintance with it after returning from a journey.*] Hadn't we better go to bed? it must be getting late.

PURDIE. Hold on to bed? [*They all brighten.*]

MATEY. [*Entering.*] Breakfast is quite ready.

[*They exclaim.*]

LADY CAROLINE. My watch has stopped.

JOANNA. And mine. Just as well perhaps!

MABEL. There is a smell of coffee.

[*The gloom continues to lift.*]

COADE. Come along, Coady; I do hope you have not been tiring your foot.

MRS. COADE. I shall give it a good rest to-morrow, dear.

MATEY. I have given your egg six minutes, ma'am.

[*They set forth once more upon the eternal round. The curious* JOANNA *remains behind.*]

JOANNA. A strange experiment, Matey; does it ever have any permanent effect?

MATEY. [*On whom it has had none.*] So far as I know, not often, miss; but, I believe, once in a while.

> [*There is hope in this for the brave ones. If we could wait long enough we might see the* DEARTHS *breasting their way into the light.*]

He could tell you.

> [*The elusive person thus referred to kicks responsively, meaning perhaps that none of the others will change till there is a tap from another hammer. But when* MATEY *goes to rout him from his chair he is no longer there. His dis-*

appearance is no shock to MATEY, *who shrugs his shoulders and opens the windows to let in the glory of a summer morning. The garden has returned, and our queer little hero is busy at work among his flowers. A lark is rising.*]

The End

THE TWELVE-POUND LOOK

*If quite convenient [as they say about cheques] you are
to conceive that the scene is laid in your own house,
and that* HARRY SIMS *is you. Perhaps the ornamenta-
tion of the house is a trifle ostentatious, but if you
cavil at that we are willing to re-decorate: you don't
get out of being* HARRY SIMS *on a mere matter of
plush and dados. It pleases us to make him a city
man, but [rather than lose you] he can be turned with
a scrape of the pen into a K.C., fashionable doctor,
Secretary of State, or what you will. We conceive him
of a pleasant rotundity with a thick red neck, but we
shall waive that point if you know him to be thin.*

*It is that day in your career when everything went wrong
just when everything seemed to be superlatively right.*

In HARRY'S *case it was a woman who did the mischief.
She came to him in his great hour and told him she did
not admire him. Of course he turned her out of the
house and was soon himself again, but it spoilt the
morning for him. This is the subject of the play, and
quite enough too.*

HARRY *is to receive the honour of knighthood in a few days,
and we discover him in the sumptuous "snuggery" of
his home in Kensington [or is it Westminster?], rehearsing the ceremony with his wife. They have been
at it all the morning, a pleasing occupation.* MRS.
SIMS *[as we may call her for the last time, as it were,
and strictly as a good-natured joke] is wearing her
presentation gown, and personates the august one who
is about to dub her* HARRY *knight. She is seated
regally. Her jewelled shoulders proclaim aloud her*

379

husband's generosity. She must be an extraordinarily proud and happy woman, yet she has a drawn face and shrinking ways as if there were some one near her of whom she is afraid. She claps her hands, as the signal to HARRY. *He enters bowing, and with a graceful swerve of the leg. He is only partly in costume, the sword and the real stockings not having arrived yet. With a gliding motion that is only delayed while one leg makes up on the other, he reaches his wife, and, going on one knee, raises her hand superbly to his lips. She taps him on the shoulder with a paper-knife and says huskily, "Rise, Sir Harry." He rises, bows, and glides about the room, going on his knees to various articles of furniture, and rises from each a knight. It is a radiant domestic scene, and* HARRY *is as dignified as if he knew that royalty was rehearsing it at the other end.*

SIR HARRY. [*Complacently.*]   Did that seem all right, eh?

LADY SIMS. [*Much relieved.*]   I think perfect.

SIR HARRY.   But was it dignified?

LADY SIMS.   Oh, very.   And it will be still more so when you have the sword.

SIR HARRY.   The sword will lend it an air. There are really the five moments—[*Suiting the action to the word*]—the glide—the dip—the kiss—the tap—and you back out a knight. It's short, but it's a very beautiful ceremony. [*Kindly.*]   Anything you can suggest?

LADY SIMS.   No—oh no. [*Nervously, seeing him pause to kiss the tassel of a cushion.*]   You don't think you have practised till you know what to do almost too well?

> [*He has been in a blissful temper, but such niggling criticism would try any man.*]

SIR HARRY. I do not. Don't talk nonsense. Wait till your opinion is asked for.

LADY SIMS. [*Abashed.*] I'm sorry, Harry. [*A perfect butler appears and presents a card.*] "The Flora Type-Writing Agency."

SIR HARRY. Ah, yes. I telephoned them to send some one. A woman, I suppose, Tombes?

TOMBES. Yes, Sir Harry.

SIR HARRY. Show her in here. [*He has very lately become a stickler for etiquette.*] And, Tombes, strictly speaking, you know, I am not Sir Harry till Thursday.

TOMBES. Beg pardon, sir, but it is such a satisfaction to us.

SIR HARRY. [*Good-naturedly.*] Ah, they like it downstairs, do they?

TOMBES. [*Unbending.*] Especially the females, Sir Harry.

SIR HARRY. Exactly. You can show her in, Tombes. [*The butler departs on his mighty task.*] You can tell the woman what she is wanted for, Emmy, while I change. [*He is too modest to boast about himself, and prefers to keep a wife in the house for that purpose.*] You can tell her the sort of things about me that will come better from you. [*Smiling happily.*] You heard what Tombes said, "Especially the females." And he is right. Success! The women like it even better than the men. And rightly. For they share. *You* share, *Lady* Sims. Not a woman will see that gown without being sick with envy of it. I know them. Have all our lady friends in to see it. It will make them ill for a week.

> [*These sentiments carry him off lightheartedly, and presently the disturbing element is shown in. She is a mere typist, dressed in uncommonly good taste, but at contemptibly small expense, and she is carrying her typewriter in a friendly*

*way rather than as a badge of slavery, as of
course it is. Her eye is clear; and in odd con-
trast to* LADY SIMS, *she is self-reliant and
serene.*]

KATE.   [*Respectfully, but she should have waited to be
spoken to.*]   Good morning, madam.

LADY SIMS.   [*In her nervous way, and scarcely noticing
that the typist is a little too ready with her tongue.*]   Good
morning.   [*As a first impression she rather likes the woman,
and the woman, though it is scarcely worth mentioning,
rather likes her.* LADY SIMS *has a maid for buttoning and
unbuttoning her, and probably another for waiting on the
maid, and she gazes with a little envy perhaps at a woman
who does things for herself.*]   Is that the type-writing
machine?

KATE.   [*Who is getting it ready for use.*]   Yes.   [*Not
"Yes, madam," as it ought to be.*]   I suppose if I am to
work here I may take this off. I get on better without it.
[*She is referring to her hat.*]

LADY SIMS.   Certainly.   [*But the hat is already off.*]   I
ought to apologise for my gown. I am to be presented this
week, and I was trying it on.   [*Her tone is not really
apologetic. She is rather clinging to the glory of her gown,
wistfully, as if not absolutely certain, you know, that it is
a glory.*]

KATE.   It is beautiful, if I may presume to say so.   [*She
frankly admires it. She probably has a best, and a second
best of her own: that sort of thing.*]

LADY SIMS.   [*With a flush of pride in the gown.*]   Yes,
it is very beautiful.   [*The beauty of it gives her courage.*]
Sit down, please.

KATE.   [*The sort of woman who would have sat down in
any case.*]   I suppose it is some copying you want done?

I got no particulars. I was told to come to this address, but that was all.

LADY SIMS. [*Almost with the humility of a servant.*] Oh, it is not work for me, it is for my husband, and what he needs is not exactly copying. [*Swelling, for she is proud of* HARRY.] He wants a number of letters answered—hundreds of them—letters and telegrams of congratulation.

KATE. [*As if it were all in the day's work.*] Yes?

LADY SIMS. [*Remembering that* HARRY *expects every wife to do her duty.*] My husband is a remarkable man. He is about to be knighted. [*Pause, but* KATE *does not fall to the floor.*] He is to be knighted for his services to— [*on reflection*]—for his services. [*She is conscious that she is not doing* HARRY *justice.*] He can explain it so much better than I can.

KATE. [*In her business-like way.*] And I am to answer the congratulations?

LADY SIMS. [*Afraid that it will be a hard task.*] Yes.

KATE. [*Blithely.*] It is work I have had some experience of. [*She proceeds to type.*]

LADY SIMS. But you can't begin till you know what he wants to say.

KATE. Only a specimen letter. Won't it be the usual thing?

LADY SIMS. [*To whom this is a new idea.*] Is there a usual thing?

KATE. Oh, yes.

> [*She continues to type, and* LADY SIMS, *half-mesmerised, gazes at her nimble fingers. The useless woman watches the useful one, and she sighs, she could not tell why.*]

LADY SIMS. How quickly you do it! It must be delightful to be able to do something, and to do it well.

KATE. [*Thankfully.*] Yes, it is delightful.

Lady Sims. [*Again remembering the source of all her greatness.*]   But, excuse me, I don't think that will be any use. My husband wants me to explain to you that his is an exceptional case. He did not try to get this honour in any way. It was a complete surprise to him——

Kate. [*Who is a practical* Kate *and no dealer in sarcasm.*]   That is what I have written.

Lady Sims. [*In whom sarcasm would meet a dead wall.*] But how could you know?

Kate.   I only guessed.

Lady Sims.   Is that the usual thing?

Kate.   Oh, yes.

Lady Sims.   They don't try to get it?

Kate.   I don't know.   That is what we are told to say in the letters.

> [*To her at present the only important thing about the letters is that they are ten shillings the hundred.*]

Lady Sims. [*Returning to surer ground.*]   I should explain that my husband is not a man who cares for honours. So long as he does his duty——

Kate.   Yes, I have been putting that in.

Lady Sims.   Have you?   But he particularly wants it to be known that he would have declined a title were it not——

Kate.   I have got it here.

Lady Sims.   What have you got?

Kate. [*Reading.*]   "Indeed, I would have asked to be allowed to decline had it not been that I want to please my wife."

Lady Sims. [*Heavily.*]   But how could you know it was that?

Kate.   Is it?

Lady Sims. [*Who after all is the one with the right to ask questions.*]   Do they all accept it for that reason?

KATE. That is what we are told to say in the letters.

LADY SIMS. [*Thoughtlessly.*] It is quite as if you knew my husband.

KATE. I assure you, I don't even know his name.

LADY SIMS. [*Suddenly showing that she knows him.*] Oh, he wouldn't like that!

> [*And it is here that* HARRY *re-enters in his city garments, looking so gay, feeling so jolly that we bleed for him. However, the annoying* KATHERINE *is to get a shock also.*]

LADY SIMS. This is the lady, Harry.

SIR HARRY. [*Shooting his cuffs.*] Yes, yes. Good morning, my dear.

> [*Then they see each other, and their mouths open, but not for words. After the first surprise* KATE *seems to find some humour in the situation, but* HARRY *lowers like a thundercloud.*]

LADY SIMS. [*Who has seen nothing.*] I have been trying to explain to her——

SIR HARRY. Eh—what? [*He controls himself.*] Leave it to me, Emmy; I'll attend to her.

> [LADY SIMS *goes, with a dread fear that somehow she has vexed her lord, and then* HARRY *attends to the intruder.*]

SIR HARRY. [*With concentrated scorn.*] You!

KATE. [*As if agreeing with him.*] Yes, it's funny.

SIR HARRY. The shamelessness of your daring to come here.

KATE. Believe me, it is not less a surprise to me than it is to you. I was sent here in the ordinary way of business. I was given only the number of the house. I was not told the name.

SIR HARRY. [*Withering her.*] The ordinary way of business! This is what you have fallen to—a typist!

KATE. [*Unwithered.*] Think of it!

SIR HARRY. After going through worse straits, I'll be bound.

KATE. [*With some grim memories.*]   Much worse straits.

SIR HARRY. [*Alas, laughing coarsely.*] My congratulations!

KATE. Thank you, Harry.

SIR HARRY. [*Who is annoyed, as any man would be, not to find her abject.*]   Eh! What was that you called me, madam?

KATE. Isn't it Harry? On my soul, I almost forget.

SIR HARRY. It isn't Harry to you. My name is Sims, if you please.

KATE. Yes, I had not forgotten that. It was my name, too, you see.

SIR HARRY. [*In his best manner.*]   It was your name till you forfeited the right to bear it.

KATE. Exactly.

SIR HARRY. [*Gloating.*] I was furious to find you here, but on second thoughts it pleases me. [*From the depths of his moral nature.*]   There is a grim justice in this.

KATE. [*Sympathetically.*] Tell me?

SIR HARRY. Do you know what you were brought here to do?

KATE. I have just been learning. You have been made a knight, and I was summoned to answer the messages of congratulation.

SIR HARRY. That's it, that's it. You come on this day as my servant!

KATE. I, who might have been Lady Sims.

SIR HARRY. And you are her typist instead. And she has four men-servants. Oh, I am glad you saw her in her presentation gown.

KATE. I wonder if she would let me do her washing, Sir Harry?

[*Her want of taste disgusts him.*]

SIR HARRY. [*With dignity.*] You can go. The mere thought that only a few flights of stairs separates such as you from my innocent children——

[*He will never know why a new light has come into her face.*]

KATE. [*Slowly.*] You have children?

SIR HARRY. [*Inflated.*] Two.

[*He wonders why she is so long in answering.*]

KATE. [*Resorting to impertinence.*] Such a nice number.

SIR HARRY. [*With an extra turn of the screw.*] Both boys.

KATE. Successful in everything. Are they like you, Sir Harry?

SIR HARRY. [*Expanding.*] They are very like me.

KATE. That's nice.

[*Even on such a subject as this she can be ribald.*]

SIR HARRY. Will you please to go.

KATE. Heigho! What shall I say to my employer?

SIR HARRY. That is no affair of mine.

KATE. What will you say to Lady Sims?

SIR HARRY. I flatter myself that whatever I say, Lady Sims will accept without comment.

[*She smiles, heaven knows why, unless her next remark explains it.*]

KATE. Still the same Harry.

SIR HARRY. What do you mean?

KATE. Only that you have the old confidence in your profound knowledge of the sex.

SIR HARRY. [*Beginning to think as little of her intellect as of her morals.*] I suppose I know my wife.

KATE. [*Hopelessly dense.*] I suppose so. I was only remembering that you used to think you knew her in the days when I was the lady. [*He is merely wasting his time on her, and he indicates the door. She is not sufficiently the lady to retire worsted.*] Well, good-bye, Sir Harry. Won't you ring, and the four men-servants will show me out?

[*But he hesitates.*]

SIR HARRY. [*In spite of himself.*] As you are here, there is something I want to get out of you. [*Wishing he could ask it less eagerly.*] Tell me, who was the man?

[*The strange woman—it is evident now that she has always been strange to him—smiles tolerantly.*]

KATE. You never found out?

SIR HARRY. I could never be sure.

KATE. [*Reflectively.*] I thought that would worry you.

SIR HARRY. [*Sneering.*] It's plain that he soon left you.

KATE. Very soon.

SIR HARRY. As I could have told you. [*But still she surveys him with the smile of Mona Lisa. The badgered man has to entreat.*] Who was he? It was fourteen years ago, and cannot matter to any of us now. Kate, tell me who he was?

[*It is his first youthful moment, and perhaps because of that she does not wish to hurt him.*]

KATE. [*Shaking a motherly head.*] Better not ask.

SIR HARRY. I do ask. Tell me.

KATE. It is kinder not to tell you.

SIR HARRY. [*Violently.*] Then, by James, it was one of my own pals. Was it Bernard Roche? [*She shakes her head.*] It may have been some one who comes to my house still.

KATE. I think not. [*Reflecting.*] Fourteen years! You found my letter that night when you went home?

SIR HARRY. [*Impatient.*] Yes.

KATE. I propped it against the decanters. I thought you would be sure to see it there. It was a room not unlike this, and the furniture was arranged in the same attractive way. How it all comes back to me. Don't you see me, Harry, in hat and cloak, putting the letter there, taking a last look round, and then stealing out into the night to meet——

SIR HARRY. Whom?

KATE. Him. Hours pass, no sound in the room but the tick-tack of the clock, and then about midnight you return alone. You take——

SIR HARRY. [*Gruffly.*] I wasn't alone.

KATE. [*The picture spoilt.*] No? oh. [*Plaintively.*] Here have I all these years been conceiving it wrongly. [*She studies his face.*] I believe something interesting happened?

SIR HARRY. [*Growling.*] Something confoundedly annoying.

KATE. [*Coaxing.*] Do tell me.

SIR HARRY. We won't go into that. Who was the man? Surely a husband has a right to know with whom his wife bolted.

KATE. [*Who is detestably ready with her tongue.*] Surely the wife has a right to know how he took it. [*The woman's love of bargaining comes to her aid.*] A fair exchange. You tell me what happened, and I will tell you who he was.

SIR HARRY. You will? Very well. [*It is the first point on which they have agreed, and, forgetting himself, he takes a place beside her on the fire-seat. He is thinking only of what he is to tell her, but she, woman-like, is conscious of their proximity.*]

KATE. [*Tastelessly.*] Quite like old times. [*He moves away from her indignantly.*] Go on, Harry.

SIR HARRY. [*Who has a manful shrinking from saying anything that is to his disadvantage.*] Well, as you know, I was dining at the club that night.

KATE. Yes.

SIR HARRY. Jack Lamb drove me home. Mabbett Green was with us, and I asked them to come in for a few minutes.

KATE. Jack Lamb, Mabbett Green? I think I remember them. Jack was in Parliament.

SIR HARRY. No, that was Mabbett. They came into the house with me and—[*With sudden horror*]—was it him?

KATE. [*Bewildered.*] Who?

SIR HARRY. Mabbett?

KATE. What?

SIR HARRY. The man?

KATE. What man? [*Understanding.*] Oh, no. I thought you said he came into the house with you.

SIR HARRY. It might have been a blind.

KATE. Well, it wasn't. Go on.

SIR HARRY. They came in to finish a talk we had been having at the club.

KATE. An interesting talk, evidently.

SIR HARRY. The papers had been full that evening of the elopement of some countess woman with a fiddler. What was her name?

KATE. Does it matter?

SIR HARRY. No. [*Thus ends the countess.*] We had been discussing the thing and—[*He pulls a wry face*]—and I had been rather warm——

KATE. [*With horrid relish.*] I begin to see. You had been saying it served the husband right, that the man who could not look after his wife deserved to lose her. It was one of your favourite subjects. Oh, Harry, say it was that!

SIR HARRY. [*Sourly.*] It may have been something like that.

KATE. And all the time the letter was there, waiting; and none of you knew except the clock. Harry, it is sweet of you to tell me. [*His face is not sweet. The illiterate woman has used the wrong adjective.*] I forget what I said precisely in the letter.

SIR HARRY. [*Pulverising her.*] So do I. But I have it still.

KATE. [*Not pulverised.*] Do let me see it again. [*She has observed his eye wandering to the desk.*]

SIR HARRY. You are welcome to it as a gift. [*The fateful letter, a poor little dead thing, is brought to light from a locked drawer.*]

KATE. [*Taking it.*] Yes, this is it. Harry, how you did crumple it! [*She reads, not without curiosity.*] "Dear husband—I call you that for the last time—I am off. I am what you call making a bolt of it. I won't try to excuse myself nor to explain, for you would not accept the excuses nor understand the explanation. It will be a little shock to you, but only to your pride; what will astound you is that any woman could be such a fool as to leave such a man as you. I am taking nothing with me that belongs to you. May you be very happy.—Your ungrateful Kate. *P.S.*—You need not try to find out who he is. You will try, but you won't succeed." [*She folds the nasty little thing up.*] I may really have it for my very own?

SIR HARRY. You really may.

KATE. [*Impudently.*] If you would care for a typed copy——?

SIR HARRY. [*In a voice with which he used to frighten his grandmother.*] None of your sauce! [*Wincing.*] I had to let them see it in the end.

KATE. I can picture Jack Lamb eating it.

SIR HARRY. A penniless parson's daughter.

KATE. That is all I was.

SIR HARRY. We searched for the two of you high and low.

KATE. Private detectives?

SIR HARRY. They couldn't get on the track of you.

KATE. [*Smiling.*] No?

SIR HARRY. But at last the courts let me serve the papers by advertisement on a man unknown, and I got my freedom.

KATE. So I saw. It was the last I heard of you.

SIR HARRY. [*Each word a blow for her.*] And I married again just as soon as ever I could.

KATE. They say that is always a compliment to the first wife.

SIR HARRY. [*Violently.*] I showed them.

KATE. You soon let them see that if one woman was a fool, you still had the pick of the basket to choose from.

SIR HARRY. By James, I did.

KATE. [*Bringing him to earth again.*] But still, you wondered who he was.

SIR HARRY. I suspected everybody—even my pals. I felt like jumping at their throats and crying, "It's you!"

KATE. You had been so admirable to me, an instinct told you that I was sure to choose another of the same.

SIR HARRY. I thought, it can't be money, so it must be looks. Some dolly face. [*He stares at her in perplexity.*] He must have had something wonderful about him to make you willing to give up all that you had with me.

KATE. [*As if he was the stupid one.*] Poor Harry.

SIR HARRY. And it couldn't have been going on for long, for I would have noticed the change in you.

KATE. Would you?

SIR HARRY. I knew you so well.

KATE. You amazing man.

SIR HARRY. So who was he? Out with it.

KATE. You are determined to know?

SIR HARRY. Your promise. You gave your word.

KATE. If I must—— [*She is the villain of the piece, but it must be conceded that in this matter she is reluctant to pain him.*] I am sorry I promised. [*Looking at him steadily.*] There was no one, Harry; no one at all.

SIR HARRY. [*Rising.*] If you think you can play with me——

KATE. I told you that you wouldn't like it.

SIR HARRY. [*Rasping.*] It is unbelievable.

KATE. I suppose it is; but it is true.

SIR HARRY. Your letter itself gives you the lie.

KATE. That was intentional. I saw that if the truth were known you might have a difficulty in getting your freedom; and as I was getting mine it seemed fair that you should have yours also. So I wrote my good-bye in words that would be taken to mean what you thought they meant, and I knew the law would back you in your opinion. For the law, like you, Harry, has a profound understanding of women.

SIR HARRY. [*Trying to straighten himself.*] I don't believe you yet.

KATE. [*Looking not unkindly into the soul of this man.*] Perhaps that is the best way to take it. It is less unflattering than the truth. But you were the only one. [*Summing up her life.*] You sufficed.

SIR HARRY. Then what mad impulse——

KATE. It was no impulse, Harry. I had thought it out for a year.

SIR HARRY. A year? [*Dazed.*] One would think to hear you that I hadn't been a good husband to you.

KATE. [*With a sad smile.*] You were a good husband according to your lights.

SIR HARRY. [*Stoutly.*] *I* think so.

KATE. And a moral man, and chatty, and quite the philanthropist.

SIR HARRY. [*On sure ground.*] All women envied you.

KATE. How you loved me to be envied.

SIR HARRY. I swaddled you in luxury.

KATE. [*Making her great revelation.*] That was it.

SIR HARRY. [*Blankly.*] What?

KATE. [*Who can be serene because it is all over.*] How you beamed at me when I sat at the head of your fat dinners in my fat jewellery, surrounded by our fat friends.

SIR HARRY. [*Aggrieved.*] They weren't so fat.

KATE. [*A side issue.*] All except those who were so thin. Have you ever noticed, Harry, that many jewels make women either incredibly fat or incredibly thin?

SIR HARRY. [*Shouting.*] I have not. [*Is it worth while to argue with her any longer?*] We had all the most interesting society of the day. It wasn't only business men. There were politicians, painters, writers——

KATE. Only the glorious, dazzling successes. Oh, the fat talk while we ate too much—about who had made a hit and who was slipping back, and what the noo house cost and the noo motor and the gold soup-plates, and who was to be the noo knight.

SIR HARRY. [*Who it will be observed is unanswerable from first to last.*] Was anybody getting on better than me, and consequently you?

KATE. Consequently me! Oh, Harry, you and your sublime religion.

SIR HARRY. [*Honest heart.*] My religion? I never was one to talk about religion, but——

KATE. Pooh, Harry, you don't even know what your religion was and is and will be till the day of your expensive funeral. [*And here is the lesson that life has taught her.*]

One's religion is whatever he is most interested in, and yours is Success.

SIR HARRY. [*Quoting from his morning paper.*]   Ambition—it is the last infirmity of noble minds.

KATE.   Noble minds!

SIR HARRY. [*At last grasping what she is talking about.*] You are not saying that you left me because of my success?

KATE.   Yes, that was it. [*And now she stands revealed to him.*]   I couldn't endure it. If a failure had come now and then—but your success was suffocating me. [*She is rigid with emotion.*]   The passionate craving I had to be done with it, to find myself among people who had not got on.

SIR HARRY. [*With proper spirit.*]   There are plenty of them.

KATE.   There were none in our set. When they began to go down-hill they rolled out of our sight.

SIR HARRY. [*Clenching it.*]   I tell you I am worth a quarter of a million.

KATE. [*Unabashed.*]   That is what you are worth to yourself. I'll tell you what you are worth to me: exactly twelve pounds. For I made up my mind that I could launch myself on the world alone if I first proved my mettle by earning twelve pounds; and as soon as I had earned it I left you.

SIR HARRY. [*In the scales.*]   Twelve pounds!

KATE.   That is your value to a woman. If she can't make it she has to stick to you.

SIR HARRY. [*Remembering perhaps a rectory garden.*] You valued me at more than that when you married me.

KATE. [*Seeing it also.*]   Ah, I didn't know you then. If only you had been a man, Harry.

SIR HARRY.   A man?   What do you mean by a man?

KATE. [*Leaving the garden.*] Haven't you heard of them? They are something fine; and every woman is loathe to admit to herself that her husband is not one. When she marries, even though she has been a very trivial person, there is in her some vague stirring toward a worthy life, as well as a fear of her capacity for evil. She knows her chance lies in him. If there is something good in him, what is good in her finds it, and they join forces against the baser parts. So I didn't give you up willingly, Harry. I invented all sorts of theories to explain you. Your hardness—I said it was a fine want of maukishness. Your coarseness—I said it goes with strength. Your contempt for the weak—I called it virility. Your want of ideals was clear-sightedness. Your ignoble views of women—I tried to think them funny. Oh, I clung to you to save myself. But I had to let go; you had only the one quality, Harry, success; you had it so strong that it swallowed all the others.

SIR HARRY. [*Not to be diverted from the main issue.*] How did you earn that twelve pounds?

KATE. It took me nearly six months; but I earned it fairly. [*She presses her hand on the typewriter as lovingly as many a woman has pressed a rose.*] I learned this. I hired it and taught myself. I got some work through a friend, and with my first twelve pounds I paid for my machine. Then I considered that I was free to go, and I went.

SIR HARRY. All this going on in my house while you were living in the lap of luxury! [*She nods.*] By God, you were determined.

KATE. [*Briefly.*] By God, I was.

SIR HARRY. [*Staring.*] How you must have hated me.

KATE. [*Smiling at the childish word.*] Not a bit— after I saw that there was a way out. From that hour you amused me, Harry; I was even sorry for you, for I saw that you couldn't help yourself. Success is just a fatal gift.

SIR HARRY. Oh, thank you.

KATE. [*Thinking, dear friends in front, of you and me perhaps.*]   Yes, and some of your most successful friends knew it. One or two of them used to look very sad at times, as if they thought they might have come to something if they hadn't got on.

SIR HARRY. [*Who has a horror of sacrilege.*]   The battered crew you live among now—what are they but folk who have tried to succeed and failed?

KATE. That's it; they try, but they fail.

SIR HARRY. And always will fail.

KATE. Always. Poor souls—I say of them. Poor soul —they say of me. It keeps us human. That is why I never tire of them.

SIR HARRY. [*Comprehensively.*]   Bah! Kate, I tell you I'll be worth half a million yet.

KATE. I'm sure you will. You're getting stout, Harry.

SIR HARRY. No, I'm not.

KATE. What was the name of that fat old fellow who used to fall asleep at our dinner-parties?

SIR HARRY. If you mean Sir William Crackley——

KATE. That was the man. Sir William was to me a perfect picture of the grand success. He had got on so well that he was very, very stout, and when he sat on a chair it was thus [*her hands meeting in front of her*]—as if he were holding his success together. That is what you are working for, Harry. You will have that and the half million about the same time.

SIR HARRY. [*Who has surely been very patient.*]   Will you please to leave my house?

KATE. [*Putting on her gloves, soiled things.*]   But don't let us part in anger. How do you think I am looking, Harry, compared to the dull, inert thing that used to roll round in your padded carriages?

SIR HARRY. [*In masterly fashion.*]   I forget what you were like. I'm very sure you never could have held a candle to the present Lady Sims.

KATE.   That is a picture of her, is it not?

SIR HARRY. [*Seizing his chance again.*]   In her wedding-gown. Painted by an R.A.

KATE. [*Wickedly.*]   A knight?

SIR HARRY. [*Deceived.*]   Yes.

KATE. [*Who likes* LADY SIMS: *a piece of presumption on her part.*]   It is a very pretty face.

SIR HARRY. [*With the pride of possession.*]   Acknowledged to be a beauty everywhere.

KATE.   There is a merry look in the eyes, and character in the chin.

SIR HARRY. [*Like an auctioneer.*]   Noted for her wit.

KATE.   All her life before her when that was painted. It is a *spirituelle* face too. [*Suddenly she turns on him with anger, for the first and only time in the play.*]   Oh, Harry, you brute!

SIR HARRY. [*Staggered.*]   Eh? What?

KATE.   That dear creature capable of becoming a noble wife and mother—she is the spiritless woman of no account that I saw here a few minutes ago. I forgive you for myself, for I escaped, but that poor lost soul, oh, Harry, Harry.

SIR HARRY. [*Waving her to the door.*]   I'll thank you— If ever there was a woman proud of her husband and happy in her married life, that woman is Lady Sims.

KATE.   I wonder.

SIR HARRY.   Then you needn't wonder.

KATE. [*Slowly.*]   If I was a husband—it is my advice to all of them—I would often watch my wife quietly to see whether the twelve-pound look was not coming into her eyes. Two boys, did you say, and both like you?

SIR HARRY. What is that to you?

KATE. [*With glistening eyes.*] I was only thinking that somewhere there are two little girls who, when they grow up —the dear, pretty girls who are all meant for the men that don't get on! Well, good-bye, Sir Harry.

SIR HARRY. [*Showing a little human weakness, it is to be feared.*] Say first that you're sorry.

KATE. For what?

SIR HARRY. That you left me. Say you regret it bitterly. You know you do. [*She smiles and shakes her head. He is pettish. He makes a terrible announcement.*] You have spoilt the day for me.

KATE. [*To hearten him.*] I am sorry for that; but it is only a pin-prick, Harry. I suppose it is a little jarring in the moment of your triumph to find that there is—one old friend—who does not think you a success; but you will soon forget it. Who cares what a typist thinks?

SIR HARRY. [*Heartened.*] Nobody. A typist at eighteen shillings a week!

KATE. [*Proudly.*] Not a bit of it, Harry. I double that.

SIR HARRY. [*Neatly.*] Magnificent!

[*There is a timid knock at the door.*]

LADY SIMS. May I come in?

SIR HARRY. [*Rather appealingly.*] It is Lady Sims.

KATE. I won't tell. She is afraid to come into her husband's room without knocking!

SIR HARRY. She is not. [*Uxoriously.*] Come in, dearest. [*Dearest enters carrying the sword. She might have had the sense not to bring it in while this annoying person is here.*]

LADY SIMS. [*Thinking she has brought her welcome with her.*] Harry, the sword has come.

SIR HARRY. [*Who will dote on it presently.*] Oh, all right.

LADY SIMS. But I thought you were so eager to practise with it.

> [*The person smiles at this. He wishes he had not looked to see if she was smiling.*]

SIR HARRY. [*Sharply.*] Put it down.

> [LADY SIMS *flushes a little as she lays the sword aside.*]

KATE. [*With her confounded courtesy.*] It is a beautiful sword, if I may say so.

LADY SIMS. [*Helped.*] Yes.

> [*The person thinks she can put him in the wrong, does she? He'll show her.*]

SIR HARRY. [*With one eye on* KATE.] Emmy, the one thing your neck needs is more jewels.

LADY SIMS. [*Faltering.*] More!

SIR HARRY. Some ropes of pearls. I'll see to it. It's a bagatelle to me. [KATE *conceals her chagrin, so she had better be shown the door. He rings.*] I won't detain you any longer, miss.

KATE. Thank you.

LADY SIMS. Going already? You have been very quick.

SIR HARRY. The person doesn't suit, Emmy.

LADY SIMS. I'm sorry.

KATE. So am I, madam, but it can't be helped. Good-bye, your ladyship—good-bye, Sir Harry. [*There is a suspicion of an impertinent curtsy, and she is escorted off the premises by* TOMBES. *The air of the room is purified by her going.* SIR HARRY *notices it at once.*]

LADY SIMS. [*Whose tendency is to say the wrong thing.*] She seemed such a capable woman.

SIR HARRY. [*On his hearth.*] I don't like her style at
all.

LADY SIMS. [*Meekly.*] Of course you know best.

[*This is the right kind of woman.*]

SIR HARRY. [*Rather anxious for corroboration.*] Lord
how she winced when I said I was to give you those ropes
of pearls.

LADY SIMS. Did she? I didn't notice. I suppose so.

SIR HARRY. [*Frowning.*] Suppose? Surely I know
enough about women to know that.

LADY SIMS. Yes, oh yes.

SIR HARRY. [*Odd that so confident a man should ask
this.*] Emmy, I know you well, don't I? I can read you
like a book, eh?

LADY SIMS. [*Nervously.*] Yes, Harry.

SIR HARRY. [*Jovially, but with an inquiring eye.*]
What a different existence yours is from that poor lonely
wretch's.

LADY SIMS. Yes, but she has a very contented face.

SIR HARRY. [*With a stamp of his foot.*] All put on.
What?

LADY SIMS. [*Timidly.*] I didn't say anything.

SIR HARRY. [*Snapping.*] One would think you envied
her.

LADY SIMS. Envied? Oh no—but I thought she looked
so alive. It was while she was working the machine.

SIR HARRY. Alive! That's no life. It is you that are
alive. [*Curtly.*] I'm busy, Emmy. [*He sits at his writing table.*]

LADY SIMS. [*Dutifully.*] I'm sorry; I'll go, Harry [*In-
consequentially.*] Are they very expensive?

SIR HARRY. What?

LADY SIMS. Those machines?

[*When she has gone the possible meaning of her*

question startles him. The curtain hides him from us, but we may be sure that he will soon be bland again. We have a comfortable feeling, you and I, that there is nothing of HARRY SIMS *in us.*]

The End.

THE OLD LADY SHOWS HER MEDALS

*Three nice old ladies and a criminal, who is even nicer,
   are discussing the war over a cup of tea. The criminal, who is the hostess, calls it a dish of tea, which
   shows that she comes from Caledonia; but that is
   not her crime.*

*They are all London charwomen, but three of them, in-
   cluding the hostess, are what are called professionally
   "charwomen and" or simply "ands." An "and" is
   also a caretaker when required; her name is entered
   as such in ink in a registry book, financial transactions
   take place across a counter between her and the reg-
   istrar, and altogether she is of a very different social
   status from one who, like MRS. HAGGERTY, is a charwoman but nothing else. MRS. HAGGERTY, though
   present, is not at the party by invitation; having seen
   MRS. DOWEY buying the winkles, she followed her
   downstairs, and so has shuffled into the play and sat
   down in it against our wish. We would remove her
   by force, or at least print her name in small letters,
   were it not that she takes offence very readily and
   says that nobody respects her. So, as you have
   slipped in, you can sit there, MRS. HAGGERTY; but
   keep quiet.*

*There is nothing doing at present in the caretaking way
   for MRS. DOWEY, our hostess; but this does not damp
   her, caretaking being only to such as she an extra
   financially and a halo socially. If she had the honour
   of being served with an income-tax paper she would
   probably fill in one of the nasty little compartments
   with the words, "Trade—charring; Profession [if any]*

405

—*caretaking." This home of hers [from which, to look after your house, she makes occasionally temporary departures in great style, escorting a barrow] is in one of those what-care-I streets that you discover only when you have lost your way; on discovering them, your duty is to report them to the authorities, who immediately add them to the map of London. That is why we are now reporting Friday Street. We shall call it, in the rough sketch drawn for to-morrow's press, "Street in which the criminal resided"; and you will find MRS. DOWEY'S home therein marked with an X.*

Her abode really consists of one room, but she maintains that there are two; so, rather than argue, let us say that there are two. The other one has no window, and she could not swish her old skirts in it without knocking something over; its grandest display is of tin pans and crockery on top of a dresser which has a lid to it; you have but to whip off the utensils and raise the lid, and, behold, a bath with hot and cold. MRS. DOWEY is very proud of this possession, and when she shows it off, as she does perhaps too frequently, she first signs to you with closed fist [funny old thing that she is] to approach softly. She then tiptoes to the dresser and pops off the lid, as if to take the bath unawares. Then she sucks her lips, and is modest if you have the grace to do the exclamations.

In the real room is a bed, though that is putting the matter too briefly. The fair way to begin, if you love MRS. DOWEY, is to say to her that it is a pity she has no bed. If she is in her best form she will chuckle, and agree that the want of a bed tries her sore; she will keep you on the hooks, so to speak, as long as she can; and then, with that mouse-like movement again, she will suddenly spring the bed on you. You thought it was a wardrobe, but she brings it down from the wall; and lo, a bed. There is nothing else in her abode [which we now see to contain four rooms—kitchen, pantry, bedroom, and bathroom] that is absolutely a surprise; but it is full of "bits," every one of which has been paid ready money for, and gloated over and tended until it has become part of its owner. Genuine Doweys, the dealers might call them, though there is probably nothing in the place except the bed that would fetch half-a-crown.

Her home is in the basement, so that the view is restricted to the lower half of persons passing overhead beyond the area stairs. Here at the window MRS. DOWEY *sometimes sits of a summer evening gazing, not sentimentally at a flower-pot which contains one poor bulb, nor yearningly at some tiny speck of sky, but with unholy relish at holes in stockings, and the like, which are revealed to her from her point of vantage. You, gentle reader, may flaunt by, thinking that your finery awes the street, but* MRS. DOWEY *can tell [and does] that your soles are in need of neat repair.*

Also, lower parts being as expressive as the face to those whose view is thus limited, she could swear to scores of the passers-by in a court of law.

These four lively old codgers are having a good time at the tea-table, and wit is flowing free. As you can see by their everyday garments, and by their pails and mops [which are having a little tea-party by themselves in the corner], it is not a gathering by invitations stretching away into yesterday, it is a purely informal affair; so much more attractive, don't you think? than banquets elaborately prearranged. You know how they come about, especially in war-time. Very likely MRS.

Dowey *met* Mrs Twymley *and* Mrs. Mickleham *quite casually in the street, and meant to do no more than pass the time of day; then, naturally enough, the word camouflage was mentioned, and they got heated, but in the end* Mrs. Twymley *apologised; then, in the odd way in which one thing leads to another, the winkle man appeared, and* Mrs. Dowey *remembered that she had that pot of jam and that* Mrs. Mickleham *had stood treat last time; and soon they were all three descending the area stairs, followed cringingly by the* Haggerty Woman.

They have been extremely merry, and never were four hard-worked old ladies who deserved it better. All a woman can do in war-time they do daily and cheerfully, just as their men-folk are doing it at the Front; and now, with the mops and pails laid aside, they sprawl gracefully at ease. There is no intention on their part to consider peace terms until a decisive victory has been gained in the field [Sarah Ann Dowey], *until the Kaiser is put to the right-about* [Emma Mickleham], *and singing very small* [Amelia Twymley.]

At this tea-party the lady who is to play the part of Mrs. Dowey *is sure to want to suggest that our heroine has a secret sorrow, namely, the crime; but you should see us knocking that idea out of her head!* Mrs. Dowey *knows she is a criminal, but, unlike the actress, she does not know that she is about to be found out; and she is, to put it bluntly in her own Scotch way, the merriest of the whole clanjamfry. She presses more tea on her guests, but they wave her away from them in the pretty manner of ladies who know that they have already had more than enough.*

MRS. DOWEY. Just one more winkle, Mrs. Mickleham? [*Indeed there is only one more.*]

[*But Mrs. Mickleham indicates politely that if she took this one it would have to swim for it. (The HAGGERTY WOMAN takes it long afterwards when she thinks, erroneously, that no one is looking.)*]

[MRS. TWYMLEY *is sulky. Evidently some one has contradicted her. Probably the* HAGGERTY WOMAN.]

MRS. TWYMLEY. I say it is so.

THE HAGGERTY WOMAN. I say it may be so.

MRS. TWYMLEY. I suppose I ought to know: me that has a son a prisoner in Germany. [*She has so obviously scored that all good feeling seems to call upon her to end here. But she continues rather shabbily.*] Being the only lady present that has that proud misfortune. [*The others are stung.*]

MRS. DOWEY. My son is fighting in France.

MRS. MICKLEHAM. Mine is wounded in two places.

THE HAGGERTY WOMAN. Mine is at Salonaiky.

[*The absurd pronunciation of this uneducated person moves the others to mirth.*]

MRS. DOWEY. You'll excuse us, Mrs. Haggerty, but the correct pronunciation is Salonikky.

THE HAGGERTY WOMAN. [*To cover her confusion.*] I don't think.

[*She feels that even this does not prove her case.*] And I speak as one that has War Savings Certificates.

MRS. TWYMLEY. We all have them.

[*The* HAGGERTY WOMAN *whimpers, and the other guests regard her with unfeeling disdain.*]

MRS. DOWEY. [*To restore cheerfulness.*] Oh, it's a terrible war.

ALL. [*Brightening.*] It is. You may say so.

MRS. DOWEY. [*Encouraged.*] What I say is, the men is splendid, but I'm none so easy about the staff. That's your weak point, Mrs. Mickleham.

MRS. MICKLEHAM. [*On the defence, but determined to reveal nothing that might be of use to the enemy.*] You may take it from me, the staff's all right.

MRS. DOWEY. And very relieved I am to hear you say it.

[*It is here that the* HAGGERTY WOMAN *has the remaining winkle.*]

MRS. MICKLEHAM. You don't understand properly about trench warfare. If I had a map——

MRS. DOWEY. [*Wetting her finger to draw lines on the table.*] That's the river Sommy. Now, if we had barrages here——

MRS TWYMLEY. Very soon you would be enfiladed. Where's your supports, my lady?

[MRS. DOWEY *is damped.*]

MRS. MICKLEHAM. What none of you grasps is that this is a artillery war——

THE HAGGERTY WOMAN. [*Strengthened by the winkle.*] I say that the word is Salonaiky.

[*The others purse their lips.*]

MRS. TWYMLEY. [*With terrible meaning.*] We'll change the subject. Have you seen thas week's *Fashion Chat?* [*She has evidently seen and devoured it herself, and even licked up the crumbs.*] The gabardine with accordion pleats has quite gone out.

MRS. DOWEY. [*Her old face sparkling.*] My sakes! You tell me?

MRS. TWYMLEY. [*With the touch of haughtiness that comes of great topics.*] The plain smock has come in again, with silk lacing, giving that charming chic effect.

MRS. DOWEY. Oho!

MRS. MICKLEHAM. I must say I was always partial

to the straight line [*Thoughtfully regarding the want of line in* Mrs. Twymley's *person*] though trying to them as is of too friendly a figure.

> [*It is here that the* Haggerty Woman's *fingers close unostentatiously upon a piece of sugar.*]

Mrs. Twymley. [*Sailing into the Empyrean.*] Lady Dolly Kanister was seen conversing across the railings in a dainty *de jou.*

Mrs. Dowey. Fine would I have liked to see her.

Mrs. Twymley. She is equally popular as maid, wife, and munition-worker. Her two children is inset. Lady Pops Babington was married in a tight tulle.

Mrs. Mickleham. What was her going-away dress?

Mrs. Twymley. A champagny cream velvet with dreamy corsage. She's married to Colonel the Hon. Chingford—"Snubs," they called him at Eton.

The Haggerty Woman. [*Having disposed of the sugar.*] Very likely he'll be sent to Salonaiky.

Mrs. Mickleham. Wherever he is sent, she'll have the same tremors as the rest of us. She'll be as keen to get the letters wrote with pencils as you or me.

Mrs. Twymley. Them pencil letters.

Mrs. Dowey. [*In her sweet Scotch voice, timidly, afraid she may be going too far.*] And women in enemy lands gets those pencil letters and then stop getting them, the same as ourselves. Let's occasionally think of that.

> [*She has gone too far. Chairs are pushed back.*]

The Haggerty Woman. I ask you!

Mrs. Mickleham. That's hardly language, Mrs. Dowey.

Mrs. Dowey. [*Scared.*] Kindly excuse. I swear to death I'm none of your pacifists.

Mrs. Mickleham. Freely granted.

Mrs. Twymley. I've heard of females that have no

male relations, and so they have no man-party at the wars. I've heard of them, but I don't mix with them.

MRS. MICKLEHAM. What can the likes of us have to say to them? It's not their war.

MRS. DOWEY. [*Wistfully.*] They are to be pitied.

MRS. MICKLEHAM. But the place for them, Mrs. Dowey, is within doors with the blinds down.

MRS. DOWEY. [*Hurriedly.*] That's the place for them.

MRS. MICKLEHAM. I saw one of them to-day buying a flag. I thought it was very impudent of her.

MRS. DOWEY. [*Meekly.*] So it was.

MRS. MICKLEHAM. [*Trying to look modest with indifferent success.*] I had a letter from my son, Percy, yesterday.

MRS. TWYMLEY. Alfred sent me his photo.

THE HAGGERTY WOMAN. Letters from Salonaiky is less common.

> [*Three bosoms heave, but not, alas, MRS. DOWEY's. Nevertheless she doggedly knits her lips.*]

MRS. DOWEY. [*The criminal.*] Kenneth writes to me every week. [*There are exclamations. The dauntless old thing holds aloft a packet of letters.*] Look at this. All his.

> [*The HAGGERTY WOMAN whimpers.*]

MRS. TWYMLEY. Alfred has little time for writing, being a bombardier.

MRS. DOWEY. [*Relentlessly.*] Do your letters begin "Dear mother"?

MRS. TWYMLEY. Generally.

MRS. MICKLEHAM. Invariable.

THE HAGGERTY WOMAN. Every time.

MRS. DOWEY. [*Delivering the knock-out blow.*] Kenneth's begin "Dearest mother."

[*No one can think of the right reply.*]

Mrs. Twymley. [*Doing her best.*] A short man, I should say, judging by yourself.

[*She ought to have left it alone.*]

Mrs. Dowey. Six feet two—and a half.

[*The gloom deepens.*]

Mrs. Mickleham. [*Against her better judgment.*] A kilty, did you tell me?

Mrs. Dowey. Most certainly. He's in the famous Black Watch.

The Haggerty Woman. [*Producing her handkerchief.*] The Surrey Rifles is the famousest.

Mrs. Mickleham. There you and the King disagrees, Mrs. Haggerty. His choice is the Buffs, same as my Percy's.

Mrs. Twymley. [*Magnanimously.*] Give me the R. H. A. and you can keep all the rest.

Mrs. Dowey. I'm sure I have nothing to say against the Surreys and the R. H. A. and the Buffs; but they are just breeches regiments, I understand.

The Haggerty Woman. We can't all be kilties.

Mrs. Dowey. [*Crushingly.*] That's very true.

Mrs. Twymley. [*It is foolish of her, but she can't help saying it.*] Has your Kenneth great hairy legs?

Mrs. Dowey. Tremendous.

> [*The wicked woman: but let us also say "Poor Sarah Ann Dowey." For at this moment, enter Nemesis. In other words, the less important part of a clergyman appears upon the stair.*]

Mrs. Mickleham. It's the reverent gent!

Mrs. Dowey. [*Little knowing what he is bringing her.*] I see he has had his boots heeled.

> [*It may be said of Mr. Willings that his happy*

*smile always walks in front of him. This smile
makes music of his life, it means that once
again he has been chosen, in his opinion, as
the central figure in romance. No one can
well have led a more drab existence, but he will
never know it; he will always think of himself,
humbly though elatedly, as the chosen of the
gods. Of him must it have been originally
written that adventures are for the adventur-
ous. He meets them at every street corner.
For instance, he assists an old lady off a bus,
and asks her if he can be of any further help.
She tells him that she wants to know the way
to Maddox the butcher's. Then comes the kind
triumphant smile; it always comes first, followed by its explanation, "I was there yesterday!" This is the merest sample of the adventures that keep MR. WILLINGS up to the
mark.*

*Since the war broke out, his zest for life has be-
come almost terrible. He can scarcely lift a
newspaper and read of a hero without remembering that he knows some one of the same
name. The Soldiers' Rest he is connected with
was once a china emporium, and [mark my
words], he had bought his tea service at it.
Such is life when you are in the thick of it.
Sometimes he feels that he is part of a gigantic
spy drama. In the course of his extraordinary
comings and goings he meets with Great Personages, of course, and is the confidential re-
cipient of secret news. Before imparting the
news he does not, as you might expect, first
smile expansively; on the contrary, there comes*

over his face an awful solemnity, which, how-
ever, means the same thing. When divulging
the names of the personages, he first looks
around to make sure that no suspicious char-
acter is about, and then, lowering his voice,
tells you, "I had that from Mr. Farthing
himself—he is the secretary of the Bethnal
Green Branch,—h'sh!"

There is a commotion about finding a worthy
chair for the reverent, and there is also some
furtive pulling down of sleeves, but he stands
surveying the ladies through his triumphant
smile. This amazing man knows that he is
about to score again.]

MR. WILLINGS. [*Waving aside the chairs.*] I thank
you. But not at all. Friends, I have news.

MRS. MICKLEHAM. News?

THE HAGGERTY WOMAN. From the Front?

MRS. TWYMLEY. My Alfred, sir?

[*They are all grown suddenly anxious—all ex-*
cept the hostess, who knows that there can
never be any news from the Front for her.]

MR. WILLINGS. I tell you at once that all is well. The
news is for Mrs. Dowey.

[*She stares.*]

MRS. DOWEY. News for me?

MR. WILLINGS. Your son, Mrs. Dowey—he has got
five days' leave. [*She shakes her head slightly, or perhaps*
it only trembles a little on its stem.] Now, now, good
news doesn't kill.

MRS. TWYMLEY. We're glad, Mrs. Dowey.

MRS. DOWEY. You're sure?

MR. WILLINGS. Quite sure. He has arrived.

MRS. DOWEY. He is in London?

MR. WILLINGS. He is. I have spoken to him.

MRS. MICKLEHAM. You lucky woman.

[*They might see that she is not looking lucky, but experience has told them how differently these things take people.*]

MR. WILLINGS. [*Marvelling more and more as he unfolds his tale.*] Ladies, it is quite a romance. I was in the—— [*He looks around cautiously, but he knows that they are all to be trusted.*] in the Church Army quarters in Central Street, trying to get on the track of one or two of our missing men. Suddenly my eyes—I can't account for it—but suddenly my eyes alighted on a Highlander seated rather drearily on a bench, with his kit at his feet.

THE HAGGERTY WOMAN. A big man?

MR. WILLINGS. A great brawny fellow. [*The HAGGERTY WOMAN groans.*] "My friend," I said at once, "welcome back to Blighty." I make a point of calling it Blighty. "I wonder," I said, "if there is anything I can do for you?" He shook his head. "What regiment?" I asked. [*Here MR. WILLINGS very properly lowers his voice to a whisper.*] "Black Watch, Fifth Battalion," he said. "Name?" I asked. "Dowey," he said.

MRS. MICKLEHAM. I declare. I do declare.

MR. WILLINGS. [*Showing how the thing was done, with the help of a chair.*] I put my hand on his shoulder as it might be thus. "Kenneth Dowey," I said, "I know your mother."

MRS. DOWEY. [*Wetting her lips.*] What did he say to that?

MR. WILLINGS. He was incredulous. Indeed, he seemed to think I was balmy. But I offered to bring him straight to you. I told him how much you had talked to me about him.

MRS. DOWEY. Bring him here!

MRS. MICKLEHAM. I wonder he needed to be brought.

MR. WILLINGS. He had just arrived, and was bewildered by the great city. He listened to me in the tactiturn Scotch way, and then he gave a curious laugh.

MRS. TWYMLEY. Laugh?

MR. WILLINGS. [*Whose wild life has brought him into contact with the strangest people.*] The Scotch, Mrs. Twymley, express their emotions differently from us. With them tears signify a rollicking mood, while merriment denotes that they are plunged in gloom. When I had finished he said at once, "Let us go and see the old lady."

MRS. DOWEY. [*Backing, which is the first movement she has made since he began his tale.*] Is he——coming?

MR. WILLINGS. [*Gloriously.*] He has come. He is up there. I told him I thought I had better break the joyful news to you.

> [*Three women rush to the window.* MRS. DOWEY *looks at her pantry door, but perhaps she remembers that it does not lock on the inside. She stands rigid, though her face has gone very grey.*]

MRS. DOWEY. Kindly get them to go away.

MR. WILLINGS. Ladies, I think this happy occasion scarcely requires you. [*He is not the man to ask of woman a sacrifice that he is not prepared to make himself.*] I also am going instantly. [*They all survey* MRS. DOWEY, *and understand—or think they understand.*]

MRS. TWYMLEY. [*Pail and mop in hand.*] I would thank none for their company if my Alfred was at the door.

MRS. MICKLEHAM. [*Similarly burdened.*] The same from me. Shall I send him down, Mrs. Dowey? [*The old lady does not hear her. She is listening, terrified, for a*

step on the stairs.] Look at the poor, joyous thing, sir.
She has his letters in her hand.

> [*The three women go.* MR. WILLINGS *puts a kind
> hand on* MRS. DOWEY'S *shoulder. He thinks
> he so thoroughly understands the situation.*]

MR. WILLINGS. A good son, Mrs. Dowey, to have written to you so often.

> [*Our old criminal quakes, but she grips the letters
> more tightly.* PRIVATE DOWEY *descends.*]

"Dowey, my friend, there she is, waiting for you, with
your letters in her hand."

DOWEY. [*Grimly.*] "That's great."

> [MR. WILLINGS *ascends the stair without one back-
> ward glance, like the good gentleman he is;
> and the* DOWEYS *are left together, with nearly
> the whole room between them. He is a great
> rough chunk of Scotland, howked out of her not
> so much neatly as liberally; and in his Black
> Watch uniform, all caked with mud, his kit and
> nearly all his wordly possessions on his back,
> he is an apparition scarcely less fearsome [but so
> much less ragged] than those ancestors of his
> who trotted with Prince Charlie to Derby.
> He stands silent, scowling at the old lady, daring
> her to raise her head; and she would like very
> much to do it, for she longs to have a first
> glimpse of her son. When he does speak, it
> is to jeer at her.*]

"Do you recognise your loving son, missis?" [*"Oh,
the fine Scotch tang of him," she thinks.*] "I'm pleased
I wrote so often." [*"Oh, but he's raized," she thinks.*]
He strides towards her, and seizes the letters roughly.
"Let's see them."

> [*There is a string round the package, and he*

*unties it, and examines the letters at his leisure
with much curiosity. The envelopes are in
order, all addressed in pencil to* MRS. DOWEY,
*with the proud words "Opened by Censor" on
them. But the letter paper inside contains not
a word of writing.*]

"Nothing but blank paper! Is this your writing in
pencil on the envelope?" [*She nods, and he gives the matter further consideration.*]

"The covey told me you were a charwoman; so I suppose you picked the envelopes out of waste-paper baskets,
or such like, and then changed the addresses?" [*She nods
again; still she dare not look up, but she is admiring his
legs. When, however, he would cast the letters into the
fire, she flames up with sudden spirit. She clutches them.*]

"Don't you burn them letters, mister."

"They're not real letters."

"They're all I have."

[*He turns to irony.*] "I thought you had a son?"

"I never had a man nor a son nor anything. I just
call myself Missis to give me a standing."

"Well, it's past my seeing through."

[*He turns to look for some explanation from the
walls. She gets a peep at him at last. Oh,
what a grandly set-up man! Oh, the stride of
him. Oh, the noble rage of him. Oh, Samson
had been like this before that woman took him
in hand.*]

[*He whirls round on her.*] "What made you do it?"

"It was everybody's war, mister, except mine." [*She beats
her arms.*] "I wanted it to be my war too."

"You'll need to be plainer. And yet I'm d—d if I care
to hear you, you lying old trickster."

[*The words are merely what were to be expected,*

*and so are endurable; but he has moved towards
the door.*]

"You're not going already, mister?"

"Yes, I just came to give you an ugly piece of my mind."

[*She holds out her arms longingly.*] "You haven't gave
it to me yet."

"You have a cheek!"

[*She gives further proof of it.*] "You wouldn't drink
some tea?"

"Me! I tell you I came here for the one purpose of
blazing away at you."

[*It is such a roaring negative that it blows her into a
chair. But she is up again in a moment, is this spirited old
lady.*] "You could drink the tea while you was blazing
away. There's winkles."

"Is there?" [*He turns interestedly towards the table,
but his proud Scots character checks him, which is just as
well, for what she should have said was that there had been
winkles.*] "Not me. You're just a common rogue." [*He
seats himself far from the table.*] "Now, then, out with it.
Sit down!" [*She sits meekly; there is nothing she would
not do for him.*] "As you char, I suppose you are on your
feet all day."

"I'm more on my knees."

"That's where you should be to me."

"Oh, mister, I'm willing."

"Stop it. Go on, you accomplished liar."

"It's true that my name is Dowey."

"It's enough to make me change mine."

"I've been charring and charring and charring as far back
as I mind. I've been in London this twenty years."

"We'll skip your early days. I have an appointment."

"And then when I was old the war broke out."

"How could it affect you?"

"Oh, mister, that's the thing. It didn't affect me. It affected everybody but me. The neighbours looked down on me. Even the posters, on the walls, of the woman saying, 'Go, my boy,' leered at me. I sometimes cried by myself in the dark. You won't have a cup of tea?"

"No."

"Sudden like the idea came to me to pretend I had a son."

"You depraved old limmer! But what in the name of Old Nick made you choose me out of the whole British Army?"

[MRS. DOWEY *giggles. There is little doubt that in her youth she was an accomplished flirt.*] "Maybe, mister, it was because I liked you best."

"Now, now, woman."

"I read one day in the papers, 'In which he was assisted by Private K. Dowey, 5th Battalion, Black Watch.' "

. . [PRIVATE K. DOWEY *is flattered.*] "Did you, now! Well, I expect that's the only time I was ever in the papers."

[MRS. DOWEY *tries it on again.*] "I didn't choose you for that alone. I read a history of the Black Watch first, to make sure it was the best regiment in the world."

"Anybody could have told you that." [*He is moving about now in better humour, and, meeting the loaf in his stride, he cuts a slice from it. He is hardly aware of this, but* MRS. DOWEY *knows.*] "I like the Scotch voice of you, woman. It drummles on like a hill burn."

"Prosen Water runs by where I was born." [*Flirting again.*] "May be it teached me to speak, mister."

"Canny, woman, canny."

"I read about the Black Watch's ghostly piper that plays proudly when the men of the Black Watch do well, and prouder when they fall."

"There's some foolish story of that kind." [*He has an-*

other careless slice off the loaf.] "But you couldn't have been living here at that time or they would have guessed. I suppose you flitted?"

"Yes, it cost me eleven and sixpence."

"How did you guess the *K* in my name stood for Kenneth?"

"Does it?"

"Umpha."

"An angel whispered it to me in my sleep."

"Well, that's the only angel in the whole black business." [*He chuckles.*]

"You little thought I would turn up!" [*Wheeling suddenly on her.*] "Or did you?"

"I was beginning to weary for a sight of you, Kenneth."

"What word was that?"

"Mister."

> [*He helps himself to butter, and she holds out the jam pot to him, but he haughtily rejects it. Do you think she gives in now? Not a bit of it.*]

[*He returns to sarcasm.*] "I hope you're pleased with me now you see me."

"I'm very pleased. Does your folk live in Scotland?"

"Glasgow."

"Both living?"

"Ay."

"Is your mother terrible proud of you?"

"Naturally."

"You'll be going to them?"

"After I've had a skite in London first."

[*The old lady sniffs.*] "So she is in London!"

"Who?"

"Your young lady."

"Are you jealyous?"

"Not me."

"You needna be. She's a young thing."

"You surprise me. A beauty, no doubt?"

"You may be sure." [*He tries the jam.*] "She's a titled person. She is equally popular as maid, wife, and munition-worker."

> [MRS. DOWEY *remembers* LADY DOLLY KANISTER, *so familiar to readers of fashionable gossip, and a very leery expression indeed comes into her face.*]

"Tell me more about her, man."

"She has sent me a lot of things, especially cakes, and a worsted waistcoat, with a loving message on the enclosed card."

> [*The old lady is now in a quiver of excitement. She loses control of her arms, which jump excitedly this way and that.*]

"You'll try one of my cakes, mister?"

"Not me."

"They're of my own making."

"No, I thank you."

> [*But with a funny little run she is in the pantry and back again. She planks down a cake before him, at sight of which he gapes.*]

"What's the matter? Tell me, oh, tell me mister."

"That's exactly the kind of cake that her ladyship sends me."

> [MRS. DOWEY *is now a very glorious old character indeed.*]

"Is the waistcoat right, mister? I hope the Black Watch colours pleased you."

"Wha—t! Was it you?"

"I daredna give my own name, you see, and I was always reading hers in the papers."

[*The badgered man looms over her, terrible for
the last time.*]

"Woman, is there no getting rid of you!"

"Are you angry?"

[*He sits down with a groan.*]

"Oh, hell!   Give me some tea."

[*She rushes about preparing a meal for him, every
bit of her wanting to cry out to every other
bit, "Oh, glory, glory, glory!"   For a moment
she   hovers   behind   his   chair.   "Kenneth!"
she   murmurs.   "What?"   he asks, no longer
aware that she is taking a liberty.   "Nothing,"
she says, "just Kenneth," and is off gleefully
for the tea-caddy.   But when his tea is poured
out, and he has drunk a saucerful, the instinct
of self-preservation returns to him between two
bites.*]

"Don't you be thinking, missis, for one minute that you
have got me."

"No, no."

[*On that   understanding   he   unbends.*]

"I have a theatre to-night, followed by a randy-dandy."

"Oho!   Kenneth, this is a queer first meeting!"

"It is, woman, oh, it is," guardedly, "and it's also a last
meeting."

"Yes, yes."

"So here's to you—you old mop and pail. *Ave atque
vale.*"

"What's that?"

"That means Hail and Farewell."

"Are you a scholar?"

"Being Scotch, there's almost nothing I don't know."

"What was you to trade?"

"Carter, glazier, orraman, any rough jobs."

"You're a proper man to look at."

"I'm generally admired."

"She's an enviable woman."

"Who?"

"Your mother."

"Eh? Oh, that was just protecting myself from you. I have neither father nor mother nor wife nor grandmama." [*Bitterly*.] "This party never even knew who his proud parents were."

"Is that." [*Gleaming*.] "Is that true?"

"It's gospel."

"Heaven be praised!"

"Eh? None of that! I was a fool to tell you. But don't think you can take advantage of it. Pass the cake."

"I daresay it's true we'll never meet again, Kenneth, but —but if we do, I wonder where it will be?"

"Not in this world."

"There's no telling." [*Leering ingratiatingly*.] "It might be at Berlin."

"Tod, if I ever get to Berlin, I believe I'll find you there waiting for me!"

"With a cup of tea for you in my hand."

"Yes, and—" [*Heartily*.] "Very good tea too."

> [*He has partaken heavily, he is now in high good humour*.]

"Kenneth, we could come back by Paris!"

"All the ladies," slapping his knees, "likes to go to Paris."

"Oh, Kenneth, Kenneth, if just once before I die I could be fitted for a Paris gown with dreamy corsage!"

"You're all alike, old covey. We have a song about it." He sings:

> "Mrs. Gill is very ill,
>   Nothing can improve her

But to see the Tuileries
And waddle through the Louvre."

[*No song ever had a greater success.* MRS.
DOWEY *is doubled up with mirth. When she
comes to, when they both come to, for there
are a pair of them, she cries:*]
"You must learn me that," and off she goes in song also:

"Mrs. Dowey's very ill,
Nothing can improve her."

"Stop!" cries clever Kenneth, and finishes the verse:

"But dressed up in a Paris gown
To waddle through the Louvre."

[*They fling back their heads, she points at him,
he points at her. She says ecstatically:*]
"Hairy legs!"
[*A mad remark, which brings him to his senses;
he remembers who and what she is.*]
"Mind your manners!" [*Rising.*] "Well, thank you for
my tea. I must be stepping."
[*Poor* MRS. DOWEY, *he is putting on his kit.*]
"Where are you living?"
[*He sighs.*]
"That's the question. But there's a place called The
Hut, where some of the Second Battalion are. They'll take
me in. Beggars" [*Bitterly*] "can't be choosers."
"Beggars?"
"I've never been here before. If you knew." [*A
shadow coming over him.*] "What it is to be in such a
place without a friend. I was crazy with glee, when I got
my leave, at the thought of seeing London at last, but after

wandering its streets for four hours, I would almost have been glad to be back in the trenches."

[*"If you knew," he has said, but indeed the old
lady knows.*]

"That's my quandorum too, Kenneth."

[*He nods sympathetically.*]

"I'm sorry for you, you poor old body." [*Shouldering his kit.*] "But I see no way out for either of us."

[*A cooing voice says, "Do you not?"*]

"Are you at it again!"

[*She knows that it must be now or never. She
has left her biggest guns for the end. In her
excitement she is rising up and down on her
toes.*]

"Kenneth, I've heard that the thing a man on leave longs for more than anything else is a bed with sheets, and a bath."

"You never heard anything truer."

"Go into that pantry, Kenneth Dowey, and lift the dresser-top, and tell me what you see."

[*He goes. There is an awful stillness. He returns, impressed.*]

"It's a kind of a bath!"

"You could do yourself there pretty, half at a time."

"Me?"

"There's a woman through the wall that would be very willing to give me a shakedown till your leave is up."

[*He snorts.*]

"Oh, is there!"

[*She has not got him yet, but there is still one
more gun.*]

"Kenneth, look!"

[*With these simple words she lets down the bed.
She says no more; an effect like this would*]

be spoilt by language. Fortunately he is not
made of stone. He thrills.]

"My word! That's the dodge we need in the trenches."

"That's your bed, Kenneth."

"Mine?" [*He grins at her.*] "You queer old divert.
What can make you so keen to be burdened by a lump
like me?"

"He! he! he! he!"

"I tell you, I'm the commonest kind of man."

"I'm just the commonest kind of old wife myself."

"I've been a kick-about all my life, and I'm no great
shakes at the war."

"Yes, you are. How many Germans have you killed?"

"Just two for certain, and there was no glory in it. It
was just because they wanted my shirt."

"Your shirt?"

"Well, they said it was their shirt."

"Have you took prisoners?"

"I once took half a dozen, but that was a poor
affair too."

"How could one man take half a dozen?"

"Just in the usual way. I surrounded them."

"Kenneth, you're just my ideal."

"You're easily pleased."

[*He turns again to the bed.*] "Let's see how the
thing works." [*He kneads the mattress with
his fist, and the result is so satisfactory that
he puts down his kit.*]

"Old lady, if you really want me, I'll bide."

"Oh! oh! oh! oh!"

[*Her joy is so demonstrative that he has to drop
a word of warning.*]

"But, mind you, I don't accept you as a relation. For
your personal glory, you can go on pretending to the neigh-

bours; but the best I can say for you is that you're on
your probation. I'm a cautious character, and we must
see how you'll turn out."

"Yes, Kenneth."

"And now, I think, for that bath. My theatre begins at
six-thirty. A cove I met on a 'bus is going with me."

[*She is a little alarmed.*]

"You're sure you'll come back?"

"Yes, yes." [*Handsomely.*] "I leave my kit in pledge."

"You won't liquor up too freely, Kenneth?"

"You're the first" [*Chuckling*] "to care whether I
do or not." [*Nothing she has said has pleased the lonely
man so much as this.*] "I promise. Tod, I'm beginning
to look forward to being wakened in the morning by hearing you cry, 'Get up, you lazy swine.' I've kind of envied
men that had womenfolk with the right to say that."

[*He is passing to the bathroom when a diverting
notion strikes him.*]

"What is it, Kenneth?"

"The theatre. It would be showier if I took a lady."

[MRS. DOWEY *feels a thumping at her breast.*]

"Kenneth, tell me this instant what you mean. Don't
keep me on the jumps."

[*He turns her round.*]

"No, it couldn't be done."

"Was it me you were thinking of?"

"Just for the moment." [*Regretfully.*] "But you have
no style."

[*She catches hold of him by the sleeve.*]

"Not in this, of course. But, oh, Kenneth, if you saw
me in my merino! It's laced up the back in the very
latest."

"Hum." [*Doubtfully.*] "But let's see it."

[*It is produced from a drawer, to which the old*

> *lady runs with almost indecent haste. The*
> *connoisseur examines it critically.*]

"Looks none so bad. Have you a bit of chiffon for the neck? It's not bombs nor Kaisers nor Tipperary that men in the trenches think of, it's chiffon."

"I swear I have, Kenneth. And I have a bangle, and a muff, and gloves."

"Ay, ay." [*He considers.*] "Do you think you could give your face less of a homely look?"

"I'm sure I could."

"Then you can have a try. But, mind you, I promise nothing. All will depend on the effect."

> [*He goes into the pantry, and the old lady is left*
> *alone. Not alone, for she is ringed round by*
> *entrancing hopes and dreadful fears. They*
> *beam on her and jeer at her, they pull her this*
> *way and that; with difficulty she breaks through*
> *them and rushes to her pail, hot water, soap,*
> *and a looking-glass. Our last glimpse of her for*
> *this evening shows her staring (not discontent-*
> *edly) at her soft old face, licking her palm, and*
> *pressing it to her hair. Her eyes are sparking.*]
> [*One evening a few days later* MRS. TWYMLEY
> *and* MRS. MICKLEHAM *are in* MRS. DOWEY'S
> *house, awaiting that lady's return from some*
> *fashionable dissipation. They have undoubt-*
> *edly been discussing the war, for the first words*
> *we catch are:*]

MRS. MICKLEHAM. I tell you flat, Amelia, I bows no knee to junkerdom.

MRS. TWYMLEY. Sitting here by the fire, you and me, as one to another, what do you think will happen after the war? Are we to go back to being as we were?

MRS. MICKLEHAM. Speaking for myself, Amelia, not me. The war has wakened me up to a understanding of my own importance that is really astonishing.

MRS. TWYMLEY. Same here. Instead of being the poor worms the like of you and me thought we was, we turns out to be visible departments of a great and haughty empire.

> [*They are well under weigh, and with a little luck we might now hear their views on various passing problems of the day, such as the neglect of science in our public schools. But in comes the* HAGGERTY WOMAN, *and spoils everything. She is attired, like them, in her best, but the effect of her is that her clothes have gone out for a walk, leaving her at home.*]

MRS. MICKLEHAM. [*With deep distaste.*] Here's that submarine again.

> [*The* HAGGERTY WOMAN *cringes to them, but gets no encouragement.*]

THE HAGGERTY WOMAN. It's a terrible war.

MRS. TWYMLEY. Is that so?

THE HAGGERTY WOMAN. I wonder what will happen when it ends?

MRS. MICKLEHAM. I have no idea.

> [*The intruder produces her handkerchief, but does not use it. After all, she is in her best.*]

THE HAGGERTY WOMAN. Are they not back yet?

> [*Perfect ladies must reply to a direct question.*]

MRS. MICKLEHAM. No. [*Icily.*] We have been waiting this half hour. They are at the theatre again.

THE HAGGERTY WOMAN. You tell me! I just popped in with an insignificant present for him, as his leave is up.

MRS. TWYMLEY. The same errand brought us.

THE HAGGERTY WOMAN. My present is cigarettes.

[*They have no intention of telling her what their presents are, but the secret leaps from them.*]

MRS. MICKLEHAM. So is mine.

MRS. TWYMLEY. Mine too.

[*Triumph of the* HAGGERTY WOMAN. *But it is short-lived.*]

MRS. MICKLEHAM. Mine has gold tips.

MRS. TWYMLEY. So has mine.

[*The* HAGGERTY WOMAN *need not say a word. You have only to look at her to know that her cigarettes are not gold-tipped. She tries to brazen it out, which is so often a mistake.*]

THE HAGGERTY WOMAN. What care I? Mine is Exquisytos.

[*No wonder they titter.*]

MRS. MICKLEHAM. Excuse us, Mrs. Haggerty (if that's your name), but the word is Exquiseetos.

THE HAGGERTY WOMAN. Much obliged. [*Weeps.*]

MRS. MICKLEHAM. I think I heard a taxi.

MRS. TWYMLEY. It will be her third this week.

[*They peer through the blind. They are so excited that rank is forgotten.*]

THE HAGGERTY WOMAN. What is she in?

MRS. MICKLEHAM. A new astrakhan jacket he gave her, with Venus sleeves.

THE HAGGERTY WOMAN. Has she sold her gabardine coat?

MRS. MICKLEHAM. Not her! She has them both at the theatre, warm night though it is. She's wearing the astrakhan, and carrying the gabardine, flung careless-like over her arm.

THE HAGGERTY WOMAN. I saw her strutting about with him yesterday, looking as if she thought the two of them made a procession.

MRS. TWYMLEY. Hsh! [*Peeping.*] Strike me dead, if she's not coming mincing down the stair, hooked on his arm!

> [*Indeed it is thus that* MRS. DOWEY *enters. Perhaps she had seen shadows lurking on the blind, and at once hooked on to* KENNETH *to impress the visitors. She is quite capable of it.*]

> [*Now we see what* KENNETH *saw that afternoon five days ago when he emerged from the bathroom and found the old trembler awaiting his inspection. Here are the muff and the gloves and the chiffon, and such a kind old bonnet that it makes you laugh at once; I don't know how to describe it, but it is trimmed with a kiss, as bonnets should be when the wearer is old and frail. We must take the merino for granted until she steps out of the astrakhan. She is dressed up to the nines, there is no doubt about it. Yes, but is her face less homely? Above all, has she style? The answer is in a stout affirmative. Ask* KENNETH. *He knows. Many a time he has had to go behind a door to roar hilariously at the old lady. He has thought of her as a lark to tell his mates about by and by; but for some reason that he cannot fathom, he knows now that he will never do that.*]

MRS. DOWEY. Kenneth. [*Affecting surprise.*] We have visitors!

DOWEY. Your servant, ladies.

> [*He is no longer mud-caked and dour. A very smart figure is this* PRIVATE DOWEY, *and he winks engagingly at the visitors, like one who*

*knows that for jolly company you cannot easily
beat charwomen. The pleasantries that he and
they have exchanged this week! The sauce
he has given them. The wit of* MRS. MICKLE-
HAM'S *retorts. The badinage of* MRS. TWYM-
LEY. *The neat giggles of the* HAGGERTY
WOMAN. *There has been nothing like it since
you took the countess in to dinner.*]

MRS. TWYMLEY. We should apologise. We're not
meaning to stay.

MRS. DOWEY. You are very welcome. Just wait [*The
ostentation of this!*] till I get out of my astrakhan—and
my muff—and my gloves—and [*It is the bonnet's turn
now*] my Excelsior.

[*At last we see her in the merino (a triumph).*]

MRS. MICKLEHAM. You've given her a glory time, Mr.
Dowey.

DOWEY. It's her that has given it to me, missis.

MRS. DOWEY. Hey! hey! hey! hey! He just pampers
me. [*Waggling her fists.*] The Lord forgive us, but
this being the last night, we had a sit-down supper at a
restaurant! [*Vehemently.*] I swear by God that we
had champagny wine. [*There is a dead stillness, and she
knows very well what it means, she has even prepared for
it.*] And to them as doubts my word—here's the cork.

[*She places the cork, in its lovely gold drapery,
upon the table.*]

MRS. MICKLEHAM. I'm sure!

MRS. TWYMLEY. I would thank you, Mrs. Dowey, not
to say a word against my Alfred.

MRS. DOWEY. Me!

DOWEY. Come, come, ladies. [*In the masterful way
that is so hard for women to resist.*] If you say another
word, I'll kiss the lot of you.

[*There is a moment of pleased confusion.*]

MRS. MICKLEHAM. Really, them sodgers!

THE HAGGERTY WOMAN. The kilties is the worst!

MRS. TWYMLEY. I'm sure. [*Heartily.*] We don't grudge you your treats, Mrs. Dowey; and sorry we are that this is the end.

DOWEY. Yes, it's the end. [*With a troubled look at his old lady.*] I must be off in ten minutes.

> [*The little soul is too gallant to break down in company. She hurries into the pantry and shuts the door.*]

MRS. MICKLEHAM. Poor thing! But we must run, for you'll be having some last words to say to her.

DOWEY. I kept her out long on purpose so as to have less time to say them in.

> [*He more than half wishes that he could make a bolt to a public-house.*]

MRS. TWYMLEY. It's the best way. [*In the important affairs of life there is not much that any one can teach a charwoman.*] Just a mere nothing, to wish you well, Mr. Dowey.

> [*All three present him with the cigarettes.*]

MRS. MICKLEHAM. A scraping, as one might say.

THE HAGGERTY WOMAN. The heart [*Enigmatically*] is warm though it may not be gold-tipped.

DOWEY. You bricks!

THE LADIES. Good luck, cocky.

DOWEY. The same to you. And if you see a sodger man up there in a kilt, he is one that is going back with me. Tell him not to come down, but—but to give me till the last minute, and then to whistle.

> [*It is quite a grave man who is left alone, thinking what to do next. He tries a horse laugh, but that proves of no help. He says "Hell!"*]

*to himself, but it is equally ineffective.   Then
he opens the pantry door and calls.*]

"Old lady."

[*She comes timidly to the door, her hand up as
if to ward off a blow.*]

"Is it time?"

[*An encouraging voice answers her.*]

"No, no, not yet.   I've left word for Dixon to whistle
when go I must."

"All is ended."

"Now, then, you promised to be gay.   We were to help
one another."

"Yes, Kenneth."

"It's bad for me, but it's worse for you."

"The men have medals to win, you see."

"The women have their medals, too."   [*He knows she
likes him to order her about, so he tries it again.*]

"Come here.   No, I'll come to you."   [*He stands gap-
ing at her wonderingly.   He has no power of words, nor
does he quite know what he would like to say.*]   "God!"

"What is it, Kenneth?"

"You're a woman."

"I had near forgot it."

[*He wishes he was at the station with* DIXON.
DIXON *is sure to have a bottle in his pocket.
They will be roaring a song presently.   But in
the meantime—there is that son business.
Blethers, the whole thing of course—or mostly
blethers.   But it's the way to please her.*]

"Have you noticed you have never called me son?"

"Have I noticed it!   I was feared, Kenneth.   You said
I was on probation."

"And so you were.   Well, the probation's ended."   [*He
laughs uncomfortably.*]

"The like of me! But if you want me you can have me."

"Kenneth, will I do?"

"Woman." [*Artfully gay.*] "Don't be so forward. Wait till I have proposed."

"Propose for a mother?"

"What for no?" [*In the grand style.*] "Mrs. Dowey, you queer carl, you spunky tiddy, have I your permission to ask you the most important question a neglected orphan can ask of an old lady?"

> [*She bubbles with mirth. Who could help it, the man has such a way with him?*]

"None of your sauce, Kenneth."

"For a long time, Mrs. Dowey, you cannot have been unaware of my sonnish feelings for you."

"Wait till I get my mop to you!"

"And if you're not willing to be my mother, I swear I'll never ask another."

> [*The old divert pulls him down to her and strokes his hair.*]

"Was I a well-behaved infant, mother?"

"Not you, sonny, you were a rampaging rogue."

"Was I slow in learning to walk?"

"The quickest in our street. He! he! he!" [*She starts up.*] "Was that the whistle?"

"No, no. See here. In taking me over you have, in a manner of speaking, joined the Black Watch."

"I like to think that, Kenneth."

"Then you must behave so that the ghost piper can be proud of you. 'Tion!'" [*She stands bravely at attention.*] "That's the style. Now listen. I've sent in your name as being my nearest of kin, and your allowance will be coming to you weekly in the usual way."

"Hey! hey! hey! Is it wicked, Kenneth?"

"I'll take the responsibility for it in both worlds. You see, I want you to be safeguarded in case anything hap——"

"Kenneth!"

"'Tion! Have no fear. I'll come back, covered with mud and medals. Mind you have that cup of tea waiting for me." [*He is listening for the whistle. He pulls her on to his knee.*]

"Hey! hey! hey! hey!"

"What fun we'll have writing to one another! Real letters this time!"

"Yes."

"It would be a good plan if you began the first letter as soon as I've gone."

"I will."

"I hope Lady Dolly will go on sending me cakes."

"You may be sure."

[*He ties his scarf around her neck.*]

"You must have been a bonny thing when you were young."

"Away with you!"

"That scarf sets you fine."

"Blue was always my colour."

[*The whistle sounds.*]

"Old lady, you are what Blighty means to me now."

[*She hides in the pantry again. She is out of sight to us, but she does something that makes PRIVATE DOWEY take off his bonnet. Then he shoulders his equipment and departs. That is he laughing coarsely with DIXON.*

[*We have one last glimpse of the old lady—a month or two after KENNETH's death in action. It would be rosemary to us to see her in her black dress, of which she is very proud; but let us rather peep at her in the familiar garments*

*that make a third to her mop and pail. It is
early morning, and she is having a look at her
medals before setting off on the daily round.
They are in a drawer, with the scarf covering
them, and on the scarf a piece of lavender.
First, the black frock, which she carries in her
arms like a baby. Then her War Savings Certificates, KENNETH'S bonnet, a thin packet of
real letters, and the famous champagne cork.
She kisses the letters, but she does not blub over
them. She strokes the dress, and waggles her
head over the certificates and presses the bonnet to her cheeks, and rubs the tinsel of the
cork carefully with her apron. She is a tremulous old 'un; yet she exults, for she owns
all these things, and also the penny flag on her
breast. She puts them away in the drawer, the
scarf over them, the lavender on the scarf.
Her air of triumph well becomes her. She lifts
the pail and the mop, and slouches off gamely
to the day's toil.]*

The End.